# Perspectives in American History

## *No. 8*
## THE RISE OF PENNSYLVANIA PROTECTIONISM

# THE RISE OF PENNSYLVANIA
# PROTECTIONISM

MALCOLM ROGERS EISELEN

**PORCUPINE PRESS**
*Philadelphia 1974*

**Library of Congress Cataloging in Publication Data**

Eiselen, Malcolm Rogers, 1902-1965.
  The rise of Pennsylvania protectionism.

  (Perspectives in American history, no. 8)
  Reprint of the ed. privately printed in Philadelphia.
  Originally presented as the author's thesis, University of Pennsylvania, 1931.
  Bibliography: p.
  1.  Tariff—United States—History.  2.  Free trade
and protection--Protection.  3.  Pennsylvania--Politics
and government.  4.  Pennsylvania--Economic conditions.
I.  Title.  II.  Series: Perspectives in American
history (Philadelphia) no. 8.
HF1754.E5  1974               382.7'3               73-18438
ISBN 0-87991-342-8


First edition 1932
(Philadelphia: privately printed, 1932)


Reprinted 1974 by
PORCUPINE PRESS, INC.
1317 Filbert St.
Philadelphia, Pennsylvania 19107


*Manufactured in the United States of America*

# CONTENTS

PAGE

I. The Foundations of Pennsylvania Protectionism, 1683-1787 . . 9

II. Protectionism under the Constitution, 1787-1815 . . . . 20

III. Post-War Protectionism, 1815-1824 . . . . . . . . 36

IV. The Tariff Enters Politics, 1824-1828 . . . . . . . . 64

V. The Climax of Early Protectionism, 1828-1832 . . . . . 90

VI. Nullification and Reaction, 1832-1839 . . . . . . . . 116

VII. The Revival of Protectionism, 1840-1844 . . . . . . . 134

VIII. The Election of 1844 . . . . . . . . . . . . . 154

IX. Fighting the Walker Tariff, 1845-1846 . . . . . . . . 172

X. The Protectionist Revolt, 1846-1848 . . . . . . . . 199

XI. Protectionism's Darkest Hour, 1849-1857 . . . . . . . 219

XII. The Triumph of Pennsylvania Protectionism, 1857-1861 . . . 244

XIII. The Dynamics of Pennsylvania Protectionism . . . . . 267

Bibliography . . . . . . . . . . . . . . . 279

*To*
*My Mother and Father*
*in affectionate acknowledgment of*
*encouragement and inspiration*

## PREFACE

A Pennsylvania legislator, weary with much contention, once suggested that "man" ought to be redefined as "an animal that makes tariff speeches." Although such a definition may not meet the rigorous standards of the lexicographer, it is likely to receive the heartfelt endorsement of those who have studied the political and economic history of the Keystone State. The tariff question has loomed very large upon the horizon of that commonwealth, which has long been recognized as the protectionist citadel of the United States.

This study undertakes to trace the origin and development of the protectionist movement in Pennsylvania, with particular reference to the period of intensive tariff agitation between 1815 and 1861. It has seemed desirable to limit the scope of the work to the policy of protection in the customary sense of fostering domestic economic interests through the medium of import duties, without considering such instruments of indirect protection as tonnage taxes, export and other bounties, and internal improvements. Within these limits, Pennsylvania protectionism has been approached from several divergent viewpoints — its economic background; its political implications; its influence on national tariff legislation; its part in contemporary propaganda; and its contribution to the development of American economic philosophy.

Much of the misunderstanding and fruitless argument which has featured the American tariff controversy may be attributed to the vagueness and ambiguity of the terminology habitually employed in such discussions. Such phrases as "a protective tariff," "a revenue tariff with incidental protection," "a tariff for revenue only" have meant all things to all men. Alexander Hamilton and Henry C. Carey were both ardent "protectionists," but the latter would have scorned the actual rates proposed by the nation's first secretary of the treasury. It has seemed desirable, therefore, to define protection in terms of intent rather than of fact. There are many cases of tariff legislation in the early days of the Republic which were below the maximum revenue standard in fact, but which were unquestionably protective in intent. It is in this sense that the word protection has been used throughout the study.

It gives me great pleasure to express my indebtedness to Professor

Albert E. McKinley and Professor Herman V. Ames of the University of Pennsylvania, under whose immediate direction this study was undertaken; to Mr. Arthur C. Bining of the same institution for suggestions concerning the early development of the Pennsylvania iron industry, and to Mr. H. H. Shenk of the Pennsylvania State Library for special courtesies in the use of the state archives at Harrisburg. To Mr. Charles H. J. Truman of Oakland, California, I am especially grateful for his generous assistance in the publication of this volume. Only a reader who shares my sense of awe in the presence of a typewriter keyboard will appreciate my obligations to my wife, Edna Truman Eiselen, for her untiring assistance in the preparation of the manuscript.

MALCOLM R. EISELEN.

# CHAPTER I

# THE FOUNDATIONS OF PENNSYLVANIA PROTECTIONISM, 1683-1787

Statesmen come and go, issues rise and wane, parties are born and pass into dissolution — but the tariff controversy is eternal. No other political or economic problem has so persistently and so recurrently claimed the attention of the American people. Since the first session of the first Congress, it has troubled legislative hall and presidential cabinet; it has turned elections and shaken political parties; it has inspired countless speeches and evoked an endless literature; and the end is not yet.

Pennsylvania and Pennsylvanians have ever been in the front lines of the tariff battle. No other state has contributed so much to the triumph and maintenance of the protective tariff as a fundamental tenet of national policy. The tireless exertions of a long line of Pennsylvania statesmen and politicians, industrialists and propagandists have served to make its name a synonym for protectionism. No state—unless it be South Carolina—has so closely identified itself with a single political formula. Rich in natural resources and pre-eminent in industrial development, Pennsylvania has always been regarded as the bulwark of the protectionist cause.

There is something of the irony of fate, therefore, in the fact that Pennsylvania's most illustrious son repudiated her favorite creed. Benjamin Franklin, at least in the ripened judgment of his more mature years, was a staunch advocate of free trade.[1] It is true that his early economic views were colored by the prevailing mercantilism of the day. Writing in 1747, he gave qualified approval to Connecticut's proposed tariff of 5 per cent. on imports on the grounds that "if you can make some of the goods, heretofore imported, among yourselves, the advanced price of five per cent. may encourage your own manufacture and in time make the importation of such articles unnecessary, which will be an advantage."[2] Again his *Observations Concerning the*

---

[1] This fact was a source of unending astonishment to Pennsylvania protectionists. As one of them naïvely remarked, "Benjamin Franklin has been constantly and confidently claimed by the Free Traders as of their school in political economy. We were sure that this could not be true, for the Doctor was preëminent for the common sense." (*Miners' Journal*, August 14, 1858.)

[2] Franklin, *Writings* (Smyth ed.), II, 313.

*Increase of Mankind,* written in 1751, advocated the prohibition of imports as a useful method of increasing population.[3] By 1767, however, Franklin had become thoroughly converted to the "laissez-faire" principles of the French physiocrats. He was still favorable to the development of domestic manufactures but not through the artificial medium of commercial restriction. On the subject of free trade he wrote, "In general I would only observe that commerce, consisting in a mutual exchange of the necessities and conveniences of life, the more free and unrestrained it is, the more it flourishes; and the happier are all the nations concerned in it. Most of the restraints put upon it in different countries seem to have been the projects of particulars for their private interest, under pretence of public good."[4] He believed that "advantageous situations and circumstances will always secure and fix manufactures,"[5] and expressed the hope that "in time perhaps Mankind may be wise enough to let Trade take its own Course, find its own Channels, and regulate its own Proportions."[6] "I find myself," he wrote, "inclin'd to adopt that modern [view] which supposes it best for every Country to leave its Trade entirely free from all Incumbrances."[7] But Franklin's economic views were not those of his adopted state. Indeed, even before his death the roots of the protective principle had been ineradicably fixed in Pennsylvania soil.

The beginnings of Pennsylvania protectionism may be traced back to the early days of the province. The first import duties were levied in 1683, when a light tax was imposed upon all imports except molasses.[8] This was superseded after 1688 by the policy of placing a heavy duty upon liquors and a few other commodities such as lumber, hops, flax and dairy products.[9] Revenue was undoubtedly the primary aim of such legislation. It is significant, nevertheless, that the particular commodities chosen for taxation were those which the authorities were most desirous to produce at home. Even then Pennsylvanians were not unmindful of the possibilities of incidental protec-

---

[3] *Ibid.* III, 69.
[4] *Ibid.* IX, 19
[5] Franklin, *Works* (Bigelow ed.), IV, 62.
[6] Franklin, *Writings* (Smyth ed.), IV, 244.
[7] *Ibid.* VIII, 261. See also Eiselen, *Franklin's Political Theories,* pp. 62-65.
[8] *Charter to William Penn,* p. 138.
[9] *Votes and Proc. of the House of Reps.,* I, 47; *Statutes at Large,* II, 105, 284, 384; III, 27, 112, 145, 150, 165, 268, 363.

tion; as early as 1704 a group from Philadelphia successfully petitioned the General Assembly for a duty on all foreign hops imported into the province.[10]

These early experiments in protectionism soon came into conflict with the growing commercial interests of Pennsylvania. As a result, all import duties were abandoned in 1725, and the province entered into a unique period of absolute free trade. Unrestricted commerce continued until 1758, when war-time emergency led to the imposition of an import duty upon liquors and sugar and a tonnage tax.[11] These laws were solely revenue measures, as were subsequent acts levying tonnage duties to provide funds for lighthouse construction.[12] Indeed, they could scarcely have been otherwise; for the watchful imperial government would have made short work of any legislation which attempted to foster colonial industry in one of Britain's most valued markets.

Although the Declaration of Independence left Pennsylvania free to formulate her own economic policies, import duties were not levied for several years, due largely to the opposition of the commercial interests. The first state duties, imposed by the act of December 23, 1780, were on a strictly revenue standard, with a basic rate of 1 per cent. ad valorem.[13] Various amendments to this act were made, but the revision of March 15, 1784 left it still a revenue measure, with practically all Pennsylvania products listed at $2\frac{1}{2}$ per cent.[14] Not until 1785 did Pennsylvania's protectionists become sufficiently vocal to make their voices heard in the state legislature.

Pennsylvania's first concerted protectionist movement had its origin in the economic reaction which followed the Revolution. During the war, the industries of the state had enjoyed a considerable degree of prosperity due to the virtual monopoly which the conflict gave to the

---

[10] *Votes and Proc. of the House of Reps.*, Vol. I, pt. 2, p. 6.

[11] *Statutes at Large*, V, 352, 409. These measures were opposed both by Philadelphia merchants and by the Executive Council, who held unanimously that "our Trade should be the last thing Taxed, that an Exemption from Duties and the Freedom of the Port had more than anything contributed to the encrease of our Trade." (*Penn. Col. Rec.*, VIII, 30, 232, 334).

[12] *Statutes at Large*, VI, 374; VII, 43.

[13] *Ibid.* X, 296.

[14] *Ibid.* XI, 262.

[15] Imports during the four years immediately preceding the war had averaged £572,189 annually. (Anderson, *Origin of Commerce*, VI, 774; Macpherson, *Annals of Commerce*, III, 339, 518, 533, 550, 564.)

home producer. At the close of hostilities, however, English merchants hastened to pour their accumulated stocks into the American market, in many cases at prices below cost. Pennsylvania received at least her share of this foreign influx, for British imports into the state in 1784 amounted to £689,491, a figure surpassed only twice during the days of colonial dependence.[15] As a result, serious protests began to appear in the press against a situation which seemed to reduce the Declaration of Independence to a hollow mockery and which seriously menaced the industrial interests of the commonwealth. A correspondent of the *Pennsylvania Gazette* expressed a not uncommon sentiment when he complained,

We have been blind to our own interest and our existence as a nation. We have encouraged the importation of British gewgaws! Our towns have swarmed with British factors! Our money has been sent in cargoes to England! and the whole trade has been wrested from our merchants, who have been obliged to sit still and see themselves hastening to destruction. . . . Ready made clothes and every article of mechanism in large quantities have been imported; so that valuable branch of men, the mechanicks, would, in a little time, be reduced to beggary.[16]

Such conditions of real and potential distress have always provided a fruitful field for protectionist agitation. To those immediately concerned, prompt action appeared necessary to preserve the infant industries of the state from utter annihilation. It was recognized that the Congress of the Confederation was powerless to take remedial measures; therefore during the winter of 1784-5, despairing manufacturers turned to the state authorities to implore protective legislation against the foreign invasion.

The legislature, composed primarily of farmers, was slow to act.[17] Committees of correspondence were therefore organized to promote action; a town meeting in Philadelphia adopted a resolution to the effect that foreign importations "ought to be discouraged; some by absolute prohibitions, others by adequate duties and imposts."[18] Finally, after six months of discussion, the General Assembly, on September 20, 1785, passed "An Act to Encourage and Protect the Manufactures of this State by Laying Additional Duties on the

---

[16] May 11, 1785.
[17] *Pennsylvania Gazette*, August 27, 1785.
[18] *Ibid*. June 22, 1785.

**Importation of Certain Manufactures which Interfere with Them.**"[19]
The protective intent of the legislation was boldly affirmed, not only
in the title, but also in the preamble, which declared:

> Whereas, although the fabrics and manufactures of Europe and other foreign
> parts imported into this country in times of peace may be afforded at cheaper
> rates than they can be made here, yet good policy and a regard to the well being
> of divers useful and industrious citizens who are employed in the making of like
> goods in this state demand of us that moderate duties be laid on certain fabrics
> and manufactures imported, which do most interfere with and which (if no
> relief be given) will undermine and destroy the useful manufactures of the like
> kind in this country.[20]

The duties levied under the act of 1785 were both specific and ad
valorem, the latter ranging from 5 to 17½ per cent. Iron manufactures,
leather goods, paper and clothing—then the most important industrial
products of the state—were all rated at 12½ per cent. A further
disposition to assist the manufacturer was reflected in the free list,
which included all kinds of raw materials. To assist Pennsylvania's
important milling industry, discriminating duties were to be levied
against Portugal so long as the latter excluded American flour from
its dominions.[21]

Not all of Pennsylvania's industrial interests were satisfied with
the protection afforded by the act of 1785, and before the end of the
year, petitions were introduced in the General Assembly asking that
the duty on nails and spikes be increased and that a tax be levied
on bar iron.[22] A special committee of the legislature reported that 300
tons of nails a year were being imported into the state and that with

---

[19] *Statutes at Large*, XII, 99.

[20] *Ibid.* p. 100.

[21] Franklin, by the irony of fate, was President of the Executive Council of
Pennsylvania when this measure was passed. Concerning it, he wrote, "I have not
lost any of the Principles of Public Oeconomy you once knew me possess'd of;
but, to get the bad Customs of a Country chang'd and new ones, though better,
introduc'd, it is necessary first to remove the Prejudices of the People, enlighten
their Ignorance, and convince them that their interest will be promoted by the
propos'd Changes; and this is not the Work of a Day. Our Legislators are all
Land-holders; and they are not persuaded, that all taxes are finally paid by the
Land. Besides, our Country is so sparsely settled . . . that the Time and Labour
of the Collector in going from House to House, and being oblig'd to call often
before he can recover the Tax, amounts to more than the Tax is worth, and
therefore, we have been forc'd into the Mode of indirect Taxes." (Franklin,
*Writings* (Smyth ed.), IX, 615.

[22] *Minutes of Tenth General Assembly*, pp. 61, 68.

proper encouragement the entire quantity might be produced at home. Accordingly, an additional duty of 1d. per pound was granted on nails and spikes. In regard to bar iron, the committee admitted that the industry was depressed and that with protection it might become self supporting; but held that bar iron was so essential to agriculture and industry that a tax at that time would be unwise.[23] Other slight revisions upward were made during the years immediately following; an additional 2 per cent. was imposed upon goods imported by aliens; while goods imported in Pennsylvania vessels received a rebate of 5 per cent. of the total duties.[24]

Today the rates of Pennsylvania's state tariff would be considered pathetically low, even according to a revenue standard. Judged by the less sophisticated criteria of that period, however, they seemed to provide a very substantial degree of protection.[25] Tench Coxe estimated that when added to the costs of importation they gave the American manufacturer an advantage of from 25 to 50 per cent. over the foreign competitor.[26] A parallel study of the Pennsylvania act of 1785 and the national act of 1789 shows that on nine-tenths of the comparable rates the state duties were higher. Glass and coal were the only articles capable of being produced in Pennsylvania which were more favored under the federal legislation and both of these industries were practically non-existent in 1785. For most of the articles in which the commonwealth was interested, the transition from state to national duties meant a reduction from a 12½ per cent. rate to 7½ per cent.

Pennsylvania was somewhat handicapped in her efforts to exclude foreign goods by the commercial policies of neighboring states. New Jersey made Burlington a free port in 1784, and most of the goods which entered there duty free ultimately reached Philadelphia.[27] Delaware, in 1786, also challenged Pennsylvania's commercial legisla-

---

[23] *Minutes of Tenth General Assembly*, p. 84; *Statutes at Large*, XII, 146.

[24] *Ibid.* XII, 403-406; XIII, 57.

[25] During the debates on the first United States tariff act, it was asserted that the protection afforded by the law of 1785 had made it possible to establish a steel furnace in Philadelphia producing 230 tons annually; that it had greatly stimulated the manufacture of candles, and that it had transformed the state from an importer into an exporter of malt liquors. (*Annals of Cong.*, 1 Cong., 1 Sess., pp. 150, 152, 153).

[26] *American Museum*, II, 253. Hamilton in his Report on Manufactures estimated the cost of importation alone at from 15 to 30 per cent. (*American State Papers, Finance*, I, 730.)

[27] *Laws of N. J.* (1800 ed.), p. 55; Carey, M., *New Olive Branch*, p. 14.

tion by opening free ports, through which it was not difficult for imported goods to invade the neighboring province.[28] It is small wonder, therefore, that Pennsylvania protectionists became leaders in the movement to grant Congress the power to regulate commerce and to levy import duties.[29]

By the close of the Confederation period, the protectionist movement had made more progress in Pennsylvania than in any other part of the country. The reason must be sought in the relatively high industrial development of the state; a development which preceded rather than followed the adoption of the protective policy. Manufactures appeared early in Pennsylvania; partly because of abundant natural resources; partly because of the large proportion of skilled artisans in the population; partly because agriculture proved relatively less profitable than in neighboring provinces.[30] Kalm reported of Germantown in 1748 that "most of the inhabitants are Manufacturers, and make everything in such quantity and perfection, that in a short time this province will want very little from England."[31] Burnaby, about 1760, found manufactures far more advanced in Pennsylvania than in New York.[32] An observer of the Confederation period believed that "the mass of manufactures in Pennsylvania, especially if we include a few adjoining counties of Delaware and New Jersey, exceeded all those of the other states together."[33] During and after the Revolution, the southern states in particular turned to Pennsylvania for manufactures as they formerly had turned to England.[34] Philadelphia was the industrial center, with 2,200 out of its 8,600 adult males engaged in manufactures in 1790.[35] Lancaster, York, and Berks counties also had developed manufactures which compared favorably with any in the country.[36] The products of the state, as enumerated by Tench Coxe about 1787, included

---

[28] *Laws of Del.* (1797 ed.), II, 831; Madison, *Writings*, II, 228.

[29] *Statutes at Large*, X, 296; XI, 162, 391; *Jour. of House Reps. of Penn., 1776-1781*, p. 564; *Pennsylvania Gazette*, June 22, 1785.

[30] The average cost of transporting a bushel of wheat 100 miles was estimated at one shilling in Pennsylvania as against two pence in New York. For this and other reasons, the profits of farming in New York were said to exceed those in Pennsylvania by 30 per cent. (Clark, *History of Manufactures*, I, 88.)

[31] Kalm, *Travels into North America*, I, 70.

[32] Burnaby, *Travels through North America*, pp. 81, 110.

[33] *House Exec. Doc.*, 22 Cong., 1 Sess., No. 308, II, 848.

[34] *Ibid.* p. 842.

[35] Coxe, *View of the United States*, p. 228.

[36] *American Museum*, XI, 189.

meal of all kinds, ships and boats, malt liquors, distilled spirits, potash, gun powder, cordage, loaf-sugar, pasteboard, cards and paper of every kind, books in various languages, snuff, tobacco, starch, cannon, musquets, anchors, nails and very many other articles of iron, bricks, tiles, potters ware, millstones and other stone work, cabinet work, trunks and windsor chairs, carriages and harness of all kinds, corn-fans, ploughs, and many other implements of husbandry, sadlery and whips, shoes and boots, leather of various kinds, hosiery, hats and gloves, wearing apparel, coarse linens and woollens, and some cotton goods, linseed and fish oil, wares of gold, silver, tin, pewter, lead, brass, and copper, clocks and watches, wool and cotton cards, printing types, glass and stone ware, candles, soap.[37]

The principal dynamic of the early protectionist movement in Pennsylvania came from the iron, textile, paper, leather and brewing industries.   The Pennsylvania iron industry, especially, very early attained the pre-eminent position which it has since maintained against all rivals.   The first iron works established in the state was a bloomery forge constructed in 1716 near Pottstown; the first furnace was built in 1720; the first pig iron was shipped to England in 1728.[38]   Acrelius, writing about 1750, reported that Pennsylvania then possessed the most advanced iron industry in the colonies.[39]   Before the Revolution, Philadelphia was exporting over 2,000 tons annually of American pig and bar iron; even after the war, the former continued to be quoted in the London market.[40]   The first furnace west of the Alleghenies was erected in 1789 in what is now Fayette county.[41]

Pennsylvania, from the days of its founder, fostered the household manufacture of textiles.   Douglass estimated that the farmers of the province made nine-tenths of their own wearing apparel.[42]   The Germans about Philadelphia, particularly, took up and developed a varied production of clothing; while the Irish settlers provided an excellent quality of linen.[43]   In 1775 the boycott of English goods gave impetus in Philadelphia to a joint stock company for the manufacture of woolens, linens, and cottons.   Through its efforts, there was brought

37 *Ibid.* p. 46.
38 Swank, *Progressive Pennsylvania*, pp. 185-187.
39 Penn. Hist. Soc., *Memoirs*, XI, 164.
40 Bishop, *History of American Manufactures*, I, 569; Clark, *History of Manufactures*, I, 296.
41 Swank, *Iron in All Ages*, p. 214.
42 Douglass, *British Settlements in North America*, II, 332.
43 Burnaby, *Travels through North America*, p. 81.

180645

to Philadelphia in that year possibly the first spinning jenny in America. The enterprise was fairly successful until interrupted by the war.[44] The factory was reopened in 1787 under the auspices of the Pennsylvania Society for the Encouragement of Manufactures and the Useful Arts. Benjamin Franklin and Robert Morris were among the subscribers to the enterprise.[45]

Paper manufacturing was another important Pennsylvania industry. The first paper mill in America was erected at Philadelphia not later than 1693 by the immediate ancestors of the eminent astronomer, David Rittenhouse.[46] Philadelphia early became the center of paper production in the colonies, due largely to the fact that more cotton and linen was worn there than in the northern provinces. At the close of the Confederation period, Pennsylvania was far ahead of all rivals, with forty-eight mills in operation and several more under construction. The annual output, estimated at 70,000 reams, was valued at $250,000.[47]

Colonial Pennsylvania also developed important leather manufactures, centering around Lancaster.[48] In order to encourage this industry, the export of hides and leather from the state was practically prohibited from 1721 to 1810.[49] Assured of abundant raw materials, Pennsylvania manufacturers built up a large export business with New York and the southern colonies.[50]

The brewing industry likewise flourished in Pennsylvania. Brissot de Warville reported in 1788 that Philadelphia had no less than fourteen good breweries.[51] Lancaster in 1786 had three breweries, and many other towns developed local enterprises of similar nature. There was also some distilling, but it was forced to compete with a veritable flood of imported spirits.[52] The growth of the brewing and distilling

---

[44] Bishop, *History of American Manufactures*, I, 383-385; Clark, *History of Manufactures*, I, 183.
[45] A portion of the subscription list and the minutes of the Society from September 11, 1787 to June 3, 1789 are in the library of the Historical Society of Pennsylvania.
[46] Bishop, *History of American Manufactures*, I, 196.
[47] Coxe, *View of the United States*, pp. 123, 299; *Annals of Cong.*, 1 Cong., 1 Sess., p. 173.
[48] Bishop, *History of American Manufactures*, I, 446.
[49] *Statutes at Large*, III, 258; *Pamphlet Laws*, 1809-10, p. 188.
[50] Bishop, *History of American Manufactures*, I, 446.
[51] Brissot de Warville, *New Travels in the United States*, p. 254.
[52] Bishop, *History of American Manufactures*, I, 261-2.

industry was important not only to those directly concerned but also to the farmer, since it afforded him a convenient market for his produce; therefore protective tariffs which sought to exclude foreign beverages were assured of a wide appeal.

Early efforts to establish glass manufactures in Pennsylvania were unsuccessful, in spite of the large quantities of siliceous rock easily available in Northampton and Berks counties.[53]  Gov. John Penn reported to the Lords of Trade in 1767 that there was only one glass works in the province, and that it was operating "to a very inconsiderable Extent, there being no other Vent for their Ware, which is of very ordinary Quality, but to supply the small demands of the Villages and Farmers in the adjacent inland Country."[54]  The first glass works at Pittsburgh was established about 1795.[55]  Not until after the adoption of the constitution, therefore, does glass become an article of protectionist solicitude in Pennsylvania.

Another important Pennsylvania industry which, however, contributed little to the early protectionist movement was the milling industry.  Madison, in the federal convention, referred to wheat and flour as the staple of Pennsylvania.[56]  Philadelphia, in 1792, exported 420,000 barrels of flour, valued at over two million dollars.[57]  The milling industry, naturally, had little direct interest in a protective policy.  The tariff act of 1785 attempted to appeal to this interest indirectly by providing retaliatory duties against Portugal for excluding Pennsylvania flour, but the discriminating provisions were repealed within a year on the grounds that they were "burdensome to the commerce of this state without producing the good effects intended thereby."[58]

The attitude of the agricultural population toward the general policy of protection was not clearly defined at this early period.  The average farmer supplied most of his own needs and therefore was little affected by taxes on foreign commodities.  His intuitive hostility to a policy discriminating in favor of another economic interest was in many·cases tempered by the hope that thereby industries might

---

53 *Ibid*. I, 235-9.
54 *Penn. Col. Rec.* IX, 354.
55 Bishop, *History of American Manufactures*, I, 243.
56 Farrand, *Records of the Federal Convention*, I, 456.
57 Coxe, *View of the United States,*'p. 64.
58 *Statutes at Large*, XII, 146, 337.

be set up in his immediate vicinity to provide a convenient market for agricultural produce. Early protectionism, therefore, evoked no clear-cut group hostility from the farm interest.

One economic interest, however, was arrayed in unremitting hostility to the protective policy. This was the powerful commercial interest, centering around Philadelphia. That city, by the close of the Revolution, had become the commercial metropolis of the country. In 1789, Pennsylvania possessed 20 per cent. of the nation's tonnage engaged in foreign trade; while the exports of the state during the fiscal year ending in 1793 represented more than one-fourth of the total for the entire Union.[59] Any legislation which restricted the freedom of international exchanges was a direct blow to this influential interest. The early protectionist struggle in Pennsylvania represents a war to the death between the industrial and commercial forces. The protective tariff became the battlefield upon which these two bitterly contending economic interests met, and the eventual triumph of the restrictive system may be measured quite accurately in the relative decline of the state's commerce after 1800.

---

[59] Seybert, *Statistical Annals,* p. 321; Coxe, *View of the United States,* p. 478.

# CHAPTER II

## PROTECTIONISM UNDER THE CONSTITUTION, 1787-1815

The federal convention which drafted the constitution of the United States assembled in Philadelphia in May, 1787. It was a body of serious and perplexed statesmen, seeking, in the midst of jealousy and forebodings, to embody in one written document the experience of the past and the aspirations of the future. Fortunately for the peace of mind of that much harrassed assemblage, the question of a protective tariff with all its endless implications was never seriously raised. There was general agreement as to the necessity of import duties; the tragic experience of the Confederation period had clearly demonstrated their desirability, both as a source of revenue and as a commercial weapon; but the possibility of using such duties for the protection of domestic industry was not discussed. Had this issue been raised endless subsequent controversy might have been averted; on the other hand, there might have been no constitution.

The attitude of the Pennsylvania delegation, had the question of protection been debated, can only be conjectured. The probability is that the vote of the state would have been cast to sanction such an application of the federal taxing power. True, Franklin was a free trader; but three of his colleagues, Fitzsimons, Clymer, and Robert Morris, subsequently expressed protectionist sentiments in Congress. Only one vote in the convention is even remotely indicative of the views of the Pennsylvanians on this point. The constitution, as adopted, forbids the states to levy import duties except with the consent of Congress. Madison wished to amend this provision so as to make the prohibition absolute. The Pennsylvania delegation voted in the negative, probably with the idea of leaving the door open for state legislation, at least as a remote contingency.[1]

As soon as the convention had completed its labors, Pennsylvania federalists eagerly seized upon the proposed constitution and urged its ratification as a potential instrument of protection. One writer promised that under the new government "heavy duties will be laid on all foreign articles which can be manufactured in this country, and . . . the manufactories of our country will flourish—our mechanics will lift up

---

[1] Farrand, *Records of the Federal Convention*, II, 441.

their heads, and rise to opulence and wealth."[2]  The Northampton County delegation to the ratifying convention, in a report to their constituents, justified their vote by advancing the same argument.[3]  A Philadelphia paper likewise pointed out the futility of attempting to protect industry by state action so long as the free ports of New Jersey and Delaware constituted an irreparable breach in the tariff wall.[4] Undoubtedly, such arguments had considerable weight in securing the adherence of Pennsylvania protectionists to the new frame of government.

After ratification had been accomplished, the manufacturers and workers of Philadelphia were not slow to claim the fulfillment of these campaign pledges.  In the Fourth of July parade in 1788, appeared such banners as "May the Union Government protect the Manufactures of America."[5]  While the members were slowly assembling for the first session of the first Congress, a Philadelphia mass meeting drew up a petition requesting that body "to lay such duties or imposts on foreign merchandise imported into these states, as will give a decided preference to our own."[6]

The Pennsylvania delegation in Congress was not slow to respond to these manifestations of protectionist sentiment.  Before Washington had taken the oath of office, the tariff question was launched upon its tumultuous and interminable career within the halls of Congress. Madison, on April 8, 1789, introduced a resolution in the House proposing a purely revenue tariff law with a few specific duties and a basic rate of 5 per cent. on all other imports.[7]  On the following day, Fitzsimons of Pennsylvania moved a substitute resolution enumerating a large number of articles upon which he advocated higher duties "calculated to encourage the productions of our country and protect our infant manufactures."[8]  This list, almost identical with the articles taxed by the Pennsylvania act of 1785, became the basis for subsequent discussion.

The Pennsylvania representatives rallied nobly to the support of the

[2] *American Museum*, II, 372.

[3] *Ibid*. III, 75.

[4] McMaster and Stone, *Pennsylvania and the Federal Convention*, p. 167.

[5] *Pennsylvania Packet*, July 9, 1788.

[6] *Ibid*. March 28, 1789; *Pennsylvania Gazette*, April 1, 1789.

[7] *Annals of Cong.*, 1 Cong., 1 Sess., p. 108.

[8] *Ibid*. p. 111.

principle of incidental protection as expressed in Fitzsimon's resolution. Hartley remarked that some might wish

to enter on this business in a limited and partial manner as it relates to revenue alone; but for my part I wish to do it on as broad bottom as is at present practicable. . . . If we consult the history of the ancient world, we shall see that they have thought proper, for a long time past, to give great encouragement to the establishment of manufactures, by laying such partial duties on the importation of foreign goods, as to give the home manufacture a considerable advantage in the price when brought to market. . . . I think it both politic and just that the fostering hand of the General Government should extend to all those manufactures which will tend to national utility.[9]

Fitzsimons, himself, envisioned a carefully balanced protective system in which each state made minor sacrifices in return for the greater good. As for his own state, he did not seek "exclusive advantages for Pennsylvania; he would contend, and undertake to prove, that by the duties already agreed to, that state sacrificed as much as any other."[10] Scott, from western Pennsylvania, seeking a duty on hemp, reminded Congress that "agriculture is entitled to its proportion of encouragement."[11]

The delegation, however, soon proved to be more united in principle than it was in detail. Fitzsimons, himself engaged in foreign commerce, was by no means an extreme protectionist.[12] He asserted that if the revenue derived from the measure exceeded the needs of the government "most certainly the duties ought to be reduced."[13] When the duty on foreign nails and spikes was under consideration, he declared that the American product was both cheaper and better, and that the refusal of protection would do "no material injury" to the Pennsylvania manufacturer.[14] Nevertheless, he joined with Clymer in urging further encouragement for the manufacture of unwrought steel.[15]

---

[9] *Ibid*. p. 114.
[10] *Ibid*. p. 135.
[11] *Ibid*. p. 161.
[12] Opponents charged him with delaying the passage of the bill until his own vessels should reach port. (Maclay, *Journal*, p. 29.)
[13] *Annals of Cong.*, 1 Cong., 1 Sess., p. 320.
[14] *Ibid*. p. 164. Compare with Hamilton's statement in the Report on Manufactures that 1,800,000 pounds of nails and spikes had been imported during the first fiscal year, and that an additional duty of 2 cents per pound would be necessary to afford adequate protection. (Hamilton, *Works*, IV, 166.)
[15] *Annals of Cong.*, 1 Cong., 1 Sess., pp. 153-4.

Clymer urged that the protection afforded the paper industry under state legislation ought to be continued.[16] Hartley opposed a duty of three cents a bushel on coal on the plea that it would be a burden on the manufacturer.[17] High duties were favored on rum and molasses, both on moral grounds and as protection to the brewing industry of the state.[18] A serious split developed in the delegation over the treatment of hemp. Fitzsimons opposed a duty as a burden upon American shipping, while Scott, speaking for western agriculture, demanded it.[19] Again, Fitzsimons favored a duty on salt, while Scott denounced it as an extremely odious tax upon an article of universal necessity.[20] Fitzsimons likewise attempted to assist the depressed shipbuilding industry of Philadelphia by including in the tariff act a discriminating tonnage duty against foreign vessels. Describing the depressed state of the Philadelphia shipbuilding industry, he testified, "Before the Revolution, 5,000 tons of shipping were annually built in that city; last year the whole tonnage was but 1,300. . . If it revives from its present languishing condition, it must be by great fostering care and protection."[21] This provision was finally removed from the revenue bill and passed as a separate measure.

Although the tariff bill in its final form provided only $7\frac{1}{2}$ per cent. ad valorem on Pennsylvania's leading products, most of the delegation seem to have been favorable to the measure as a whole. More than that cannot be said, since the bill was adopted on May 16, 1789 without a roll call. From the House it went to the Senate, where the Keystone State was represented by William Maclay and Robert Morris, the latter renowned as one of the nation's outstanding merchants.

Of the two Senators, Maclay was the more thorough-going protectionist. He favored an increase of all the House rates except that on salt.[22] He pointed out that under the new rates, Pennsylvania's chief industries would enjoy 5 per cent. less protection than under the state law, and, invoking the now familiar "vested interests" argument,

---

[16] *Ibid.* p. 173.
[17] *Ibid.* p. 177.
[18] *Ibid.* pp. 131, 137, 204.
[19] *Ibid.* p. 157.
[20] *Ibid.* pp. 166, 173.
[21] *Ibid.* p. 295.
[22] Maclay, *Journal,* pp. 73, 83.

declared "that although the United States were not absolutely obliged to make good the engagements of the State to individuals, yet as individuals had embarked their property in these manufactures, depending on the State laws, I thought it wrong to violate those laws without absolute necessity."[23]

Morris, like Fitzsimons in the House, was torn by a desire to serve two masters. As a friend of commerce, he secured a reduction of the rates on cables and cordage, and blocked increases on leather goods, canes and whips, clothing, gold and silver ware, jewelry, and manufactures of tin and pewter.[24] As a friend of industry, he urged higher rates on iron manufactures and other articles.[25] He was sufficiently protectionist, however, to receive, along with Maclay, the denunciation of the low-tariff men. Strong of Massachusetts, for instance, accused the Pennsylvania delegation of seeking to burden New England with an undue proportion of the impost.[26] Lee of Virginia denounced the duty on loaf sugar as a tax upon "three millions of people . . . to support half a dozen people in Philadelphia."[27]

The measure was finally passed by the Senate on June 11 without roll call; minor differences between the two houses were adjusted; and it was signed by President Washington on the Fourth of July. From the standpoint of the Pennsylvania protectionist, the new act left much to be desired. It has been pointed out that, as contrasted with the state revenue system which it replaced, the new measure represented an average loss of about 5 per cent. ad valorem. Duties were increased on distilled spirits, but sharply reduced on malt liquors. Coal was taxed for the first time—2 cents a bushel—but the importance of this resource was not yet appreciated in Pennsylvania. The 5 per cent. increase on glass in no way compensated for the equal decrease suffered by the vastly more important paper, leather, clothing and iron industries. At the same time, two important raw materials, cotton and hemp, were removed from the free list. Years later, Mathew Carey wrote,

> It is a melancholy operation . . . to compare the tariff of 1789, and the principles on which it is predicated with the preamble to a law of the state of

---

23 Maclay, *Journal,* p. 62.
24 *Ibid*. pp. 54, 63.
25 *Ibid*. pp. 47, 63.
26 *Ibid*. p. 65.
27 *Ibid*. p. 56.

Pennsylvania, passed anno 1785. . . . The sound policy, the fostering care of its citizens and the resources of the state displayed in the latter form a strong and decisive contrast with the utter impolicy of the tariff.[28]

The protectionist, however, had at least the cold comfort that the new measure would be administered on a national basis, and that its barriers, though low, could not be overthrown by adverse legislation in adjacent states.

To sum up the controversy over the first tariff act, it is evident that Pennsylvania in 1789 was not yet consolidated either as to economic interests or as to tariff objectives. Protection, as a general principle was supported by the industrialist, tolerated by the farmer, and regarded with suspicion and hostility by the merchant. Even among its friends, the tariff still afforded perplexing problems. There was still no general agreement as to what commodities most needed protection, or how to correlate the needs of raw material and manufactured product. Until the War of 1812, the tariff movement in Pennsylvania represents a guerrilla warfare rather than a sustained offensive, a campaign conducted for the most part without leadership and without plan.

Perhaps the most consistent advocates of protectionism during the early period were the various societies organized at about this time for the encouragement and promotion of domestic industry. The sponsors of these organizations seem to have been motivated partly by patriotism and partly by less disinterested considerations. Typical of such associations was the Pennsylvania Society for the Encouragement of Manufactures and the Useful Arts, mentioned in the preceding chapter. This body was organized primarily to foster industrial development through the introduction of improved machinery and manufacturing methods.[29] Samuel Slater, the "father of American manufactures," was attracted to the United States by an advertisement of the Society offering a reward for improved cotton machinery.[30] Nevertheless, its members had no objections to promoting industry by legislative as well as mechanical devices. To quote an official report, "It was deemed of great importance, by the Society, to procure

[28] Carey, M., *New Olive Branch*, p. 30.
[29] *Plan of the Pennsylvania Society*, p. 7.
[30] White, *Memoir of Samuel Slater*, p. 37.

the adoption of such modifications of the state and federal revenue laws in the years 1787 and 1789, and on some occasions since, as would raise the necessary pecuniary supplies by impositions on foreign goods which rivaled our own manufactures."[31] Several months before the first Congress of the United States assembled at New York, the Society made a survey of American industry, designed "to collect together such a stock of information, to lay before Congress, as may enable them to regulate the impost duty, in the manner best calculated to raise a revenue and to protect domestic manufactures."[32]

The Pennsylvania Society was the first of several such organizations, partly industrial, partly educational, and partly propagandist, to be established in various parts of the state. Most of them, like the Philadelphia body, quickly became hotbeds of strong protectionist sentiment, and helped to give some degree of continuity to the early movement for higher duties. An interesting exception was the Germantown Society for Promoting Domestic Manufactures, established in 1790, which provided in its constitution that "Being of opinion that every manufacture, amongst us, should be supported by its intrinsic value . . . the Society shall never use its influence with government, to prevent foreign manufactures from being introduced; but on the contrary, shall exert itself to promote a free unlimited commerce, which is the true interest of every country."[33] Such self-denying devotion to the principles of the Classicists, however, was not characteristic of manufacturing societies in Pennsylvania at this or any other period.

Pressure was also exerted in more desultory fashion through memorials and petitions to Congress from specific industries. There was no unified plan behind these appeals; they were merely the expressions of local groups seeking legislative encouragement for their own particular interest. Uniformly they presented a vivid picture of depression and distress, due, it was alleged, to excessive importations. Some of these pleas seem to represent interests genuinely depressed by foreign competition; others must be discounted as the efforts of unprofitable units in generally flourishing industries to

---

[31] *A Communication from the Pennsylvania Society*, (1804), p. 18. See also *American Museum*, III, 179.
[32] *Ibid*. V, 210.
[33] *Constitution of the Germantown Society*, Article IX.

prolong an inherently unsound existence through legislative aid. Such marginal producers have always played an untiring and plausible role in the unending fight for higher duties.

In spite of general industrial prosperity from 1789 to 1815, Pennsylvania produced a fair proportion of such memorials. Perhaps the most comprehensive was the memorial of the artisans and manufacturers of Philadelphia which was presented to the House of Representatives on December 9, 1803. This asserted that "the competition that the manufacturing citizens of the United States are, by the laws of the country, obliged to sustain with the manufacturers of a foreign country is . . . unjust," and that "an infant manufacture must have some protection to enable it to contend with an old establishment." Specifically, the memorial suggested that prohibitive duties be levied on manufactures of wood, fur, leather, horn, bone or rags, since domestic production in these lines was assured. Manufactures of hemp, flax, cotton and iron required extensive capital and therefore should also receive governmental assistance. Revenue requirements might be met through duties on luxuries.[34] Other petitions, more modest in their scope, presented the protectionist claims of the arms manufacturers, hat and umbrella makers, and the printers of the state.[35] Sometimes the memorials threw interesting light on the divergent interests which existed even within the industrial group itself. In 1794, for instance, the "merchants, manufacturers of iron, and shipbuilders" of Philadelphia requested that bar iron be placed upon the free list. This evoked a counter memorial from Pennsylvania iron masters praying that the duty be left untouched.[36] Their petition having been denied, the iron manufacturers then asked for "such countervailing duties on imported wrought iron, as will secure a just and reasonable reward to your petitioners."[37] On the whole, these petitions and memorials seem to have had very little immediate influence on Congress; most of them were either completely ignored or were reported unfavorably by the committees to which they were referred.

There were not many literary propagandists of protection active in

---

[34] *Annals of Cong.,* 8 Cong., 2 Sess., p. 1467; *American State Papers, Finance,* II, 61.

[35] *Ibid.* pp. 22, 118; *Annals of Cong.,* 7 Cong., 2 Sess., p. 1235.

[36] *Ibid.* 3 Cong., 1 Sess., pp. 474, 523.

[37] *American State Papers, Finance,* II, 553.

Pennsylvania during this early period. Among desultory writers upon the subject, one notes with considerable surprise the name of Dr. Thomas Cooper, then a resident of the state. Long before he became the flaming evangel of free trade and nullification in South Carolina, protectionist Pennsylvania knew Cooper as the staunch advocate of the restrictive system.[38] As an economist, Cooper did not deny the contentions of the Classicists as to the theoretical advantages of free trade. Nevertheless, he declared,

It will be a horrible fraud to entice our citizens to embark in the troublesome and hazardous speculation of new manufactures, and then on a sudden peace leave them to all the malignity of british competition in our own market. . . . With us, it will be, not a measure of economy, so much as a measure of protection and defence. Our markets ought to be more at home; more under our command; and this will call for permanent not temporary regulations.[39]

In another passage, which might have been taken verbatim from the writings of Henry C. Carey, Cooper thus enumerated the benefits to be derived from domestic manufactures,

As a mean of national defence and national independence, as a mean of propagating among our citizens the most useful and practical kinds of knowledge — as a mean of giving that energetic, frugal, calculating and foreseeing character to every branch of our national industry, that does not exist but among a manufacturing people — as a mean of multiplying our social enjoyments by condensing our population — and as a mean of fixing the consumers and the producers in the immediate neighborhood of each other — I would encourage the commencement at least of home manufactures.[40]

To obtain these advantages he believed it expedient "so far to aid the introduction of manufactures in this country by protecting duties as to afford a reasonable prospect of safety to the prudent investment of capital and the industrious pursuit of business; but no bounty to wild speculation, to negligent workmanship or to smuggling."[41] In short, Cooper's economic views at this time were thoroughly Pennsylvanian. During the nullification excitement they were quoted triumphantly

---

[38] Hezekiah Niles testified that Cooper's writings had helped in his youth to confirm his belief in the protective policy. (*Niles' Register*, XXVI, 36.)

[39] Letter to Jefferson, December 4, 1808, quoted in Malone, *Public Life of Thomas Cooper*, p. 193.

[40] *The Emporium*, I, 9.

[41] *Ibid.* p. 10.

against the Doctor by opponents, who intimated that he was unduly susceptible to environmental influences. He was said, however, to have abandoned his protectionist views after a thorough study of the subject during the winter of 1818-19, while still resident in Pennsylvania.[42]

The Pennsylvania delegation in Congress prior to 1815 was strongly though not quite unanimously protectionist. Between 1789 and 1816 there were some twenty-seven revisions of the tariff, of which several provided for material increases in the duties levied. All of these increases had their immediate origin in the pressing revenue needs of the government. Nevertheless, an intention to afford incidental protection is apparent both in the debates and in the articles chosen for increased rates. Furthermore, the proceedings and votes on these measures show that the Pennsylvania members of Congress, with few exceptions, were quick to recognize and welcome the protection thus afforded. The first test of protectionist sentiment came on the tariff act of 1790 which raised the rates on many articles, including steel, glass, paper and coal. The Pennsylvania delegation in the House supported the measure by unanimous vote.[43] The fact that the increase was intended as a substitute for the unpopular whisky tax may have helped to hold western representatives in line.[44] In the Senate, Morris supported the proposition, but Maclay for some reason voted in the negative.[45] The tariff was again revised in 1792 so as to embody some of the protectionist recommendations of Hamilton's Report on Manufactures. Again the increase commanded the unanimous support of Pennsylvania in the House.[46]

Revenue needs were made the excuse for further protective increases in 1794. Here for the first time opposition developed within the state delegation. Hartley, himself a farmer and representing an agricultural community, opposed further increases because they would raise the price of farm labor and would impose unjust bur-

---

[42] *Democratic Press,* March 31, 1824.

[43] *Annals of Cong.,* 1 Cong., 2 Sess., p. 1741.

[44] One may only speculate to what extent Pennsylvania's deep-seated antipathy for direct taxation facilitated the triumph of protectionism in the state. Condy Raguet once observed, "I have been frequently struck with the extreme repugnance manifested by the people of Pennsylvania to the payment of a direct tax, while they so readily agree to the imposition of an indirect tax to any amount." (*Banner of the Constitution,* February 16, 1831.)

[45] *Annals of Cong.,* 1 Cong., 2 Sess., p. 1055.

[46] *Ibid.* 2 Cong., 1 Sess., p. 572.

dens upon the consumer.[47] Fitzsimons, however, "hoped that the House would do something for the manufactures of the country."[48] He especially defended a proposed increase in the duties on coal on the grounds that the United States would soon be able to provide her own supply.[49] The measure was finally passed without a roll call.

A proposal to increase the duty on salt from 12 to 20 cents a bushel in 1797 developed a significant divergence of interest and opinion among the Pennsylvania representatives. The western part of the state as yet brought its salt from the seaboard, and Gallatin, especially, opposed the increase as an oppressive tax upon an article of common necessity. Eastern representatives countered with the conventional protectionist arguments. The final passage found the group evenly divided, with four supporting and four voting against the measure.[50] Salt was destined long to remain a point of weakness in the usually united front of Pennsylvania protectionism.

No further changes seriously involving Pennsylvania interests were made until 1804. The revision of that year transferred a large number of articles from the ad valorem to the specific schedules, and resulted in a real protective duty on window glass. Pennsylvania in the House supported it with a vote of fourteen to one.[51] Perhaps more than any other measure from 1794 to 1816, this may be regarded as a test vote on the principle of protection. The delegation's unanimous support a few days later of the general 2½ per cent. increase to support the Mediterranean fleet was not significant since protectionist and anti-protectionist united in passing the measure.[52]

The period from the passage of Jefferson's Embargo Act to the signing of the Treaty of Ghent constituted an extremely abnormal era in American commercial relations. First the embargo policy and then the war reduced imports to unusually low levels. Nevertheless, protectionist efforts in Congress continued unabated during these years. Diminished revenues and increased expenditures were result-

---

[47] *Annals of Cong.,* 3 Cong., 1 Sess., p. 291ff.
[48] *Ibid.* p. 421.
[49] *Ibid.* p. 699.
[50] *Ibid.* 5 Cong., 1 Sess., p. 447.
[51] *Ibid.* 8 Cong., 1 Sess., p. 1205.
[52] *Ibid.* 8 Cong., 1 Sess., p. 1225.

ing in an ever-mounting deficit in the national finances. To many Pennsylvania Congressmen the situation seemed to afford a heaven-sent opportunity to raise the rates, under cover of the emergency, to at least a maximum revenue basis. Accordingly, much of the legislation sponsored by Pennsylvanians during these years, while ostensibly designed to relieve the treasury, was at heart intended to establish a protective system which would continue to operate even after the return of normal conditions. In 1809 the delegation voted thirteen to three in favor of a general 50 per cent. increase. The measure was defeated in the Senate, however, with Leib voting for it and Gregg voting against it.[53] An effort was made to amend Macon's Bill No. 2 so as to impose a 50 per cent. increase of duty on French and British goods. The intent of the amendment was clearly protective rather than retaliatory. In the House, Adam Seybert made a powerful appeal in behalf of the measure. He argued that protection was needed, not on account of comparative labor costs—which he found as high in England as in America—but because of the inferior foreign products which were sold as American goods. He sought to show that such measures would not bear unjustly upon the South, and that when the infant industries had reached maturity, the protection might be abandoned.[54] The amendment was finally passed in the House, with the Pennsylvania repre-sentatives divided eleven to one in its favor, but was defeated in the Senate.[55]

The outbreak of hostilities in 1812 made an increase in the exist-ing rates absolutely necessary. On April 25, after the preliminary embargo but before the final declaration of war, Roberts of Penn-sylvania introduced a resolution in the House to double all existing duties.[56] Four days after war was declared, the measure was passed, with sixteen affirmative and two negative votes from Pennsylvania. One of the latter was cast by the only Federalist on the delegation and may have been primarily an anti-war vote.[57] In the Senate, Leib voted for the increase while Gregg did not vote.[58] Even in

---

[53] *Ibid.* 10 Cong., 2 Sess., pp. 454, 1448.
[54] *Ibid.* 11 Cong., 2 Sess., pp. 1891-1900.
[55] *Ibid.* p. 1915.
[56] *Ibid.* 12 Cong., 1 Sess., p. 1333.
[57] *Ibid.* p. 1531.
[58] *Ibid.* p. 309.

the midst of a none too successful war, Pennsylvania Congressmen did not cease from their protectionist labors. Samuel Ingham, on April 5, 1814, introduced a resolution requesting the Secretary of the Treasury to report a general tariff act "conformably to the existing situation of the general and local interests of the United States." The resolution was supported by Seybert and Ingersoll, who declared that the existing ad valorem rates were not high enough, and was passed without objection.[59]

The congressional proceedings prior to 1816, therefore, show substantial unanimity in the Pennsylvania delegation in support of every measure for increasing the tariff duties. The strong protectionist inclinations of the group become even more apparent when compared with the votes of other states or of the body as a whole.[60] The few negative votes were cast either for partisan purposes or by isolated individuals from the agricultural sections. The bulk of the farmers at this time supported tariff increases either as preferable to direct taxation, or in the hope of developing domestic markets for agricultural produce. The commercial classes seemed to have become rather indifferent toward the issue, at first because of the great prosperity which the European wars brought to the American carrying trade; then, during the period of restriction and war, because they suffered from other far greater grievances.

Fostered thus by legislation and by war, Pennsylvania manufactures developed very rapidly during this period. The manufacturing census of 1810 showed the state clearly leading the union in both quantity and diversity of industrial product. At the same time, however, the commercial interests of the state were declining with equal rapidity. Senator Plumer noted, as early as 1805, that "the number of buildings in Philadelphia annually encrease—but their trade declines."[61] Two years later, Jefferson observed that "Philadelphia, particularly, is becoming more manufacturing than commercial."[62] The commercial statistics of the period tell the same

---

[59] *Ibid.* 13 Cong., 2 Sess., p. 1959.

[60] It is a fallacy to say, as some writers have done, that these early votes cannot be called protectionist because the rates involved were usually below the maximum revenue standard. Early protectionists could not afford to scorn the day of small beginnings. Governmental policies are not accustomed to spring into being, like the Greek goddess, full-armed from the brain of Jove.

[61] Plumer, *Memorandum*, p. 328.

[62] Jefferson, *Writings*, XI, 397.

story. Pennsylvania in 1789 supplied 20 per cent. of the nation's tonnage in foreign trade; by 1816 the figure had fallen to less than 10 per cent.[63] The inevitable result of the rise of industry and the decline of commerce was to send Pennsylvania into the post-war tariff struggle with a greatly enhanced and unified protectionist sentiment.

The manufacturing census of 1810 gives an unusually complete picture of the industrial development of the nation.[64] Pennsylvania's annual production was estimated at $33,691,111 out of a national total of $172,762,676, or about 19 per cent. of the whole. This exceeded by one-third the production of the closest competitor, New York. As compared with other states, Pennsylvania led in the production of iron and steel, hides and leather manufactures, distilled liquors, paper and hats; was second in glass, and third in textiles. On the basis of value, products worth over a million dollars annually were iron and steel, 6 millions; hides and leather manufactures, almost 5 millions; textiles and distilled liquors, approximately 4 millions each; and hats, a million and a quarter.

The Pennsylvania iron industry was not only the most extensive single interest, but also was particularly prosperous during most of this period. Hamilton, in 1791, reported that since the Revolution the average price of bar iron had risen from $64 to $80 per ton, due to the increased demand for manufacturing purposes.[65] Furnaces that had ceased operation during the Revolution and the succeeding depression were reestablished and new ones were erected.[66] In 1832, a Pennsylvania iron manufacturer testified that "the greatest fortunes made in this country in the iron manufacture were made prior to the late war . . . and this, too, at a time when the duty was only from 5 to 15 per cent."[67] According to the census of 1810, the value of Pennsylvania iron production amounted to 41 per cent. of the national total. There were at that time in operation within the state 44 blast furnaces, 6 air furnaces, 78 forges, 4 bloomeries, 18 rolling and slitting mills, 50 trip hammers, 5 steel furnaces and 175 naileries. The furnaces accounted for 26,878 tons of cast iron, or

---

[63] Seybert, *Statistical Annals*, pp. 320-322.
[64] *American State Papers, Finance*, II, pp. 746-763.
[65] Hamilton, *Works*, IV, 165.
[66] Bishop, *History of American Manufactures*, II, 54n.
[67] *Sen. Doc.*, 21 Cong., 2 Sess., No. 67, p. 52.

50 per cent. of the domestic production; while the forges worked up 10,969 tons of bar iron, or 44 per cent of the total.[68]

Geographically, the greatest industrial concentration was in the southeastern portion of the state, but important enterprises of various kinds were already beginning to spring up in the interior. Philadelphia county produced about 36 per cent. of the total, including especially leather goods, manufactured iron, textiles, hats and distilled liquors. The iron industry in its various phases centered around Philadelphia, Delaware, Chester, Lancaster and Berks counties in the East, in Cumberland and Huntingdon in the middle, and in Fayette and Allegheny in the Pittsburgh region. Leather and leather goods were produced chiefly in the southeastern tier of counties. Philadelphia and Lancaster counties led by a wide margin in the number of distilleries. The chief textile producers were Philadelphia, Berks and Bucks counties in the East and Washington county in the West. The latter was easily the leading area in the production of wool. The newly-established glass industry was found principally in three widely separated counties, Allegheny, Wayne and Philadelphia.

Even at this early period, **Pittsburgh was beginning to come** forward as a growing manufacturing center. Michaux reported, as early as 1802, that Pittsburgh was shipping bar iron, coarse linen, bottles and whisky down the river to New Orleans.[69] Visiting the city a year later, Harris found "most of the manufactures that are to be met with in any other part of the United States."[70] Niles referred to it in 1814 as the "Birmingham of America" and enthusiastically predicted that it was destined to become "the greatest manufacturing town in the world."[71] At this time the future iron metropolis boasted four iron foundries and one steel furnace, from

---

[68] *American State Papers, Finance*, II, 695-6.

[69] Thwaites, *Early Western Travels*, III, 158.

[70] *Ibid.* III, 343.

[71] *Niles' Register*, VI, 208. English travelers derived much amusement from the "Birmingham of America." Birkbeck thought that it resembled the Birmingham of a century and a half before, and cautioned Americans against thus confusing the future subjunctive with the present indicative. (*Notes on a Journey in America*, p. 41.) Fearon suggested that "if the inhabitants of Pittsburgh are determined to call the place after some English town, I should propose that . . . it be denominated, with relation to the humidity of its climate 'the American Manchester,' for I remained at this place for several days during which time the rain never ceased." (*Sketches of America*, p. 201.)

which cannon and munitions were supplied to Perry's fleet on Lake Erie and Jackson's army at New Orleans.[72] A local census in 1815 reported 1960 workers employed in manufactures and a total output valued at $2,617,833. Of this sum the manufacture of iron constituted about $800,000.[73] Thus even in the far western part of the state there was being laid the economic basis for a strong protectionist sentiment, which, with the coming of peace, was soon to unite with its seaboard prototype in a despairing cry for legislative assistance.

---

[72] Jones, *Pittsburgh in 1826*, p. 54; Swank, *Iron in All Ages*, p. 227.
[73] *American State Papers, Finance*, III, 641; *Hazard's Register*, IV, 168.

# Chapter III

## POST-WAR PROTECTIONISM, 1815-1824

The treaty of Ghent brought to a majority of the American people a welcome deliverance from a none too glorious conflict. To the manufacturers of the country, however, peace meant the abrupt loss of the virtual monopoly under which they had been rapidly and profitably expanding their establishments. They realized that, regardless of treaties, Britain was still their foe; relentlessly determined to reconquer her former markets and to "stifle in the cradle" the infant industries which had developed in the United States during the war. There seemed cold comfort in a peace which merely transferred the struggle from the battlefield to the market place and substituted for armed conquest a scarcely less menacing commercial invasion.

The termination of the war necessarily reopened the tariff question; since the double duties were to expire one year after the close of hostilities. Pennsylvania protectionists eagerly seized the opportunity to demand that the wartime rates be maintained as a bulwark against the anticipated influx of foreign goods. Even before imports had reached competitive proportions, the manufacturers of Philadelphia informed Congress that they could not "divest themselves of anxiety and dread for the fate of the infant manufactures, whose existence and prosperity are unquestionably of vital importance to the whole community."[1] A correspondent of the Philadelphia *Aurora* suggested that immediate duties of 50 per cent. should be imposed, which might be reduced gradually to a permanent level of 35 per cent.[2] Another writer, viewing protection as a moral obligation upon the government, declared,

Should it not, therefore, be the hope and the wish of every true friend to the genuine interests of our country, that the confidence manifested by our manufacturers in their government during the war, by increasing their different establishments to the utmost of their abilities, and by the erection of new works of different kinds . . . should not, in time of peace, be found to be misplaced, founded as it was, on the hopes they entertained, that on the restoration of peace, the fos-

---

[1] *Annals of Cong.*, 13 Cong., 3 Sess., p. 1195.
[2] February 25, 1815.

tering hand of the constituted authorities would be immediately extended to their relief, support and patronage. Can we for a moment suppose that these hopes, these reasonable expectations, will be blasted? — No! Congress will do their duty; they will realize all the reasonable expectations of their manufacturers . . . by continuing the double duty on articles imported.[3]

The growing intensity of feeling in favor of protection was further evidenced by the fact that now for the first time the Pennsylvania state authorities ventured to exert their official influence in a sphere supposedly reserved to the federal government. Governor Snyder opened the legislative session with a warm plea for protection,[4] and the lower house responded by adopting with a large majority a resolution favoring such duties "as will effectually protect those manufactures in which our country has already engaged.[5] The measure was defeated in the Senate, however, by a vote closely following the lines of economic interest in the state.[6] Such incursions by executive and legislature into the realm of tariff controversy soon came to be a stereotyped feature of the protectionist agitation in Pennsylvania.

The principal objective of the post-war movement in Pennsylvania, as elsewhere, was increased protection for the textile industry. One newspaper correspondent went so far as to suggest a total prohibition on the importation of foreign fabrics;[7] while the more practical woolen manufacturers of the state asked Congress for at least the continuation of the war duties. These industrialists asserted that the American producer needed protection because of "first, the higher prices he pays here for the wool, the machinery, and the workmanship; second, the probable depression of wool and cloth abroad; thirdly, the enormous import sold here below their cost; and, lastly, the prejudice of the country in favor of foreign fabrics."[8] Next to textiles, the iron interests of the state were perhaps the most vocal in their appeal to the national legislature for a degree of

---

[3] *Pittsburgh Mercury*, October 21, 1815.
[4] *Pennsylvania Archives*, Fourth Series, IV, 890.
[5] *House Journal*, 1815-16, pp. 553, 563-5. The provision restricting protection to industries already in existence was inserted at the suggestion of James Buchanan, then as ever, the advocate of the middle road in tariff legislation. (*Harrisburg Chronicle*, March 11, 1816.)
[6] *Senate Journal*, 1815-16, p. 354.
[7] *Aurora*, February 25, 1815.
[8] *Annals of Cong.*, 14 Cong., 1 Sess., p. 1711.

protection which in some cases, at least, approached the point of absolute prohibition.[9]

No actual legislation on the tariff was possible until the Fourteenth Congress convened in December, 1815. As soon as the session opened, however, the manufacturers of Philadelphia dispatched an able delegation of three men to Washington to present in as favorable light as possible their claims for governmental encouragement.[10] The nature of their appeal may be surmised from the following excerpt, written by a member of this lobby to one of the most prominent members of the Pennsylvania delegation,

The double duties you must continue if you do not you will ruin Three Fourths of our merchants and shopkeepers for their stores are full of goods at the double duties and . . . if the double duties are taken off the manufacturers abroad will come in with their goods and undersell the present holders — and moreover our own manufacturers require the Double duties. . . . We never can say we are independent when we are obliged to send to England for our Coat and to Ireland for our Shirt.[11]

It quickly became apparent that the protectionist forces in Congress, while numerous, were not sufficiently strong to retain the double duties. It was voted, however, to continue the war rates until June 30, 1816 in order to permit adequate time for deliberation on the new measure. Sergeant of Pennsylvania suggested a further extension to January 1, 1817, on the grounds that so abrupt a termination would tend "to alarm the whole manufacturing interest, which was now looking up to the Government for additional support, instead of expecting an early reduction of the existing duties."[12] This proposal, although supported by three-fourths of the Pennsylvania representatives, was overwhelmingly rejected by the House.[13]

The basis for the revision was a report submitted by the Secretary of the Treasury, Alexander Dallas, himself a Philadelphian. To serve at once the requirements of protection and of revenue, the Secretary divided the rates into three classes. Goods already produced in sufficient quantities to satisfy the home demand should

9 *Cf.* Wm. Montgomery to Sergeant, December 12, 1815; Sergeant MSS.
10 *Aurora,* November 27, December 4, 1815.
11 Thomas Leiper to Sergeant, January 2, 1816; Sergeant MSS.
12 *Annals of Cong.,* 14 Cong., 1 Sess., p. 675.
13 *Ibid.* p. 690.

be thoroughly protected, since "a wise Government will surely deem it better to sacrifice a portion of its revenue, than to sacrifice those institutions which private enterprise and wealth have connected with public prosperity and independence." Manufactures not yet adequate to meet domestic requirements, but which might become so with proper cultivation, should receive such duties "as will enable the manufacturer to meet the importer in the American market upon equal terms of profit and loss." The remaining articles, produced in small quantities or not at all, should be taxed solely with an eye to revenue.[14] In short, the tariff recommended by Dallas was sufficiently Pennsylvanian to bring into issue the whole general subject of protection.

The debates upon the bill are very imperfectly reported, but the Pennsylvania delegation seems to have played a comparatively minor part in the proceedings. This was perhaps due to a natural lack of enthusiasm for a measure which, while paying lip service to the protective principle, actually effected a considerable reduction in duties. Nevertheless, Samuel Ingham contributed an able speech in defence of the proposed bill, in the course of which he boldly declared that "the great principle involved in this bill was not a revenue proposition . . . Its great primary object was to make such a modification of duties upon the various articles of importation, as would give the necessary and proper protection and support to the agriculture, manufactures, and commerce of the country. The revenue is only an incidental consideration." He asserted that the tariff was not "a mere contrivance to collect taxes from the people in the easiest way, without their knowing it, but a measure intended and calculated to increase their comfort, happiness, and wealth, and of course their disposition and ability to pay whatsoever the exigencies of the Government may require, and as a necessary consequence to increase and perpetuate the security, the peace, and especially the independence of the nation." He believed further that "we ought to promote every species of internal industry . . . in which the conditions of the country and the inclination and capacity of the people may authorize a reasonable prospect of success."[15]

Indirectly replying to Ingham, John Ross of Northampton county

---

[14] *Ibid.* p. 1685.
[15] *Annals of Cong.*, 14 Cong., 1 Sess., pp. 1239-45.

delivered a few days later one of the most unique tariff speeches ever made by a Pennsylvania Congressman. He rose, he said, to reply to those

who maintained that the Government was pledged to afford a high protection to manufactures, and against the rage for fostering them to the exclusion of every other pursuit. He desired the independence of the people as well as national independence, and wished not to see one class of the community enslaved by another. . . . If the extravagant duties proposed were not necessary for revenue, he could see no strong necessity for them. . . . All manufactories were conducted with slaves, because the occupation had a tendency to degrade and debase the human mind. . . . The only kind of manufactures he wished to see flourishing, were those conducted in families; any others would prove destructive to the liberties of this Republic, by combinations effecting a revolution in this House and in the Government. There was already great necessity for a strong country party to withstand the manufacturing and commercial parties here.[16]

Ross, true to his principles, opposed the tariff at every stage of its passage. On one occasion he expressed the wish that "the ambassadors from the cotton factories had at once made a treaty with the Committee of Ways and Means, which the House might have swallowed and left the other manufactories to themselves, and not be burdening the people in every possible way under the plea of protection."[17] In spite of such heterodoxy, Ross was reelected to the succeeding Congress—clear evidence that in 1816 the protectionist conquest of Pennsylvania was not yet complete.

The profound antipathy to manufactures displayed by the Northampton Representative was by no means shared by the majority of his colleagues. Whenever the protectionist issue was clearly drawn, the delegation consistently supported the higher duties. The proposal to strike out the minimum valuation on cottons affords possibly the best test vote of the entire proceedings on the abstract principle of protection. The change would have substituted very moderate for almost prohibitive rates on course cotton goods, and was accordingly opposed by sixteen out of the nineteen Pennsylvanians voting.[18] Only two members of the delegation approved the reduction of the duty on hammered bar iron from 75 cents to 45 cents per hundred-

16 *Ibid.* p. 1272.
17 *Ibid.* p. 1284.
18 *Ibid.* p. 1348.

weight, a serious blow to the iron interest of the state.[19] In spite of this and other reverses, the delegation was inclined to accept the bill as affording the best protection obtainable, and on the final roll call contributed seventeen affirmative and three negative votes.[20] The debate in the Senate has not been recorded, but both Pennsylvania Senators assisted in passing the measure.[21]

The tariff act of 1816 as passed was considerably less protective than the emergency war duties it replaced; indeed, in several particulars, its rates were decidedly lower than those recommended by the Secretary of the Treasury. Course cottons were well cared for through the workings of the minimum principle, but woolen manufactures, for which much of the raw material had to be imported, obtained little real relief. The rates on iron, in which Pennsylvania felt a peculiar interest, were for the most part low. The new act imposed a tax of $1.50 per hundredweight on rolled bar iron, but only 45 cents per hundredweight on the hammered article. In the case of the former, which was not then produced in America, the duty afforded really vigorous protection; but the latter impost was only equivalent to about 18 per cent. on the average price of bar iron in England.[22] Pig iron was admitted at the comparatively low rate of 20 per cent. ad valorem. The tariff as adopted, therefore, can scarcely be considered a particularly Pennsylvanian measure, either in its authorship or in its provisions.

The tariff of 1816 evoked little comment at the time of passage. It soon became evident, however, that the measure was hopelessly inadequate to stem the long pent-up flood of English merchandise seeking an outlet regardless of price. The strain of over-supply and consequent low prices bore hard on the domestic manufacturers and many of them were compelled to close their factories and discharge their workmen. At the same time food prices and rents remained excessively high; so that there was intense suffering among the Philadelphia poor during the winter of 1816-17. As a result of the existing distress, Pennsylvania papers became increasingly critical

---

[19] *Ibid.* p. 1326.
[20] *Ibid.* p. 1352.
[21] *Ibid.* p. 331.
[22] See tables of prices in Scrivenor, *Comprehensive History of the Iron Trade*, pp. 377, 407, 409.

of the government and its tariff policy. Discussing the origin of the act of 1816, the *Aurora* declared,

Whether it was English influence which operated on the tariff, or private mercantile interest operating to the prejudice of the most sacred and safest policy for an independent nation . . . the whole of the manufacturing capital was sacrificed by the abandonment of the double duties and the adoption of an insidious and contemptible theory which was reprobated as fallacious at the period in question, but which has now realized even more than was then said of it.[23]

Early in 1817, a committee of the state Senate reported that "in all parts of the country our manufactures are rapidly declining and sinking under a foreign combination and forced importation, and the unwillingness of the government to protect and uphold them."[24] At the same time, a resolution easily passed both houses of the Assembly which urged the Pennsylvania members of Congress "to use their endeavors to have such measures adopted, as will effectually protect and encourage the manufactures of the United States."[25]

The chief petitioners for additional protection at this time were the ironmasters of the state, who felt that their industry had been discriminated against under the existing law. During the first two months of 1817 some ten memorials were introduced in Congress from Pennsylvania manufacturers.[26] A typical appeal recited that "the manufacturers of iron are at present in a very depressed state, owing to the great influx of foreign iron and the reduced price at which it is sold. They believe that unless timely aid is afforded, this important branch of our national industry must sink into total ruin."[27] Relief was not immediately forthcoming, but the attack was renewed in the following session of Congress under the able leadership of John Sergeant.[28] Chiefly through the efforts of the Pennsylvania delegation, an act was passed imposing a specific duty of 50 cents per hundredweight on pig iron, and increasing the rate on hammered bar iron from 45 cents to 75 cents a hundredweight.

---

[23] December 7, 1816.
[24] *Senate Journal*, 1816-17, p. 255.
[25] *Ibid.* p. 260; *House Journal*, 1816-17, p. 464.
[26] Carey, M., *New Olive Branch*, p. 48.
[27] *Niles' Register*, XIII, 149.
[28] *Annals of Congress*, 15 Cong., 1 Sess., pp. 1726-7.

At the same time legislation was adopted extending the duration of the cotton and woolens duties imposed in 1816. Both measures were supported unanimously by the Pennsylvania representatives, who regarded them as important victories for the policy of protection.[29]

Meanwhile the state was on the eve of an event of most far-reaching significance in the development of Pennsylvania protectionism. Since the war, the whole economic structure of the commonwealth had been resting upon the uncertain foundations of a recklessly inflated currency. Forty-one banks with an aggregate capital of $17,000,000 had been chartered by the legislature during the single year of 1814; thirty-seven of these had actually gone into operation. Expansion and depreciation of the currency was the inevitable result. On the day when the tariff of 1816 went into effect the paper of the Pennsylvania banks was circulating at a discount of from 17 to 25 per cent.; or sufficient to nullify completely most of the duties imposed by that measure.[30] Thus a depreciated currency and swelling imports set up a sort of vicious circle to undermine the industrial stability and economic equilibrium of the state. Banking manias, however, are wont to carry within themselves the seeds of their own destruction, and in this case the bubble of inflation burst abruptly in the latter part of 1818. Prices began to fall rapidly and heavily, as the country entered upon an era of deflation and financial readjustment. Everyone was involved; the fall of wages affected the laborer; the decline of food prices injured the farmer; and the lowering of rents impoverished the landowner. The result was that the whole community was made to experience the same distress which had already overtaken the manufacturer because of heavy importations and low prices. It is not surprising, therefore, that the feeling of economic interdependence thus engendered had a profound unifying effect upon the attitude of Pennsylvania toward the tariff question.

The general distress which began in 1818 reached its climax during the following year, but the readjustment to a new scale of monetary exchange was not fully completed until the latter part of 1821. The effects of the depression were naturally most conspicuous in Philadelphia with its concentrated working population and inflated real estate values. Flint found, in December, 1818, that "the pre-

---

[29] *Annals of Congress,* 15 Cong., 1 Sess., pp. 1740, 1743.
[30] *Hunt's Merchants' Mag.,* **X**, 318.

dominance of British goods has shut up many workshops that were employed during the late war."[31] The number of unemployed in the city during 1819 was variously estimated at from 7,288 to 20,000 out of a total population of about 110,000.[32] A committee appointed to take emergency measures for relief reported that "unless some early change takes place in the affairs of the community . . . the suffering of the poor will far exceed anything that America has heretofore witnessed."[33] One of the directors of the Bank of the United States, writing to a friend in England, thus described the rapid fall of prices which had occurred, "Houses which rented for $1200 now rent for $450; fuel which cost $12, now costs $5½; flour which was $10 and $11 is now $4½; beef 25 cents, now 8 cents."[34]

Much the same situation existed in the Pittsburgh region, where the industrial interest had been hard pressed ever since 1816. A committee report in that year represented that "the manufacture of cottons, woolens, flint glass, and the finer articles of iron, has lately suffered the most alarming depression. Some branches which had been several years in operation have been destroyed or partially suspended, and others of a more recent growth, annihilated before they were completely in operation."[35] The English observer, Birkbeck, who visited Pittsburgh two years later, found that "the manufacturers are under great difficulties, and many are on the eve of suspending their operations, owing to the influx of depreciated fabrics from Europe."[36] Evans, whose "pedestrious tour" took him to the western metropolis at about the same time, reported a similar decline of business.[37] A local survey, contrasting conditions in 1815

---

[31] Thwaites, *Early Western Travels*, IX, 58.

[32] The lower figure was probably more nearly correct. Nevertheless, a survey of Philadelphia industries at the height of the depression revealed an astonishing decline in employment. The number of workers reported in three of the leading lines of production was:

|                     |   | 1814 | 1816 | 1819 |
|---------------------|---|------|------|------|
| Cotton manufacture  | . . . | 1761 | 2325 | 149  |
| Woolen manufacture  | . . . | 1310 | 1226 | 260  |
| Iron casting        | . . . . . | 1093 | 1152 | 52   |

For various estimates on unemployment see *Hazard's Register*, IV, 168; *Niles' Register*, XVII, 117; Thwaites, *Early Western Travels*, IX, 274; Carey, M., *Appeal to Common Sense*, p. 63; *Pittsburgh Statesman*, November 9, 1819.

[33] *Aurora*, September 8, 1819.

[34] Unidentified clipping in Mathew Carey scrapbooks.

[35] *Niles' Register*, XII, 130.

[36] Birkbeck, *Notes on a Journey in America*, p. 41.

[37] Thwaites, *Early Western Travels*, VIII, 248.

with those in 1819, found that employment had decreased from 1960 to 672; while the value of the product had fallen from \$2,617,833 to \$832,000.[38] Such pessimistic accounts are at least partially confirmed by the manufacturing census of 1820, which reported many factories in western Pennsylvania either closed or depressed.[39]

Less conspicuous than the industrial distress, but none the less real, was the hardship inflicted upon the farmers of the state by the collapse of the circulating medium. Heavy exportations of foodstuffs had served to keep agricultural prices at extremely high levels for several years after the war. By 1819, however, the combined effect of the English corn laws and good harvests in Europe had largely closed this outlet, and left the American market glutted. The price of foodstuffs fell ruinously; flour in Philadelphia dropped from \$14.75 per barrel in March, 1817, to \$3.62 in March, 1821—a shift in four years from the highest to the lowest quotations to be found between the Revolution and the Civil War.[40] At the same time this staple was selling in Pittsburgh as low as a dollar per barrel.[41] Other farm prices suffered equally rapid declines; wool, for instance fell from \$1.50 to 50 cents a pound within a comparatively short time.[42] The inevitable result was a corresponding drop in land values, in many cases to one-half or one-third the original figure.[43]

As has been pointed out, the primary cause of this widespread depression was a faulty banking structure and an inflated currency. Excessive imports followed inevitably, but they were the symptoms of economic maladjustment rather than the disease itself.[44] Never-

---

[38] *Pittsburgh Gazette,* January 11, 1820.

[39] *American State Papers, Finance,* IV, 104-123.

[40] See table of monthly flour prices in Grosvenor, *Does Protection Protect?* p. 110.

[41] *Pittsburgh Mercury,* May 23, 1821.

[42] *Aurora,* February 28, 1818.

[43] *Pittsburgh Gazette,* September 15, 1818.

[44] This was the view adopted by a special committee of the Pennsylvania Senate, appointed in 1820 to inquire into the extent and causes of the existing crisis. The committee found "that a distress unexampled in our country since the period of its independence, prevails throughout the commonwealth." They believed, however, that the cause thereof was "to be found chiefly in the abuses of the banking system, which abuses consist first in the excessive number of banks, and secondly in their universal bad administration. . . . The want of protection to domestic manufactures, although it may apply in a great degree to the operations of manufacturing towns, yet it is not valid as relates to the great mass of people of the commonwealth, who can perceive in the banking institutions the immediate causes of their embarrassments." (*Senate Journal,* 1819-20, pp. 222-31.)

theless the flood of foreign merchandise was visible and tangible and appealed to the popular imagination as no abstract monetary theory could have done. The result was that as the distress continued public opinion turned increasingly to a protective tariff as a panacea for existing economic ills.

Perhaps the most striking feature of this accelerated protectionist movement was its strength among the hitherto apathetic agricultural population. As far back as 1787 Pennsylvania protectionists had been wooing the farmer with a seductive picture of tariff-born industries at his doorstep, eager to consume his produce and to enrich his coffers.[45] So long, however, as war-torn Europe provided a sufficient demand to sustain the price of foodstuffs, a home market continued a matter of secondary importance to the average agriculturalist. The financial crisis of 1819 quickly dispelled this indifference. Rightly or wrongly, the farmer attributed his difficulties to the lack of a constant and permanent market close at home, and argued that the growth of domestic industry would not only supply the deficiency, but also by the transfer of workers from the field to the factory would convert unwelcome competitors into welcome customers. Such a hypothesis once adopted, the protectionist conquest of the agricultural element of the state was both easy and rapid. As early as 1820 the farmers of Allegheny county were actually petitioning Congress for more adequate protection to domestic industry.[46] Five years later, Hezekiah Niles believed that "the farmers of Pennsylvania are unanimously favorable to the tariff."[47] Such a statement, while not literally true, was substantially accurate. Three years of hard times had done more than a generation of abstract reasoning to reconcile the agriculturalist to the tariff policy of the manufacturer. Thereafter, in most sections of the state, the two interests worked harmoniously and effectively together in the cause of protection.

Another marked feature of Pennsylvania sentiment at this time was the intense protectionism which was manifest even in the regions most remote from the Atlantic seaboard and Europe. The people of Pittsburgh, in particular, attributed their troubles to the

---

[45] *Cf. American Museum*, II, 361.
[46] *Pittsburgh Gazette*, February 8, 15, 1820.
[47] *Niles' Register*, XXIX, 50.

tariff rather than the currency, and zealously advocated an increase in the existing duties. The intemperate nature of public sentiment on the subject is suggested by the following extract from one of the leading journals of the city:

The peace has glutted our country with English goods, even to loathing, and the importation of British manufactures has affected our western establishments with a deadly palsy. Our capital is rushing in floods to the seaboard to satisfy European claims; we are bleeding at every pore, and we can look but to two sources for relief from evil, to a constant state of war, or to a systematic encouragement of manufactures. The idea is horrible that in a civilized country, a refined people should sigh for a state of perpetual hostility; that the genius of prosperity, like the Asiatic Juggernaut, can only be conciliated by the blood of human victims. Yet self-defence and self-interest must suggest these wishes, if Congress do not extend to us the fostering hand of encouragement.[48]

The question naturally arises as to how far these interior sections of the country were really affected by foreign imports, which could be obtained only after slow and costly transport by rough mountain roads or by long and circuitous water routes. Examination of the evidence on this point indicates that the geographical barrier, while partially effective, was not wholly so; and that European merchandise in considerable quantity and variety was actually competing with the domestic product in the western market. Even before the war, observers noted the prevalence of British goods beyond the Alleghenies. Michaux reported in 1802 that "seven-tenths of the manufactured articles consumed in Kentucky . . . are imported from England."[49] Harris and Cuming both were surprised to find many foreign products selling almost as cheaply on the Ohio as at the port of entry.[50] Cramer in 1811 estimated that Pittsburgh merchants were handling each year about one million dollars worth of imported goods, "which are the great sore of our country, and will be as long as the balance of trade is against us on the sea."[51] Interrupted during the war, the influx was resumed on a larger scale after the restoration of peace. The goods reached Pittsburgh by any one of three routes; one overland by wagon from Philadelphia or

[48] *Pittsburgh Gazette*, September 11, 1818.
[49] Thwaites, *Early Western Travels*, III, 203.
[50] *Ibid*. III, 343; IV, 229.
[51] Cramer, *The Navigator*, 1811, p. 72.

Baltimore; another by way of the Hudson, Mohawk and Allegheny rivers, broken by a short land portage; the third, by boat from New Orleans. The latter method was best adapted to more bulky commodities, such as sugar, coffee, liquors, salt, iron, and salted fish, but its terminus on the Gulf was remote from the established lines of commerce.[52] The normal cost of carriage from Philadelphia to Pittsburgh was about $5 per hundredweight, although in times of stress it went as high as $11 per hundredweight.[53] Transport by way of the New York rivers also cost about $5 per hundredweight but was slower than the overland route,[54] while goods could be brought from New Orleans to any part of the Ohio valley for from $2.50 to $3 per hundredweight.[55] A committee of the New York Assembly estimated that the value of the goods involved in this trade would run at least $200 to the hundredweight; if so, the cost of transport from the coast to Pittsburgh would average less than 10 per cent. of the selling price, and on items of great value in small compass the proportion would be much less.[56] There is reason to believe, therefore, that the heavy importations of the post-war period actually afforded serious competition to the infant industries of western Pennsylvania and thus provided a real and immediate basis for the virulent protectionism which for the first time swept that section of the state.[57]

The financial crisis in one other way gave added impetus to the protectionist movement in Pennsylvania; for it brought into the arena one of the most persistent propagandists who ever wielded a pen—Mathew Carey of Philadelphia. Carey had long been known as one of the city's leading publishers and most fearless and aggres-

---

[52] *Niles' Register*, XXII, Supplement, p. 69.

[53] *American State Papers*, Miscellaneous, II, 117; Birkbeck, *Notes on a Journey in America*, p. 36; Thwaites, *Early Western Travels*, VIII, 249; Ringwalt, *Development of Transportation Systems*, p. 27; *Pittsburgh Gazette*, July 31, 1818.

[54] *Niles' Register*, XV, 267; *Pittsburgh Gazette, December 22, 1818.*

[55] Meyer, *History of Transportation in the United States*, pp. 88, 111.

[56] *Public Documents Relating to the New York Canals*, p. 392.

[57] The amount of foreign imports brought into the Pittsburgh region cannot be determined with any degree of accuracy. During the years of post-war depression the land carriage westward from Philadelphia to Pittsburgh averaged about 21,000,000 pounds annually. (*Penn. Senate Journal*, 1822-23, p. 150.) This included both domestic and foreign commodities, but the latter must have constituted a considerable proportion of the whole.

sive journalists. Heredity had given him the enthusiastic temperament of the Celt, with its proverbially eager quest for the controversial and its instinctive revulsion to fancied wrong. His early writings had revealed an intense love for his adopted country; a violent hatred for England; and a strong humanitarian zeal for promoting the public welfare. All these impulses were outraged by the distress of 1819, in which he saw a ruthless attempt upon the part of Britain to reduce the United States to a condition of economic vassalage. He had long been a believer in the desirability of domestic manufactures as an instrument of national growth and independence and had been a member of the manufacturers' lobby at Washington in 1815, but otherwise had taken no active part in the tariff controversy. The monetary collapse and the suffering which followed induced him to abandon this passive rôle and to embrace the cause of protection with all the fervor of an inspired crusader. For the next fifteen years he labored, as he said, "with full as much zeal and ardour as if my temporal and eternal salvation depended on it."[58]

Carey's great objective was to arouse an irresistible body of public opinion favorable to the restrictive system. He believed that the desirability of protection was so apparent that if he could but carry the facts to the people, its triumph was assured.[59] Mindful of Tom Paine's revolutionary successes, he determined to make the pamphlet his chief medium of agitation, and accordingly entered upon a career of intensive literary production. Never an easy writer, he often spent twelve to fourteen hours a day at his desk.[60] The quantity of his output is astonishing. He, himself, declared that "probably there never was so great a number of publications issued by one man on any one subject."[61] A mere enumeration of titles includes over sixty tracts, comprising some 2500 pages. Such a list, however, gives no adequate idea of his total production; since many of these pamphlets appeared in several editions, constantly revised and enlarged. More than half of these publications were printed and distributed at his own expense; the remainder were financed by

---

[58] Carey, M., *Autobiographical Sketches*, p. 2.
[59] *Ibid.* p. 4.
[60] Carey, M., *The Olive Branch*, No. III, p. xi.
[61] Carey, M., *The Crisis*, p. 21.

intermittent contributions from friends of the cause. To Carey's flaming zeal, such assistance appeared pitifully inadequate to the work at hand, and he published many unseemly diatribes against those manufacturers who failed to support with lavish hand his ambitious projects.[62]

Carey, in his pamphlets, utterly repudiated the hackneyed formula of revenue with incidental protection. He defined a sound tariff as one which "renders revenue subservient to the promotion of individual industry and national prosperity,"[63] and believed that "the higher the duty on any article the greater and speedier the benefit to the public."[64] Concerning the futility of free trade he wrote, "Decay, decrepitude, and ruin have uniformly attended such a system, in all past ages; and, by the eternal laws of the moral world, cannot fail to produce the same effect to the end of time."[65] These and equally dogmatic assertions were supported, not with the calm detachment of the philosopher but with the crude give and take of the polemical journalist. His arguments consisted for the most part of casual accumulations of fact and figures which a contemporary euphemistically described as displaying "a longing after victory rather than a desire for truth."[66] The weapons of his armament were not great in number, but were of a kind well adapted to his purpose. The constitutionality of the tariff was supported with long compilations of extracts from the utterances of the Fathers. Similar quotations were exhumed to prove the tariff inconsistencies of Calhoun, McDuffie, and Thomas Cooper. He repeatedly turned to Great Britain, France, and Russia for illustrations of the happy workings of the restrictive system and in contrast depicted the ruinous desolation of the unprotected American economic structure. He sought again and again to show how commerce and agriculture had been the recipients of legislative favors ever since the establishment of the government, while industry had been as uniformly neglected. Again, somewhat inconsistently, he urged the protective policy for the special benefit it would bring to the American farmer. The alleged distress of the South was sometimes discounted; sometimes attributed to the over-

---

[62] *Cf.* Carey, M., *Autobiographical Sketches*, pp. 4, 113; *Collectanea*, p. 18.
[63] Carey, M., *New Olive Branch*, p. 25.
[64] Carey to J. S. Johnston, May 2, 1824; Johnston MSS.
[65] Carey, M., *Essays on Political Economy*, p. 229.
[66] *Democratic Press*, June 25, 1825.

production of cotton, caused by inadequate protection to the cotton mills of the North. Free trade memorials and reports were subjected to the closest scrutiny and then elaborately refuted. In the way of fundamental arguments for protection, Carey originated nothing. His task was to take the familiar arguments and recast them into new and striking forms, or to endow them with pleasing reality by means of statistical and other illustrative material. Many a protectionist speech of that day found its bone and sinew in one of Carey's pamphlets, and many of his assertions have survived to take a permanent place in the protectionist creed.

Carey's literary contributions, though voluminous, represented but one phase of his protectionist activity. No agency was too humble, no instrument too obscure for the eager publicist. With circular letters and petitions, through the college and the press, in public meetings and manufacturers' organizations, he ceaselessly labored to impart to others the faith that was within him. For printing, traveling expenses and postage, he expended over $4,000 of his own money, exclusive of the value of his time.[67] In 1824 he established and edited a weekly paper, *The Political Economist*, dedicated to the protectionist cause, but the project had to be abandoned after four months of intermittent publication for want of support.[68] He even offered to contribute $500 a year to the University of Maryland toward the expense of a professorship in political economy to be held by Daniel Raymond, whose treatise, he declared, contained "more sound practical truths than I have ever seen in any book on the subject." This offer was not accepted, possibly because of Raymond's outspoken views in opposition to slavery.[69] Carey himself, later characterized this project as "absurd," since he believed that the same amount expended in the dissemination of pamphlets would have been more useful.[70]

The period of distress from 1818 to 1821 represented, therefore, a real turning point in the development of Pennsylvania protectionism. It provided three important elements of strength which had formerly been lacking. In the first place, it effected the conversion of the

[67] Carey, M., *The Crisis*, p. 18.
[68] Carey, M., *Autobiographical Sketches*, p. 109.
[69] *Ibid.* p. 112.
[70] Carey, M., "Autobiography," *New England Magazine*, VII, 483.

previously apathetic agricultural interest, comprising two-thirds of the total population. Secondly, it proved for the first time to the industrialists of western Pennsylvania that they, too, had a direct, vital interest in the policy of protection.[71] Finally, the accession of Mathew Carey made certain that the tariff propaganda in the state would henceforth be pushed with relentless persistence and untiring zeal. Thus it was that perhaps the most lasting result of the years of depression in Pennsylvania was to produce a tariff movement better organized, more aggressive, more intolerant and infinitely more powerful than any which had preceded.

The dawn of a more intense and more militant protectionism was heralded as early as 1819 by many indications. One of these was the revival of societies for the encouragement of domestic manufactures, somewhat similar to those which had sprung up in the early years of the Republic but which had long since passed into oblivion. Two such bodies were organized in Philadelphia during 1819, both sponsored by the indefatigable Mathew Carey.[72] Their avowed purpose was to encourage the use of American manufactures and to work toward the adoption of a protective policy. Similar bodies, with like objectives, were organized at Lancaster, Harrisburg, Pittsburgh and elsewhere.[73] These societies hastened to exert pressure on both President and Congress in behalf of higher duties.[74] The propagandist efforts of one of the Philadelphia organizations drew the fire of Representative Whitman, who complained:

---

[71] It is significant that for the next decade, Pennsylvania's most active protectionists in Congress came from the western part of the state.

[72] The existence of so many Philadelphia societies with almost similar names has been a source of great confusion—especially among foreign writers. Those most likely to be confused, with dates of organization, are:
1. The Pennsylvania Society for the Encouragement of Manufactures and the Useful Arts (August, 1787).
2. The Philadelphia Society for the Encouragement of Domestic Manufactures (March, 1806).
3. The Philadelphia Society for the Promotion of National Industry (March, 1819).
4. The Pennsylvania Society for the Encouragement of American Manufactures (September, 1819).
5. The Pennsylvania Society for the Promotion of Manufactures and the Mechanic Arts (December, 1826).

[73] *Aurora*, August 23, October 8, November 1, 1819; *United States Gazette*, September 10, 1819; *Harrisburg Reporter*, November 19, December 10, 1819.

[74] *Cf. Niles' Register*, XVI, 219.

An association in Philadelphia, calling itself a Society for the Promotion of National Industry, has its branches in every part of the Union, with which it corresponds, and which it directs, and instigates, and sets in motion, by the means of pamphlets and newspaper essays. Its inflammatory and unfounded statements have pervaded every part of the Union. Each member of the present Congress has been favored with enough to make two large volumes at least. And these have, for a moment, deluded the people, and made them believe it is wise to annihilate commerce, in order to build up great manufactories.[75]

Another evidence that Pennsylvanians were beginning to treat the tariff question very seriously is found in the action of a Philadelphia mass meeting in the fall of 1819, where it was agreed "that at all future elections for members of the state legislature or the Congress of the United States, we will vote for no man who is known to be unfriendly to the support and protection of domestic manufactures."[76] However, no concerted measures for carrying this threat into effect seem to have been taken. Some of the manifestations of protective enthusiasm at this time verged upon the unconventional. For instance, the grand jury of the Eastern District of Pennsylvania drew up an address to the other grand juries of the United States, in which they outlined what they would regard as an acceptable tariff act.[77] Another Pennsylvanian evolved an ingenious device whereby foreign manufactures might be excluded by state action. He held that while the state authorities had no power to regulate commerce, they did have a right to prohibit it completely, as in the case of a quarantine; and he suggested that Pennsylvania invoke its police power "to subject that commerce to a long quarantine which is ruinous to the morals, the industry, and the political health of their people generally, and is bringing starvation to the door of a large portion of their most useful citizens."[78] Meanwhile, the shoemakers of Philadelphia had become so impressed with protectionist reasoning that they petitioned the governor and state Assembly for legislation prohibiting the sale of New England shoes in Pennsylvania, on the grounds that the New Englanders were "a species of foreigners."[79]

---

[75] *Annals of Cong.*, 16 Cong., 1 Sess., p. 2002.
[76] *Aurora*, August 23, 1819.
[77] *Ibid.* November 13, 1819.
[78] Unidentified clipping dated December 29, 1819 in Mathew Carey scrapbooks.
[79] *United States Gazette,* April 25, 1818.

While the "lunatic fringe" of Pennsylvania protectionism was thus searching for ingenious ways to override the Constitution, more practical friends of domestic industry were turning to Congress with a demand for a general revision of the tariff laws. The House of Representatives which convened in December, 1819 was strongly favorable to the protective policy. This was indicated by the appointment, for the first time, of a standing Committee on Manufactures, with Henry Baldwin of Pittsburgh as chairman.[80] Baldwin was well known as a staunch protectionist; indeed the tariff question had been made the principal issue in his election.[81] This committee proceeded to report three bills, embracing a comprehensive program for the relief of the manufacturing interest. These provided for a tax on sales by auction, the payment of import duties in cash, and a complete upward revision of the tariff. The latter measure increased existing rates by from 20 to 100 per cent. on practically all articles manufactured in Pennsylvania.[82]

Baldwin, as chairman of the committee, opened the debate upon the tariff bill with a long and powerful speech defending its provisions.[83] He frankly admitted that the proposed measure was protective in principle and in detail, and expressed the hope that he should see the day when, "in full command of our consumption and means of defence, our resources retained at home, our great interests safe from foreign competition, we shall be in fact, as well as in name, free and independent States." He believed that the ideal revenue system should provide adequate protection for every article which could be made at home; while any deficit should be met with an excise tax on the domestic manufactures thus fostered. The two taxes of course were to be carefully adjusted so as to be still thoroughly protective.

Baldwin appears to have been rather sensitive concerning the charge that the interested manufacturers had taken an unduly active part in framing the provisions of the bill. Speaking for the committee, he assured the House that "our motives rise higher than the interest of manufacturers; whether they make or lose money now;

---

[80] *Annals of Cong.*, 16 Cong., 1 Sess., p. 710.
[81] *Pittsburgh Gazette*, August 4, September 4, 1818.
[82] *Annals of Cong.*, 16 Cong., 1 Sess., pp. 1913-16.
[83] *Ibid.* pp. 1916ff.

whether it tends to enrich one or another, or all classes of society, had scarcely entered into our consideration." He especially resented the imputation that the bill was over-solicitous concerning the interests of his own city. Taking up this point, he declared,

This has been called a Pittsburgh, a cut-glass bill, local, partial in its operations; and I have been charged with framing it from interested motives. . . . I tell the house frankly, that I have not lost sight of the interest of Pittsburgh, and would never perjure myself if I had; but the charges shall be met plainly, and if you are not convinced that the interests of that place are identified with the nation; that cut glass can be defended on national grounds, then I agree that Pittsburgh, its Representative, its favorite manufacture and the tariff, may go together.

He pointed out that he whole-heartedly approved the enhanced duties on iron, in spite of the fact that his district was dependent upon outside sources for its supply; for iron was "an all essential article for private consumption and national defence." In short, he favored the proposed bill, not on selfish local grounds, but on the "national principle, that we ought to feed, clothe and be able to defend ourselves."

While Baldwin was leading the Pennsylvania delegation in the fight for higher duties, the once-powerful commercial interests of the state were rallying their reduced forces in opposition to the proposed measure. Numerically, this element constituted less than 4 per cent. of the state's population, but they still exerted considerable influence over the press of Philadelphia.[84] The Chamber of Commerce of that city addressed a long remonstrance to Congress, in which they asserted that

the duties on imports are already so high that the consumption decreases daily . . . . The result of the proposed tariff promises to be the destruction at one sweeping blow of our whole commercial and agricultural systems. . . . Your memorialists respectfully remark that they are opposed not only to the principle of the proposed tariff, but also to the details to which it is applied; and that, so far from adding one cent to the present duties, it is our opinion that an increase of revenue and an improvement in our general condition can only be expected by a diminution in the existing duties.[85]

As the event proved, the forebodings of the Philadelphia merchants were needless, at least for the moment. The Baldwin measure easily

---

[84] Carey, M., *Appeal to Common Sense*, p. 97; *Aurora*, May 9, 1820.
[85] *Annals of Cong.*, 16 Cong., 1 Sess., p. 2424ff.

passed the House of Representatives, with only one Pennsylvania vote recorded against it.[86] The Senate, however, decided by a majority of one to defer consideration of the bill until the next session. Both Pennsylvania Senators voted against the postponement, which in effect meant the defeat of the proposed tariff.[87] The other two protectionist measures reported by the Committee on Manufactures suffered an equally ignominious fate. The bill to require the cash payment of duties had been designed to curb the influx of goods for purely speculative purposes. Baldwin pointed out that the existing credit system really amounted to a loan for the amount of the duties to the needy foreign manufacturer.[88] Nevertheless, the innovation seemed too drastic, and was rejected by the House, although the Pennsylvanians supported the measure, sixteen to six. The auction sales bill had been intended to check a practice through which foreign merchandise had been able to secure a wide distribution at very low prices. So far as Pennsylvania was concerned the measure was supported by all except the auctioneers and the importers.[89] The proposal was voted on in various forms and received the support of a large majority of the Pennsylvania representatives, but was ultimately rejected by the House.[90]

The tariff maneuvers of the winter of 1819-20, therefore, ended in a complete triumph for the anti-protectionists. Nevertheless, the commercial interests of Pennsylvania realized that the margin of victory had been narrow, and that the Baldwin tariff might yet be accepted by the Senate. In anticipation of the next session of Congress, therefore, a convention of merchants assembled at Philadelphia in November, 1820, and drew up a set of resolutions which sanctioned a tariff for revenue only, warned against the dire consequences which would attend the enactment of the pending bill, and opposed a system of cash duties.[91] When Congress assembled, however, it was found that the protectionist forces were weaker than at the preceding session. Baldwin, in behalf of the Committee on

---

[86] *Ibid.* p. 2155.
[87] *Ibid.* p. 672.
[88] *Ibid.* p. 1969.
[89] *Aurora*, February 5, 8, 1820; Silas Weir to Sergeant, January 29, 1820; Sergeant MSS.
[90] *Annals of Cong.*, 16 Cong., 1 Sess., pp. 2178, 2184.
[91] *Aurora*, November 9, 1820.

Manufactures, presented a tariff bill, accompanied by a report which Mathew Carey characterized as "one of the most powerful state papers that have appeared in this country."[92] This measure aroused little enthusiasm and the session adjourned with the existing rates still intact.

The year 1821 was marked by something of a lull in the Pennsylvania tariff excitement. Secretary Crawford informed the President's cabinet that there had been considerable reaction against high duties even in Pittsburgh.[93] This seems to have been due not so much to the protectionist reverses as to the gradual improvement of economic conditions. The financial readjustment had slowly worked itself out, and business was beginning to accommodate itself to the new regime. In Philadelphia it was estimated that 4,000 new looms had been put in operation within six months.[94] It was reported from Lancaster that manufactures "flourish better than in former times, although the tariff is not as high as some politicians would have it."[95] At the same time, the western part of the state, in spite of transportation difficulties, was beginning to ship linens, glass, and hardware to Philadelphia and Baltimore.[96] The immediate result of this general industrial recovery was to silence temporarily the vehement protectionism of the preceding years.

The unnatural calm which thus settled upon the Pennsylvania tariff controversy was not broken until the session of Congress which opened in December, 1822. Baldwin was absent because of serious illness, and his place as chairman of the Committee of Manufactures was taken by John Tod, also of Pennsylvania. Although the complexion of the House was not encouraging, Tod in due course reported a bill "for the more effectual encouragement and protection of domestic manufactures."[97] The most interesting feature of the debate which followed was James Buchanan's maiden speech upon the tariff, delivered February 7, 1823.[98] In view of the equivocal

---

[92] *Annals of Cong.*, 16 Cong., 2 Sess., p. 1553; Carey, M., *Autobiographical Sketches*, p. 87.
[93] Adams, *Memoirs*, V, 411.
[94] *Niles' Register*, XXI, 39.
[95] *United States Gazette*, September 4, 1821.
[96] *Democratic Press*, April 14, 1821.
[97] *Annals of Cong.*, 17 Cong., 2 Sess., p. 544.
[98] *Ibid.* pp. 893ff.

position which Buchanan was later forced to take toward the subject, it is of interest to note his sentiments at this time, when presumably they were unaffected by any considerations of party expediency or personal ambition. Discussing the general principles which should govern American tariff policies, he asserted,

In selecting the objects of additional duty, I would do so with a view to the encouragement of such domestic manufactures as are necessary for the defence of the nation, and for the consumption of the great mass of your people; and more particularly those articles of which your country furnishes the raw material in abundance. By this means, whilst you raise revenue, you indirectly, but gradually, encourage such manufactures as will render you more independent of foreign nations. . . . We do not ask the same encouragement for the growth and manufacture of any article that has been afforded to that of cotton. For one, I desire at present no prohibitory duty on any other article. All that we ask of you is that, as you must raise revenue, you should do it in such a manner as to give some indirect encouragement to the agriculture and manufactures of the middle portion of the Union. . . . This policy, which accommodates itself to our circumstances, is infinitely better than either the dreams of political economists, who, on the one hand, would cast off every restriction and open your ports to all the world, or the systems of those who, on the other, are so devotedly the friends of domestic manufactures, that they would sacrifice the commercial, and injure the agricultural interests of the country for their promotion. . . .

The farmers are the most useful, as they are the most numerous class of society. No measure ought ever to be adopted by the government which would bear hardly upon them. . . . My constituents are principally farmers, and I should feel it both my duty and my inclination to resist any measure which would be pernicious to their interest. . . . I will never consent to adopt a general restrictive system, because that class of the community would then be left at the mercy of the manufacturers. . . . If this bill proposed a system which would lead to such abuses, it should not receive my support. I consider this bill as a revenue measure. . . .

After manufactures have been fairly brought into existence, if they cannot support themselves without extraordinary duties, or in other words, without continual contributions from the consumers, they must be abandoned by the Government.

Buchanan then turned to a consideration of specific items in the bill. In the interests of agriculture, he favored the additional tax on linen, hemp, and spirits. At the same time he heartily endorsed the increased rates on iron; especially since the depressed condition of the industry had seriously injured the farmer in his home market. However, he vigorously opposed as prohibitive the proposed minimum valuation of 80 cents per yard on woolens. In short, Buchanan's sentiments at this time were protectionist, but moderately so; indeed, they are strikingly consistent with those which he entertained throughout his public career. His middle-of-the-road attitude toward the tariff was later seriously criticized as dictated by a weak desire to placate both the protectionists of Pennsylvania and the free trade leaders of the Democracy. Nevertheless, it must be said that few politicans have spent four decades in public life with less fluctuation in their expressed attitude upon the subject than James Buchanan. In 1823, Pennsylvania protectionists hailed him as a kindred spirit; in 1860, they denounced him as an apostate. In both cases, Buchanan's views were essentially the same; it was Pennsylvania protectionism which had changed its objectives and its ideals.

The House as a whole shared little of Buchanan's enthusiasm for. the proposed revision. The best measure of protectionist sentiment was the vote to discharge the Committee of the Whole from the consideration of the bill, so as to bring it directly before the House. Pennsylvania supported the motion with only one dissenting voice, but the proposition was overwhelmingly defeated and there was no further discussion of 'the question.[99] Instead, the protectionists determined to postpone the agitation until the next Congress, in which the new apportionment would greatly strengthen their forces.

As soon as the new Congress had assembled, the protectionists of Pennsylvania opened with unprecedented vigor their campaign for higher duties. In response to the suggestion of Governor Schulze, the state Assembly adopted a joint resolution, requesting the Representatives and instructing the Senators from Pennsylvania to exert their influence in favor of a tariff revision.[100] Some question was raised in the lower house as to the legislature's constitutional right to "instruct" a Senator, but the doubtful word was finally retained by a vote of 56 to 35.[101] At the same time the customary private

---

[99] *Annals of Cong.*, 17 Cong., 2 Sess., p. 1015.
[100] *Pennsylvania Archives*, Fourth Series, V, 496; *Pamphlet Laws*, 1823-24, p. 241.
[101] *Harrisburg Chronicle*, January 22, 1824.

memorials were poured into Washington. One of these, signed by members of the Assembly who were likewise farmers, illustrates the new spirit of cooperation between industry and agriculture which was springing up in Pennsylvania. This document affirmed that

your memorialists, wholly cultivators of the soil, and not otherwise concerned in manufactures than in their own families, are firmly persuaded that the solid interests of the nation require that an efficient protection be afforded to the manufacturing portion of their fellow citizens who, with few exceptions, have been greatly depressed ever since the return of peace. . . . The idea which, in common with the majority of our agricultural brethren, we long entertained, of the advantages resulting from purchasing goods abroad, because they can be had cheaper than at home, has been proved, by experience, to be ruinously fallacious. . . . We, therefore, respectfully request that you will adopt such a modification of the existing tariff, as may afford complete protection to the manufactures of our common country.[102]

To offset such appeals the Philadelphia merchants submitted a counter-memorial, drafted by Horace Binney, which declared that the industries of the country were already flourishing, and that any revision of the tariff would be fatal to commerce and to agriculture.[103]

Meanwhile, the Committee on Manufactures had reported the bill which provided the basis for the tariff of 1824. As introduced in the House it was thoroughly protectionist in its provisions, and the Pennsylvania delegation, with one exception, rallied enthusiastically to its support. Tod and Buchanan were the most active in the advocacy of the measure; the latter declared, "I would vote for this bill upon the same principle that I would for the erection of a necessary fortification or the building of a navy."[104] The other Representatives, however, were by no means inactive; as Daniel Webster, arrayed in opposition to the bill, wrote to a friend, "We have had much from the Philadelphia school of the adverse balance of trade, exportation of specie, loss of foreign markets, etc."[105] The only dissenting voice was that of Breck, representing the shipping interest, who declared that the bill was "monstrous" and would

---

102 *Annals of Cong.*, 18 Cong., 1 Sess., pp. 3109ff.
103 *American State Papers, Finance*, IV, 482-6; Binney, *Life of Binney*, p. 87.
104 *Annals of Cong.*, 18 Cong., 1 Sess., p. 2263.
105 Webster, *Writings*, XVII, 348.

injure commerce and industry alike through the exclusion of cheap raw materials.[106]

Pennsylvania's most bitter battle was over the duties on iron. During 1822 and 1823 the English price of bar iron had dropped more than $10 a ton, while American prices remained stationary.[107] As a result, importation had increased rapidly, while American ironmasters frantically appealed for legislative assistance.[108] The Committee on Manufactures, accordingly, had recommended that the rate on hammered iron bars be raised from 75 cents to $1.12 per hundredweight. This proposal aroused a storm of opposition, on the grounds that it imposed a tax upon the whole people for the benefit of a few Pennsylvania iron manufacturers. Fuller of Massachusetts declared that the insatiable ironmasters of the Keystone state were already prosperous, and that no other section had asked for higher duties.[109] A memorial of the New Haven Chamber of Commerce pointed out that most of the imported iron was used by the manufacturers and shipbuilders of New England and observed further that "the beneficent Creator has wisely placed mines of iron ore in the interior of Pennsylvania, which were undoubtedly designed for the supply of the inhabitants there; but it would be unreasonable and unjust to compel the inhabitants of other distant States to go there for a supply of iron, when at the same time they have a much cheaper and more convenient resource."[110] John Randolph grimly remarked that "the true remedy, and the only one, for the iron manufacturer of Pennsylvania . . . would be to lay on the table of this House a declaration of war in blank, and then go into a Committee of the Whole, to see what nation in the world it would be most convenient to go to war with."[111]

It must not be supposed that the Pennsylvania delegation remained silent, while the iron interest of their state was under this heavy fire. Buchanan attempted to reply to the charge that the iron manufacturers of the state were already prosperous. He explained that a

---

[106] *Annals of Cong.*, 18 Cong., 1 Sess., pp. 1736-38.
[107] Scrivenor, *Comprehensive History of the Iron Trade*, pp. 377, 406-410; *Sen. Doc.*, 62 Cong., 1 Sess., No. 21, pp. 327-8.
[108] *House Exec. Doc.*, 29 Cong., 1 Sess., No. 6, pp. 168-9.
[109] *Annals of Cong.*, 18 Cong., 1 Sess., pp. 1706-7.
[110] *Ibid.* p. 3152.
[111] *Ibid.* p. 2371.

few of the ironmasters had been able through large capital and inland location to survive the general ruin and to gain control of the market at monopoly prices, but that such cases were the exception. The majority of producers had failed, with consequent loss to the whole countryside.[112] Stewart declared that if Congress were unwilling to grant the iron duties for the sake of the manufacturer, "he asked it for the sake of the farmer; for the sake of the revenue; for the merchant; for the nation; it was demanded by everything American—by every proud and patriotic feeling."[113] The question was finally settled by adopting a compromise rate of 90 cents per hundredweight, although every member of the delegation except Breck voted in the negative.[114] Even less successful was the attempt to secure additional duties on pig iron. Several members of the delegation spoke in favor of a motion to increase the rate on this article from 50 cents to 75 cents per hundredweight, but the proposal was rejected by the House.[115]

Although from the standpoint of the manufacturer the iron duties left much to be desired, the measure as a whole represented a decided gain for the principle of protection. The final vote, therefore, showed twenty-four Pennsylvanians in favor of the bill, with only Breck opposed.[116] The tariff then went to the upper house, where the state's two Senators were at least morally obligated to support it under their instructions from the Assembly. Although they seem to have taken little part in the discussion, their protectionist sympathies were clearly reflected by their votes in opposing every reduction of the House rates and in favoring the passage of the bill.[117] After considerable deliberation the measure was finally adopted by the Senate in amended form; the differences between the two houses were eliminated through reconsideration and conference; and the bill received the approval of the President on May 25, 1824.

As written into law, the tariff act of 1824 was considerably less protective than the measure originally reported by the Committee on Manufactures. Nevertheless, for the time being, it was received

---

112 *Ibid*. p. 1709.
113 *Ibid*. p. 2275.
114 *Ibid*. p. 2287.
115 *Ibid*. p. 1751.
116 *Ibid*. p. 2429.
117 *Ibid*. p. 744.

throughout Pennsylvania with general approbation. By 1825, economic conditions in the state were much improved; Philadelphia and Pittsburgh reported that all the old factories were busy and that new ones were rapidly going into operation.[118] The iron industry, especially, was benefitted by a sharp upward trend of prices both at home and abroad. Indeed, so great was the British demand for iron that considerable quantities of pig metal were actually exported from Pennsylvania to England during the year.[119] The manufacture of coarse cottons was likewise so far advanced that even Hezekiah Niles was forced to admit that no further protection was required.[120] At the same time, a Pittsburgh writer noted with considerable satisfaction that the glass of western Pennsylvania was known and sold from Maine to New Orleans.[121] As usual, the prevalent prosperity operated to quiet the protectionist agitation. Moreover, public attention was being seriously diverted to the matter of internal improvements, a subject made especially pertinent by the completion of the Erie canal project in New York. Indeed, had not the tariff question made its first serious incursion into the realm of politics during the presidential election of 1824, the eighteen months immediately following the passage of the new law would have been completely devoid of protectionist excitement.

---

[118] *Democratic Press*, January 7, March 22, 1825.
[119] *Ibid.* March 17, April 5, 1825.
[120] *Niles' Register*, XXVIII, 147.
[121] Jones, *Pittsburgh in 1826*, p. 69.

CHAPTER IV

## THE TARIFF ENTERS POLITICS, 1824–1828

The protectionist agitation in Pennsylvania prior to 1824 was almost exclusively an economic movement, with only desultory incursions into the realm of politics. During the era of Republican and Federalist rivalry before the war of 1812, party lines were drawn on other issues than the tariff. After the conflict, the factional nature of Pennsylvania politics was not conducive to the development of any very fundamental differences of principle. Occasionally, however, the tariff issue was injected into a campaign. In 1816, the cotton manufacturers of Philadelphia threatened to invoke the ballot to enforce their demands for protection.[1] Hiester, running for governor in 1817 and 1820, was attacked because as a member of Congress in 1816 he had voted for lower rates on textiles and iron.[2] During the painful period of financial readjustment, it was frequently asserted that protection must be made the dominant political issue of the future; for instance, the *Aurora* opposed Monroe's reelection in 1820 because of his alleged hostility to American manufactures.[3] The tariff question likewise appeared in some form in every Pittsburgh congressional election from 1816 to 1822.[4] In the latter year, Philadelphia protectionists headed by Mathew Carey drew up a separate ticket of approved candidates for Congress and the state legislature. The sponsors fell into disagreement over the nominations, however, and only a few scattering votes were polled.[5] Nevertheless, such cases as these were decidedly exceptional; for the most part the approach of an election served to quiet rather than to stimulate the protectionist agitation. Generally speaking, the tariff question was a negligible factor in Pennsylvania politics prior to 1824.

The presidential election of 1824 was the first in which the tariff question was seriously raised in Pennsylvania. The appearance of

---

[1] W. Duane to Sergeant, January 27, 1816; Sergeant MSS.

[2] *Harrisburg Chronicle,* June 30, 1817; *Harrisburg Republican,* October 7, 1817; *Pittsburgh Statesman,* August 11, 18, 1820.

[3] *Aurora,* November 3, 1819; May 9, November 1, December 8, 1820.

[4] *Pittsburgh Mercury,* September 14, 1816; September 23, 1820; September 21, 1822; *Pittsburgh Gazette,* September 4, 1818.

[5] *Aurora,* October 2, 10, 1822.

the issue at this time was due in part to the growing feeling that a friend of the American system should occupy the White House; but more especially it was an outgrowth of the violent partisanship which marked the campaign. Adherents of the respective candidates, in their eager quest for votes, could not afford to ignore the well-recognized and deep-seated protectionist sentiment of the state. Nor were the friends of the tariff in Pennsylvania at all averse to the introduction of the question into politics, although as the event proved, their cause was greatly weakened thereby.[6] Encouraged by the general acceptance of protection as an economic principle, they anticipated that the political conquest of the state would be equally rapid and easy. Indeed, but for the abrupt emergence of Andrew Jackson as a presidential candidate, this expectation might easily have proved correct. No one could foresee that Pennsylvania's infatuation for the "Old Hero" would submerge even the tariff as an issue and would set in motion forces sufficiently strong to delay for a generation the political triumph of the protectionists.

The opening of the campaign of 1824 revealed that Jackson had developed a tremendous political following in Pennsylvania. Even his followers do not seem to have appreciated the overwhelming strength of his personal appeal, and they spared no pains to present him to the electorate as a loyal supporter of the protective system. To this end, they gave wide publicity to Jackson's so-called Coleman letter, written April 26, 1824, which for many years constituted his one significant public utterance on the tariff question. In this letter, written while the act of 1824 was still pending, he declared,

So far as the Tariff before us embraces the design of fostering, protecting and preserving within ourselves the means of national defence and independence, particularly in a state of war, I would advocate and support it. . . Providence has filled our mountains and our plains with minerals—with lead, iron and copper, and has given us a climate and a soil for the growing of hemp and wool. These being the grand materials of our national defence, they ought to have extended to them adequate and fair protection, that our own manufactories and laborers may be placed in a fair competition with those of Europe; and that we may have within our own country a supply of those leading and important

---

[6] Van Buren warned the manufacturers at about this time that "if they suffered their interests to become identified with a political party (any one) they would share the fate of that party, and go down with it whenever it sunk." (Benton, *Thirty Years View*, I, 34.)

articles so essential to war. Beyond this, I look at the Tariff with an eye to the proper distribution of labor and revenue; and with a view to discharge our national debt. . . . Draw from agriculture the superabundant labor, employ it in mechanism and manufactures, thereby creating a home market for your bread-stuffs, and distributing labor to a most profitable account, and benefits to the country will result. . . . It is, therefore, my opinion that a careful and judicious tariff is much wanted, to pay our national debt, and afford us the means of that defence within ourselves, on which the safety of our country and liberty depends; and last but not least, give a proper distribution to our labor, which must prove beneficial to the happiness, independence and wealth of the community.[7]

This statement, although not altogether free from ambiguity, was hailed by Jackson's Pennsylvania friends as a clear-cut expression in favor of the protective policy. As confirmatory evidence, it was pointed out that Jackson in the Senate had voted for the tariff of 1824 and had especially supported higher rates on iron. On the other hand, his opponents alleged that he had revealed his anti-protectionist tendencies in his votes on wool and woolen goods.[8]

The four remaining candidates, Clay, Adams, Crawford, and Calhoun, were all likewise presented to the people of Pennsylvania as advocates of the protective system. Mathew Carey warmly supported Clay, and had a place upon the latter's electoral ticket.[9] A Philadelphia mass meeting, with Carey presiding, expressed their appreciation of the Kentuckian's "distinguished talents and un-equalled exertions" in the protectionist cause.[10] On the other hand, the Adams forces characterized Clay as a man of one idea, who would be unwilling to grant due recognition to all the great interests of the country.[11] Although Calhoun's anti-tariff views were not yet so pronounced as they afterwards became, they attracted consider-able adverse comment during the early stages of the campaign.[12] Crawford and Adams largely escaped such attacks, principally because public attention was directed to other and more vulnerable points of assault.

Measured in terms of actual votes, the influence of the tariff issue

---

[7] Bassett, *Correspondence of Andrew Jackson*, III, 249-51; *Niles' Register*, XXVI, p. 245.

[8] *Pittsburgh Statesman*, June 19, 1824.

[9] Clay, *Works*, IV, 102; *United States Gazette*, October 29, 1824.

[10] *Niles' Register*, XXVII, 61.

[11] *United States Gazette*, October 25, 1824.

[12] *Democratic Press*, February 3, March 17, 1824.

in the election was probably not very great. Had the question never been raised, it is likely that Jackson's victory would have been just as complete and the defeat of his opponents just as overwhelming.[13] The dominant feature of the whole campaign was the tremendous personal appeal of the "Hero of New Orleans;" so far as governmental policies were discussed at all, the issues of caucus nominations and internal improvements both carried greater weight than the tariff. Protection, therefore, was an incidental not a decisive factor in the result. Nevertheless, the election of 1824 marks an important turning point in the development of Pennsylvania protectionism; from that time the emphasis rapidly shifts from the economic to the political aspects of the question.

The election excitement of 1824 was followed by a complete cessation of the tariff agitation, an interlude which lasted through the following year. The rates established by the act of 1824 seemed to give general satisfaction; Pennsylvania industry was flourishing; and public interest was centered upon the subject of internal improvements. Even Mathew Carey turned his versatile pen from the tariff to a discussion of improved methods of transportation. The protectionist, however, has never been inclined to remain long content with the status quo, and in this case the mild economic revulsion which developed during the winter of 1825-26 resulted in a swift revival of the whole question. This depression was in large measure the aftermath of the speculative crisis which seriously affected Great Britain in 1825. Bankrupt English manufacturers poured their surplus stocks into the United States at very low prices, and the resultant competition caused considerable suffering among the less effective units of American industry. It was claimed for instance, that three-fourths of the 4,000 hand looms in the vicinity of Philadelphia had been forced to suspend operations due to the influx of foreign goods.[14] At the same time, many farmers suffered from a sharp decline in the price of flour and wool.[15] The extent of the revulsion was in no way commensurate with that of a few years be-

---

[13] The popular vote was: Jackson, 35,929; Adams, 5,436; Crawford, 4,182; Clay, 1,705. (*Smull's Legislative Handbook*, 1921-22, p. 739.)

[14] *Niles' Register*, XXX, 239; Carey, M., *Reflections upon the Subject of Emigration*, p. 27.

[15] Grosvenor, *Does Protection Protect?* p. 110; *House Exec. Doc.*, 38 Cong., 1 Sess., No. 2, 287.

fore; nevertheless it was sufficient to arouse the protectionists of Pennsylvania to renewed exertions in behalf of their favorite principle.

The immediate objective of the revived agitation was a readjustment of the rates on wool and woolen goods. The tariff of 1824 had increased the duties on woolens to 33⅓ per cent., but had counterbalanced this by raising the tax on wool to 30 per cent. Inasmuch as most of the raw material had to be imported, it is estimated that the net protection afforded the manufacturers of woolen goods was only about 18⅓ per cent.[16] The mill owners claimed that this amount was entirely inadequate and pointed to the fact that imports of woolen goods into the United States during 1825 had been unusually large. At the same time the sheep raisers of the country alluded to the steadily declining price of wool and demanded that their interests likewise be considered in any revision of the duties.

Although Massachusetts was the chief seat of the woolen industry, Pennsylvania's investment in this form of manufacture was by no means negligible. In addition, the state contained about two million sheep, some of which produced an unusually fine grade of wool.[17] Moreover, the other economic interests of Pennsylvania rather welcomed an excuse to reopen the tariff question in the hope that a general revision might ensue. For all these reasons, Pennsylvania protectionists preceded even those of New England in demanding a readjustment of the rates on wool and woolens.[18] Dissatisfaction with the existing duties appeared for the first time during the winter of 1825-26 and quickly gained strength. To carry on the agitation, Mathew Carey helped to establish in 1826 the Pennsylvania Society for the Promotion of Manufactures and the Mechanic Arts. The body had between sixty and seventy members, of whom about nine-tenths were manufacturers, and for some time constituted the most active protectionist organization in the state.[19]

By the time Congress had assembled in December, 1826, the demand for a revision in behalf of wool and woolens had become too persistent to be ignored. Accordingly, the Committee on Manufac-

---

16 Taussig, *Tariff History of the United States,* p. 75.
17 *Niles' Register,* XXIX, 88.
18 *Ibid.* XXXIV, p. 187.
19 Carey, M., *Autobiographical Sketches,* p. 13.

tures hastened to draw up and report the measure commonly known
as the woolens bill of 1827. Without any change in the nominal rate
of duty on woolens, the desired protection was to be obtained
through a cleverly devised system of minimum valuations. The bill
provided that all goods costing less than 40 cents a square yard were
to pay duty as if they had cost 40 cents; all valued at more than
40 cents and less than $2.50 were to be charged as if they had cost
$2.50; and all between $2.50 and $4 were to be assessed at the latter
figure. This amounted in substance to a specific duty of 13⅓ cents
a yard on woolens of the first class, 83⅓ cents on those of the second class, and $1.33⅓ on those of the third class. Since the goods
most commonly imported were worth about a dollar a yard, the
manufacturers would enjoy, under cover of the existing rates, an actual protection of approximately 83⅓ per cent.[20] The same principle
was to be applied in respect to the raw material. The ad valorem
rate for unmanufactured wool was to be increased to 40 per cent.,
and all wool costing between 10 and 40 cents a pound was to be
rated at 40 cents.

The introduction of this ingeniously constructed measure left
many of the Pennsylvania Representatives confronted with a serious
dilemma. They realized that there was a decided sentiment among
their constituents in favor of higher duties for wool and woolens.
Nevertheless, the bill which had been laid before them was open to
valid criticism, even from the protectionist point of view. For one
thing, its rates were cumbersome and presented a strong incentive
to fraudulent undervaluation. Moreover, woolens had been granted
a more generous increase than wool, and this discrimination might
be resented in the agricultural districts. Also, the proposed bill afforded no relief to other interests of the state which might feel that
they too were entitled to legislative assistance. To these considerations of an economic nature was added another which was entirely
political. A large majority of the Pennsylvania delegation were
friendly to the presidential ambitions of Andrew Jackson, and the
deliberations upon the woolens bill seemed to present an admirable
opportunity to promote his candidacy. The defeat of the measure,
if discreetly accomplished, would serve to discredit the Administra-

---

[20] Taussig, *Tariff History of the United States*, p. 94.

tion in the eyes of northern manufacturers, especially in New England, and would materially diminish President Adams' chances for reelection. Many Pennsylvania Congressmen, therefore, found themselves in that painful state of doubt and uncertainty which sometimes overtakes those who seek to serve two masters.

Confronted with the final decision, however, most of the Pennsylvanians yielded to the supposed wishes of their constituents and gave orthodox protectionist votes in favor of the measure. "Tariff Andy" Stewart contributed the state's most enthusiastic endorsement of the bill. Speaking of the American system, he declared that

it was a system he never would abandon; it was a subject on which he could make no compromise. . . . This system was intimately and inseparably connected with the best interests of the State from which he came, as he believed it was with those of the whole Union. . . . Regarding the bill under consideration as a part of that system, it should have, through all its vicissitudes, his cordial and unwavering support. . . . What State in the Union had been so uniform, so consistent, so steady, and unwavering, as Pennsylvania in maintaining the principles and policy of this bill? . . . Sir, the farmers of Pennsylvania and New York know that it is better for them and better for the nation, to save the ten millions a year which is now sent abroad for woolens, and to get them at our own manufacturing establishments for an exchange of equivalents, by exchanging wool and flour for cloth.[21]

The final roll call, however, revealed a degree of opposition within the delegation that was quite unusual, especially in view of the clear-cut protectionist intent of the measure. Seven negative votes were cast, all of them by Jackson adherents. The dissentients were Addams of Reading, Buchanan of Lancaster, Ingham of New Hope, Kremer of Lewisburg, Stevenson of Pittsburgh, and Kittera and Wurts of Philadelphia.[22] Of these, Buchanan was easily the most outspoken in his denunciation of the bill. His opposition to the measure was based upon five counts: first, because of its unjust system of minimums; second, because under its provisions, Pennsylvania would not be able to compete with the already well-established manufactures of New England; third, because it did not give adequate protection to the wool grower; fourth, because it failed to provide additional duties on spirits and hemp; fifth, be-

---

21 *Cong. Debates*, 19 Cong., 2 Sess., pp. 911, 1081, 1083.
22 *Ibid.* p. 1099.

cause it paved the way for smuggling and evaluation frauds.[23] He believed that the rates established in 1824 provided a fair measure of protection and should be preserved intact for all time.[24] Lest he be accused of apostasy, he took pains to affirm that, "in regard to myself, I have ever been the friend of what has been called the tariff policy. The new doctrines of political economy which have been preached in England have no charms for me. They have never been practiced by British statesmen; and there is much reason to believe that they have been manufactured, not for home consumption but for foreign markets."[25] In another speech, he asserted, "I have always been, and believe I ever shall be, the decided friend of domestic manufactures. The duties, however, which we impose, should be protecting merely, not prohibitory. They should only enable the domestic manufacturer to sustain a fair competition in the domestic market."[26]

It is commonly assumed that the objections raised by Buchanan were mere equivocations to conceal his real political motive for opposing the measure. Stanwood, for instance, speaks of his "well-simulated excitement" over the hemp duties.[27] Such an interpretation does Buchanan an injustice. While he was perfectly willing to defeat the bill in the interests of Jackson's candidacy, nevertheless the objections which he brought forward seem to have been real and sincere. The views which he expressed at all stages of the woolens discussion are identical to those presented in his speech of February 7, 1823, where no political issue was involved. Both speeches reveal the utmost solicitude for the agricultural interest, and in both Buchanan demands additional protection for hemp and spirits. Further comparison shows that in 1823 as in 1827 he opposed the minimum principle in its application to woolens. Moreover, the general tone of moderate protectionism is very similar in both cases. A confidential letter written by Buchanan on February 13, 1827 is of interest in this connection, as well as for the light it throws upon the attitude of the Pennsylvania delegation. Speaking of the woolens bill, the writer declares that if passed it would

[23] *United States Gazette,* July 18, 1827.
[24] *Cong. Debates,* 19 Cong., 2 Sess., p. 913.
[25] *Ibid.* p. 912.
[26] *Ibid.* p. 749.
[27] Stanwood, *American Tariff Controversies,* I, 257.

raise the price of every poor man's coat at least for some years fifty per cent. Its most odious feature is that it will operate only on the clothes worn by the poor and middling classes of society. It has been carried through the House by the coalition between the East and the West and by the votes of 19 Pennsylvanians who whilst many of them disapproved the Bill believed their constituents to be so Tariff mad that they were afraid to vote against it. This however is between ourselves. I endeavored to protect our whisky and our hemp and my attempt would have succeeded, had not the previous question been sustained and of course a direct vote on my proposition been evaded. . . . I have but little doubt that the coalition intend to endeavor to connect the opposition to the Woolen Bill with the cause of Gen. Jackson in Pennsylvania.[28]

The tone of this letter rather tends to reinforce the conclusion that insofar as Buchanan was playing politics he was able to do so in substantial harmony with his own convictions upon the tariff question.

The other Pennsylvanians who opposed the woolens bill followed very closely the lines of argument laid down by Buchanan. Although there is no direct evidence as to their motives in voting against the measure, it was generally recognized at the time that political considerations bulked large, with perhaps an additional commercial influence in the case of the two Philadelphia members. Kremer and Ingham, especially, were accused of subordinating the economic interests of the state to the presidential ambitions of Andrew Jackson.[29] Whatever Ingham's motives may have been he was particularly careful to temper his vote with an ostentatious display of protectionist zeal. In explaining his opposition, he declared,

I have been devoted to the system of protecting the domestic industry of the country, and my zeal has sometimes been deemed infatuation; and with the greatest reluctance could I give a vote against a measure intended for that protection. I have examined this bill with an anxiety to find in it some feature that would justify a vote in its favor. This search has been unsuccessful.[30]

The legislative history of the woolens bill may be outlined very briefly. After a month of debate, in which the Pennsylvanians took an active part on both sides, the measure was passed by the House

---

[28] Buchanan to Thomas Elder; Gratz Collection.
[29] *Democratic Press*, February 26, 1827; Sargent, *Public Men and Events*, I, 151n.
[30] *Cong. Debates*, 19 Cong., 2 Sess., p. 833.

with a vote of 106 to 95. The opponents of revision were sufficiently strong in the Senate, however, to prevent all discussion, and ultimately the bill was laid upon the table by the casting vote of Vice President Calhoun. Both Pennsylvania Senators voted against such action, which was equivalent to defeat.[31]

Meanwhile, the discussions in Congress had engendered a considerable degree of public feeling in Pennsylvania. Aside from a small minority made up of intense partisans and the commercial interests of Philadelphia, general sentiment was strongly favorable to the proposed bill.[32] It was asserted that wool could be grown in the state more cheaply than elsewhere, and that "were a due protection given, Pennsylvania would soon manufacture more woolens than any other state in the Union."[33] It was pointed out that protectionist Pennsylvania had given more votes against the bill than any other northern state and the dissenting seven Congressmen were attacked both individually and collectively for their vote.[34] A "Wool raiser" addressed an open letter to Ingham in which he declared,

You are a farmer and have been a wool grower. . . . I am therefore at a loss to imagine any honest motive which could have induced you to vote against that bill. . . . I am ashamed of you, Mr. Ingham. As for Mr. Wurts and Mr. Kittera our City Representatives, they are lawyers and are not expected to understand our interests. I pity but do not blame them.[35]

Nevertheless, both Ingham and Buchanan were sufficiently strong in their home districts to obtain public votes of approbation for their conduct.[36] Stevenson of Pittsburgh was less fortunate. A local observer believed that "there is not one man in ten in Allegheny county who does not condemn the vote of our representative."[37] A public meeting adopted a resolution of censure for his

[31] *Ibid.* p. 496.
[32] *Democratic Press*, February 19, June 25, 1827; *Niles' Register*, XXXI, 401; XXXII, 265, 295.
[33] *United States Gazette*, April 17, 1827.
[34] *Democratic Press*, February 26, 1827.
[35] *Ibid.* February 27, 1827.
[36] *Ibid.* June 20, 1827; *Niles' Register*, XXXII, p. 314.
[37] Unidentified clipping in Mathew Carey scrapbooks. Yet, with a strange lack of political perception, Stevenson wrote Buchanan, "I find my course on the woolens bill has gained me many firm friends. I never was stronger." (Stevenson to Buchanan, August 3, 1827; Buchanan MSS.)

part in opposing the bill, and he was defeated for reelection the following year.[38]

The defeat of the woolens bill convinced the protectionists of Pennsylvania that if relief was to be attained, more concerted action would be necessary. This realization found its material expression in two so-called Harrisburg conventions, which met at the state capital during the summer of 1827. The origin of this movement is a bit obscure. Possibly Henry Clay furnished the first impetus;[39] or perhaps it came from the wool raisers of Washington county, who were suffering from a continued decline of prices.[40] At any rate the first public sponsor of the project was the Pennsylvania Society for the Promotion of Manufactures and the Mechanic Arts, which on May 14, 1827 issued a call for a national convention of "farmers, manufacturers, and friends of both branches of industry" to meet at Harrisburg on July 30.[41] Shortly thereafter, the Society announced a state convention to be held at the same place in June to choose delegates to the national gathering.[42]

The Pennsylvania state convention, which assembled on June 27, consisted of sixty-three delegates, representing twenty-one different counties.[43] The heaviest representation was from the southern and eastern portions of the commonwealth, but the influence of Buchanan and Ingham had been sufficient to keep Lancaster and Bucks counties from sending delegates.[44] Mathew Carey was pres-

---

[38] *Harrisburg Pennsylvania Intelligencer*, July 3, 1827.

[39] The following letter written by Clay to Benjamin W. Crowninshield on March 18, 1827 may be significant in this connection: "I have sketched a plan of co-operation. . . . If the first movement takes place in Philadelphia, no pains should be spared to make it numerous, reputable and imposing. Let all persons (friends of D[omestic] M[anufactures], I[nternal] I[mprovements] and the Admin.) without regard to party denominations heretofore existing, be brought out. Let Ch. Justice Tilghman or Judge Barnes preside. Get M. Carey to attend. Let the meeting publish an address, well drawn, temperate in language, but firm in purpose and eloquent in composition. This meeting will form a nucleus." (This letter is printed in the *Quarterly Journal of Economics*, II, 491.)

[40] *Democratic Press*, May 15, 1827.

[41] *Proceedings of the General Convention at Harrisburg*, p. 1.

[42] *United States Gazette*, May 25, 1827.

[43] The counties represented were Philadelphia, Chester, Cumberland, Berks, Northumberland, Union, Bedford, Franklin, Montgomery, Dauphin, Lebanon, Luzerne, Huntingdon, Beaver, Allegheny, Mifflin, Delaware, Somerset, Lycoming, Adams, and Centre. Delegates had been appointed but failed to attend from Washington, Fayette, and Greene counties. (*Journal of a Convention of Delegates of the State of Pennsylvania*, p. 3.)

[44] *Democratic Press*, June 20, 1827; *Niles' Register*, XXXII, p. 314.

ent and took a leading part in the proceedings, but two of the state's outstanding protectionists refused to be present. John Tod had been chosen a delegate, but did not attend because he regarded the whole movement as a political scheme of the anti-Jackson men.[45] Henry Baldwin likewise declined an appointment on the grounds that as an opponent of the woolens bill he would not be representing the sentiments of his townspeople.[46] Although the call for the convention had been issued primarily in the interests of agriculture, actual farmers were in a decided minority. According to a contemporary tabulation, the body included sixteen farmers; eleven lawyers; twenty-one manufacturers; three merchants; three printers and book sellers; two bankers; one physician; one waterman; and five whose occupation was unknown.[47]

The work of the convention was brief. An address was drawn up and adopted, recommending adequate protection for every form of manufacture which could be produced at home. This document was drafted by Charles Jared Ingersoll, vice president of the Pennsylvania Society and a staunch protectionist, although not so extreme and unyielding in his views as Carey.[48] A memorial was also drawn up for submission to the state legislature, which requested that body to adopt a suitable resolution for the guidance of the Pennsylvania representatives in Congress.[49] Finally, a delegation of sixteen, including both Carey and Ingersoll, were appointed to represent the state at the general convention to follow.[50]

The national convention which assembled at Harrisburg on July 30 contained representatives from thirteen states.[51] Among the members were several protectionists of national reputation such as Mathew Carey, Hezekiah Niles, Abbott Lawrence of Massachusetts, and Rollin Mallary of Vermont, chairman of the House Committee on Manufactures. Joseph Ritner, later governor of Pennsylvania,

---

[45] Clipping from *Bedford Gazette* in Mathew Carey scrapbooks.
[46] *Pittsburgh Mercury*, July 24, 1827.
[47] *Ibid.*
[48] *Journal of a Convention of Delegates of the State of Pennsylvania*, p. 12.
[49] *Ibid.* p. 10.
[50] *Journal of a Convention of Delegates of the State of Pennsylvania*, p. 16.
[51] The states represented were Connecticut, Delaware, Kentucky, Maryland, Massachusetts, New York, New Hampshire, New Jersey, Ohio, Pennsylvania, Rhode Island, Vermont, and Virginia. (*Proceedings of the General Convention at Harrisburg*, p. 1.)

was elected chairman, as a tribute to the wool growers of Washington county where he resided.[52] According to Niles, a majority of the members of the convention were practical farmers.[53] The men who dominated the proceedings, however, were the politicians such as Mallary, the manufacturers such as Lawrence, and the journalists such as Niles and Carey.

The fate of the woolens bill had convinced American protectionists of the futility of attempting to put through a tariff revision which appealed only to a single interest. At the very beginning of the convention, therefore, Carey urged that they should not confine their attention to wool and woolens, for as he said, "The greater the variety of interest, the greater the prospect of success."[54] The protectionists present, with no opposition to fear within their ranks, responded enthusiastically to this suggestion, and committees were appointed to inquire into the expediency of higher duties on various products of industry and agriculture. The Pennsylvania delegates showed particular interest in behalf of printed cottons, wool and woolens, iron, and spiritous liquors.[55] On the basis of the committee reports and the general discussion, a series of resolutions were finally adopted which embraced the recommendations of the convention. The most urgent and most explicit proposals were those relating to wool and woolens. The ad valorem rate on woolen goods was to be gradually increased to 50 per cent. and was to be assessed on minimum valuations of fifty cents, two dollars and a half, four dollars, and six dollars a yard. The duties thus proposed would mean absolute prohibition for many classes of goods and high protection for all. The duties on wool costing more than 8 cents a pound were to be increased gradually to 50 cents, an utterly prohibitive figure. Largely at the behest of Pennsylvania, the convention urged that the duty on hammered bar iron be raised to one cent a pound. Other increases were recommended on flax, hemp, printed cottons, and spirits. The committee on glass was the only one to report that further protection would not be necessary.[56]

While the members of the Harrisburg Convention were thus

52 *United States Gazette,* August 2, 1827.
53 *Niles' Register,* XXXIII, 65.
54 Unidentified clipping in Mathew Carey scrapbooks.
55 *United States Gazette,* August 3, 1827.
56 *Proceedings of the General Convention at Harrisburg,* p. 19.

busily engaged in rearranging the tariff rates to their own satisfaction, a bitter controversy was springing up in many quarters as to the real significance of the gathering. No sooner had the project been launched than the charge began to recur that it was simply a political device to lure Pennsylvania into the support of the Administration. Some degree of plausibility was lent to this assertion by the fact that the Pennsylvania Society which had proposed the convention was made up entirely of Adams men.[57] Typical of such charges was the following extract from a letter published in a Pittsburgh newspaper:

We look upon the whole scheme of a convention at Harrisburg as a contemptible maneuver to operate on public sentiment in your state. Doubtless there are manufacturers among its members, who think they have an interest in its proceedings; but the greater part of them are unquestionably actuated only by a desire to seduce Pennsylvania from the cause of Jackson, under false pretences that himself and friends are opposed to a tariff, while Mr. Adams is in its favor.[58]

In the same vein, a public meeting at Harrodsburgh, Kentucky, resolved that "the real design of this convention at Harrisburg is not to advance American industry, but to organize a political club under the direction of the Administration of the general government to direct and control public sentiment and particularly to operate upon the election in the state of Pennsylvania.[59] John C. Calhoun was another who believed that the gathering had its origin in the insidious designs of intriguing politicians.[60] All these insinuations, however, were indignantly denied by the sponsors of the convention. Carey asserted that the Pennsylvania Society had always carefully held itself aloof from the political controversies of the day.[61] Niles pointed out that in the convention, "the president, and one of the vice-presidents, and many of the members were friendly to the election of General Jackson to the presidency of the United States."[62] An Adams paper advanced the further argument that "the friends of Domestic Manufactures would have been madmen to break down

---

[57] *Niles' Register*, XXXII, p. 350.
[58] *Pittsburgh Mercury*, July 31, 1827.
[59] *Ibid.*
[60] Calhoun, *Correspondence*, p. 250.
[61] *Niles' Register*, XXXII, 350.
[62] *Ibid.* XXXIV, p. 187.

their strength by mingling the economical plans with political matters. . .The friends of the American system are anxious that there may be unanimity upon the subject, and certainly will not mix up anything with the main object that might tend to invite opposition."[63]

As often happens, the truth was probably somewhere between these two extremes. Clay's letter to Crowninshield, cited above, indicates that the Adams leaders were indeed making a deliberate attempt to identify the Administration with the protectionist cause. Likewise it should be noted that the Pennsylvania delegation to the convention contained a large proportion of active politicians; of the sixteen members, one later became governor and seven others served at some time in Congress. The Jackson men had already shown how to use the tariff as a campaign weapon in the case of the woolens bill, and it would have been indeed strange if some of the Administration leaders had not profited by the example. On the other hand there were at Harrisburg men like Mathew Carey who were absolutely incapable of subordinating the tariff to any political end. Carey's utter contempt for partisan considerations is clearly indicated in the following passage, which was written in the interval between the state and national conventions:

I am myself decidedly in favor of the administration but can never consent to be instrumental in amalgamating the question of the presidency with that of the protection of manufactures. The former question I consider as comparatively insignificant. It is in my opinion deplorable that twelve millions of people are almost ready for mortal combat to decide who shall administer their affairs, when there are probably five hundred men in the nation fully competent. . . . We realize the truth of Swift's maxim "party is the madness of the many for the benefit of the few."[64]

It is altogether probable, therefore, that there were present at Harrisburg two very distinct elements, each seeking a different goal through a common medium. So far as numbers were concerned, however, the sincere protectionists undoubtedly constituted a large majority of the convention.

The protectionist movement of 1827 not only produced the Harrisburg convention; but also brought forward in Pennsylvania

---

[63] *Democratic Press,* May 31, 1827.
[64] *Niles' Register,* XXXII, p. 350.

a new propagandist to share the labors of Carey and Ingersoll. This was Friedrich List, the German economist, whose later writings were destined to exercise a profound influence upon European tariff policies. List had emigrated from his native land to Pennsylvania in 1825, partly to escape government persecution at home, partly to seek material wealth, and partly to find in a new environment additional evidence to support his economic theories. He had settled in the vicinity of Reading, acquired a farm and a German newspaper, and set himself to an intensive study of the American life about him. His particular interest in economic problems soon led him to take an active part in the tariff struggle.

Many authors insufficiently acquainted with List's earlier writings have declared that he was first converted to the protective principle during his sojourn in America.[65] It would indeed contribute much to the prestige of Pennsylvania protectionism could it be proved that the theories which won Europe to the tariff system had their origin in the hospitable environment of that state. The evidence is conclusive, however, that List had become a protectionist before leaving Europe. On the eve of his departure for America, he wrote,

When will the sight of such manufacturing prosperity bring the obstinate worshippers of Adam Smith into the right road? However much this teacher of national economy may have been of service to the world from other points of view, all his services cannot compensate for the incalculable mischief which he has caused by instilling the dream of so-called "free intercourse" into the minds of some of our theorists. . . . I hope that the United States will afford me a fine example in proof of my assertion. They followed Smith's theories till their whole industry lay in ruins, and then began to follow the system which the theorists abhor. We shall see how they fare under it.[66]

Thus it is clear that Pennsylvania had nothing new to offer List in the way of fundamental principles. Nevertheless, his American experience admittedly did much to establish and confirm the details of the elaborate economic philosophy which he was even then developing. He was delighted to find in Pennsylvania a state of society which seemed to harmonize perfectly with the theories which he had already evolved. Fired with boundless enthusiasm, he wrote,

---

[65] *Cf.* Sherwood, *Tendencies in American Economic Thought,* p. 15.
[66] Quoted in Hirst, *Life of Friedrich List,* p. 33.

My destiny having afterwards called me to the United States, I left behind all my books; they would only have led me astray. The best book on Political Economy in that new country is the volume of life. There were solitudes rapidly being converted into rich and powerful States. There for the first time I obtained a clear idea of the gradual development of the economy of a people. A process which in Europe would require the lapse of centuries, takes place in America before one's very eyes; there society is seen passing from the savage state to pastoral life; from this condition to agriculture, and from agriculture to manufactures and commerce. There one may easily observe how the rent of land rises gradually from nothing to a high level. There the humblest farmer knows better than the most learned scholars of the Old World the means of making agriculture prosperous and augmenting rents; he endeavors to attract manufactures to his neighborhood. There the contrasts between agricultural and manufacturing countries are exemplified in the most decided manner, and cause the most disastrous revulsions. . . . That book I have read earnestly and assiduously, and lessons drawn from it I have tried to harmonize with the results of my previous studies, experience, and reflections.[67]

.List's residence in Pennsylvania likewise helped to shape his later career by bringing him into association with some of the leading American protectionists of the day. Ingersoll in particular was impressed with his ability and zeal, and induced him in 1827 to write a popular pamphlet in support of protection. Accordingly, List produced a tract entitled *Outlines of American Political Economy,* which was really a brief presentation of the ideas later expounded in his more famous *National System.* The production attained an immediate success; it was distributed by the Pennsylvania Society to the extent of several thousand copies; and was widely republished by the press. List records that he was congratulated on his effort by some of the most distinguished men of the country, including James Madison and Henry Clay.[68] This contribution was followed by two other pamphlets also published under the auspices of the Society.[69] He was likewise invited by the Philadelphia organization to prepare a two-volume scientific treatise upon the subject of political economy, but the work was never completed.[70] The purchase of a rich coal mine in the Schuylkill region diverted his attention to the problems

---

[67] List, *Das Nationale System* (Eheberg ed.), Intro., p. x.
[68] *Ibid.* pp. xi, xii.
[69] *Ibid.* p. 364.
[70] *Ibid.* pp. xi, xii.

of mining and transportation, and from that time until his return to Germany in 1830, his literary efforts were confined to these topics.[71]

List's career as a Pennsylvania protectionist is of interest chiefly because of its bearing upon his later work. His efforts extended over too short a period to gain an enduring place in American tariff literature. Nevertheless, for a brief span he enjoyed considerable repute as a protectionist even in a state where such sentiments were almost taken for granted. The Pennsylvania Society on November 3, 1827 gave a complimentary dinner in his honor.[72] The same body, in giving public endorsement to his works, declared that he "has founded a new and true system of political economy and has thus rendered an eminent service to the United States."[73] The strongly protectionist *Miners' Journal* characterized him as one of the "most able champions of the American System in the United States."[74] Even the intense free-trade partisans of the South deemed his efforts of sufficient importance to receive their ridicule and abuse. Hamilton of South Carolina dryly observed that "we appear to have imported a Professor from Germany, in absolute violation of the doctrines of the American system, to lecture upon its lessons—to convict Adam Smith of stupidity and Ricardo of error."[75] McDuffie was even more severe than his colleague in his remarks concerning

a certain German Professor of Political Economy and Necromancy in Pennsylvania, who has been recently introduced to the American public by a member of the Harrisburg Convention. . . . We are certainly relapsing into the age of alchemy; and I challenge any man to find a parallel in the pretended discoveries of Paracelsus, Roger Bacon or any of their followers, to the grand discovery in political alchemy made by this notable German professor![76]

The tariff agitation in Pennsylvania continued unabated after the adjournment of the Harrisburg convention. It was still essentially a wool and woolens movement; indeed, the other industries of the state had little real cause for complaint. Wool prices continued low; the residents of Washington county, for instance, com-

[71] Hirst, *Life of Friedrich List,* p. 55.
[72] *Democratic Press,* November 10, 1827.
[73] List, *Das Nationale System* (Eheberg ed.), Intro., pp. xi, xii.
[74] March 15, 1828.
[75] *Cong. Debates,* 20 Cong., 1 Sess., p. 2432.
[76] *Ibid.* p. 2394.

plained that a sheep which cost a dollar a year to maintain provided only 75 cents worth of wool.[77] Protectionist sentiment, however, seemed to be somewhat divided as to the exact measures to be taken. Some, under the leadership of Mathew Carey, favored a fearless application of the Harrisburg recommendations;[78] others preferred the reintroduction of the woolens bill, suitably amended so as to provide for a more general revision.[79] A very interesting tariff discussion took place in the Pennsylvania legislature when that body convened in December. Early in the session, a resolution was introduced in the House to the effect that "the present tariff system of the government of the United States is wholly insufficient to render that protection to our domestic manufactures and agricultural interests which they need to relieve them from present embarrassment and secure them from impending ruin.[80] Objection was quickly made that this passage was too strong. One member particularly protested against the reference to a "state of impending ruin," which he declared was "entirely destitute of foundation."[81] The resolution as finally adopted by both houses employed much milder phraseology, but was still thoroughly protectionist. It specifically requested additional duties on woolen and fine cotton goods, glass, spirits, flax, chinaware, hemp, wool, and bar iron."[82]

The Twentieth Congress met for its first session in December, 1827. It was futile, however, to expect any rational consideration of the tariff question from that politically infatuated body. The Jackson party was in control of the House of Representatives, and the leaders immediately set in motion an ingenious but risky scheme to discredit the Administration among the protectionists of the northern states. The plan was to introduce a bill providing for extremely high duties, but at the same time containing specific provisions so thoroughly obnoxious to the manufacturing interest that the Adams men of New England would be compelled to ally themselves with the free traders of the South in defeating the measure.

---

[77] *Hazard's Register,* I, 128.
[78] *Cf.* Carey, M., *Memorial of the Citizens of Philadelphia to Congress,* November 9, 1827.
[79] *Cf. Pittsburgh Mercury,* June 19, 1827.
[80] *Harrisburg Reporter,* December 11, 1827.
[81] *Ibid.* December 18, 1827.
[82] *Pamphlet Laws,* 1827-28, p. 496.

Thus it was hoped they would ineffaceably brand themselves as foes to the protective system. At the same time, the Jackson men representing the northern industrial states could safely support the measure without any danger of its passage, and so be able to approach the electorate with the plausible argument that they were the real and exclusive friends of the tariff. By this device it might be possible to break down the Adams strength in the decidedly protectionist states of New York, Pennsylvania and Ohio.

Accordingly, the Committee on Manufactures, which was made up largely of Jackson sympathizers, dutifully reported a bill designed to carry out the foregoing plan. Manufactured articles, with one significant exception, were granted extremely high duties, which in some cases even exceeded the amount requested by the producers themselves. Only woolen goods, the particular interest of New England, were deliberately slighted. These were not only taxed at 40 per cent. instead of 50 per cent. as requested at Harrisburg, but also were afforded a much less favorable scale of minimum valuations. In order to alienate further the manufacturers of New England, very high duties were placed on important raw materials such as iron, flax, hemp, wool, and molasses.

The fate of the committee bill may be recorded very briefly. The Jackson men staunchly resisted all proposed amendments, lest the measure become too palatable to those who were expected to defeat it. Special efforts were made to defeat the so-called Mallary amendment, which sought to substitute the recommendations of the Harrisburg convention for those of the committee. The plans of the conspirators progressed smoothly at every point until the final vote was reached; then, too late, they discovered that they had underestimated one factor—the reluctance of New England to play into the hands of the opposition by causing the defeat of the measure. To the surprise and consternation of its authors, the bill passed both houses by a narrow margin, and the "tariff of abominations" became the law of the land.

The Pennsylvanians in both House and Senate gave unanimous support to the bill on its final passage.[83] It is not surprising that they should have done so; since with all its defects, the measure still

---

[83] *Cong. Debates*, 20 Cong., 1 Sess., pp. 786, 2471.

afforded extreme protection on most articles. Moreover, most of the delegation were staunch Jacksonians, whose part in the whole scheme was to affect the most extreme solicitude for the bill. As between the two motives, it is clear that a large majority were partisans first and protectionists second. This was shown by the vote upon the Mallary amendment, which would have made the measure far more acceptable to the friends of industry, but which would have largely thwarted its political objectives. On this proposition, Pennsylvania, acting in unnatural alliance with the free traders of the South, gave only five affirmative as against eighteen negative votes.[84] Political motives are likewise reflected in the debates, where certain remarks were dropped with the obvious intent of goading the Adams men into opposition to the bill. Stevenson's assertion, for instance, that the operation of the iron clauses of the bill would transfer to Pennsylvania all the rolling and slitting mills of New England was clearly designed not to gain votes but to repel them.[85] Bates of Massachusetts later took up this remark and openly accused the Pittsburgh member of seeking thereby to arouse political animosity against the measure.[86] Buchanan likewise had much to say against the "grasping spirit" of New England and especially supported the high duty on molasses, a provision which was extremely obnoxious to that section.[87] He also strongly opposed any system of minimum valuations upon woolens.[88] This action, while entirely consistent with Buchanan's previously expressed views, could not help but be especially galling to eastern manufacturers. With such devices as these, therefore, the Jackson men labored unceasingly to discredit the protectionist claims of the Adams forces and to erect the highest possible barrier of suspicion and jealousy between New England and Pennsylvania.

While Pennsylvania congressmen were thus earnestly striving to legislate Andrew Jackson into the White House, their constituents at home were following the tariff battle with intense interest. Public sentiment on the whole was severely critical of the bill as reported by the Committee on Manufactures. Meetings in all parts of the

---

[84] *Ibid.* p. 2245.
[85] *Ibid.* p. 1760.
[86] *Ibid.* p. 2000.
[87] *Ibid.* pp. 2106, 2346.
[88] *Ibid.* p. 2044.

state approved the recommendations of the Harrisburg convention and expressed regret that these had not been followed more closely in the proposed legislation. The principal objection was centered upon the rates on wool and woolens, which were held to be utterly inadequate.[89] Nevertheless, the general attitude seems to have been that the committee measure was infinitely preferable to no revision at all. This feeling may have been strengthened by a minor financial crisis which struck Philadelphia while the bill was still pending in the House; a local observer, commenting upon the occurrence, declared that "an anti-tariff meeting would not be very fully attended, were it called just now."[90] At any rate, Buchanan was warned that the people of Pennsylvania would hold the Jackson majority in Congress strictly responsible for the success of the measure, and that its rejection might have very serious political consequences.[91]

Once passed, the tariff of 1828 was accepted with considerable enthusiasm, especially by the Jacksonians, who did not hesitate to claim for themselves the credit for its adoption. One paper declared that the act "could not have been more protective to our manufacturing and agricultural interests, if Pennsylvania alone would have had the formation of it."[92] Baldwin hailed it as a measure "which will produce more benefits to the country than any bill ever before passed. . .It is the most important bill which was ever adopted."[93] Mathew Carey, on the other hand, was too unyielding and too uncompromising a protectionist to share such sentiments. He characterized the act of 1828 as a "crude mass of imperfection" and asserted that it had failed to meet the expectations of its friends.[94] Carey's attitude, however, was by no means representative of the general reaction to the new revenue law. Most friends of the American system in Pennsylvania were quickly reconciled to its provisions, which in actual operation proved to be far more protective than had been anticipated.

The passage of the act of 1828 left the presidential question in

---

[89] *American State Papers, Finance,* V, 705, 710, 717, 760, 900, 901, 943, 972.
[90] *Niles' Register,* XXXIV, 35.
[91] William B. Fordney to Buchanan, April 15, 1828; Buchanan MSS.
[92] *Harrisburg Reporter,* June 6, 1828.
[93] *Cincinnati National Republican,* June 6, 1828.
[94] Carey, M., *Olive Branch,* No. IV, p. 3; *Common Sense Addresses,* p. xi.

full and undisputed possession of the Pennsylvania scene. As a matter of fact, ever since the summer of 1827, the political waters had been seething around the contending personalities of Andrew Jackson and John Quincy Adams. There is reason to believe that the Administration leaders would have liked to take the offensive in Pennsylvania with protection as their principal issue, but the vigor with which the "bargain and corruption" charge was pressed very soon threw them upon the defensive. The Jackson men were more aggressive on the tariff question than might have been expected in view of their embarrassing Southern affiliations, but as the campaign advanced they too found it expedient to say less and less upon the subject. Personalities and democracy were easily the dominant issues of the election; nevertheless, the tariff played an interesting though not decisive part in the struggle.

Both candidates maintained throughout the campaign a dignified reticence upon the subject of protection. Adams' tariff views were never too clearly defined; while Jackson discreetly referred all interrogators to the Coleman letter in 1824.[95] Jackson's unwillingness to express himself on the question is well indicated by his answer to a Pennsylvania correspondent who had urged a reaffirmation of his tariff views as necessary to prevent serious defections in that state.[96] Jackson replied,

I ask you as one of my friends whether Mr. Stewart, Mr. Lawrence and Mr. Ritner would be better satisfied than they now are, were I to *reiterate* to the world my expressions to Dr. Coleman sustained as they are by my votes in the senate of the United States. . . . Those gentlemen act uncandidly—they rather desire me to come out under present circumstances that I may incur the charge of electioneering and afford my enemies a new subject for misrepresentation and distortion. . . . My real friends have confidence in me; they are satisfied with the sincerity of the sentiments expressed in my letter to Dr. Coleman and with the illustration afforded by my public votes. My enemies would not be satisfied with anything I could now say.[97]

Despite Jackson's reticence concerning the tariff, his Pennsylvania supporters bestirred themselves to make the most of the

95 *Cf.* Jackson's letter to Governor Ray of Indiana in *Niles' Register*, XXXIV, p. 158.
96 John J. Steele to Jackson, December 28, 1827; Jackson MSS.
97 Jackson to John J. Steele, February 17, 1828; Jackson MSS.

material at hand. The Coleman letter was industriously circulated, and much emphasis was laid upon Jackson's protectionist efforts while in the Senate.[98] At the same time the General's friends challenged their opponents to "produce any letter, speech or act, in which John Q. Adams has expressed an opinion, or declared himself in favor of protecting domestic manufactures."[99] More specifically, it was pointed out that neither in Adams' inaugural address nor in his three annual messages was there any reference to this vital national question.[100] Turning to their candidate for the Vice-Presidency, the Democrats depicted Calhoun as one who had "urged with resistless force the claims of the American manufacturer to legislative protection," and quite ignored the fact that the characterization no longer applied.[101] The proceedings of Congress were likewise scanned for evidence that the Jackson men were the real friends of the tariff. They pointed out, for instance, that an Adams man had contributed Pennsylvania's only vote against the act of 1824. Moreover, it was argued rather inconsistently that Jackson votes had passed the woolens bill in the House, and would have done so in the Senate but for the absence of Administration members.[102] As a matter of course, the Democrats claimed credit for the passage of the act of 1828, which they claimed had been "forced under the reluctant wing of government by your Jackson representatives."[103]

Needless to say, the Administration forces regarded the tariff issue of the campaign in a far different light. Adams and Rush were depicted as the bulwarks of the American system; Jackson on the other hand was described as "a southern man with southern feelings, the deadly enemy of the American System."[104] One paper asserted that "wherever Jacksonism prevails, opposition exists to Domestic Manufactures and the American System. Opposition to the American System and opposition to the Administration are convertible terms."[105] Another Adams journal believed it to be "as

---

[98] *Cf. Democratic Press*, June 14, 1827; *Harrisburg Reporter*, December 12, 1827.
[99] *Harrisburg Reporter*, December 12, 1827.
[100] *Pittsburgh Mercury*, February 26, 1828.
[101] *American Sentinel*, January 14, 1828.
[102] *Philadelphia Gazette*, June 26, 1827.
[103] *American Sentinel*, October 31, 1828.
[104] *United States Gazette*, August 4, 1828.
[105] *Democratic Press*, July 31, 1827.

clear and irresistible as proofs of Holy Writ . . . that Jackson has been, is now, and will continue to be, deadly hostile to the American system and all the great interests of the north."[106]  To refute Jackson's claims in respect to the tariff of 1824, it was pointed out that on many of the individual items he had favored the adoption of lower rates.[107]  It was pointed out that Calhoun, by his casting vote, was responsible for the defeat of the woolens bill, and that he was "avowedly an enemy of the American System."[108]  Much was also made of the fact that on the woolens bill, Adams men contributed 96 out of the 106 ayes; while 85 out of the 95 noes came from the Jackson side of the House.[109]  The fantastic charge was made that £1,000,000 of British gold had been thrown into the contest in behalf of the free trade candidate—Andrew Jackson.[110]  This seems to have been the first appearance of this extravagant accusation, which soon became a regular quadrennial visitant in Pennsylvania.

It is difficult to say just what effect the tariff argument had upon the final result of the election.  Stewart and Ritner and a few other extreme protectionists ostentatiously bolted the Democratic party on the grounds that Jackson was hostile to American industry.[111]  On the other hand, Baldwin, who was himself an iron manufacturer, loyally supported the General's candidacy.[112]  It is not likely, all things considered, that the tariff question did Jackson much harm; indeed, one observer believed that he had been greatly benefited by the passage of the act of 1828.[113]  As the bank controversy was to show subsequently, Jackson's personal popularity in Pennsylvania was too overwhelming to be seriously affected by any issue.  The congressional elections in October resulted in a sweeping victory for the Democratic candidates, and clearly foreshadowed the Jackson

---

[106] *Harrisburg Intelligencer*, April 3, 1828.

[107] *Miners' Journal*, March 22, 29, 1828.

[108] *Harrisburg Intelligencer*, April 10, 1828; *United States Gazette*, August 19, 1828.

[109] *United States Gazette*, January 4, 1828.

[110] *Harrisburg Intelligencer*, October 7, 14, 28, 1828.

[111] John J. Steele to Jackson, December 28, 1827; Jackson MSS.; Stewart, *Speeches on the Tariff Question*, p. 5; Sargent, *Public Men and Events*, p. 152n.

[112] Baldwin to Jackson, April 11, 1828; Jackson MSS.; *Harrisburg Reporter*, June 26, 1828.

[113] Joseph Lescure to Buchanan, June 11, 1828; Buchanan MSS.

triumph which was to follow. After this preliminary test of strength, the *Harrisburg Intelligencer* lamented that

The result of the late election has shown us that the people of this state are irrevocably chained to the car of the great idol. And such is their infatuation and so completely are they blinded by their idolatry, that reason, argument and facts are alike lost on them. . . . "Huzza for Jackson" is the sum of their answer to every argument, and to dance around a hickory pole the ultimatum of their love of country and patriotic feeling. . . The great question at issue in the present contest is whether the northern tariff or the southern anti-tariff shall prevail. Pennsylvania has already arrayed herself under the standard of the latter; her dearest interests have been cast at the feet of the great Moloch, and her neck bowed to the wheels of his car.[114]

The returns of the presidential election more than verified this editor's doleful anticipations. The Jackson ticket swept Pennsylvania by a popular vote of two to one.[115] Adams was able to carry only five counties in the entire state, namely, Delaware, Bucks, Adams, Beaver, and Erie.[116] A close analysis of the returns reveals no discernible relation between the tariff question and the distribution of the vote. There is not a particle of evidence to indicate that Jackson's overwhelming victory reflected any diminution of tariff enthusiasm in the state; indeed, as will be seen, Pennsylvania was entering upon a period when protectionist sentiment was more intense and more nearly universal than ever before in her history.

---

[114] October 21, 1828.
[115] The official returns were: Jackson, 101,652; Adams, 50,848. (*Smull's Legislative Handbook,* 1921-22, p. 740.)
[116] *American Sentinel,* November 14, 1828.

CHAPTER V

## THE CLIMAX OF EARLY PROTECTIONISM, 1828-1832

Early protectionist sentiment in Pennsylvania reached its zenith during 1830 and the first months of 1831. These years represent the culmination of the steady and irresistible tariff movement which had been gaining momentum ever since the close of the second war with Britain. Already there were apparent upon the horizon new political and economic forces which were destined to shake the protectionist cause even in its Pennsylvania citadel; but both friend and foe agreed that for the moment the triumph of the tariff system was complete and overwhelming. An interesting description of the intensity of protectionist sentiment at this time has been furnished by Condy Raguet, the able spokesman of the state's negligible free-trade element. Writing in 1830, he declared:

There is not now in the whole state of Pennsylvania a single paper that will circulate the doctrines of Free Trade. Even in Philadelphia, a city which has so many commercial advantages, there is not an editor who will openly avow himself as an opponent of the American System, nor do we know of one who would give free admission to essays intended to show the fallacies of the restrictive philosophy.[1]

Raguet described his native city of Philadelphia as "the very head-quarters of the American system."[2] Concerning the other industrial metropolis of the state, he asserted:

The City of Pittsburgh is one of the strongholds of the American system. It is quite probable that there is not, in the whole population, a single individual who ever opens his lips on the subject of Free Trade unless it be to denounce it, whatever he may think in relation to it. To attempt, therefore, to convert such a community to the true faith, would be almost as vain as to attempt to convert the Turks to Christianity. . . . The people of Pittsburgh would no doubt be as much astonished to hear it asserted that the restrictive system was injurious to their prosperity, as the people of Brazil are when foreigners tell them that the use of carts . . . having the axletree to turn around with the wheels is not an advantageous custom.[3]

Possibly Raguet's free trade predilections caused an element of

---

[1] *Banner of the Constitution,* June 9, 1830.
[2] *Free Trade Advocate,* II, 14.
[3] *Banner of the Constitution,* March 30, 1831.

exaggeration to creep into his writings; nevertheless, his general conclusions are fully substantiated by protectionist observers. It was commonly believed that at least nine-tenths of the state's inhabitants were friendly to the tariff system.[4] Particular emphasis was laid upon the unanimity of protectionist sentiment among the farmers of the state.[5] Indeed, a report submitted to the Secretary of the Treasury in 1832 went so far as to say that in western Pennsylvania "the agricultural classes are fully satisfied with the present system; they are firm in the belief that it is just as beneficial to them as to those who are engaged in manufacturing. This opinion is universal."[6] This statement was undoubtedly overdrawn; but it is clear that the tariff of 1828, with its high duties on raw materials, was very well received by the farmers of the state.

Few Pennsylvanians during these years had either the inclination or the hardihood to protest against the "tariff of abominations" and the policy which it represented. To do so was to incur the risk of intellectual and political ostracism;; to experience the loneliness and futility of the proverbial voice crying in the wilderness. Nevertheless, the feeble minority of anti-protectionists was not completely silenced. In March, 1830, a meeting of Philadelphia blacksmiths and other ironworkers petitioned Congress for lower duties upon essential raw materials. They declared that they were taxed from 140 to 250 per cent. on the raw and semi-manufactured iron they required, whereas the hardware they produced received a protection of only 25 per cent. Their memorial was tactfully sent to the presiding officers of the respective Houses, "in order to cause no uneasiness to the Representatives or Senators from this district, as we suppose a majority of their constituents are on the other side: that is, tariff men.[7] In the Senate, the petition was referred to the Committee on Manufactures, which reported that the blacksmiths had just cause for complaint, but recommended that relief be sought by raising the duties on hardware rather than by lowering the rates on raw materials.[8] The Philadelphia ironworkers, accordingly, re-

---

[4] *Cf. United States Gazette,* March 9, September 23, 1831; *Review of the Report of a Committee of the Citizens of Boston,* p. 54.
[5] *Cf. Democratic Press,* September 19, 1827; *United States Gazette,* March 14, 1828; *Free Trade Advocate,* I, 30.
[6] *House Exec. Doc.,* 22 Cong., 1 Sess., No. 308, Vol. II, p. 235.
[7] *Banner of the Constitution,* April 7, 1830.
[8] *Ibid.* May 22, 1830.

newed their request at the following session of Congress.[9] This time
the memorial was referred to a select committee, with Senator Hayne
as chairman. This committee brought in a vigorous report, which
denounced the protective system in theory and in practice, while it
commended "the wisdom and virtue which have enabled the petitioners to discern the true policy of the country."[10] In spite of this
favorable consideration, no further action was taken upon the
blacksmiths' memorial.

It was during this period, also, that Condy Raguet first entered
the arena as one of the few men who have ventured to preach without equivocation or reservation the gospel of free trade in Pennsylvania. Raguet's earlier years had been devoted primarily to commercial pursuits and to service in the state legislature where he had
won considerable recognition for his careful study of banking and
currency problems. During this period his tariff views appear to
have been rather fluctuating. In view of his mercantile interests,
it is not surprising that he at first opposed the protective policy as
an unwarranted curb upon commercial development.[11] However,
the tariff movement which swept the country after the War of 1812
numbered him among its converts, and by 1819 he came forward
as an earnest worker in the cause. He contributed, in that year, a
series of essays sufficiently protectionist to be published as an appendix to a volume by Mathew Carey.[12] He also served as secretary of a large tariff meeting at Philadelphia, and was placed upon
the committee chosen to draft a memorial to Congress.[13] At about
the same time, he introduced in the Pennsylvania Senate a resolution which asserted that "the helping hand of government is requisite to overbalance those difficulties which are invariably presented to infant enterprises" and asked Congress for such laws
"as may afford to the manufacturing interests of the country a fair
.prospect of success against a forced foreign competition."[14] Nevertheless, Raguet could not even then be considered as an extreme
protectionist. He opposed, for instance, an amendment to his reso-

---

[9] *Ibid.* January 19, March 2, 1831.
[10] *Sen. Doc.*, 21 Cong., 2 Sess., No. 67, p. 6.
[11] *Aurora*, September 19, 1819.
[12] Carey, M., *Addresses of the Philadelphia Society*, 4th edition.
[13] *Aurora*, August 23, 1819.
[14] *Senate Journal*, 1819-20, pp. 455-457.

lution which would have recommended the iron industry of Pennsylvania to the special attention of Congress.[15] Also, at this session he was chairman of the special committee of the Senate which found that an unwise banking policy rather than excessive imports was the cause of the prevailing distress in the state.[16]

This protectionist period represented merely a transitory stage in the development of Raguet's economic philosophy. He was one of those who suffered heavy reverses during the depression of 1819. As a result he lost his entire fortune and was glad to accept an appointment in 1822 as United States consul at Rio de Janeiro. He served there as consul and charge d'affaires for five years, during the tumultuous period of Brazil's struggle for independence. He returned to Philadelphia in 1827, completely purged of all protectionist tendencies. The influences at work within him during this period can only be surmised. Perhaps his own private losses seemed to point the moral that a policy of artificial commercial restriction had no place in an enlightened economic order. Perhaps an enforced five years' meditation in a foreign land had brought him to a renewed appreciation of Adam Smith as a propounder of universal truth. Certainly he was impressed by Brazil's experience as to the beneficent results of a more liberal commercial policy.[17] Be the causes of his conversion what they may, it is certain that Raguet returned from South America an undeviating advocate of the free trade system for every nation, at every time, and under every circumstance.

For the theoretical basis of his new doctrines, Raguet went directly to the writings of Adam Smith, Say, and Senior. He held that both individuals and nations should be permitted to purchase freely in their natural markets; for, he inquired, "Is it not unwise—is it not cruel—nay, is it not wicked—for governments to compel people to labor for two days to procure the bread or the clothing which one

---

[15] *Ibid.* p. 457.

[16] See p. 45n, *supra*.

[17] Prior to 1808 the ports of Brazil had been closed to all nations except Portugal. In that year, Prince John, fleeing to America to escape the armies of Napoleon, threw open Brazilian ports to foreign commerce. An era of unprecedented prosperity ensued. Some years after his return, Raguet wrote, "A residence of near five years in South America . . . had given us a practical opportunity of judging the importance of foreign commerce under a system of free trade." (*Banner of the Constitution,* December 31, 1832.)

day's labor could command if they were left free to employ their industry in the way known to them to be most conducive to their private interest?"[18] Any departure from that principle he held to be "a tax upon one portion of the community for the benefit of another portion,"[19] or as he picturesquely phrased it "robbing Peter of one dollar to pay Paul half-a-dollar."[20] In like manner he disposed of the "vested interests" argument, holding it an absurdity that the manufacturers should be entitled to "an eternal tax upon the industry of the country."[21] He also had nothing but contempt for the economic fiction, so often encountered in tariff discussions, of a "favorable" balance of trade. He realized that commerce in the long run must result in the exchange of equivalents, and held that the nation which attempted through a protective tariff to force her economic streams into unnatural channels was guilty of a "voluntary annihilation of a portion of her wealth creating power."[22] Such a nation, seeking by fatuous policy to shut itself off from the rest of the world, he compared to "Robinson Crusoe in his goat-skins."[23] Nor did he believe that a nation must combat error with error; that if other nations employed the restrictive system, the United States must imitate them in self-defense. So clear, so overwhelming did he regard the advantages of free trade, that in the last tariff utterance of his life, he declared, "If ninety-nine out of a hundred nations adopt the restrictive system, it is the true policy of the remaining one to adhere to the principles of free trade."[24]

Fired with the zeal of a recent convert, Raguet diligently set out to promulgate his economic doctrines. His paramount duty as he saw it was to attempt to rally the broken free trade forces of the North; and as he surveyed the battlefield, nowhere could he find a more needful scene for his labors than in his native city of Philadelphia. Thus it was that in 1829 he established his *Free Trade Advocate* in what a southern contemporary called "the very den of monopoly and injustice."[25] This journal was the first periodical in the country to be

---

18 *Ibid.* November 14, 1832.
19 *Free Trade Advocate*, I, 9.
20 Raguet, *Essays on the Principles of Free Trade*, p. 105.
21 *Ibid.* pp. 155-158.
22 *Free Trade Advocate*, I, 9, 10.
23 *Hunt's Merchants' Magazine*, VI, 19.
24 *Ibid.* p. 14.
25 *Charleston Mercury*, quoted in *Free Trade Advocate*, I, 409.

devoted entirely to advancing the cause of free trade. Its slogan was the battle cry of the Classicist, "Laissez-nous faire," and its professed purpose was to combat the extensive propaganda and the "erroneous opinions" of the protectionists.[26] The paper received a hearty welcome in the South, where it was hailed as "the most formidable adversary the restrictionists have yet had to encounter."[27] It also received some support in the commercial centers of the North, even in Philadelphia. Nevertheless, Raguet was not satisfied with the limited circulation of the paper. Before the end of the year, therefore, he rechristened it the *Banner of the Constitution* and transferred the place of publication to Washington. He hoped thereby to give the paper the status and prestige of a national journal; to be closer to the official sources of information; and to be able to watch first-hand the dramatic struggle within the halls of Congress.[28] Here again the periodical was welcomed in the South as a worthy antidote for the weekly draught of protectionism administered by Hezekiah Niles.[29] Nevertheless, the editor found to his sorrow that no paper could flourish in Washington which failed to make party alignments or refused to subordinate principles to personalities. Raguet refused absolutely to do either. Consequently, in 1830, he removed the paper to New York, in the hope that it would command the support of the large commercial interests of that city.[30] In this he was disappointed; in fact he found that he had more subscribers in Philadelphia than in New York.[31] Accordingly after only four months in the metropolis, he moved the entire establishment to Philadelphia for what he called "an attack on Pennsylvania."[32] Once more, however, the expected support failed to materialize. The circulation of the *Banner of the Constitution* never exceeded 1600 and as the stigma of nullification brought free trade principles more and more into disrepute, the subscription list dwindled.[33] By the end of 1832, Raguet was ready to admit defeat. He could no longer see "the slightest prospect of any abandonment for many years to come of the American System from

---

[26] *Free Trade Advocate*, I, 15.
[27] *Charleston Patriot*, quoted in *Free Trade Advocate*, II, 14.
[28] *Banner of the Constitution*, December 5, 1829.
[29] *Niles' Register*, XXXV, 425; XXXVII, 66.
[30] *Banner of the Constitution*, December 1, 1830.
[31] *Ibid*. April 13, 1831.
[32] *Ibid*. April 20, 1831.
[33] *Ibid*. December 31, 1832.

any returning sense of justice or any change of opinion as to its expediency or constitutionality."[34] So on the last day of the year, he **laid down his pen, not without a sigh of relief**; for the lot of a free trade editor in Pennsylvania has never been an enviable one.[35] A protectionist paper announced his retirement with the comment that "the Free Trade flag may be considered forever struck — never to be hoisted again in Pennsylvania."[36] Raguet, however, found it impossible to withdraw permanently from the struggle. The excitement attending the culmination of the nullification movement in South Carolina brought him once more to the firing line. He established, in 1833, *The Examiner,* a bi-weekly paper published at Philadelphia and "devoted to the advancement of the cause of states rights and free trade."[37] At one time the journal enjoyed 7,500 subscribers, but the settlement of the immediate issues soon terminated the need for such a periodical.[38]

In all of these numerous projects, Raguet reveals himself as the unyielding and uncompromising foe of the protective system. As he phrased it, "Everyone who has read our paper knows that we have always handled the American system without gloves; that we have attacked it with small sword and broad sword; that we have assailed it in every honorable manner we could invent, with the weapons of argument, of irony and of ridicule."[39] As an editor, he assiduously assembled official documents, legislative proceedings, statistical compilations, and essays upon the theory and practice of foreign trade and political economy. These he presented in excellent form, with a

---

[34] *Ibid.* September 12, 1832.

[35] Raguet vividly described the treatment which the Pennsylvanians of that day accorded to tariff heterodoxy: "In our social relations we have encountered many painful feelings. The great body of our personal acquaintances are in favor of the Tariff and of government practically without limitation of powers; and the odium to which we have been subject for four years has at times been so great as almost to amount to excommunication. There are even gentlemen, with whom we have been on terms of friendship, who have suspended intercourse with us altogether, merely because they have pecuniary or political interests which they suppose have been injured by our publication; and there are thousands, who in 1818 assisted to elect us for four years to the Senate of the State, who would not at this day give us their suffrages for the dignified station of a County commissioner, if our ambition should happen to run in that line." (*Ibid.* November 14, 1832.)

[36] *Miners' Journal,* August 11, 1832.

[37] *Examiner,* I, 16.

[38] *Ibid.* p. 419.

[39] *Banner of the Constitution,* December 31, 1832.

moderation and dignity which won the respect of friend and foe alike. Unlike most editors of the day, his columns were open to the arguments of either side. His original contributions surpass those of Mathew Carey both as to felicity of expression and diversity of content. For instance, he made effective use of the ironical petition, a clever device for bringing the arguments of the protectionists to a logical *reductio ad absurdum*.[40] Like most propagandists, Raguet occasionally fell into grave inconsistencies in the development of his arguments. Sometimes, for instance, he denies outright that protection is a benefit to the industrialist; elsewhere, he accuses the manufacturer of piling up exorbitant profits under the tariff system. In one place, he may assert that American industry is strong enough to compete on equal terms with every rival; while in another passage, he will argue that we cannot compete with the foreign producer, and hence will save money through importation. On the whole, however, he seems to have been guilty of fewer inconsistencies than most of the contemporary writers who opposed him.[41]

Raguet not unjustly regarded Pennsylvania as the keystone of the protectionist arch. He entertained the fond hope that "if she can be detached from her allegiance to the American System, the fabric will crumble to atoms."[42] Furthermore, he seems to have been strangely confident that there was in Pennsylvania a latent anti-tariff sentiment ready to spring to life if given the proper leader. He pointed out how the state's attitude toward internal improvements and the national bank had reversed itself almost overnight under the mystical persuasiveness of Andrew Jackson. So, he continued,

We do not see how any man, not blind by self interest or party delusion, can fail to perceive that, if General Jackson shall at some future day say, "Down with the tariff," down it will go. There is, in this very state of Pennsylvania—aye and in the very iron counties supposed to be most interested in the Protective Policy—a party which is only waiting for the watchword, and who are prepared

---

[40] Bastiat in his *Sophismes Economiques* made effective use of the same device. Possibly he derived the idea from Raguet; at any rate the French work did not appear until 1847.

[41] Few writers on either side of the tariff question have been able to escape entirely the pitfalls of self-contradiction. This is due to the fact that most of them, while paying lip service to the inductive method, have consciously or unconsciously developed their arguments through the deductive process.

[42] *Banner of the Constitution*, March 30, 1831.

to prove that Pennsylvania is, at heart, no more attached to the Tariff than she was to the internal improvements or to the Bank.[43]

Fired with this delusive hope, Raguet labored mightily to prepare for the day when the people should be led forth out of economic bondage. For example, he attempted in 1831 to raise a fund to distribute a thousand free subscriptions to the *Banner of the Constitution* through all the counties of Pennsylvania.[44] This project, however, had to be abandoned for want of financial support. In a further effort to mobilize anti-tariff sentiment within the state, he helped to organize the Free Trade Convention which met at Philadelphia in September, 1831.[45] Fifteen of the maritime and southern states were represented at this gathering. Pennsylvania sent sixteen delegates, drawn almost exclusively from the mercantile interests of Philadelphia.[46] Aside from paying the expenses of the convention the local men do not seem to have taken a very active part in the proceedings. The protectionists manifested much amusement over the unrepresentative character of the delegation, which they alleged had been appointed by a meeting of fifteen persons in Philadelphia.[47] So far as Pennsylvania was concerned, therefore, the convention accomplished little except to indicate in striking fashion the weakness of the free trade movement within the state.[48]

As was to be expected, Raguet's most appreciative audience was found in the South. The redoubtable Senator Hayne paid tribute to "the distinguished services he has rendered to the cause of civil liberty and human happiness," and commended his journal as "an enduring monument of the talents, learning, disinterestedness and public virtue of its distinguished editor."[49] A Georgia paper called him "the most powerful and enlightened opponent of the restrictive system in the

---

43 *Ibid.* November 28, 1832.
44 *Ibid.* May 4, 1831; *Niles' Register*, XL, 178.
45 *Niles' Register*, XL, p. 393
46 *Journal of the Free Trade Convention*, p. 4; *Banner of the Constitution*, October 12, 1831.
47 *Niles' Register*, XL, p. 393.
48 In sharp contrast was the attitude of the state toward the convention of Friends of Domestic Industry held at New York in October, 1831. Pennsylvania sent 100 delegates; William Wilkins of Pittsburgh presided; Ingersoll helped to write the Address; while Carey and several others took a very active part in the proceedings. (*Address of the Convention of Friends of Domestic Industry*, p. 43; *Harrisburg Intelligencer*, November 5, 1831.)
49 *Banner of the Constitution*, November 11, 1832.

Union."[50] A correspondent from the same state wrote that "no man had done so much in so short a time . . . to eradicate error and enforce truth."[51] An enthusiastic Virginian assured him that "if your paper could be generally circulated, even among the people of Pennsylvania, I have no doubt that, in a few years, there would be an entire revolution in public opinion on the subject of protecting duties."[52]

As a matter of fact, Raguet's prodigious efforts seem to have won few converts in his own state. Nevertheless, his ability and sincerity were generally recognized and respected, even by those who bitterly condemned his theories. The protectionist *United States Gazette* declared of him, "A writer has appeared, who, for a wonder, is able to say something new, ingenious, and not pedantic, on the anti-protective side . . . He has said more in favor of abolishing all protecting duties than the whole body of nullifiers have been able to utter in the last five years."[53] The same editor lauded the *Banner of the Constitution* as "unquestionably the most powerful on the nullification and anti-tariff side, of all we read."[54] The *Miners' Journal* called him "The Free Trade Goliah," and was sorry to find "a man of such extensive attainments so deluded as to advocate the cause of Free Trade in Pennsylvania."[55] Even Mathew Carey, who seldom praised an opponent, regarded him as "a man of mind and of respectable character."[56] Raguet was, therefore, not without honor in his own country, even though it be the unrelenting protectionist soil of Pennsylvania. It was his misfortune, however, to write at a time when the nullification excitement in the South and the unprecedented prosperity in the North had united to bring free trade sentiments into exceptional disrepute. No theories, however luminous, no arguments, however powerful, could make headway in the face of a combined appeal to national patriotism and economic self-interest.

All observers agree that Pennsylvania enjoyed an unusual degree of prosperity and industrial expansion under the tariff of 1828. The most significant development, perhaps, was found in the iron and coal

---

[50] *Augusta Chronicle,* quoted in *Banner of the Constitution,* February 27, 1830.
[51] *Ibid.* April 13, 1831.
[52] *Ibid.* April 6, 1831.
[53] *United States Gazette,* August 19, 1831.
[54] *Ibid.* August 20, 1831.
[55] August 27, 1831, July 21, 1832.
[56] Carey, M., *The Protecting System,* No. 1, p. 1.

industries of the state. One of the "abominations" of the new tariff had been to grant the iron manufacturers an increase of duties which even they had not solicited. Although the Harrisburg convention had only asked for a slight increase in the rates on hammered bar iron, the act as adopted provided for a general upward revision. The duty on pig iron was increased from 50 to 62½ cents per hundredweight, that on hammered bar from 90 to 112 cents per hundredweight, and that on rolled bar from $30 to $37 per ton. The rates on iron manufactures were raised in proportion. On the basis of average foreign prices in 1828, the new impost was equivalent to an ad valorem rate of 46 per cent. on pig iron, 35 per cent. on hammered bar, and 86 per cent. on rolled bar, the article in which European competition was most dreaded. This protection was further augmented by a decline in foreign prices during the years immediately following, so that by 1832 the rates amounted to 57 per cent. on pig iron, 44 per cent. on hammered bar, and 113 per cent. on rolled bar.[57] At the same time the duties on many forms of iron manufactures ran well over 100 per cent.[58] Besides the protection afforded by the tariff, it was estimated that the freight from England to the United States was equivalent to an addition of 5 per cent. on hammered iron and 10 per cent. on rolled iron, while upon articles of hardware it was considerably more.[59]

The fact should be noted in partial justification for these extremely high duties that about 1828 there appeared a sudden and decided increase in the differential between European and American iron prices. While American prices remained relatively static, there was a sharp decline in the European market, due largely to improved methods of manufacture.[60] The free trade minority in Pennsylvania claimed that if domestic iron manufacturers would only adopt similarly advanced processes, they could easily compete with British producers.[61] Concerning this point, one anti-tariff writer asserted in 1832,

---

[57] Computed from treasury statistics in *House Exec. Doc.*, 29 Cong., 1 Sess., No. 6, pp. 168-9.

[58] *Niles' Register*, XLII, p. 213.

[59] *Banner of the Constitution*, June 13, 1832.

[60] For comparative prices at this period see *Senate Document*, 62 Cong., 1 Sess., No. 21, pp. 327-8.

[61] *Banner of the Constitution*, August 22, 1832.

In Pennsylvania little or no improvement has been introduced into the manufacture of iron. Since the year 1828, we are informed by a highly intelligent rolling master, American bar iron has actually deteriorated. The furnaces, he remarks, which made good iron before, still continue to do so; but most of the new furnaces make very poor iron. . . . The old process of charcoal and the hammer is the only one known; and the most perfect indifference has prevailed with regard to every improvement and we have the evidence of the iron masters themselves of their unwillingness to come into any economical or more perfect form of making iron in their recent opposition to a company about to be incorporated in Pennsylvania to make iron by the coking process. It may with perfect truth be asserted that the tariffs of 1824 and 1828, so far from improving the manufacture of iron in the United States, have only had the effect, by removing further competition, of deadening invention, discouraging ingenuity.[62]

In justice to the iron manufacturers thus attacked, it should be pointed out that their failure to adopt improved methods was due, at least in part, to causes beyond their control. The use of coke was made costly by the remoteness of the bituminous coal fields from the center of population, and by the absence of adequate transportation facilities.  Anthracite coal was more available, but the technical problems involved in the use of this fuel had not yet been solved either in the United States or in England.

Even with due allowance for an increasing differential in favor of the European producer, the iron duties established in 1828 afforded a very real protection to the American manufacturer.  An inquiry sponsored by the Secretary of the Treasury in 1832 showed most of the Pennsylvania iron men perfectly satisfied with the existing duties; indeed several went so far as to say that lower rates would not ruin them.[63] Under the provisions of this act, the iron industry of the country enjoyed a period of extremely rapid growth.  According to the best statistics available, the pig iron production of the United States increased from 130,000 tons in 1828 to 191,000 tons in 1831.[64] Definite figures for Pennsylvania are wanting, but it is a fair assumption that its output grew in much the same proportion. It was asserted that the iron rolled at Pittsburgh alone had in-

---

[62] *Exposition of the Unequal, Unjust, and Oppressive Operation of the Present Tariff*, p. 8.

[63] *House Exec. Doc.*, 22 Cong., 1 Sess., No. 308, Vol. II, pp. 204-629.

[64] *Journal of the Proceedings of the Friends of Domestic Industry*, Reports of Committees, p. 16; Carey, H., *Harmony of Interests* (2d ed.), p. 12.

creased from 3,000 tons in 1828 to more than 9,000 tons in 1831, and that thirty-four new furnaces had been erected in the region west of the Alleghenies under the tariffs of 1824 and 1828.[65] A Venango county iron manufacturer' thus described the profits obtainable under the prices which prevailed during this entire period:

With proper management, a furnace will make from 300 to 1000 tons per annum, which can be made at an expense of from $22 to $24 per ton according to the price of provisions; and with ore, timber, etc. convenient and good, at about $18 to $20. Under proper management and good materials, a furnace will clear at present prices ten thousand dollars per annum.[66]

So prosperous was the iron industry as a whole that many manufacturers hastened to throw new establishments into operation without due regard for the consequences. The inevitable result was that the field quickly became overcrowded, with a corresponding reduction in profits. Some foresighted protectionists had very early seen the danger that excessive duties might thus defeat their own purpose. Quite possibly this realization helps to explain the reluctance of the ironmasters present at the Harrisburg convention to ask for a general increase of duties.[67] Mathew Carey, as early as 1829, had noted the tendency toward unwise industrial expansion and had warned against

the cupidity of gain, which is one of the greatest of the besetting sins of the country, whereby production has been immoderately forced—a sin which blasts and withers industry in all its various branches. Whenever any pursuit proves profitable, too many rush into it and involve themselves and others in difficulty—often in total ruin. Production outruns consumption. Glutted markets—reduced prices—and not merely a cessation of profits, but actual losses, are the necessary consequence.[68]

By 1832, this trend of the iron industry was generally recognized, and the responses to the questionnaire of the Secretary of the Treasury in that year showed more complaint against the domestic than against the foreign competitor. A Centre county ironmaster, for instance, reported that

after the last war provision and store goods decreased in price, and labor sunk

---

[65] *Cong. Debates*, 22 Cong., 1 Sess., p. 473.
[66] Unidentified clipping in Mathew Carey scrapbooks.
[67] *Cf. Niles' Register*, XXXVIII, p. 350.
[68] Carey, M., *Common Sense Addresses*, p. xi.

accordingly, which enabled the ironmasters, who survived the shock occasioned by the reduction of duties to make a handsome profit till 1828; then the rage for iron works became so great that provisions and labor rose rapidly in price, so that the greatest economy and attention became requisite to make much profit.[69]

It seems clear, however, that the difficulties represented by such complaints were relative rather than absolute. Although the excessive profits ushered in by the tariff of 1828 were soon curtailed by domestic competition, the iron industry as a whole continued reasonably prosperous throughout the four years the measure was in operation.

Before leaving the article of iron, it is necessary to note the emergence at this time of a movement destined to cause much mental anguish to the protectionists of Pennsylvania. This was the proposal to admit foreign iron free of duty where it was to be used for railroad purposes. Such a project, if carried into effect, would necessarily constitute a serious breach in the nation's tariff barrier. The issue first appeared in 1828, when the Baltimore and Ohio Railroad petitioned Congress for permission to import its iron duty free. The proposition was bitterly opposed by the Pennsylvanians in both Houses on the grounds that the iron manufacturers of their state could easily supply all domestic requirements, and the measure was ultimately postponed to death.[70] Two years later, however, the attack was renewed more successfully. At that time, the protectionists of Congress passed a tariff measure designed to strengthen the protective system through the elimination of various abuses in the collection of the revenue. Because of these features the Pennsylvania delegation supported the bill unanimously.[71] A rider was attached to the measure, however, which reduced the duties on railroad iron to 25 per cent. Thus protectionist Pennsylvania was maneuvered into the anomalous position of supporting a bill for the reduction of the duties upon one of its principal products. The railroad interests scored a further legislative triumph in 1832, when an act was passed which provided for a remission of the duties on railroad iron when used within three years. Neither

---

[69] *House Exec. Doc.*, 22 Cong., 1 Sess., No. 308, Vol. II, p. 289.
[70] *Senate Journal*, 20 Cong., 1 Sess., pp. 235, 326; *Cong. Debates*, pp. 682-687, 689, 692, 2505, 2761.
[71] *Cong. Debates*, 21 Cong., 1 Sess., p. 987.

the debate nor the final vote upon this measure is recorded, but the provision, which remained upon the statute books until 1841, continued to be an extremely sore point with Pennsylvania protectionists.[72]

The anthracite coal industry, like the iron interest, enjoyed an almost phenomenal growth under the act of 1828. Pennsylvania, for various reasons, had been comparatively slow to exploit this valuable natural resource. Anthracite had been brought from the Pottsville district to Philadelphia as early as 1800, but few persons showed any inclination to experiment with the new fuel.[73] Indeed, it was not until 1820 that coal was shipped to the seacoast upon a commercial scale. In that year 365 long tons were sent from the Lehigh region to Philadelphia. From this humble beginning the output grew with extreme rapidity, especially after 1825 when the Schuylkill district was first opened to navigation. Between 1828 and 1832 total production mounted from 77,516 tons to 363,871, an increase of 469 per cent. As a result of this rapid development, the anthracite region of Pennsylvania had become by 1829 the leading coal producing area in the country.[74]

As usual, the growth of a new economic interest preceded rather than followed the appearance of protectionist agitation in its behalf. The tariff of 1816 provided for a tax of five cents per bushel upon foreign coal, which was increased to six cents in 1824. This duty seems to have been regarded as adequate until about 1827, when a mild agitation was launched in favor of higher rates.[75] This movement had its origin, not in any prevailing distress, but rather in the growing strength of the industry, which made it eager to obtain a monopoly upon the home market. The agitation was temporarily silenced by the wild era of speculation which struck the Pottsville region in 1829. While the boom lasted, production was rapidly increased, coal lands brought fabulous prices, town sites were recklessly laid out and sold to eager purchasers.[76] The inevitable crash

---

[72] The duties remitted under the act of 1832 amounted to the considerable sum of $6,372,079. (*Sen. Exec. Doc.*, 34 Cong., 3 Sess., No. 55, pp. 8, 9.)

[73] Bowen, *Coal Regions of Pennsylvania*, p. 21.

[74] Pennsylvania Bureau of Statistics of Labor and Agriculture, *Annual Report*, 1872-73, pp. 213-216; *Mineral Resources of the United States*, 1915, II, 358.

[75] *Cf. Democratic Press*, June 1, 1827; *Miners' Journal*, February 9, 1828.

[76] Bowen, *Coal Regions of Pennsylvania*, pp. 27-31; *Hunt's Merchants' Mag.*, XXI, 273.

came in the latter part of 1830, accompanied by a serious decline in coal prices and land values.[77] The resulting disillusionment evoked an immediate cry for legislative relief. Particular resentment was expressed at the suggestion brought forward by Governor Wolf in 1830 that the state should impose a small tax upon each ton of coal mined.[78] It was pointed out that the anti-protectionists of the country would certainly seize upon such a levy as unmistakable evidence that even Pennsylvania considered the industry sufficiently established to stand upon its own feet without further legislative assistance.[79] Indeed, it was suggested that the General Assembly might much more fittingly "use their influence to procure from congress a greater duty on foreign coal, than to be employed in burdening still more our own."[80] Accordingly, a resolution was presented in the legislature, requesting the Pennsylvanians in Congress to work for an additional impost upon foreign coal.[81] Although no official action was taken upon this proposal, its introduction is significant as indicating that a new economic interest had definitely come forward to ally itself with the protectionist forces in Pennsylvania.

Another powerful economic factor which helped at this period to strengthen the protectionist movement in Pennsylvania was the state's heavy investment in internal improvements, which began about 1820 and reached a climax during the latter part of the decade. Expenditures approximating $40,000,000 were made in opening to navigation the Lehigh, Schuylkill, and Susquehanna rivers and in constructing the great Pennsylvania canal from Philadelphia to Pittsburgh. This heavy outlay affected the protectionist controversy in two ways. In the first place, it appeared necessary to stimulate domestic industry in order to create sufficient traffic to make the investment a profitable one. As a tariff meeting at Harrisburg viewed the situation,

Pennsylvania, having by her government and citizens constructed within her limits extensive canals and not less than sixty railroads, making near nine hundred miles of internal improvements, exclusive of turnpikes, and costing upwards of

---

[77] David S. Hassinger to George Wolf, July 25, 1831; Wolf MSS.
[78] *Pennsylvania Archives*, Fourth Series, V, 884, 920.
[79] *Miners' Journal*, January 29, 1831.
[80] *Poulson's American Advertizer*, January 7, 1831.
[81] *House Journal*, 1830-31, I, 67.

$40,000,000, for the purpose of making available her iron, her coal, her salt, her agricultural and manufactured commodities, all depending on an efficient tariff for a market, has interests too substantial to be yielded as a peace offering to causeless discontent, or to be staked on the fortunes of political men or parties.[82] In the second place, it could be argued quite plausibly that improved transportation facilities would make it all the easier for the European competitor to invade the American market; or, as a Centre county ironmaster put it, "I am apprehensive that our railroads and canals will enable foreigners to pester us . . . in our own vicinity."[83] Thus every dollar spent on internal improvements was made to appear as an additional reason for the extension and maintenance of the protective system.

Meanwhile, in the South an inflamed public sentiment was grimly mobilizing for a repeal of the "tariff of abominations." Even in protectionist Pennsylvania, the gravity of the situation was fully realized. As Samuel Ingham ably summarized the divergent points of view,

To continue permanently upon the people taxes equal to 10,000,000 of dollars, the amount of the present sinking fund, more than will be required for the current expenses of the government, will, I most conscientiously believe, hazard the existence of this Union. . . . On the other hand, suddenly and indiscriminately to reduce the impost duties to the scale of revenue for the current expenditure would cause a scene of ruin which cannot be described.[84]

Mathew Carey described the crisis even more succinctly when he declared, "The Southern people will not submit to the tariff—and we neither can nor will abandon it."[85] While recognizing the seriousness of Southern opposition, most Pennsylvania protectionists united with Carey in unyielding support of the tariff system. Governor Wolf, in his annual message of 1831, warned against undue sympathy for Southern complaints, "lest in lending ourselves to aid in relieving them from an imaginary oppression, we put ourselves in a condition to be seriously oppressed."[86] The *Miners' Journal* declared emphatically that "the present tariff should be sustained without any modification."[87] Similarly, a meeting at Pittsburgh

---

[82] *United States Gazette,* June 18, 1832.
[83] *House Exec. Doc.,* 22 Cong., 1 Sess., No. 308, Vol. II, p. 290.
[84] *Banner of the Constitution,* July 13, 1831.
[85] M. Carey to J. S. Johnston, December 17, 1831; Johnston MSS.
[86] *Pennsylvania Archives, Fourth Series,* V, 964.
[87] May 19, 1832.

insisted that "the principle of protection should not be waived, either in form or substance, either presently or prospectively, but that it be in its fullest extent maintained, and that neither local jealousies, political arrangements, nor menaces of resistance, ought to induce a compromise of the interests of any of the industrious classes of the American people."[88] An attempt was made in 1830 to send Carey to Congress to exert his talents more directly in defence of the act of 1828, but he declined the honor on the grounds that he had uniformly disavowed all ambitions of a political nature.[89]

The proceedings of the Pennsylvania legislature clearly reflected the overwhelming protectionist sentiment of the state. A resolution was adopted in 1830 upholding both the expediency and the constitutionality of the existing duties. Only two negative votes were cast in the Senate and one in the House.[90] Concerning the latter, Raguet mournfully remarked, "We have seen that the legislature of . . . Pennsylvania has proclaimed with a voice, unanimous, with the exception of the single vote of a highly enlightened friend to our cause, that she is beyond the reach of science and philosophy."[91] The following year, similar resolutions were overwhelmingly adopted, together with one invoking special consideration for the article of iron. Another resolution providing for the distribution of the treasury surplus among the several states encountered considerable opposition in the lower house, but was finally passed by a vote of 51 to 35.[92] The temper of the legislature during the session of 1831-32 was, if anything, even more unyielding than before. Early in the session, the two Houses adopted without the formality of a rollcall a resolution opposing "any reduction of duty on articles which may be produced or manufactured in the United States."[93] The lower

---

[88] *House Doc.*, 22 Cong., 1 Sess., No. 285.

[89] *Niles' Register*, XXXVIII, 417; *United States Gazette*, August 2, 1830. Commenting on his refusal, the *Richmond Whig* declared, "Conduct like this is an Oasis in the desert of Politics—a green spot which relieves the eye, wearied and disgusted with contemplating the slanders, lying hypocrisy, selfishness, disingenuousness, tergiversation, and universal degeneracy, which mark the epoch." (Quoted in *United States Gazette*, August 17, 1830.)

[90] *Senate Journal*, 1829-30, I, 179; *House Journal*, I, 125, 194.

[91] *Banner of the Constitution*, April 21, 1830.

[92] *Pamphlet Laws*, 1830-31, p. 505; *House Journal*, I, 427-9, 665-71; *Senate Journal*, I, 565.

[93] *Pamphlet Laws*, 1831-32, p. 625; *House Journal*, I, 311; *Senate Journal*, I, 156, 270.

House voted down overwhelmingly a conciliatory amendment to the effect that "the protection of American manufactures should be fostered as far as is compatible with the peace and harmony of the Union."[94] Later in the year, as actual tariff reduction became imminent, the Assembly adopted by unanimous vote a series of seven resolutions protesting against any abandonment of the protective system and favoring the recharter of the national bank.[95] One other resolution was reported by committee to the effect that

so satisfied are we of the value of the protection afforded to the agriculture and manufactures of the country by the protective duties, that, however painful it may be for us to say so, and however we may deplore such a result, we firmly believe that a secession of a portion of our brethren from the Union of the States would be less disastrous than the prostration of the manufacturing and agricultural interests of our prospering country.[96]

Such a sentiment, however, was too extreme even for Pennsylvania, and the resolution was eventually withdrawn. Even with this omission, Raguet believed that the resolves which were adopted had considerable influence in nullifying the spirit of conciliation in Congress.[97] Others beside the Pennsylvania free trader commented adversely upon the state's unrelenting attitude in the face of a national emergency. Clayton of Georgia declared that "her conduct is more inexorable, more uncompromising, and less magnanimous than any of the States in reference to this selfish and destroying System."[98] Even a Northerner like John Quincy Adams wrote impatiently of Pennsylvania,

She has taken the lead of the general policy of the country and she is exercising it certainly for her own advantage—it might deserve enquiry whether for that of the whole Union. . . . The tariff was her tariff. The bank was her bank. They are now before us for further enquiry, and it might be well to consider the subject with reference to the interests of the whole as well as to the special interests of Pennsylvania. . . . Pennsylvania has become the domineering State, and her exercise of her supremacy is not encouraging.[99]

While Pennsylvania protectionism was thus speaking in no un-

---

94 *Banner of the Constitution*, February 15, 1832.
95 *Pamphlet Laws*, 1831-32, p. 644; *House Journal*, I, 925, 945; *Senate Journal*, I, 793.
96 *Banner of the Constitution*, June 6, 1832.
97 *Ibid.* July 4, 1832.
98 *Cong. Debates*, 22 Cong., 1 Sess., p. 3562.
99 Adams, *Memoirs*, VIII, 474.

certain tones at home, the state's representatives in Washington were laboring no less industriously to preserve intact the provisions of the act of 1828. During the sessions of the Twenty-first Congress, covering the period from 1829 to 1831, repeated efforts were made by the South to effect both general and specific reductions in the existing duties. Except for a slight defection upon the article of salt, Pennsylvania resisted all such proposals with practical unanimity. The prevailing sentiment was well expressed in Denny's vigorous denunciation of McDuffie's proposal to reduce the rates to the level of the act of 1816. Concerning this project, the Pittsburgh representative declared,

It aims a death blow at the best interests of Pennsylvania; it strikes at her iron, her salt, and other extensive manufactures. Pass it, and you will spread ruin and distress where now is to be met the cheering hum of industry; and scenes will arise more calamitous than any that ever yet visited that State. . . . Upon my native city, which, from her numerous and extensive manufacturing establishments, has been called the Birmingham of America, this amendment would inflict the most disastrous effects; adopt it, and you pass a ploughshare over a city of twenty thousand inhabitants, and consign that now flourishing and growing place to depopulation and ruin.[100]

At about this time, Pennsylvania protectionists played an interesting part in the historic Jefferson day banquet in 1830 at which Andrew Jackson uttered his famous defiance of Southern nullification. John Quincy Adams believed that the primary object of the gathering was to trick Pennsylvania Congressmen into drinking anti-tariff and nullification toasts. At any rate, eight members of the delegation, all dyed-in-the-wool Jeffersonian Republicans, agreed to attend. Upon their arrival at the hall, however, they asked to see the set toasts which were to be given, and upon examination found them so obnoxious that they refused to remain and retired in great indignation.[101] An ingenious interpretation of the whole episode was put forward by the anti-Jackson party in Pennsylvania. As the Pittsburgh *Gazette* sought to explain,

It is true that the President, at the late Jefferson dinner, gave a toast which may be construed into a declaration that the *Tariff must be sustained,* and the threatened resistance of the South put down; but it is equally true that this same toast

---

[100] *Cong. Debates,* 21 Cong., 1 Sess., p. 920.
[101] Adams, *Memoirs,* VIII, 228.

may mean that the *Tariff must be repealed to pacify the South Carolinians.* Duff Green asserts most positively that the latter was the true meaning of the toast. Duff's reasoning on this subject is very plausible. . . . We would suppose that if the sentiments of the President were similar to those of the Pennsylvania delegation, the toasts which drove them off would also have disturbed his feelings.[102]

When the Twenty-second Congress convened in December, 1831, it was generally recognized that some revision of the tariff would be forthcoming. A surplus revenue and Southern discontent made some changes inevitable; the only hope of the protectionists was to direct the modification into channels where it would not seriously affect American industrial interests.[103] A bill was accordingly reported by the House Committee on Manufactures, based very largely upon recommendations made by the Secretary of the Treasury. This measure provided for a general reduction of duties to about the level established in 1824. Particularly galling to the protectionists was the bill's complete abandonment of the system of minimum valuations on woolens. For this and other reasons, Pennsylvania's general reaction to the proposed measure was anything but favorable. One paper declared that, "the tariff bill now before Congress lies like a torpedo at the root of our prosperity and there is danger that without immediate action the interests of this great and growing state will be sacrificed to appease the painted Juggernaut of Southern jealousy."[104] The National Republican state convention characterized the measure as "insidious in its design and impractical in its execution."[105] It was asserted that the enactment of the bill would reduce the protection on wool by 80 per cent., and that the wool growers of the state were therefore opposed to it "in solid phalanx."[106]

In Congress, Andrew Stewart was Pennsylvania's most outspoken critic of the proposed measure. He boldly claimed for his state the honor of having founded the tariff system and expressed the hope that she would ever be unanimous in maintaining it.[107] He declared

---

102 May 7, 1830.

103 C. F. Ingersoll suggested that the Pennsylvania delegation should agree to yield something on the tariff if the Administration would give its sanction to a modified national bank. (*Correspondence of Nicholas Biddle*, p. 188.)

104 *Harrisburg Telegraph*, May 23, 1832.

105 *United States Gazette*, June 14, 1832.

106 *Ibid.* May 23, 25, 1832.

107 *Cong. Debates*, 22 Cong., 1 Sess., p. 3281.

that if South Carolina wished to secede unless allowed to have her own way, "I say, for one, let her go."[108] As a substitute for the Committee bill, Stewart introduced a measure of his own, which provided that most of the rates should be reduced 10 per cent. annually over a two-year period, that negro clothing should be admitted free, and that non-competitive duties should be drastically lowered.[109] This proposal, however, was soon lost from sight in a hopeless tangle of amendments. Several of Stewart's colleagues, on the other hand, were inclined to accept the Committee's bill as the lesser of two evils. It was feared that the alternative might be the very radical reduction already reported by the Committee on Ways and Means. Moreover, Pennsylvania interests, especially iron, had fared comparatively well in the general downward revision.  Because of these mixed motives, the final vote found the delegation in the House quite evenly divided, with fourteen members recorded in the affirmative and twelve in the negative.[110] Party lines were not strictly followed, but on the whole the Jackson men showed much more enthusiasm for the bill than did their opponents.

Pennsylvania was represented in the Senate by William Wilkins, a Pittsburgh iron manufacturer, and George M. Dallas, who later gave the historic casting vote upon the tariff in 1846. The latter's views at this time were thoroughly Pennsylvanian. "I am inflexible," he declared, "as to nothing but adequate protection."[111] He asserted that his native state would be "thrown back a century" by the abandonment of the tariff policy.[112] Free trade, he observed, "has no existence but in books. It never has been tested, and it never can be tested, without the Utopian resort to a Congress of nations . . . a resort, which, like another Congress, that of Panama, will prove 'introuvable', anxiously and pompously sought, but never found."[113] In framing the nation's tariff laws, he wished "to give to domestic manufactures, if possible, the whole aid of the whole revenue; to reserve all duties from imported articles which do not enter into competition with our own produce or fabric, and to make their

---

[108] *Ibid.* p. 3271.
[109] *Ibid.* p. 3272.
[110] *Ibid.* p. 3830.
[111] *Ibid.* p. 485.
[112] *Ibid.* p. 474.
[113] *Ibid.* p. 470.

entry free."[114] Both Senators supported the tariff upon its final passage, and Wilkins was a member of the conference committee appointed to adjust the differences between the two Houses.[115] Henry Clay charged that in this capacity his solicitude for iron had made him too submissive where other interests, especially woolens, were involved. Wilkins retorted that he had stood out for the higher duties as long as possible and had yielded only when compelled to do so in order to save the whole bill.[116]

The tariff of 1832, once passed, seems to have proved generally acceptable to Pennsylvania protectionists. The iron duties, which were restored to the level of 1824, were declared to be adequate.[117] The rates on cotton goods, glass, and coal remained unchanged. The abolition of the woolens minimums was counteracted at least in part by lower rates upon the necessary raw materials. All things considered, Pennsylvania interests came out of the contest practically unscathed, and it was freely charged that this preferred treatment was an administration scheme to gain the state's support both for the passage of the bill and for the reelection of President Jackson.[118]

The act of 1832 was passed upon the eve of another exciting presidential contest in Pennsylvania. It was inevitable, therefore, that the question of tariff and nullification should quickly be carried into the political arena. As in the previous election, the canvass of 1832 was largely dominated by the inspiring personal appeal of Andrew Jackson. Moreover, the veto of the bank bill during the summer launched a new issue which quickly surpassed even the tariff question in popular interest. Nevertheless, protectionist sentiment in Pennsylvania was too strong and too militant to be completely eclipsed by any personality or any issue. The tariff views of the various candidates, therefore, soon became the subject of careful scrutiny and vehement contention.

The campaign of 1832 was the first in which Henry Clay's candidacy evoked any real enthusiasm in Pennsylvania. The Kentuckian, in 1824, had made an extremely poor showing in the Keystone State. Even Allegheny county, which later became an im-

---

114 *Ibid.* p. 1284.
115 *Ibid.* p. 1219.
116 *Ibid.* pp.1275-6.
117 *Niles' Register*, XLII, 184.
118 *United States Gazette*, April 10, May 8, 1832.

portant Whig stronghold, had given him only 18 votes.[119] Moreover, the "bargain and corruption" charge which followed the election was not calculated to endear him to the Jacksonians of the state. Indeed, so intense had been the feeling against him during 1825 that he was actually burned in effigy in Pittsburgh.[120] Nevertheless, as early as 1830 there began to appear unmistakable evidences of a popular movement in his behalf. Possibly, the knowledge that the tariff of 1828 was in danger helped to rally Pennsylvania protectionists to his support. At any rate, "Clay for President" meetings were held in many parts of the state during 1831.[121] It was asserted that "Henry Clay has done more for Pennsylvania than all that class of politicians which have received her favor for the last four years,"[122] and a Philadelphia meeting lauded him "because he is a sincere, ardent, efficient, and tried friend of the American system, and has at all times sustained it, in peace and in war, at home and abroad, in public and in private, with unwavering constancy and resolution."[123] From the protectionist standpoint, the National Republican ticket was strengthened by the nomination of John Sergeant for Vice President. Sergeant was a Philadelphian, who had consistently advocated the tariff system during a long career in Congress. It was Clay's ill fate, however, to encounter the full tide of the Anti-Masonic movement in Pennsylvania, and the National Republican ticket was discreetly withdrawn shortly before the election. Most of his supporters went over to Wirt, the Anti-Masonic candidate, whose views upon the tariff were rather obscure. Nevertheless, the Jackson papers made a last-minute attempt to discredit the latter by depicting him as hostile to the protective system and to American industry.[124]

The chief struggle of the campaign, however, naturally centered about the tariff views of the President. Universally Jackson was hailed by his admirers as a friend of the protective system. Ingersoll, addressing a meeting in Philadelphia, declared,

The ablest vindication of the constitutionality of the protecting system is con-

---

[119] *Pittsburgh Gazette,* November 4, 1831.
[120] *Wilson, History of Pittsburgh,* p. 762.
[121] *United States Gazette,* July 28, 1831.
[122] *Poulson's American Advertizer,* April 5, 1831.
[123] *Poulson's American Advertiser,* April 5, 1831.
[124] *American Sentinel,* November 1, 2, 1832.

tained in his messages to Congress on the subject. The most secure, satisfactory and solid settlement of the Tariff is embodied in the late act of Congress; for which manufacturers are mainly indebted not merely to his official recommendation, but to his personal and active interposition and influence. For the manufacturing interest to turn upon and sting such a benefactor, would not be merely ingratitude, but infatuation, the madness of reckless party. . . . In General Jackson, manufacturers have a patron whose patronage is all important to them.[125]

Even Democrats who had resisted the tariff revision to the last ditch, before election day were hailing the act of 1832 as one of the greatest triumphs of the administration.[126] It was asserted that this was the "judicious" tariff for which Jackson had always contended and that he was "unquestionably attached to the protective system."[127]

No less positive were the supporters of Clay and Wirt in asserting the President's utter hostility to the restrictive principle. Horace Binney, while admitting that Jackson had once been friendly to the tariff, declared that his views had completely changed.[128] The address of the National Republican state convention inquired if "there is an article, which Pennsylvania can make, or sell, or raise, whose price must not be ruinously affected by the *judicious* change, which General Jackson would introduce?"[129] Much wonder was expressed at the infatuation which had led Pennsylvania to subordinate its economic interests to political ends, and the hope was expressed that "this great state, which, by the arts of deception, and by promises to support her favorite system of policy, was lured into the support of Andrew Jackson, is now rousing from her delirious enthusiasm for a man, to the support of those great national principles which lie at the foundation of her prosperity.[130]

Those who anticipated the overthrow of political Jacksonism in Pennsylvania, however, were destined to receive a rude disappointment. The President carried the state by a comfortable margin, although the returns gave him a reduced popular vote and a greatly

125 *Ibid*. October 31, 1832.
126 *Ibid*. August 16, 1832.
127 *Ibid*. February 13, 1832; *Miners' Journal*, August 25, 1832.
128 *Speech Delivered by Horace Binney*, October 20, 1832, p. 7.
129 *United States Gazette*, June 9, 1832.
130 *Poulson's American Advertiser*, July 26, 1831.

diminished majority.[131] His heaviest loss was in Philadelphia city and county, which, after giving Jackson a majority of 5817 in 1828, went for Wirt by 1880 votes. In Allegheny county the General's majority dropped from 2200 to 336. Very heavy losses were likewise suffered in Lancaster, Chester, Washington, and Bucks counties.[132] Because of the complications introduced by the bank issue, it is difficult to say just how far the tariff question influenced the result. Probably, the bank was the chief factor in Philadelphia and the tariff in Allegheny. Jackson's reduced majority in Washington county may very well have been occasioned by the unpopular wool provisions of the act of 1832; in spite of his losses, however, the President still carried the county by a wide margin. For the state as a whole, the bank, the tariff, and the improved organization of the opposition all undoubtedly contributed to reduce the margin of victory. Nevertheless, Jackson's hold upon Pennsylvania was still strong, as evidenced by the fact that no presidential candidate until Abraham Lincoln was able to equal the majority he achieved in 1832.

---

[131] The popular vote was: Jackson, 91,949; Wirt, 66,689 (*Smull's Legislative Handbook*, 1921-22, p. 740). Jackson's popular vote was 9,703 less than in 1828, while his majority dropped from 50,804 to 25,260.

[132] *Harrisburg Intelligencer*, November 18, 1828; *Harrisburg Telegraph*, November 21, 1832.

# CHAPTER VI

NULLIFICATION AND REACTION, 1832-1839

The storm of South Carolina nullification, long threatening upon the horizon, burst at last in November, 1832. In rapid succession came the Ordinance of Nullification, declaring the tariff acts of 1828 and 1832 null and void within the borders of the Palmetto state, and the President's Proclamation, asserting in clear and forceful language his intention to uphold the Union and to enforce its laws by every means at his command. Thus at last the issue was clearly and unmistakably drawn, with the whole future of the protective system apparently at stake. Such a struggle was certain to arouse the utmost concern in Pennsylvania, where it was generally believed that the entire economic prosperity of the state rested upon a tariff foundation.

Pennsylvania protectionists quickly arrayed themselves in unyielding and uncompromising opposition to the demands of the nullificationists. Indeed, the prevailing temper of the state was almost as extreme in one direction as was that of South Carolina in the other. The sentiments of Jackson's Proclamation were generally applauded, even by those who had opposed his reelection.[1] It was freely asserted that the state had surrendered all that was possible by the act of 1832, and that further concession was out of the question.[2] A Pittsburgh paper declared that

if the Tariff is really oppressive to South Carolina, we would, at once, rather than abandon the protective policy, agree that the free states should buy her out —aye! buy her out, lands, houses, negroes, and all, and transport them to a more fertile soil!—to Louisiana, or Texas, or as many of them would no doubt prefer, to the dominions of his Majesty, King William the Fourth.[3]

Even more extreme was a resolution adopted by a public meeting in Somerset county to the effect that

notwithstanding we know and feel the value of the Union, for which our fathers fought, yet we sincerely believe that the removal or abolition of the Tariff at this time would be more destructive of our peace and prosperity than the secession of any one State of the Union; therefore we cannot consent to see our trade,

---

[1] *Cf. Pittsburgh Gazette,* December 25, 1832.
[2] *Cf. American Sentinel,* January 26, 1833; *Harrisburg Telegraph,* January 30, 1833.
[3] *Pittsburgh Gazette,* January 18, 1833.

commerce and manufactures sacrificed to appease the nullifying devotees of the South.[4]

Other more penetrating observers realized that it would be utterly impossible to maintain the protective system if the South Carolina nullification movement succeeded. As early as 1830, the Pittsburgh *Gazette* had warned its readers that

if we sustain the Tariff in this state, after it is nullified in Carolina, we must be ruined. Charleston will become the great shipping port of the Union, because merchandise can be brought there duty free, while it pays a heavy duty in Philadelphia, New York, etc. Perhaps indeed, the merchants in the latter cities might import the goods into Charleston and reship them to the other cities for distribution—thus evading the Tariff entirely.[5]

The prevailing sentiment of the General Assembly was just as unyielding as that of the press. Breck, in the Senate, expressed the views of many members when he declared that "he, for one, would take Disunion with Commerce and Manufactures, in preference to Union without them."[6] Conciliatory resolutions introduced by Buttz in the House and by Petrikin in the Senate were most unceremoniously rejected.[7] Petrikin, in particular, was subject to the most violent condemnation as a "traitor to his state and country," who, it was asserted, was animated by the "same desires for notoriety that prompted the Grecian to set fire to the famous Temple of Diana."[8] Early in the session, both Houses adopted by almost unanimous vote a series of resolutions asserting "that it is the clear and undisputable right of Congress to impose duties upon importations" and offering the support of the Commonwealth in all measures for the enforcement of the federal laws.[9] Later, another resolution was adopted, specifically opposing any reduction of duties "calculated to affect the successful prosecution of our domestic manufactures, or in any way to impair the faith of the government, by which the

---

[4] *American Sentinel,* February 12, 1833.

[5] April 2, 1830.

[6] *United States Gazette,* January 24, 1833. This was the same Samuel Breck who, as a free-trader, had given Pennsylvania's only adverse vote upon the tariff of 1824. (See p. 60, *supra.*)

[7] *House Journal,* 1832-33, I, 139; *United States Gazette, December* 21, 1832; *Harrisburg Chronicle,* January 7, 1833.

[8] *Harrisburg Telegraph,* January 19, 1833.

[9] *Pamphlet Laws,* 1832-33, p. 484; *House Journal,* I, 45; *Senate Journal,* I, 139.

enterprise of our own citizens would be checked, and successful domestic competition retarded."[10]

Nowhere in the Union, therefore, did the forces of nullification encounter a more stubborn resistance than in Pennsylvania. Nevertheless, even in that state there had developed by 1833 a slight reaction from the intense protectionism of the preceding years. Here and there, even in Pennsylvania, a courageous voice was beginning to suggest that American industries were now strong enough to stand alone, and to demand that the Union should not be sacrificed upon the altar of an outworn economic shibboleth. Condy Raguet, in particular, hailed the nullification movement as a portent of the impending overthrow of the restrictive system.[11] He believed that the country had reached the point where it must choose between the protective tariff and the Union, and he urged that the crisis be met, not with force, but with conciliation.[12] He even went so far as to advocate a national constitutional convention to clear up disputed interpretations as to internal improvements, the tariff, the national bank, the jurisdiction of the Supreme Court and the powers of the executive.[13] When President Jackson met nullification with a resounding affirmation of national supremacy, Raguet denounced him as an apostate who had basely deserted the very "principles upon which our liberties and institutions are founded."[14] Prophetically, indeed, he foresaw at this time the possibility of a rupture of the Union, terminating in the establishment of a Southern Confederacy.[15]

A preacher of such doctrines could not hope for widespread popularity in Pennsylvania, but, as the nullification crisis became more acute, an occasional disciple did appear to plead for conciliation and lower duties. Raguet reported that by the close of 1831 there were ten free-trade papers in the state as compared with only one at the beginning of the year.[16] A Pittsburgh paper went so far as to declare that "if, by an abandonment of the protective policy, the

---

[10] *Pamphlet Laws*, 1832-33, p. 486; *House Journal*, I, 222; *Senate Journal*, I, 245.

[11] *Banner of the Constitution*, November 14, 1832.

[12] *Ibid.* November 21, December 19, 1832.

[13] *Ibid.* December 12, 1832.

[14] *Ibid.* December 31, 1832.

[15] *Ibid.* December 26, 1832.

[16] *Ibid.* December 14, 1831.

South can be tranquilized, their attachment to the constitution restored, and the Union preserved, let the sacrifice be made."[17] A
group of citizens from the important iron-manufacturing county of
Huntingdon expressed themselves in a memorial to Congress as

> believing that, as the national debt is paid, there is no good reason why heavy
> taxes should be raised from the people in the shape of duties on imports, when
> the funds are not required for the legitimate expenses of government, and being
> skeptical in the doctrines of heavy duties protecting the domestic industry of
> our country, your memorialists are led to believe that they have a tendency to
> disqualify a great portion of our citizens from making a living in any other
> manner than in a manufactory. . . . Your memorialists would respectfully
> represent that it is their desire to see the duties reduced to the economical wants
> of government.[18]

Public meetings in other parts of the state likewise went on record
as favoring lower duties upon grounds of both expediency and
justice.[19] Even Mathew Carey's staunch protectionism wavered for
a moment, and in March, 1832, he suggested a compromise measure,
providing for an annual reduction of 10 per cent. until all duties
were at a horizontal level of 25 per cent.[20] Justifying his act, he
declared that "to preserve the Union, scarcely any sacrifice can be
too great."[21] Within less than a month, however, he withdrew the
proposal, since more mature consideration had convinced him that
it would be "highly pernicious to some of the important interests
of the country."[22] Nevertheless, Carey's defection and similar in-
cidents were joyously seized upon by the South as evidence that the
protectionist movement in Pennsylvania was upon the verge of disintegration.[23] Such hopes were destined to remain unfulfilled. While
Pennsylvania tariff sentiment in 1833 and for several years thereafter was slightly less intense and less universal than during the

---

[17] *Pittsburgh American Manufacturer,* quoted in *Pittsburgh Gazette,* November 18, 1832.

[18] *House Exec. Doc.,* 22 Cong., 2 Sess., No. 50.

[19] *Cf. American Sentinel,* September 13, October 26, 1832; *Harrisburg Chronicle,* February 11, 1833.

[20] Carey, M., *Olive Branch,* No. III, pp. 29, 30. The project which Mathew
Carey thus sponsored originated with his son, Henry C. Carey, who was at that
time a free trader.

[21] *United States Gazette,* April 4, 1832.

[22] *Niles' Register,* XLII, 110.

[23] *Cf. Cong. Debates,* 22 Cong., 2 Sess., p. 369; *United States Gazette,* May 12,
1832.

climactic years of 1830 and 1831, nevertheless, the state continued to be generally recognized as the protectionist stronghold of the nation.

While the protective issue was being thus fiercely debated in Pennsylvania, there was taking place in Congress the decisive struggle between tariff and anti-tariff, between national sovereignty and states rights. Discussion in the House first centered around the so-called Verplanck bill, sponsored by one of the most earnest and consistent free traders in Congress. This measure provided for a decided reduction in most of the existing duties. The wool and woolens rates were sharply cut; the minimum valuation on cotton goods was abolished and the duty lowered; and many other articles suffered a heavy loss of protection. Iron and its manufactures fared comparatively well in the proposed revision; the tax was left unchanged for one year, and then was to be reduced only 20 per cent. The debate upon this measure dragged along in the House for several weeks; and then the bill was abruptly dropped in favor of a project which had been introduced in the Senate by Henry Clay. This was the historic Compromise of 1833, which provided for a gradual lowering of all duties to a horizontal maximum of 20 per cent. All rates above 20 per cent. were to suffer a biennial reduction amounting to 10 per cent. of the excess, beginning on December 31, 1833. Thus, by 1840, four-tenths of the duties over 20 per cent. would be removed. Then, on December 31, 1841 one-half of the remaining excess was to be taken off; and on June 30, 1842 the other half was to go. After that date, therefore, there would be no rates above 20 per cent. ad valorem. The measure also enlarged the free list, but the high-tariff party secured the important concession that after 1842 duties must be paid in cash and upon the basis of American rather than foreign valuation. In this form, the Compromise was adopted by both Houses and became the basis for a temporary alleviation of Southern discontent.

The prolonged discussions upon the Verplanck bill found the Pennsylvania delegation in the House overwhelmingly opposed to its passage. Watmough declared, "I have not been able to discover one feature of the bill . . . to which I can give my sanction. . . It ruins nineteen-twentieths, and is unpalatable to the residue. . . It leaves not one particle of protection to any one interest."[24] He asserted that the attempt to conciliate Pennsylvania by offering com-

---

[24] *Cong. Debates,* 22 Cong., 2 Sess., p. 1295.

paratively high duties on iron was an insult to the "high-minded freemen of that State."[25] McKennan, who represented the wool growers of Washington county, declared upon this same point,

Why has the discrimination been made in the bill in favor of the iron interest? Why are some kinds of this article to be protected with a duty of 79 per cent. whilst woolen and cotton fabrics are protected with the trifling duty of 20, and the interests of the wool grower by the nominal duty of 15. I impute no improper motives to the committee; but for what reason was this discriminating principle adopted? Was it to render the obnoxious features of the bill palatable to the people of Pennsylvania? Was it by gilding the bitter pill to induce them to swallow it? If these were the views entertained, let me tell gentlemen they will find themselves egregiously mistaken. Pennsylvania supports the system as a whole, and in all its parts. She knows that if a single interest in the protective system is laid low, no part can stand; that if a single link be stricken from the chain, the whole must go.[26]

Stewart, far from sanctioning a reduction, suggested that the rates upon all competing articles be raised to the point of prohibition. Thus at one stroke, he declared, the country would secure adequate protection and a reduction of the embarrassing treasury surplus.[27] Indeed, the only Pennsylvania voice raised in support of the Verplanck bill was that of Gilmore from the Pittsburgh district, who had helped to frame the measure as a member of the Committee on Ways and Means. He believed that the bill afforded a "fair and reasonable protection to those great interests which have grown up under the faith of the government."[28] Undoubtedly, the comparatively favorable iron duties which the measure provided had much to do with determining his attitude.[29] Gilmore's conduct, however, does not seem to have met the approval of his constituents, who passed a vote of censure against him, while one Pittsburgh paper went so far as to place him in the unflattering company of Benedict Arnold and Aaron Burr.[30] The state legislature was likewise decidedly hostile to the Verplanck bill and adopted by an overwhelming majority a resolution opposing its passage.[31]

---

[25] *Ibid.* p. 1297.
[26] *Ibid.* p. 1092.
[27] *Ibid.* p. 1120.
[28] *Ibid.* p. 1078.
[29] *Ibid.* pp. 977, 1079.
[30] *Pittsburgh Gazette,* January 15, February 12, 1833.
[31] *Pamphlet Laws,* 1832-33, p. 486; *House Journal,* I, 222; *Senate Journal,* I, 245.

Henry Clay's compromise measure when presented, proved no more satisfactory to Pennsylvania protectionists than the House bill which it supplanted. Clay later asserted that he had conceived the plan while upon a visit to Philadelphia, and had submitted it in confidence to some of the manufacturers and political leaders of that city, who approved it.[32] Nevertheless, the opposition to the measure when publicly announced was both immediate and unrestrained. Both Wilkins and Dallas voted against the Compromise in the Senate.[33] The latter, in particular, opposed the measure on the grounds that with its passage "the overthrow of the protective system might be looked upon as almost certain; and the inevitable consequence would be that thousands, tens of thousands, and hundreds of thousands would be thrown out of employment and become paupers."[34] In the House, the Compromise was acted upon with very little discussion. The final vote showed four Pennsylvanians supporting and twenty-one opposing the measure.[35]

The immediate purpose of the Compromise had been to avert the menace of South Carolina nullification or worse. In this, it was entirely successful. Many Pennsylvania protectionists, however, believed that the country had paid too high a price even for the boon of domestic tranquility. One editor voiced a very general feeling when he declared that "the bill is an entire abandonment of the American system. . . We cannot doubt that the country is on the verge of ruin."[36] Mathew Carey wrote despondently to a friend,

Considered as a mere manufacturing question, it is perhaps the best arrangement that could have been made. But the manufacturing view of the subject fades into comparative insignificance alongside of the constitutional view, and the permanence and dignity and efficiency of the government all of which in my opinion have received a mortal wound. The union may drag on a sickly, consumptive existence for a few years, but its fate is, I am satisfied, sealed. The question ought to be settled at once and forever whether our government has efficiency enough to enforce the execution of the laws. . . . This question must be settled one day or other, and it can never be settled under more favorable auspices. . . . I am sick, sick, sick, of the prospects of the country.[37]

---

32 Clay, *Works*, IV, 353; *Pittsburgh Post*, April 10, 1844.
33 *Cong. Debates*, 22 Cong., 2 Sess., p. 808.
34 *Ibid.* p. 794.
35 *Ibid.* p. 1810.
36 *Miners' Journal*, March 2, 1833.
37 M. Carey to J. S. Johnston, March 21, 1833; Johnston MSS.

Other protectionists found comfort, however, in the expectation that the provisions of the Compromise would never be carried into effect, and that a new tariff law would be passed before 1842 ushered in the period of drastic reduction.[38] It was very evident that the tariff men of the state regarded the settlement as a truce and not a surrender. No one realized this better than Condy Raguet, who in his valedictory to the *Banner of the Constitution* wrote prophetically,

Should the tariff be materially reduced at the present session of Congress, it is easy to foresee that all the casualties at the North, resulting, in the next few years, from bad speculations, overtrading, excessive issues of banks, the devastations of the cholera, failure of crops, and Western floods, and every other imaginable cause, will be ascribed to the overthrow of the American system.[39]

Raguet's penetrating observation was destined to find an abundant verification in the course of subsequent tariff controversies in Pennsylvania.

In the midst of the general attack upon the Compromise of 1833, the sponsor of the measure could not hope to escape violent denunciation. Bitter reference was made in the press to Clay's "apparent aberration" in sponsoring these "parricidal propositions."[40] Before the final passage of the Compromise Act, a Philadelphia paper reported that "there appears to be considerable fluttering among the supporters of Mr. Clay in this quarter. The politicians are generally mum; but the persons most deeply interested, and who formed the most numerous portion of his supporters at the late election, express their dissatisfaction in no measured terms."[41] Similar testimony came from the other extremity of the state, where a Pittsburgh editor declared, "We have watched, carefully, the course of the old friends of Mr. Clay, since his abandonment of the protective policy, and are truly gratified in finding such unanimity in condemning his conduct. With one or two exceptions his most zealous and oldest supporters have proclaimed that, as he has deserted the Tariff, they will desert him."[42] It is very clear that Clay's sponsorship of the act of 1833 had a most blighting effect upon his newly-born popu-

---

[38] *Cf. Miners' Journal*, March 9, 1833.

[39] *Banner of the Constitution*, December 31, 1832.

[40] *United States Gazette*, February 26, 1833; *Miners' Journal*, February 23, 1833.

[41] *American Sentinel*, February 18, 1833.

[42] *Pittsburgh Gazette*, February 26, 1833.

larity in Pennsylvania. As the election of 1844 was to show, his prestige never completely recovered from his apparent betrayal of American industry in its hour of need. Many Pennsylvania protectionists in the first heat of their indignation against the Kentuckian spoke or wrote angry sentiments which were resurrected with telling political effect eleven years later.

The first outburst of resentment against the Compromise Act quickly died away, however, and for the next few years the tariff agitation in Pennsylvania was almost entirely stilled. This was due in part to the fact that during these years the bank issue completely dominated the stage as the one great object of universal contention; and partly to the prevalent high prices and general prosperity which seemed to belie the direful prognostications of the protectionists. A mild flurry of excitement was caused during the winter of 1833-34, when the existing high price of fuel induced the New York city authorities to petition Congress for a repeal of the duty on coal.[43] The Pennsylvania legislature adopted a resolution declaring that if any change were made, the duty should be increased rather than diminished.[44] The approach of spring and a marked decline in the price of coal ended the agitation at least temporarily. The issue was again raised in December, 1836, when Jackson's annual message to Congress suggested that the surplus be relieved by abolishing the duties upon articles of common necessity such as coal.[45] Remonstrances against the proposed reduction poured into the General Assembly, which accordingly adopted a strong resolution instructing the state's Senators and requesting its Representatives to oppose any modification of the existing duties.[46] Pennsylvania protectionists were thus compelled by the force of circumstance to become the staunchest adherents of the measure which they had so recently condemned. Buchanan, for instance, asserted that Congress was under a moral obligation not to overturn the Compromise Act.[47] Even the strongly protectionist *United States Gazette* believed that "honor and honesty

---

[43] *Miners' Journal,* January 11, June 21, 1834.

[44] *Pamphlet Laws,* 1833-34, p. 574; *House Journal,* I, 888; *Senate Journal,* I, 734, 761.

[45] Richardson, *Messages and Papers of the Presidents,* III, 251.

[46] *Pamphlet Laws,* 1836-37, p. 398; *House Journal,* I, 364, 450; *Senate Journal,* I, 326, 334.

[47] *Cong. Debates,* 24 Cong., 2 Sess., p. 949.

require that the compromise should be considered the settled law of the land until the time limited."[48] Few persons realized that the state was upon the verge of an economic catastrophe destined to arouse Pennsylvania protectionism from its apathy and to precipitate a militant and aggressive crusade for the overthrow of the Compromise Act.

The panic of 1837 broke abruptly in April and immediately overwhelmed Pennsylvania along with the rest of the country. There ensued that deadly progression of economic woes which always follow in the wake of a financial collapse: the suspension of specie payments, mercantile paralysis, general bankruptcy, a rapid and ruinous fall of prices, and industrial stagnation. The effects of the first shock gradually wore off, and the Philadelphia banks resumed specie payments, perhaps prematurely, in August, 1838. During the latter months of 1839, however, a second revulsion took place. Specie payments had to be suspended once more in October, and extreme depression was again experienced by both the manufacturing and mining interests of the state.[49]

It has come to be almost an axiom of the protectionist faith that the panics of 1837 and 1839 were caused by the operation of the Compromise Act. Both Stanwood and Taussig erroneously attribute the origin of this economic fallacy to the writings of Henry C. Carey.[50] As a matter of fact, Carey merely appropriated for his own use an idea which had come to be quite generally accepted in his own state even before his first protectionist works appeared. The process by which this curious perversion of economic history gained a foothold in Pennsylvania affords an interesting illustration of the way in which legends are born.

Pennsylvania's first reaction to the crisis was to attribute it, as does the historian, to the unsound financial policies of the government, the inflation of the currency, and the reckless speculative mania which had gripped the country. Within a few months, however, protectionists were beginning to attribute the prevailing distress to the rapid increase of importation which had occurred since

[48] December 14, 1836
[49] *Niles' Register*, LVII, 143, 214; *Miners' Journal*, August 24, December 7, 1839.
[50] Stanwood, *American Tariff Controversies*, II, 9; Taussig, *Tariff History of the United States*, p. 116 and note.

1833.[51] The Pittsburgh *Advocate and Statesman,* for instance, in its issue of August 4, 1837, declared,

This paper has always been an advocate of the American system. To the abandonment of this system we may trace the origin of the evils that have fallen upon the country . . .It appears obvious to us, upon the whole, that no plan can be devised, for the regulation of the currency, which can be relied upon as permanent in its operation, unless accompanied by a tariff of duties, at least as high as that which was departed from at the time of the "compromise". Under the operation of our present tariff, and more particularly so when it shall have reached its minimum, what check can be interposed against excessive importations? What security have we that we shall not find ourselves, every three or four years, in precisely the situation we now find ourselves? . . . Nothing but a resort to the much abused American System can save us.

Commenting upon this article, a Democratic editor remarked with just a trace of irony,

A few months ago, a whig statesman or a whig journal which should have dared to ascribe the financial embarrassments of the country to any other cause than the gold bill, the specie circular, the refusal to recharter a national bank, or the removal of the deposites would have been denounced as a recreant and traitor to his party . . . The Pittsburgh *Advocate* . . . now comes out in a serious and deliberate article, charging these embarrassments—not to the refusal to charter the Bank, not to the removal of the deposites, not to "tinkering the currency"— but to the abandonment of the American System and the compromise bill of Mr. Clay—to the excessive imports which bank and foreign credit have induced—to the squandering of the general means, by the merchants, in lands, stocks, paper cities, etc.[52]

Nevertheless, the argument that the tariff was to blame for the prevailing distress does not seem to have made much headway until the second crisis broke in 1839. To many Pennsylvanians, however, this recurrence of disaster seemed to afford unmistakable confirmation of the protectionists' worst forebodings. The Philadelphia banks, in their official statement explaining the causes of their second suspension, declared that British manufacturers had been flooding the country with foreign products and selling them at a loss in order to obtain specie for their own needs.[53] It was charged that under

---

[51] Imports had increased in value from 101 million dollars in 1833 to over 176 millions in 1836. The latter figure exceeded the imports of any preceding year by over 30 millions. (*Statistical Abstract of the United States,* 1888, p. 12).

[52] *Pittsburgh Mercury,* August 9, 1837.

[53] *Niles' Register,* LVII, 154.

the reduced rates English coal had actually been imported into Schuylkill county, an interesting variation upon the proverbial "coals to Newcastle" which probably had slight basis in fact.[54] At any rate, a gathering of Schuylkill miners expressed the belief that the "present embarrassment in the pecuniary affairs of the country and the consequent suspension of specie payments by the banks of this commonwealth is less owing to the mismanagement of our monied institutions, than to the creation of a foreign debt by the excessive importation of foreign goods which ought to be manufactured at home."[55] Such sentiments were echoed by public meetings and newspapers in many parts of the state.[56] The Pennsylvania Senate, in 1840, adopted a resolution which recited that "the present reduced condition of the tariff is one of the prime causes of the unparalleled prostration of individual and national credit, of the reduced price of agricultural and domestic products, of the languishing and depressed condition of all branches of industry, of the ruined and depreciated state of our national currency which so fatally prevails."[57] The House does not seem to have taken any action at this time, but in 1843 they adopted, by a vote of 45 to 40, a resolution asserting that "the compromise of the Tariff . . . may be regarded as one of the causes which has produced not only the embarrassed state of the finances, but also operated ruinously upon the great manufacturing interests of the country, and to a great extent destroyed our home industry, the only true sources of national as well as individual wealth and prosperity."[58] Since Henry C. Carey's first protectionist work did not appear until 1848, it is clear that he must be regarded as the disseminator rather than the originator of the idea that the Compromise of 1833 brought about the economic disasters which followed.

One effect of the crisis of 1839 was to bring Mathew Carey once more into the tariff arena, whence he had retired after the passage of the Compromise Act. The venerable warrior announced his inten-

---

[54] *Miners' Journal,* December 14, 1839.

[55] *Harrisburg Reporter,* March 6, 1840.

[56] *Cf. Niles' Register,* LVII, 143; *Pittsburgh Gazette,* October 18, 1839; *United States Gazette,* December 9,1839, March 10, 1840; *Franklin Repository,* January 21, 1840; *Miners' Journal,* November 2, December 7, 1839. For evidence that the idea was not confined to Pennsylvania, see *Niles' Register,* LVII, 170-172.

[57] *Senate Journal,* 1840, I, 9, 513; *Niles' Register,* LVII, 375.

[58] *House Journal,* 1843, I, 130, 426.

tion to undertake a discussion of the protective principle in connection with the existing depression, but death intervened on September 17, 1839 before he could carry the project into effect.[59] Thus passed from the stage one of Pennsylvania's most tireless and unselfish and uncompromising defenders of the protectionist faith. There is something of the tragic in the career of this economic Don Quixote. His whole later life was embittered; for his almost pathetic belief in the omnipotence of the protectionist argument made him intolerantly impatient with all those who could not accept his creed. He was denied even the satisfaction of living to see the triumph of his principles; since he died at a time when the country, under the provisions of the Compromise Act, was moving ever farther from the protectionist ideal. As perhaps the most bitter irony of all, his son, Henry C. Carey, had taken up his father's pen and was using it in an unfilial glorification of free trade and laissez faire.[60]

It is not easy to measure the actual influence which Carey exerted upon the tariff movement of his day. Public opinion is too imponderable, too intangible an entity to be traced confidently and accurately to its source. Obviously, Carey's appeal cannot be estimated by present-day standards, which would condemn his most passionate outbursts as well-nigh unreadable. His influence, therefore, must be evaluated very largely in the light of contemporary judgments, which happily have survived in exceptional profusion.[61] As was to be expected, the country received his offerings with emotions which ranged from the most flattering approval to the equal extreme of profound aversion. Naturally, the most bitter opposition came from the South. In Columbia, South Carolina, he shared with Henry Clay the dubious distinction of being burned in effigy.[62] In many places in the South, persons refused to purchase Bibles which bore his name as publisher.[63] Governor Giles of Virginia lamented that he should have "become enamoured with the most despotic, antiquated, and

---

[59] Carey, M., *The Querist*, p. 10.

[60] Henry C. Carey's conversion to protection did not take place until 1844.

[61] After the manner of many another purveyor of universal panaceas, Carey collected and published long compilations of testimonials, each attesting to the constancy and efficacy of his labors. His scrapbooks, preserved in the collections of the Philadelphia Library Company, also afford a wealth of contemporary comment, both critical and laudatory.

[62] *Niles' Register*, XXXIV, 416.

[63] Carey, M., *Autobiographical Sketches*, p. 48.

almost obsoleted doctrines of the most despotic governments of Europe."[64] In Congress, Representative Wilde of Georgia referred derisively to "the new economical gospel of Mathew."[65] McDuffie of South Carolina, ever outspoken in his dislikes, declaimed against the deluding influence of "Mathew Carey's interminable masses of statistical nonsense."[66] The free trade press was no less critical of what one editor called the "fallacious sophistries of Mathew Carey."[67] A Southern paper reported that

Mathew Carey—armed cap-a-pie and mounted on a Merino Ram—still winds his screeching, discordant, hollow and deceitful sounds . . . He knows that the blast of rams' horns prostrated the walls of Jerico in days of old; and in his Quixotisms he imagines that two or three bold Bah-Bahs! from him and the Ram together, will tumble the strongholds of political economy about the ears of Dr. Cooper.[68]

According to another journal, "Mr. Carey and Mr. Niles seem to have divided the labor and set up to manage the whole affair: Mr. Niles attends the counter at Washington; Mr. Carey the out-door business. Mr. Niles has secured a majority of Congress; Mr. Carey is laboring to secure a majority of the people."[69] One editor, striking a satirical vein, declared,

The grand university of the Careyans is established at Philadelphia, under the auspices of their patriarch—a venerable scribe . . . The Achilles, the sword and shield of the Careyans sits calmly amidst the smoke and thunder of forges . . . ever and anon sending forth a rocket to illuminate the pages of the *Patron of Industry,* or of *Niles' Weekly Register* . . . These crying Philosophers disturb the nation by harping on misfortunes which they never can alleviate, and by chanting the funeral dirge of our prosperity, anxiously expecting responsive notes from every hill and valley in the land. These unhappy victims of patriotic sensibility will never be soothed till all the states join in one sad chorus of lamentation mingled with the sighs of the wilderness and the mournful surge of the ocean.

---

[64] *United States Gazette,* September 17, 1827.

[65] *Cong. Debates,* 20 Cong., 1 Sess., p. 2700.

[66] *Ibid.* 19 Cong., 2 Sess., p. 1004. Stewart of Pennsylvania replied that "although the views of Adam Smith, and other British writers, may suit the purposes of the gentlemen from New York and South Carolina, yet they must give me leave to say, that I would not give one page of the 'statistical nonsense' of Mathew Carey, on this subject, for all the theories of Adam Smith, and their long and learned speeches into the bargain."

[67] *Banner of the Constitution,* June 1, 1831.

[68] Clipping from *Sumter Gazette* in Mathew Carey scrapbooks.

[69] Unidentified clipping in Mathew Carey scrapbooks.

The object of all this weeping and wailing is to persuade the people of the United States that they are all perfectly miserable, and that relief can only be found in the embraces of the Careyans—who by their lugubrious cries, would attract victims only to devour them.[70]

More significant than this abuse and ridicule, which was to be expected, was the universality with which even free traders paid reluctant tribute to the efficacy of Carey's labors. Governor Giles admitted that his writings had "attracted more attention than could have been expected from the preposterous notions contained in these political nostrums."[71] Senator Parris of Maine, in a speech of May 8, 1828, found occasion to say:

I will not mention names, but will merely point the attention of gentlemen to a single gentleman in Philadelphia who has been laboring with ability on this subject for years, and who has done more to promote what is called the "American System" than has been done by any individual or association, in either or all of the six Eastern states.[72]

Condy Raguet, who as a free trader had slight respect for the validity of Carey's argument, declared that the latter "has been more instrumental than any other individual in this country in the establishment of the Restrictive system. . . His writings are looked upon as almost oracular."[73] Speaking of his own state, Raguet declared that Carey "has done more to inoculate the State of Pennsylvania with the Tariff mania, than all other writers put together."[74] Again, referring to Philadelphia, Raguet asserted that Carey "absolutely converted a free trade population to the opposite side of the question."[75] Another writer believed that the Philadelphian had "made more converts, and done more to mislead and hoodwink the public, than all the eloquence of all the statesmen put together."[76] The hostile New York *Journal of Commerce* declared, "Mr. Carey of Philadelphia and Mr. Niles of Baltimore have long been distinguished as advocates of the American System, and have probably done more than any other writers to secure its success."[77] Similarly,

---

[70] *Ibid.*
[71] *Richmond Enquirer*, September 14, 1827.
[72] *Cong. Debates*, 20 Cong., 1 Sess., p. 742.
[73] *Banner of the Constitution*, August 25, 1830.
[74] *Ibid.* April 11, 1832.
[75] *Ibid.* April 6, 1831.
[76] *Ibid.* June 1, 1831.
[77] April 27, 1832.

the *Southern Review* asserted, "Mr. Niles and Mr. Carey have contributed more than any two men in the United States—we make no exception—to spread the delusion which prevails in certain parts of the Union, on the subject of making the nation wealthy by shackling and destroying its most profitable commerce."[78] The *Richmond Enquirer* found that "the statistics of Messrs. Niles and Carey, with their inconsequent conclusions, are sent throughout the country, and furnish the data and arguments by which the tariffites everywhere sustain themselves."[79] The New York *Evening Post* characterized these two journalists as

the instructors and guides of the orators and politicians who are employed in supporting the "American System." They have not only furnished the raw materials of most of the speeches made in Congress and elsewhere, but there is not even in the orations of Mr. Clay, as far as we have read, a single argument which cannot be traced to the dull pages of *Niles' Register,* or the interminable essays of Mathew Carey.[80]

The protectionists of the country were no less willing to testify concerning Carey's services to the cause. Not infrequently, he was the guest of honor at testimonial dinners, at which his admirers paid tribute to their venerable champion.[81] Resolutions which were adopted at tariff meetings and conventions frequently expressed their appreciation for his timely labors.[82] Many eminent leaders in public life spoke of his efforts in equally laudatory terms. Henry Clay, speaking in the House of Representatives, said of him, "I seize with great pleasure the occasion to say that he merits the public gratitude for the disinterested diligence with which he has collected a large mass of highly useful facts, and for the clear and convincing reasoning with which he generally illustrates them."[83] At the same time the Kentuckian informed Carey that every additional pamphlet "proves what an irreparable loss we should sustain, if you were to withdraw from that cause, which is so much identified with you."[84] Buchanan wrote, "The American people are under great

---

[78] Quoted in *Free Trade Advocate,* I, 129.
[79] *Ibid.* p. 411.
[80] Quoted in *Niles' Register,* XXXVIII, 82.
[81] Cf. *Niles' Register,* XX, 345; XXXIV, 337; *United States Gazette,* July 15, 1828.
[82] Cf. *Niles' Register,* XVII, 229; *Democratic Press,* June 4, 1827; *United States Gazette,* February 3, 1831.
[83] *Annals of Cong.,* 18 Cong., 1 Sess., p. 1991.
[84] Carey, M., *Pamphlet Dedicated to the Great Manufacturing Capitalists,* p. 5.

obligations to you for your disinterested, able, and persevering efforts in a cause so vitally connected with the future prosperity of our country."[85] Daniel Webster believed that Carey's "various short tracts on the subject of the Constitution and the attempts at Nullification have done much good; and would have done more, had they been more widely circulated."[86] William Henry Harrison openly acknowledged that he had been converted to protection by the cogency of Carey's presentations.[87] Two other presidents of the United States, John Adams and James Madison, in the rich perspective of their later years paid tribute to his ability and zeal.[88] Mallary of Vermont, one of the leading protectionists of Congress, admitted that he had drawn heavily upon Carey's pamphlets in the preparation of his speeches.[89] Two other prominent New Englanders, Abbott Lawrence and Oliver Wolcott expressed similar appreciation for the Philadelphian's untiring exertions.[90]

By friend as well as foe, the names of Mathew Carey and Hezekiah Niles were frequently linked as the outstanding protectionists of the day. An Illinois journal referred to them as the "Jachin and Boaz of the American system."[91] Niles, himself, commented on the number of times he found Clay, Carey and Niles mentioned together "as a sort of triumvirate engaged in the work of deluding the people and spreading 'artful sophistries' through the land and doing bad things enough to sink the nation."[92] The editor of the *Weekly Register* was ever generous in praise of the services of his co-worker in the cause. Speaking of Carey, he declared, "It is a proud thing to hear one's name associated with his—for a more honest, charitable and disinterested patriot never lived than Mathew Carey. . . When the ephemeral politicians of the day . . . shall have passed into nothingness, his name and labors will be blessed by millions of happy

---

[85] *Ibid.*
[86] Webster, *Writings*, XVI, 231.
[87] Carey, M., *Autobiographical Sketches*, p. 52.
[88] Carey, M., *Pamphlet Dedicated to the Great Manufacturing Capitalists*, pp. 4, 5.
[89] *Ibid.* p. 6.
[90] *Ibid.* pp. 4, 5.
[91] Quoted in *Banner of the Constitution*, August 3, 1831. Jachin and Boaz were the two bronze pillars that stood before the temple of Solomon.
[92] *Niles' Register*, XXXVII, 353.

freemen."[93] Another generous tribute was paid by the editor of the Providence *Journal,* who asserted that Carey's writings

had done much in saving the country from impending ruin . . . By his writings on political economy, the most stubborn in opposition to his views, after a fair examination, have been led to confess their former errors of opinion in regard to our nation's greatness . . . A different spirit among the inhabitants happily exists in favor of manufactures and national industry; and it is not saying too much to assert that in this respect, Mathew Carey has been one of the greatest of the founders of our real national independence . . . Thomas Paine, it was said, prepared the minds of the people in the Revolutionary struggle for independence. Mathew Carey has prepared the minds of the citizens for real independence and a perpetuation of liberty . . . Thomas Jefferson wrote the Declaration of Independence. Mathew Carey has caused its principles to be put into successful practice by changing the opinion of the people . . . Mathew Carey has written equally as sound as Hamilton . . . Notwithstanding the opposition and prejudices his writings have had to contend with, they have effected a decided change in the minds of a majority of the people . . . But few Americans are as well known and as justly appreciated abroad as this distinguished individual.[94]

The New York *Mirror* believed that "Mr. Carey has done more to spread before the people of the Union correct views, and to remove narrow prejudices in relation to these fountains of national strength, independence and riches than any other man living, or that has lived in this country. This gives him, as we think, a pre-eminent claim to the honorable title of 'Father of the American System'."[95] Many other similar quotations might be adduced to indicate the high esteem in which the Philadelphian's protectionist labors were commonly held. There is excellent reason to believe, therefore, that Carey's writings—uninteresting as they seem to twentieth-century readers—were welcome pabulum to the less jaded literary appetites of the nineteenth, and that their incessantly reiterated arguments carried conviction to many a skeptic of the northern states.

[93] *Ibid.* XXXVI, 2.
[94] Clipping in Mathew Carey scrapbooks.
[95] *Ibid.*

# Chapter VII

## THE REVIVAL OF PROTECTIONISM, 1840-1844

The tariff agitation which burst upon Pennsylvania during the latter part of 1839 seems to have been unforeseen, even by the protectionists themselves. In spite of the panic of 1837, many of them had come to believe that the question had been settled forever by the Compromise Act and that American industry was now sufficiently developed to stand without further legislative assistance. Richard Rush, who had been regarded as a good protectionist while Secretary of the Treasury under John Quincy Adams, wrote in 1839,

In Pennsylvania, we all approved of them [the acts of 1824 and 1828] but we did not contend for perpetual protection to our manufacturing industry—that position was never taken. We only asked adequate protection for a proper time as a helping hand to us, against the pre-existing skill of olden times. This we have had. It has served us to a point beyond which we could not justly ask anything more, consistently with the coequal claims and rights of other portions of the confederacy.[1]

Even the *United States Gazette,* long recognized as one of the most ardent protectionist papers in the state, declared that

there was a time when our infant manufactures required protection to enable them to get under way, to go alone. Through the labored exertions of Henry Clay, Mathew Carey, Hekekiah Niles, and other kindred and patriot spirits, this protection was given. It is now no longer needed, but this protection has given wealth and prosperity to the country, and particularly to Pennsylvania.[2]

Such optimistic utterances were completely falsified by the event; for the ensuing ten years were destined to witness one of the most bitter periods of tariff agitation in Pennsylvania history. The protectionists, once aroused from their lethargy, were as persistent and unyielding as ever in their appeals for government assistance. At the same time, however, it was very noticeable that the Democrats and free traders generally were becoming more aggressive and more outspoken in their opposition to the tariff system. Consequently, the protectionist struggle in Pennsylvania, beginning about 1840, presents a much more diversified and contentious aspect than had been the case a decade earlier.

---

[1] *American Sentinel,* November 30, 1839.
[2] May 30, 1839.

From the protectionist point of view, many economic factors combined to produce a revived interest in the tariff question. The cumulative effect of the panics of 1837 and 1839 has already been noted. Another contributing factor was the heavy importation of foreign goods during 1839. After a temporary slump due to the financial crisis, imports in that year amounted to 156 millions, a figure surpassed only during the wild speculative era of 1836.[3] Moreover, with the passage of time, the drastic tariff reductions scheduled for 1841 and 1842 were rapidly becoming something more than a remote contingency. For all these obvious reasons, Pennsylvania protectionists by the close of 1839 were growing increasingly restive under the inexorable workings of the Compromise Act.

Another economic factor, more obscure but none the less real, must be noted as contributing to the revived protectionism of this period. This was the first successful application of anthracite coal to the smelting of iron ore. Prior to this time, charcoal had been the universal fuel, and the growing scarcity of timber in eastern Pennsylvania served to keep production costs high in the area most exposed to foreign competition. Until the hot-blast principle was introduced in America in 1833 the use of anthracite had been out of the question. The first experiments with the new process were undertaken in Schuylkill county, where a limited quantity of pig iron was produced in 1836 with hard coal as the exclusive fuel. Other trials followed, but it was not until 1840 that the problem was completely solved in both its engineering and commercial aspects. At the end of that year there were six anthracite furnaces in operation.[4] Thereafter the number increased rapidly, so that by 1846 forty-two furnaces were producing practically one-third of the pig iron in Pennsylvania.[5]

The introduction of anthracite iron served in several ways to strengthen the protectionist movement in Pennsylvania. In the first place the ensuing development greatly increased the number of employees and hence the voting strength of the iron interest. Not only were more persons engaged in iron production than in any other form of industry, but also from the nature of the employment every

---

[3] *Statistical Abstract of the United States*, 1888, p. 12.
[4] Swank, *Iron in All Ages*, pp. 354, 360, 362.
[5] *House Exec. Doc.*, 31 Cong., 1 Sess., No. 4, p. 810.

worker was a voter or a prospective voter.[6] In the second place, the
introduction of cheaper and more efficient methods of production
placed the manufacturers of charcoal iron at a serious disadvantage.
Their difficulties were increased by the marked decline in prices
which occurred between 1837 and 1843 as a result of improved processes in America and overproduction in England. While the cost
of making charcoal iron remained constant, the prices on the American market declined from 30 to 50 per cent. during these years.[7]
The result was that many of the less efficient producers suffered
heavy losses; it was claimed for instance that twenty furnaces in
Pennsylvania were forced into bankruptcy during the single year of
1842.[8] In the face of a two-fold competition and declining prices,
the manufacturers of charcoal iron turned with renewed intensity to
Congress with pleas for legislative relief. In the third place, the use
of anthracite for fuel served to create an effective working alliance
between the iron and coal interests of the state.  Thereafter, a depression in the iron industry was certain to react disastrously upon
the coal producer as well. Thus, whenever the tariff question was
raised subsequent to 1840, the protectionists could count upon a
full concert of policy and action between these two great economic
interests of the state.  In various ways, therefore, the development
of anthracite iron not only provided a strong economic motive for a
renewed tariff agitation in Pennsylvania, but also tended to confirm
the position of the iron industry as the keystone of the protectionist
arch in that state.

   The Pennsylvania tariff agitation, once launched, rapidly gained
in violence as the period of drastic reductions under the Compromise
became increasingly imminent. A meeting held in Independence
Square, Philadelphia, declared that the declining duties were "the
one great cause of the present embarrassments of the country."[9] A
Pittsburgh gathering believed that "nothing but a restoration of the
tariff or a war with Great Britain could restore our former prosperity."[10]  A similar meeting at Harrisburg asserted that

---

[6] *Compendium of the Sixth Census*, pp. 358-361.
[7] *House Exec. Doc.*, 38 Cong., 1 Sess., No. 2, pp. 306-320; Swank, *Iron in All
Ages*, p. 514; Clark, *History of Manufactures*, III, 387; *Hunt's Merchants' Mag.*,
XVI, 591; *American Laborer*, I, 52.
[8] *Documents Relating to the Manufacture of Iron in Pennsylvania*, p. 109.
[9] *Public Ledger*, March 31, 1842.
[10] *Harrisburg Keystone*, March 3, 1841.

the establishing of no National Bank, Independent Treasury, Fiscal agent, Board of Exchequer by the general government; or suspension resolutions or law to compel the resumption of specie payments by the States will restore confidence or credit, or create a permanently sound currency until a check is first put to excessive importations of foreign goods, and a stop to the drain of American specie by a sound, discriminating tariff.[11]

Slight attention was paid to the argument, often heard in other parts of the Union, that the Compromise must be maintained as something sacred and inviolable. This contention was lightly dismissed by a group of Pittsburgh protectionists, who declared,

We aver that neither in the Act, nor in the circumstances attending its passage, is there to be found a particle of the terms or conditions of either compromise or contract:—it was a *victory* or rather it was the *articles of submission* yielded to the victors by the timid sentinels whom we had placed in the Halls of Congress. Such terms, thus obtained, we are at liberty to discard on the first fitting occasion.[12]

Possibly the loudest cry for additional protection during this period came from the anthracite coal industry of the state. From 1824 to 1832, foreign coal had been subject to a specific duty of $1.68 a ton, which under the workings of the Compromise Act would be ultimately reduced to about 40 cents a ton. The anthracite producers were much disturbed at the prospect and declared that under such rates they could not hope to compete with Nova Scotia coal on the New York and Boston markets.[13] It was freely asserted that nothing less than $2 a ton would afford adequate protection to the Pennsylvania mining interest; indeed, a fifty-foot petition was sent to Congress from Schuylkill county asking for a duty of $2.80 a ton.[14] The economic basis for this agitation is to be found not so much in excessive imports as in the low prices which prevailed at this time. In 1842, when the movement was at its height, Pennsylvania produced 67 per cent. of the entire national consumption; while imports constituted only about 5 per cent. of the total.[15] At the same time, however, anthracite prices in Philadelphia reached

---

[11] *Ibid.* February 19, 1842.
[12] *Pittsburgh Weekly Gazette,* January 7, 1842.
[13] *Miners' Journal,* January 29, 1842.
[14] *Ibid.* March 19, 26; April 9, 23, 1842.
[15] Computed from tables in *Mineral Resources of the United States,* 1915, II, 358 and Insert; Pennsylvania Bureau of Statistics of Labor and Agriculture, *Annual Report,* 1872-73, pp. 213-216.

the lowest level in the history of the coal trade.[16] It is clear that imports had nothing to do with the decline; since prices continued to fall during 1843 and 1844 when very little foreign coal entered the country. Nevertheless, Pennsylvania protectionists eagerly seized upon the drastic reductions of the Compromise Act as a convenient and plausible explanation for the depressed condition of the coal industry.

In the face of this revived protectionist sentiment, the increasing boldness of the anti-tariff forces in Pennsylvania requires a word of explanation. Undoubtedly, the most important single factor must be sought in the political exigencies of the Democrats, who were compelled by the fiscal developments of the Jacksonian era to stress an independent treasury and a hard currency above all other issues. To divert Northern attention from the tariff to the circulating medium, it was necessary to woo the manufacturer with the argument that real protection was unobtainable so long as an inflated currency operated as a bounty to the foreign producer. Buchanan as early as 1836, had been urging a reform of the currency as the most effective method of protecting the domestic producer against European competition.[17] Ingersoll, running for Congress in the following year, had ventured to assert, "Of what use is our impost on foreign goods of 25 per cent. while we add 33 per cent. to their relative value, by making our money so much worse than foreign money?. . .Hard money is the only effectual tariff."[18] The classic presentation of this argument, however, appeared in a speech delivered by Buchanan in the Senate on January 22, 1840. Although dealing primarily with the question of an independent treasury, the Pennsylvania Senator took the opportunity to point out the anti-protective effect of an inflated currency, and to demonstrate the advantage enjoyed by the hard-money countries of Europe in their commercial dealings with the United States.[19] Although his argument was unimpeachable both in theory and in fact, seldom has a speech been subject to such brutal misrepresentation and distortion. The Whigs adduced figures to show that the workers in these hard-

---

[16] See table of prices in Swank, *Statistical Abstract*, p. 22.
[17] Buchanan to Dauphin Co. Democrats, June 30, 1836; Buchanan Mss. Library of Congress.
[18] *Niles' Register*, LII, 269.
[19] *Cong. Globe*, 26 Cong., 1 Sess., App., pp. 129-137.

money countries received only a few cents a day in wages, and they charged Buchanan with a desire to reduce American labor to a similar servile condition.[20] Thus was born the appellation of "Ten-Cent Jimmy," which pursued him to the close of his public career. In spite of such misrepresentation, there were many in Pennsylvania who recognized the difficulty of maintaining tariff barriers in the face of an inflated currency. A Pittsburgh paper declared that "in the present state of our currency, it is folly to think of giving prosperity to the country by tariff laws, and until our infamous system of banking is reformed and the constitutional currency restored, all levying of tariffs will be but to increase the burthens of the people."[21] A Philadelphia journal urged that the country "reform the currency, and our manufacturers can take care of themselves, without levying an indirect tax upon the people to afford them an artificial existence."[22] A Pennsylvania Congressman even dared to assert that "wherever we have the raw material in abundance, we can, under a sound currency, compete with the English manufacturer without any tariff whatever."[23]

At the same time that the Democratic politicians of Pennsylvania were making a deliberate attempt to subordinate the tariff question to that of the currency, the small free-trade minority of the state was deriving considerable encouragement from contemporary economic trends both at home and abroad. To many disinterested observers in the United States, it appeared that American industry had outgrown the stage of dependent infancy. It was felt that the protection originally asked by the manufacturers of the country had already been afforded with superabundant generosity, and that thereafter the domestic producer should be required to stand upon his own feet.[24] Moreover, many Americans were being considerably impressed by the trend of economic thought in England, where the rapid progress of free-trade sentiment seemed to portend the speedy overthrow of the protective system. Friends of the tariff had consistently admitted that free trade was a highly desirable ideal, but

---

[20] *Ibid.* pp. 157-159.
[21] *Pittsburgh Manufacturer,* January 22, 1842.
[22] *Public Ledger,* February 8, 1840.
[23] *Pennsylvanian,* June 24, 1840.
[24] That this idea was making progress even in Pennsylvania is indicated by the quotations on page 134, *supra.*

that, so long as England clung to the restrictive policy, the United States must do likewise in self-defense. When Britain lowered her tariff barriers, it was argued, then the United States might safely abandon her commercial restrictions. Now, unexpectedly, England seemed about to throw her ports open to the products of the world, and the proposed repeal of the corn laws threatened to deprive American protectionists of one of their most effective arguments. Even in Pennsylvania, there were those who accepted the anti-tariff revulsion abroad as evidence that the commercial millenium was at hand, and, for the first time in years, the theoretical advantages of free trade were openly avowed by some of the most influential newspapers in the state. This was especially true of the Philadelphia *Pennsylvanian,* the state's outstanding Democratic organ, and the Philadelphia *Public Ledger,* an independent paper claiming the largest circulation in the commonwealth.[25] "What are protecting tariffs," inquired a *Public Ledger* editorial, "but devices to tax the many for the benefit of the few, sure to produce nabobs and beggars, palaces and almshouses, princes and paupers?"[26] Such duties were characterized as "a tax upon consumption, and not upon property, upon necessity, and not ability, upon the necessity of living and not the ability of paying."[27] Noting with satisfaction the marked trend toward free trade in England, the same paper observed,

The world is growing wiser upon the subject of trade. It is beginning to discover that trade . . . to produce the good for which it was designed in the highest degree, must be *let alone,* left as much as possible to its own laws, and restrained as little as possible by human laws . . . All restraints beyond the necessity of enforcing natural laws, never fail to do mischief . . . We call the attention of our statesmen . . . to this subject, involving the temporal affairs of every human being in our country. While other nations are bursting the fetters forged in darker ages, and escaping from a system founded in periods of ignorance, we trust that our enlightened republicanism will not pick up and wear such cast off manacles. If men in other countries have been able to see the truth through the clouds and smoke which had been accumulating around them for ages, let *us* not be blind in a clear atmosphere.[28]

---

[25] Condy Raguet was an early member of the *Public Ledger's* editorial staff and helped to institute its free trade tendencies, which persisted until the Civil War. (*Miners' Journal,* July 24, 1841.)

[26] *Public Ledger,* September 2, 1841.

[27] *Ibid.* August 10, 1842.

[28] *Ibid.* June 8, 1841.

The *Pennsylvanian* enunciated the conventional free-trade doctrine that "it appears highly probable, if not absolutely certain, that several branches of our manufactures will be increased in amount and in real profitableness to the labourer, by a general reduction of the tariff."[29] In the course of a series of theoretical essays entitled "Tariff Fallacies," it declared, "We doubt not that the iron business of Pennsylvania, and the manufacture of the heavier articles from our agricultural products will continue gradually to increase under a system of free trade; but if it would not do so, then it would be wiser to let the ore remain for our grandchildren, and buy manufactures with the produce of our farms."[30] The same paper reprinted an extremely laudatory essay upon Adam Smith, the tenor of which may be judged by the following extract:

He was the first to reveal in the glory of its simplicity and beauty the eternal doctrine of Free Trade . . . He established on immutable foundations the safety, profitableness, the moral uses, of an unrestrained prosecution of industry and an unfettered intercourse among nations . . . As Paul had carried Christianity into all the cities of the Heathen world, and as Bacon had applied the torch of a true method to the logomachies of the schoolmen, so Smith lifted up the light of the glorious principle of Free Trade, in the midst of the hosts who rallied around the banners of monopoly and restriction.[31]

Ten years before, it would have been difficult to find a eulogy of Adam Smith or of the free-trade system in any representative Pennsylvania newspaper. It is clear, therefore, that both sides entered the renewed tariff struggle after 1840 with new elements of strength and new points of weakness. In numbers and in zeal, the protectionists seem to have gained more than the opposition. Nevertheless the accessions to the free-trade party were sufficient to permit it to play an interesting and occasionally an effective role in the ensuing discussions.

The first engagement of the renewed tariff struggle was fought in connection with the presidential election of 1840. It was a skirmish rather than a battle, however, for the political leaders on both sides were uncertain as to the attitude which they should take upon the subject. Neither party deemed it expedient to make the question of

[29] *Pennsylvanian*, June 29, 1842.
[30] *Ibid*. December 23, 1841.
[31] *Ibid*. November 17, 1840.

protection a decisive issue in the campaign, yet neither dared ignore the subject entirely. The Democrats discreetly borrowed Jacksonian phraseology to depict Van Buren as the friend of a "judicious" tariff.[32] For the most part, however, they preferred to stress the question of an independent treasury and a metallic currency, and they asserted that if these were established no protective tariff would be necessary. The Democrats indignantly denied the protectionist claims of their opponents and gave wide circulation to statements by both Harrison and Tyler in favor of the Compromise Act.[33]

The Whigs were rather handicapped in their tariff utterances during the campaign by the fact that both Harrison and Clay were publicly urging the maintenance of the principles of the Compromise.[34] They contented themselves for the most part with vague declarations identifying their candidate with a protective tariff and high wages. They pointed out that Harrison had given tariff votes in the Ohio legislature in 1819; that he had supported the act of 1828 while in Congress; and that he had written a series of strongly protectionist letters to Calhoun in 1831.[35] They also gave a wide circulation to a letter by McDuffie in which the South Carolinian declared concerning the tariff question, "General Harrison has always been an extremist on this subject, and Mr. Webster, his Prime Minister apparent, has avowed his determination to revive it, regardless of the Compromise, to which he has always been violently opposed."[36] Tyler attempted to propitiate Pennsylvania restrictionists by pointing out that the Compromise Act which he favored would actually afford about 40 per cent. protection because of its provisions for American valuation and cash payments.[37] On the other hand, it was asserted that Van Buren had always been a bitter foe of the tariff and would resort to direct taxes to meet the deficit rather than approve any increase in the import duties.[38] It is difficult to say just how much effect such appeals had upon the final result in Pennsylvania. In that wildly emotional campaign of

---

32 *Cf. Pennsylvanian*, June 3, 1840.
33 *Pittsburgh Mercury*, October 12, 1840; *Harrisburg Reporter*, July 3, October 20, 1840.
34 Norton, *Reminiscences of the Log Cabin and Hard Cider Campaign*, p. 209.
35 *Franklin Repository*, July 30, 1840; *Pittsburgh Gazette*, October 14, 1840.
36 *Pittsburgh Gazette*, October 22, 1840.
37 *Ibid.* October 27, 1840.
38 *Franklin Repository*, July 9, 30, 1840.

coonskins, log cabins, and hard cider, it is not likely that the tariff or any other serious question influenced many votes, but inasmuch as Harrison carried the state by a majority of only 334, the growing discontent with the Compromise Act may well have represented the margin of victory.

As usual, the revived tariff agitation very quickly invaded the Pennsylvania state legislature. During the session of 1840, the conventional protectionist resolutions were passed by the Senate, but the House refused to consider them.[39] The Whigs used their control of the next legislature, however, to pass resolutions in favor of higher duties and the distribution of the proceeds from the public lands.[40] Buchanan was informed that the real purpose of these obnoxious instructing resolutions was to force his resignation from the Senate.[41] Far from being embarrassed thereby, he seems to have welcomed them as affording a convenient excuse to justify a break with his party in support of the revenue act of 1841.[42] Nevertheless, the Whigs attempted to repeat the maneuver during the legislative session of 1842, in spite of the fact that the Democrats had regained control of the lower House. Instructing resolutions were introduced, therefore, denouncing free trade as an "idle theory" and calling upon Congress to impose protective or even prohibitive duties.[43] Buchanan was extremely anxious to be left free to act according to his own discretion upon the tariff question and accordingly urged his friends to defeat the measure.[44] Acting under instructions from Washington, the Democratic majority in the House adopted an ingenious policy of delay and emasculation. In other words to render the resolutions as obnoxious as possible to the Whigs, amendments were adopted approving a tariff for revenue only and denouncing distribution as "impolitic and inexpedient." Then having forced their opponents into the invidious position of voting against their own resolutions, the Democrats quietly put the measure to sleep by refusing to permit a third reading.[45]

---

[39] *Senate Journal,* 1840, I, 513; *House Journal,* 1840, I, 1002, 1246.
[40] *Pamphlet Laws,* 1841, p. 434; *Senate Journal,* I, 119; *House Journal,* I, 143.
[41] A. J. Wilson to Buchanan, January 22, 1841; Buchanan Mss.
[42] *Cong. Globe,* 27 Cong., 1 Sess., p. 438.
[43] *House Journal,* 1842, I, 73.
[44] Buchanan, *Works,* VI, 74.
[45] *House Journal,* 1842, I, 147, 342, 363, 498, 999, 1027, 1029, 1031.

The clash of tariff and politics which produced these strange maneuvers at Harrisburg had an exact counterpart in the legislative proceedings at Washington. The Twenty-Seventh Congress was convened in extraordinary session on May 31, 1841 to deal with the problem of a constantly growing deficit in the treasury. To meet the situation, at least in part, the revenue act of 1841 was passed, which raised the duty to 20 per cent. ad valorem on most articles previously free or paying less than that figure. This measure, as adopted by the House, was distasteful to the tariff party because of the tax imposed on tea and coffee which would provide revenue without affording protection. Accordingly, the Pennsylvania delegation gave only ten votes for and seventeen against the bill.[46] In general, the Whigs supported the measure while the Democrats opposed it. The Senate greatly improved the bill from the protectionist point of view by restoring tea and coffee to the free list and by inserting a 20 per cent. duty on railroad iron. Buchanan was very largely responsible for the latter provision.[47] In its amended form, both Buchanan and Sturgeon supported the bill.[48]

The adoption of the act of 1841 failed to silence, even momentarily, the tariff agitation. The additional revenue which it provided was small and was almost entirely offset by the provision for the distribution to the states of the proceeds of the public lands, put through at the same session of Congress for purely political reasons. The treasury deficit, therefore, not only remained, but threatened to become even greater as a result of the drastic reduction of duties impending under the Compromise Act. Moreover, the question was raised whether any duties could be legally collected after June 30, 1842, unless Congress prescribed the necessary administrative regulations for effecting the change from foreign to American valuations. The protectionists, therefore, opened the regular session of Congress, in December, 1841, with a vigorous agitation for the overthrow of the Compromise and the reenactment of the high duties prevailing before 1833.

---

[46] *Cong. Globe,* 27 Cong., 1 Sess., p. 274.

[47] *Ibid.* pp. 402, 403, 431.

[48] *Ibid.* p. 438. In explanation of Buchanan's vote, Calhoun wrote, "His state is a Tariff state, made so by the iron business, and still more by the want of decision on his part. He had to yield, or go out of public life, and to go out in Pennsylvania is to be finally lost politically." (Calhoun, *Correspondence,* p. 491).

Before a general revision was attempted, it seemed desirable to pass a provisional tariff act, repealing the last reduction scheduled under the Compromise. Accordingly, the so-called "little tariff bill" was introduced, extending the duration of the existing duties to August 1. At the same time, the Whigs sought to make political capital by inserting a provision retaining the distribution scheme, which originally had been limited to the duration of the Compromise Act. As a result of this maneuver, the Pennsylvania delegation in both Houses cast their votes upon a strictly partisan basis, with the Whigs supporting and the Democrats opposing the measure.[49] Although the "little tariff bill" was passed by Congress, President Tyler hastened to veto the measure because of its ill-advised distribution proviso. Ordinarily, this exercise of the Executive power would have evoked well-nigh universal condemnation in Pennsylvania, but upon this occasion political considerations produced a curiously divided reaction among the people of the state. A Whig meeting at Pottsville denounced the veto as "one of the most tyrannical and daring acts of usurpation, which has ever characterized the Executive Branch of this government."[50] The Democrats, on the other hand, warmly commended the wisdom and courage shown by the President's action.[51] The Whigs were not sufficiently strong in Congress to override the veto; so of necessity they turned to a consideration of the general tariff bill already introduced in the House by the Committee on Ways and Means. This measure had been prepared by the Secretary of the Treasury, Walter Forward of Pittsburgh, who was said to have abandoned the Democratic party because of Jackson's hostility to the protective policy.[52] The bill established the duties at about the general level of the act of 1832, but once more contained the obnoxious distribution clause. As before, the Pennsylvania delegation split upon a strictly partisan basis. The typical Democratic attitude was well expressed by Fornance, who declared, "I am desirous that some tariff bill shall pass; but no tariff bill can purchase my vote for the distribution of the public lands."[53] A noticeable feature of the debate was the unusually

[49] *Cong. Globe,* 27 Cong., 2 Sess., pp. 637, 679.
[50] *Miners' Journal,* July 9, 1842.
[51] *Cf. Pittsburgh Mercury,* July 6, 1842.
[52] *Niles' Register,* LXI, 98.
[53] *Cong. Globe,* 27 Cong., 2 Sess., App. p. 495.

moderate protectionism openly avowed by several of the Pennsylvania Democrats. Ingersoll, for instance, declared,

I lay it down as a demonstrable axiom which all experience, particularly our own, has incontestably proved, that the lowest duties are the best, because they are the most permanent, in a confederated country, consisting, like ours, of various separated States . . . As a private individual, having contributed to bring about the tariff of 1828, I confess its extravagance. It was too stimulant—over bountiful . . . The iron business of Pennsylvania, the woolens, and perhaps other pursuits, instead of flourishing, declined, under the highest duties . . . It is the paramount interest (as I conceive) of this country to cultivate the utmost freedom of trade, by treaties introducing the reciprocity principle, and by tariffs imposing no duties but such as are absolutely indispensable . . . The cost of transportation from Europe, freight, insurance, and other charges (without counting home valuation) I reckon as equal with cash duties to at least twenty per cent.—which added to the twenty per cent. ad valorem on all hands conceded, affords a protection which ought to be sufficient.[54]

The final passage found the delegation divided, with twelve Whigs supporting and fourteen Democrats opposing the measure.[55] In the Senate, both Buchanan and Sturgeon, as Democrats, voted against the bill.[56]

The general measure was open to precisely the same objections as the provisional bill, and Tyler promptly invoked his veto power against it. At the same time, he intimated that the tariff, if passed without the distribution clause, would receive his approval. As before, the President's action was generally commended by the Democrats of Pennsylvania. The *Pennsylvanian* characterized the vetoed measure as "the new bill of abominations."[57] A Pittsburgh paper asserted that "the reasons given by the President for this act must satisfy everyone who is not carried away by party madness."[58] Many Democratic journals expressed serious doubts as to the sincerity of the Whigs in posing as the friends of the protective system. One editor declared impatiently, "If the Whigs really desire to promote the great interests of the country and rely upon a tariff as a means, why do they not abandon these petty expedients, and pass

---

[54] *Ibid*. p. 644.
[55] Ibid. p. 762.
[56] Ibid. p. 852.
[57] August 11, 1842.
[58] *Pittsburgh Chronicle*, August 14, 1842.

a tariff bill at once, which shall strictly be a tariff bill, unconnected with Distribution or any other measure."[59] A Democratic meeting in Schuylkill county adopted a resolution declaring

that the clamor now raised by the Federalists throughout the country on the subject of a high tariff is intended only to make political capital for the next Presidential election to supply the vacuum created by the explosion of log cabins, coon skins and hard cider . . . that they have no desire to pass a Tariff Bill at the present session of Congress . . . but that their main object is to "head Capt. Tyler" to procure a situation for Capt. Clay.[60]

The Whigs, on the other hand, exhorted their party associates not to yield upon the distribution question. As one of the leading protectionist papers of the state explained, "Nothing like duration can be expected in a tariff, until it is relied upon solely to supply the revenues of this government. . .The necessity of giving permanency to the Tariff system—justice to the states—their increasing wants—the will of the people—all demand that the proceeds of the lands shall be distributed to the states."[61] Another editor vehemently asserted, "If Congress submits to the dictation of John Tyler, they will deserve the execration of the people and of every friend of liberty throughout the world. . .We would sooner see John Tyler meet the fate of his great prototype, Charles the 1st, than the principle should be established that Congress must bow to the dictation of a would-be despot."[62]

Meanwhile, Pennsylvania Democrats were attempting to evolve an acceptable basis of compromise upon which both parties might unite. One such proposal was sponsored by Buchanan in the Senate and by Ingersoll and Fornance in the House. Their project was, briefly, to restore the duties as they stood in 1839, after the first three minor reductions had taken place under the Compromise. Several of the extremists in the Democratic party rejected the proposal, however, and it had to be abandoned. Nevertheless, Buchanan later expressed the belief that Congress, by this refusal, had lost an excellent opportunity to effect a permanent settlement of the tariff question upon a fair and reasonable basis.[63]

---

59 *Pittsburgh Mercury,* August 10, 1842.
60 *Harrisburg Keystone,* August 17, 1842.
61 *North American,* August 25, 1842.
62 *Miners' Journal,* August 13, 1842.
63 *Cong. Globe,* 27 Cong., 2 Sess., App., p. 493; Buchanan, *Works,* VI, 74; *Pennsylvanian,* August 3, 1842.

Actually, the situation had reached the point where there was no alternative for the Whigs but complete surrender, lest they brand themselves as selfish political intriguers, indifferent to the fate of the protective system. Accordingly, the tariff bill, minus the distribution clause, was reintroduced and, after a bitter struggle, was passed by both houses. Of the Pennsylvanians, ten Whigs and ten Democrats voted for the bill in its revised form. Although no member of the delegation opposed the measure, three Whigs and five Democrats were either absent or not voting on the final roll call.[64] In the Senate, both Buchanan and Sturgeon voted for the bill, although the former did so under protest. As he declared,

I admit, most cheerfully, that the bill is extravagant in the protection which it affords; and in some instances, is altogether prohibitory. It is a bill of which I do not approve, and for which I would not vote, were it not for the present unparalleled condition of the existing law, the treasury, and the country . . . I think I shall hazard little in declaring that, at the least, four-fifths of those whose will I am bound to obey, if placed in my situation, would vote for the present measure.[65]

In spite of Buchanan's lack of enthusiasm for the measure, his protectionist adherents later made much of the fact that without his vote the act of 1842 could not have passed the Senate.[66] The Pennsylvania Whigs, on the other hand, attributed the success of the bill to Secretary Forward, who drafted the bill, the Representative McKennan of Washington county, who directed the contest in the House.[67]

The tariff of 1842 involved a return to the same general level of protection which had existed before the Compromise. There were, however, numerous differences of detail. The rates were lower than in 1832 upon wool and woolens, but higher upon cottons. There was a reduction of from 10 to 15 per cent. in the duties upon the more important forms of iron. Glass enjoyed an extremely high protection; while the duties upon paper and leather goods were lowered. Coal was granted a specific rate of $1.75 per ton. Although this was

---

[64] *Cong. Globe,* 27 Cong., 2 Sess., p. 926.

[65] *Ibid.* pp. 951, 960.

[66] *Cf. Pennsylvanian,* January 23, May 4, 1844.

[67] *Cong. Globe,* 29 Cong., 1 Sess., App., p. 1091; Blaine, *Twenty Years of Congress,* I, 191; *Pennsylvanian,* September 14, 1842; *Pittsburgh Chronicle,* August 27, 1842.

less than the mining interests had requested, they professed themselves as entirely satisfied with the tax, which at the prevailing low price of coal was equivalent to about 80 per cent.[68] The provision for the cash payment of duties was carried over from the Compromise Act, but the system of American valuation was abandoned. When allowance is made for the technical improvements which had been taking place in many lines of American industry, the tariff of 1842 actually afforded more adequate protection than that of 1832.

Pennsylvania's general reaction to the new tariff act was extremely favorable. The *North American* declared, "The Tariff will give sufficient revenue and afford quite as much protection as the friends of American industrial interest should require. . . It is considered a very good tariff."[69] Wildest enthusiasm prevailed in the anthracite regions, where, it was reported,

The inhabitants of Danville . . . greeted its passage with a spirited jubilee—all the bells in the town rang out a merry peal, and the repeated booming forth of cannon told to the neighborhood their feelings at the result . . . The citizens of Mauch Chunk also received the news of its passage with great rejoicing. Cannons were fired—bells rung, and every window in the streets were illuminated.[70]

The Democratic press likewise expressed quite general approval of the provisions of the new act. One such paper declared, "This we believe is as good a tariff bill as could be got, under the peculiar circumstances in which we are situated in this country; and although portions of it may be somewhat objectionable, still we think it will tend to invigorate every branch of manufactures and the mechanic arts."[71] Even the *Pennsylvanian* and *Public Ledger,* whose free-trade tendencies have been noted, were only mildly critical of the new law. The editor of the former commented,

We have never been advocates of the high tariff system, but situated as the country and the government was, and would have been had not some bill been passed, it was the part of wisdom and patriotism for those who had the moral courage to do it, to give up some of their predilections, and adopt the best measures that could be obtained.[72]

---

[68] *Miners' Journal,* September 3, 1842 ; August 31, 1844.
[69] August 25, 1842.
[70] *Miners' Journal,* September 10, 1842.
[71] *Harrisburg Keystone,* September 7, 1842.
[72] *Pennsylvanian,* September 3, 1842.

The *Public Ledger* urged that the new tariff should be given a fair trial, for, it asserted,

If it be bad, a point about which no two interests agree, it is at least useful at present, in diminishing imports, and leaving our abundant exports to be paid for in coin; and as we now want coin more than anything else, the tariff is the best that we could have now . . . Let us try it and let Congress *let it alone.*[73]

Pennsylvania protectionists very quickly realized that only eternal vigilance could preserve the tariff of 1842 from a speedy overthrow. The margin of victory had been too narrow for comfort—two votes in the House and one in the Senate. A temporary truce followed the passage of the new revenue law, but by 1844 the foes of protection were mobilized for an attack upon the tariff system from several directions. From abroad came the news that Henry Wheaton had negotiated a reciprocity agreement with the Zollverein, providing for marked tariff reductions in favor of German cotton and woolen clothing, manufactures of flax, hemp, and silk, leather goods, certain kinds of glass, and a few other articles.[74] Many Pennsylvania protectionists regarded this agreement as an extremely dangerous innovation in American commercial policy. A Pittsburgh paper, for instance, warned against the influx of German glass which would follow the ratification of the treaty, and predicted that "if Tyler can squeeze it through, it will be the entering wedge by which the tariff will be nullified, even if not repealed."[75] The fear proved groundless; for the Senate rejected the treaty upon the ostensible grounds that it was an unconstitutional interference with the tariff-making powers of Congress. Of the two Pennsylvanians, Sturgeon opposed the treaty, while Buchanan did not vote, although he had been present in the Senate earlier in the day.[76] Buchanan's failure to vote, if intentional, may have been influenced by the personal appeal in behalf of the treaty which Wheaton addressed to him from Berlin.[77]

Pennsylvania protectionists were likewise confronted during 1844 by a serious agitation to revive the privilege of importing railroad iron free of duty. A bill to this effect was introduced in the Senate,

---

[73] December 12, 1842.
[74] Laughlin and Willis, *Reciprocity*, p. 8n.
[75] *Pittsburgh Gazette*, November 26, 1844.
[76] *Sen. Exec. Jour.*, VI, 347.
[77] Wheaton to Buchanan, March 27, 1844; Buchanan Mss.

where Buchanan and Sturgeon led the opposition to it. The former characterized the proposal as an attempt "to crush the vast iron interest of Pennsylvania, Maryland, and New Jersey for the benefit of railroad companies" and declared that a bill "so unequal and unjust should never pass, whilst he entertained any hope of resisting it successfully."[78] The combined iron and coal interests of the state declared that the measure, if passed, "would introduce a system of legislation much more pernicious to the country and its industry than the wildest notions of the advocates of horizontal duties and free trade."[79] The proposal was finally tabled by the close vote of 21 to 20, but was revived periodically thereafter; so that it remained for years an ever-present threat against the iron interest of Pennsylvania.[80]

The most comprehensive assault upon the existing duties, however, was represented by the so-called McKay bill, introduced in the House in 1844. This measure, although not so drastic as the Compromise Act, did provide for a general reduction of duties. The rate on pig iron was to be cut from $9 to $7 per ton, on rolled bar from $25 to $20 per ton, and on hammered bar from $17 to $15 per ton. The duty on coal was to be reduced from $1.75 to $1 a ton.[81] Nevertheless, observers saw in the provisions of the bill a deliberate discrimination in favor of Pennsylvania products. A New York paper denounced it as "sneaking in its exceptions in behalf of iron and sugar—in the hope of propitiating Louisiana and Pennsylvania to Van Burenism."[82] Niles, also, believed that

Mr. McKay's tariff bill was drawn up with an especial eye in a number of its provisions to conciliate the vote of the senators and representatives in Congress from Pennsylvania as well as if possible to enlist the people of that state in the project of modifying the existing tariff . . . But the bait appears to have most signally failed. There are few instances of a whole community like Pennsylvania with such numerous ramifications of parties and interests, rallying so promptly and so unequivocally to the support of any debatable object.[83]

---

[78] *Cong. Globe*, 28 Cong., 1 Sess., App., p. 680.
[79] *Letter to the Hon. George Evans against the Repeal of the Duty upon Railway Iron*, p. 3.
[80] *Cong. Globe*, 28 Cong., 1 Sess., App., p. 682.
[81] *North American*, March 13, 1844.
[82] *New York American*, quoted in *Niles' Register*, LXVI, 33.
[83] *Niles' Register*, LXVI, 89.

Pennsylvania's opposition to the McKay bill was, as Niles said, immediate and well-nigh unanimous. The legislature adopted resolutions instructing the Senators and requesting the Representatives "to oppose any change in the present tariff which might prove injurious to the manufacturing and agricultural interests of this commonwealth, sternly to resist any reduction in the present duties on iron, coal, and wool, and to omit no effort to sustain all the great interests of the nation, calculated to foster and promote American industry."[84] Only one vote was recorded against this resolution in either House, and that was given by a member who thought that the instructions were not sufficiently mandatory.[85] Public meetings of both parties strongly denounced any interference with the existing rates. One such gathering memorialized Congress to the effect that

the present bill has more than realized the best expectations of its friends, in reviving trade and in furnishing revenue to the government . . . Our furnaces, forges, cotton mills, and workshops, that but one year ago were abandoned, are now again full of life and activity, and the employment that was lately given to foreign capitalists and artizans is now secured for our own people. Our banks are able to retain their specie, and the gloom and despondency which lately prevailed is now dissipated . . . We therefore pray you to abstain from all legislation upon the subject and thereby give peace and prosperity to the country.[86]

Another meeting predicted that the proposed bill "would utterly destroy the great Iron interests of Pennsylvania, throw out of employment upwards of twelve thousand hands, and sink ten millions of capital now employed in that business in this state alone."[87] Samuel Ingham expressed regret that southern free traders by such persistent and ill-advised attacks upon the tariff were driving Northern manufacturers into an ominous alliance with the abolitionists.[88] In Congress, Pennsylvanians of both parties vied with each other in denouncing the McKay tariff. The Democrats, especially, were much more assertive in their protectionism than they had been two years before. The delegation, on May 10, 1844, unanimously supported the motion to lay the bill upon the table, which, as the event proved,

---

[84] *Pamphlet Laws*, 1844, p. 601.
[85] *Senate Journal*, 1844, I, 481.
[86] *Sen. Doc.*, 62 Cong., 1 Sess., No. 72, p. 1606.
[87] *North American*, March 26, 1844.
[88] Ingham to Duff Green, July 12, 1844; Green Mss.

ended further discussion upon the subject.[89] With the immediate danger of adverse legislation thus averted, Pennsylvania protectionists were able to concentrate their attention upon the exciting presidential election of 1844, in which, so far as the Keystone State was concerned, the tariff easily overshadowed all other issues.

---

[89] *Cong. Globe.,* 28 Cong., 1 Sess., p. 622.

# CHAPTER VIII

## THE ELECTION OF 1844

In American political history, the presidential election of 1844 is usually written in terms of "the reannexation of Texas and the reoccupation of Oregon." Nevertheless, this clash of "manifest destiny" and anti-slavery produced few reverberations in Pennsylvania, where the tariff became in unprecedented measure the dominant issue of the campaign. This was due in part to the personality of the candidates; with Henry Clay, consecrated by long tradition as the "Father of the American System," opposed to James K. Polk, whose protectionism was justly open to serious question. Another contributing factor was the feeling that the tariff of 1842 was in real danger, and that its ultimate fate would depend upon the attitude of the next administration at Washington. The Democratic leaders of Pennsylvania, in view of their party's rather uncertain ground upon the question of protection, would have preferred to keep the tariff in the background, and accordingly they sought to create a diversion in favor of Texas and in opposition to a national bank. Neither issue took hold, however, and from first to last the tariff was the one outstanding topic of political controversy. It was found desirable to interpret even the question of Texas with an eye to its protectionist implications. The Whigs, for instance, maintained that the annexation of that region would bring six additional Southern states into the Union and that the votes of their twelve Senators would break down the tariff system for all time.[1] The Democrats, on the other hand, predicted that Texas, as an independent nation, would constitute an irreparable breach in the American tariff barrier; since British goods would be imported there free of duty and then would be smuggled across the border to carry "ruin and bankruptcy into every manufacturing district of the United States."[2]

Clay, himself, struck the keynote of the Whig campaign in Pennsylvania when he wrote to one of his most trusted lieutenants,

It seems to me that in Pennsylvania the points to be pressed are the tariff and Col. Polk's hostility to it, and the Distribution of the proceeds of the Public

---

[1] *Pittsburgh Gazette,* August 29, 1844.
[2] *Pittsburgh Post,* April 17, 1844.

Lands. The strongest proofs should be laid before the Public of that hostility. On the other hand my known attachment to both these measures of policy should be urged on all suitable occasions.[3]

Although Clay, with an eye to the Southern vote, would have preferred to avoid too definite an expression of his tariff views, he found it necessary, as the campaign advanced, to reassure Pennsylvania protectionists in progressively stronger terms of his loyalty to the American system. Early in June, he informed the Whigs of Dauphin county that he favored "raising in time of peace, the amount of revenue requisite to an economical administration of the government, exclusively from foreign imports, by a tariff so adjusted that, by proper discriminations, just and reasonable encouragement shall be extended to American industry."[4] Democratic attacks upon this rather ambiguous declaration soon compelled him to amplify it with the so-called Cope letter, in which he observed, "I have everywhere maintained that in adjusting a tariff for revenue, discriminations ought to be made for protection; that the tariff of 1842 has operated most beneficially, and that I am utterly opposed to its repeal."[5] Finally, in September, he made a further bid for Pennsylvania support with the flat assertion, "I am of opinion that the operation of the Tariff of 1842 has been eminently satisfactory; that I am decidedly opposed to its repeal; that I should regard its repeal as a great national calamity; and that I am unaware of the necessity of any modification of it."[6]

Clay's protectionist utterances were given a wide circulation by the Whigs of Pennsylvania. All friends of domestic industry were urged to "vote for Henry Clay, the father of the American system— the man whose principles are the life blood of the Protective policy."[7] An ardent Whig paper eloquently declared, " 'The poison which passed the lips of Socrates penetrated the vitals of Greece— the axe which fell upon the neck of Cicero severed the head of Rome!'—the ostracism of Henry Clay by Pennsylvania would be alike the suicidal act of party madness."[8] When the Democrats

---

[3] Clay to J. M. Clayton, August 29, 1844; Clayton Mss.
[4] *Niles' Register,* LXVI, 235.
[5] *Ibid.* p. 325.
[6] *Pittsburgh Gazette,* September 23, 1844.
[7] *North American,* November 1, 1844.
[8] *Ibid.* October 29, 1844.

adduced the Compromise Act as evidence of Clay's anti-tariff pro-
clivities, the Whigs replied that he had sponsored the measure only
to avert a much more drastic reduction.[9] One Whig orator, carried
by his enthusiasm into the realms of sheer fancy, attempted the following unique interpretation of the Compromise provisions:

The principles of the Compromise Act are, too frequently, misapprehended. It
is generally supposed to be a duty of twenty per cent. upon all articles of importation; this is not true—it provides an average duty of twenty per cent.,
which, with home valuation and cash payments, was then deemed by our manufacturers equivalent to thirty per cent. Now this average was affected in this
way; upon articles which required protection, the duty would range between
50 and 100 per cent. as seemed expedient, while upon articles which needed no
protection, it might be as low as. five per cent.[10]

The Democrats, at the same time, were giving an equally wide dissemination to certain of Clay's recent utterances upon the subject,
which were alleged to reveal not only his unrelenting hostility to the
protective system, but also his pusillanimous intention to espouse the
tariff in the North and free trade in the South.  They laid much
emphasis upon Clay's admonition to the Senate, delivered on January 21, 1842, to "carry out the spirit of the Compromise Act. Look
to revenue alone for the support of government. Do not raise the
question of protection which I had hoped had been put to rest. There
is no necessity of protection, for protection."[11] Wide publicity was
also given to the so-called Bronson and Meriwether letters, written
by Clay in 1843 to residents of Georgia. In the former, Clay declared:

In comformity with the principle announced in the compromise act, I think
that whatever revenue is necessary to an economical and honest administration
of the General Government ought to be derived from duties imposed on Foreign
imports. And I believe that in establishing a tariff of those duties, such a discrimination ought to be made, as will incidentally afford reasonable protection
to our national interests.

I think there is no danger of a high tariff being ever established; that of
1828 was eminently deserving that denomination. I was not in Congress when
it passed, and did not vote for it; but with its history and with the circum-

---

9 Williams, *Address on the Subject of the Tariff,* p. 20; *Prospect before Us,
or Loco Foco Impositions Exposed,* p. 5.
10 *Miners' Journal,* August 17, 1844.
11 *Cong. Globe,* 27 Cong., 2 Sess., p. 156.

stances which gave birth to it I am well acquainted. They are highly discreditable to American legislation, and I hope for its honor, will never again be repeated.

After my return to Congress in 1831 my efforts were directed to the modification and reduction of duty contained in the act of 1828. . . I had resigned my seat in the Senate when the act of 1843 was passed. . . Without intending to express any opinion upon every item of this last tariff, I would say, that I think the provisions, in the main, are wise and proper. If there be any excesses or defects in it, (of which I have not the means of judging) they ought to be corrected.

My opinion that there is no danger hereafter of a High Tariff is founded on the gratifying fact that our manufactories have now taken a deep root. In their infancy, they needed a greater measure of protection; but, as they grow and advance, they acquire strength and stability, and consequently will require less protection. Even now some branches of them are able to maintain in distant markets successful competition with rival foreign manufactures.[12]

The Meriwether letter expressed much the same idea, together with the assertion, eagerly seized upon by the Democrats, that "I never was in favor of duties being so high as to amount to a prohibition of articles on which they were laid. I have thought it best for all interests that there should be competition. . . I should have preferred that the Compromise, in all its parts, including the Home valuation, could have been adhered to."[13] Other isolated fragments of speeches and letters were brought forward, which, as is usual in such cases, scarcely did justice to Clay's views; but which were nicely calculated to arouse distrust as to the sincerity of the Whig candidate's protectionist professions.[14]

As was to be expected, the Democrats used such excerpts as a text from which to draw a most unflattering picture of Clay's tariff record. A meeting at Harrisburg declared "that we regard with emotions of disgust the Janus-faced policy pursued by Mr. Clay on the tariff question, as utterly unworthy an honest, candid, and ingenuous man. He is for protection at the North, against protection at the South, and for deception everywhere."[15] The *Pennsylvanian* took

---

[12] *Harrisburg Democratic Union,* November 8, 1843.

[13] *Niles' Register,* LXV, 203.

[14] Cf. *Pennsylvanian,* July 1, 1844; *Pittsburgh Post,* March 25, April 6, September 7, 1844.

[15] *Pennsylvanian,* June 8, 1844.

pains to point out that "Henry Clay did not vote for the Tariff of 1816—1824—nor 1828. In 1831 he directed all his efforts to reduce the Tariff of 1828. He voted for the tariff of 1832 which lowered the previous protection. In 1833, he introduced and advocated the Compromise Act which cut up the whole policy of protection."[16] It was declared that the Kentuckian's vote in favor of the tea and coffee tax in 1841 was clear evidence of his hostility to the tariff system, and it was confidently asserted that he would have opposed the act of 1842 had he been in Congress at the time.[17] One of the leading Democratic organs of the state even charged that he had voted against the tariff of 1828.[18] In western Pennsylvania, the opposition revived, with considerable effect, a letter written by Harmar Denny at the time of the Compromise, in which that ardent Whig protectionist declared, "Clay has left his Tariff friends and united with Calhoun. The project submitted by Mr. Clay is believed to have previously received the approbation of Mr. Calhoun. Some think it originated with that individual."[19] As further evidence of Clay's convenient political pliability it was pointed out that in 1832 he had strongly opposed the distribution of the proceeds of the public lands as being both unwise and unconstitutional.[20]

The vigor of the Democratic attacks upon Clay in the Keystone State was partially due to certain inherent weaknesses in their own ticket, which made an attack the safest mode of defence. The nomination of James K. Polk and George M. Dallas threw the Democratic leaders of Pennsylvania into a real state of consternation. Their feelings were eloquently summarized by Ingham's exclamatory outburst in a letter to Buchanan, "James K. Polk President U. S.!!!!!!!!!!!!!!!!!!!!!!!!!!!!!"[21]. The nomination of Dallas, although he was a Pennsylvanian, was equally unpalatable to the dominant Buchanan wing of the Democratic party in the state.[22]

Polk's great weakness lay in his clearly defined record as an anti-

---

[16] November 1, 1844.
[17] *Pittsburgh Post*, August 10, 15, 1844.
[18] *Harrisburg Democratic Union*, August 7, 1844.
[19] *Pittsburgh Post*, August 24, 1844.
[20] *Harrisburg Democratic Union*, November 29, 1843; April 13, 1844. For Clay's early views upon the subject of distribution see his *Works*, IV, 315; *Cong. Debates*, 22 Cong., 1 Sess., p. 70.
[21] S. D. Ingham to Buchanan, June 3, 1844; Buchanan Mss.
[22] J. W. Forney to Buchanan, June 11, 1844; Buchanan Mss.

protectionist. As a member of Congress from 1825 to 1839 he had earnestly supported every proposal for lower duties. That his sentiments had undergone no change was shown by his open letter to the people of Tennessee, written in 1843, during an unsuccessful campaign for governor. Concerning the tariff, Polk had declared in most unmistakable language,

All who have observed my course know that I have at all times been opposed to the "protective policy." I am for laying such moderate duties on imports as will raise revenue enough when added to the income from the sale of lands and other incidental sources to defray the expenses of Government economically administered. I am in favor of a tariff for revenue, and opposed to a tariff for protection. I was a member of Congress during the period that this subject excited greatest interest. I was opposed to the protective tariff of 1828 and voted against it. I voted for the act of 1832 because it reduced the tariff of 1828 to lower rates. That made some reduction though not as much as I desired to have made. I voted for the act of March 2d, 1833 (commonly called the compromise act) which reduced the rates of 1832 to still lower rates. . . By the tariff act of the 30th of August, 1842, the compromise act was violated and repealed. I am opposed to the act of 1842, not regarding it to be a revenue tariff, but in many of its provisions highly protective and oppressive in its character. I am in favor of the restoration of the compromise act of 1833.[23]

A candidate who had recently enunciated such sentiments as these could scarcely be welcome, either to the protectionists of Pennsylvania or to those politicians whose sole hope of victory rested upon protectionist votes.

It is not surprising, therefore, that letters of advice began to pour in upon Polk from Pennsylvania Democrats, urging extreme discretion in his tariff utterances.[24] Dallas suggested that the tariff was a question on which "brevity would be the soul of wit."[25] Muhlenberg, the Democratic candidate for governor in Pennsylvania, urged Polk to be

cautious and prudent in regard to it, as it is as far as Pennsylvania is concerned, a dangerous one. . . If therefore you could devise some mode of giving us in Pennsylvania some moderate declaration respecting a revenue tarif [sic]

---

[23] *Answers of Ex-Gov. Polk,* p. 21.
[24] It is significant that the Polk Papers in the Library of Congress contain ten letters from Pennsylvania dealing with the tariff for every one which concerns Texas or the Bank.
[25] G. M. Dallas to Polk, June 26, 1844; Polk Mss.

adopted to the wants of the Government embracing the principle of discriminating duties and incidental protection it would do much to give the Whigs a complete Waterloo with us in this state at least. . . . If you cannot give us Pennsylvanians a helping hand in our moderate views you will at least not give us a knockdown blow. A little concession often produces a great good.[26]

The editors of the Pittsburgh *Post* informed Polk that "many Democrats believe that the vote of Pennsylvania depends on what you may be able to say upon the question," and suggested that he issue a tariff declaration couched in the exact phraseology of Clay's Bronson letter.[27] John K. Kane, one of the leaders of the Democratic organization in Philadelphia, hastened to write,

There is but one question on which in some parts of our State we are vulnerable. Pennsylvania has, or imagines she has, tariff interests,—and the timidity of some of our Statesmen, who ought to have led opinion to the right track, has made the subject one on which even our party sentiment is unsound. Will you pardon me for saying that a dignified reserve on this topic, such reserve as characterized the language of Gen. Jackson when a candidate will assist us in our canvass.[28]

Several correspondents deemed it necessary to warn Polk that Pennsylvania Whigs disguised as Democrats were attempting to draw him into incautious tariff utterances which might be used to his detriment.[29] Concerning Texas, slavery, and the tariff, Fornance wrote to one of Polk's political advisers,

I do most seriously and solemnly protest against any long, wishy-washy, milk and water epistles on these or any of these questions. His friends here are willing to go it blind, and as to our enemies it is none of their business. . . The time is now so short that I think he can or may avoid answering those questions at all, but if he is compel'd to answer, I hope each question will be answered in a single sentence.[30]

Even Robert J. Walker added his word of warning that in Pennsylvania the tariff question was "irresistible." He declared that Polk's

---

[26] H. A. Muhlenberg to Polk, June 3, 1844; Polk Mss.

[27] Phillips & Smith to Polk, June 7, 1844; Polk Mss.

[28] J. K. Kane to Polk, May 30, 1844; Polk Mss. It was in reply to this communication that Polk wrote the much-discussed exposition of his tariff views known as the Kane letter.

[29] Wm. Riley to Polk, July 31, 1844; I. G. McKinley to Polk, August 17, 1844; Polk Mss.

[30] J. Fornance to A. V. Brown, May 31, 1844; Polk Mss.

further silence upon the subject would defeat the Democratic ticket in that state, and suggested a rather ambiguous formula in favor of "fair and reasonable" incidental protection.[31] Before Walker's letter was received, however, Polk had written his important letter to John K. Kane of Philadelphia, which was destined to constitute his sole tariff utterance of the campaign.

The Democratic candidate realized early in the struggle that he could not long avoid an expression of opinion upon the tariff, and he observed that while "I shall answer frankly and independently I shall desire to do so prudently."[32] Hoping, therefore, to forestall embarrassing interrogations, he wrote, on June 19, the Kane letter, in which he declared,

I am for a tariff for revenue, such an one as will yield a sufficient amount to the Treasury to defray the expenses of the Government economically administered. In adjusting the details of a revenue tariff, I have heretofore sanctioned such moderate discriminating duties as would produce the amount of revenue needed, and at the same time afford reasonable incidental protection to our home industry. I am opposed to a tariff for protection merely and not for revenue. Acting upon these general principles it is well known that I gave my support to the policy of Gen'l Jackson's administration on this subject. I voted against the tariff of 1828. I voted for the act of 1832, which contained modifications of some of the objectionable provisions of the act of 1828. As a member of the Committee of Ways and Means of the House of Representatives I gave my assent to a Bill reported by that Committee in December 1832, making further modifications of the act of 1828, and making also discriminations in the imposition of the duties which it imposed. That bill did not pass, but was superseded by the Bill commonly called the Compromise Bill, for which I voted.[33]

In my judgment it is the duty of the Government to extend, as far as it may be practicable to do so, by its revenue laws and all other means within its power, fair and just protection to all the great interests of the whole

---

[31] R. J. Walker to Polk, June 18, 1844; Polk Mss.

[32] Polk to C. Johnson, June 8, 1844. Reprinted in *Letters of James K. Polk to Cave Johnson*, 1833-1848.

[33] The rough draft among the Polk Papers in the Library of Congress shows that at this point Polk had originally written and then crossed out the following sentence: "My opinions upon the subject of the tariff have undergone no change." The alteration is significant. Had this sentence been included in the letter as published it would have been much more difficult for Pennsylvania Democrats to depict Polk as a friend of the tariff of 1842. This is evidently one point at which the Democratic candidate chose to reply "prudently" as well as "frankly and independently."

Union, embracing agriculture, manufactures, the mechanic arts, commerce and navigation. I heartily approve the Resolutions upon the subject passed by the Democratic National Convention lately assembled at Baltimore.[34]

Polk seems to have doubted the advisability of publishing the letter, but agreed to leave the question to the discretion of Kane, Dallas, and Henry Horn.[35] More mature consideration, however, convinced his political advisers of the unwisdom of such publication, and on July 2 Gideon Pillow wrote, with Polk's approval, asking that the letter should be withheld from the press.[36] Only the day before, however, the *Pennsylvanian* had printed the letter in full, cleverly paralleled with almost identical sentiments taken from a speech delivered by Clay at Raleigh, North Carolina, in April.[37] As the event proved, it was fortunate for Polk that the Kane letter was not recalled; for it is very doubtful whether he could have carried Pennsylvania without it.

The Democratic leaders of Pennsylvania greeted the Kane letter with extreme enthusiasm. Dallas wrote Polk, "Your Tariff letter . . . has given entire satisfaction."[38] Buchanan and Simon Cameron believed that it ensured a Democratic victory in Pennsylvania.[39] Richard Rush characterized it as a "jewel."[40] Wilson McCandless, a prominent Democrat of Pittsburgh, wrote, "After your nomination we dreaded the promulgation of your sentiments on the subject of the Tariff, as exhibited by our adversaries, but your letter to Mr. Kane . . . has satisfied our mechanics and operatives that you are as good a Tariff man as Clay, who by his infamous Compromise bill brought down the duties to a horizontal 20%."[41] Robert J. Walker, representing the Southern wing of the Democratic party, believed that the letter had done much good and that its sentiments "could not be bettered in any way."[42]

Pennsylvania Democrats were equally emphatic, however, that

---

34 Polk to J. K. Kane (rough draft), June 19, 1844; Polk Mss.
35 *Ibid.*
36 G. J. Pillow to H. Horn and J. K. Kane, July 2, 1844; Polk Mss.
37 *Pennsylvanian*, July 1, 1844.
38 G. M. Dallas to Polk, July 6, 1844; Polk Mss.
39 J. K. Kane to Polk, July 2, 1844; Polk Mss.; S. Cameron to Buchanan, July 2, 1844; Buchanan Mss.
40 R. Rush to Polk, July 19, 1844; Polk Mss.
41 W. McCandless to Polk, August 11, 1844; Polk Mss.
42 R. J. Walker to Polk, July 10, 1844; Polk Mss.

Polk must say absolutely nothing further upon the subject of the tariff, lest he destroy the favorable impression which the Kane letter had created. They were especially alarmed by a letter to Buchanan from A. V. Brown, a member of Polk's board of strategy, in which the writer declared,

I know the strength of the Tariff question in your state but suppose Col. Polk to have gone a pretty satisfactory length in his Kane letter and there is no danger of that letter being disturbed. He may be forced to say whether he is for the tariff of 1842—which he must answer in the negative—all his speeches here and his circular letters will compel him to do so. . . Pickens of South Carolina complains a little of the Kane letter but I am corresponding with him on the subject and there is no danger of an audible murmuring about it. You know how hard it is to reconcile those Southern *furiosi* on that subject.[43]

It was perhaps in response to this communication that Buchanan wrote the following emphatic letter:

"For Heaven's sake let our friend the Colonel write nothing more on the subject." His letter to Kane was discreet; and we can get along with it very well. Let him stand upon that; & I think he may rely with confidence on the vote of Pennsylvania. I should very much dread the effect of a declaration under his own hand at the present moment against the Act of 1842; and surely this cannot be necessary to sustain our cause in the South. Both my regard for the Col: & my state pride make it a subject of the deepest interest & feeling to me, that we shall give him the Keystone by a handsome majority. Let us alone and we shall do it—I have a right to speak on this Tariff question, as I expressed a strong opinion myself against portions[44] of the present Tariff & offered to accept the Compromise Act as it stood in 1839. I retain these opinions whilst I am a strong advocate of reasonable discriminations with a view to incidental protection.[45]

Simon Cameron, also, strongly urged against any attempt to elaborate upon the views expressed in the letter to Kane. During the latter part of the campaign, he wrote to Polk,

The tariff question . . . I consider settled in this state for the present. We have succeeded in fixing the belief that you "are as good a tariff man as Clay." Your

---

[43] A. V. Brown to Buchanan, August 22, 1844; Buchanan Mss.

[44] The rough draft of this letter in the Buchanan papers shows that Buchanan had originally written "the extravagances" and then with characteristic caution substituted the less revealing word, "portions".

[45] Buchanan to ————— (rough draft), September 6, 1844; Buchanan Mss. The letter is also printed in Buchanan, *Works*, VI, 70.

letter to Kane was well done—but if you had written one more . . . you would never have touched bottom here. No man can get the state believed to be opposed to a protective tariff. But "sufficient for the day is the evil thereof." I look to your elevation as a means of preserving the great principles of the democratic party in their purity.[46]

Polk heeded these admonitions from Pennsylvania and maintained a studied silence upon the tariff throughout the remainder of the campaign, even in the face of the most persistent pressure from his political adversaries.[47]

Polk's reticence left the Democrats of Pennsylvania free to depict his protectionism in the most alluring colors. Buchanan toured the state, declaring from his personal knowledge of the two candidates that James K. Polk was as good a tariff man as Henry Clay.[48] The Harrisburg *Democratic Union* declared,

*Col. Polk holds the doctrine of Free Trade in unqualified abhorrence.* HE NEVER HAS ADVOCATED IT, AND NEVER WILL. He is in favor of a judicious revenue tariff, affording the amplest incidental PROTECTION TO AMERICAN INDUSTRY. He is the especial friend and advocate of the COAL AND IRON INTEREST, those two great objects of solicitude with Pennsylvanians, and believing PERMANENCE in our laws to be of incalculable value, *is opposed to the disturbance of the existing tariff.* These facts we state upon *the very best authority.*[49]

As evidence that Polk was as good a protectionist as Clay, it was pointed out that *"neither* James K. Polk *nor* Henry Clay voted for the Tariff of 1828; that *both* of them voted for the tariff of 1832; that *both* of them voted for the compromise act of 1833, which continued in operation until the 30th of June, 1842; and that *both* of

---

[46] S. Cameron to Polk, October 18, 1844; Polk Mss.

[47] Polk's greatest difficulty arose during the latter part of September, when a meeting at Pulaski, Tennessee, addressed a series of tariff questions to him, which were so specific in character that it would be very difficult to give an evasive answer. (The questions appear in *Niles' Register,* LXVII, 125). Polk and his advisers felt that some sort of a response must be made. Several laborious drafts in the Polk papers testify to his earnest endeavor to give the semblance of a reply without committing himself upon the question. In general, these tentative replies took the ground that his public record was too well known to require further discussion and that his tariff views were already adequately expressed in the Kane letter. Finally, in despair, Polk abandoned the attempt and fell back upon a shallow pretext to justify his refusal to return any answer.

[48] Buchanan to ———, July 13, 1846; Buchanan Mss.; *Cong. Globe,* 29 Cong., 1 Sess., App., p. 716; *Pennsylvanian,* July 15, 1846.

[49] *Harrisburg Democratic Union,* June 5, 1844.

them had left Congress before the present tariff act was passed."[50]
The assertion was even made that "although James K. Polk has not
talked so much about a Tariff as Henry Clay, he has done more
for a Tariff than Henry Clay has done."[51] Polk's adherents also
derived considerable satisfaction from a letter written by Wilson
McCandless to the Democrats of Clarion county, which predicted
that Clay, if elected, would give the tariff of 1842 "the same *support*
that the rope does the hanging man—instant death, and 'without
benefit of clergy'."[52]

As election day approached, the Democratic leaders made a definite effort to divert public attention from the tariff question to the
bank. Buchanan appears to have been the originator of this
maneuver, which was vigorously pushed both from the platform
and in the press.[53] The *Pennsylvanian* observed, "The Whigs may
prate about a tariff to their hearts content; but the people are not
to be deceived. They have been taught from experience that the
issue is Bank or no Bank."[54] Elsewhere, speaking of the Whigs,
the editor declared, "Is not all their zeal for the *Tariff* a mere cloak
to cover their secret object—a UNITED STATES BANK? Is not
that what they want from Mr. Clay?—that which again and again
prostrated the whole industry of the country when it had the
*highest tariffs*."[55] This attempt to invoke the spirit of political
Jacksonism in behalf of Polk appears to have had little real effect; to
the very end of the campaign, the Democrats were forced by their
opponents to devote their major attention to the tariff issue.

The Whigs, meanwhile, welcomed an excuse to turn from a rather
forced glorification of Clay's dubious tariff record to a whole-
hearted assault upon the protectionist professions of the Democratic
candidate. The Kane letter, in particular, was subject to the most

---

[50] *Ibid.* August 7, 1844. This specious argument is an excellent example of a
truth which is only a half-truth. It conceals the important difference that Polk
actually voted against the act of 1828; while Clay, as Secretary of State, had no
chance to express himself. Had he enjoyed a vote, it probably would have been
cast in the affirmative. Both Kentucky Senators actually did vote for the measure, which carried a high duty on hemp.

[51] *Pennsylvanian*, August 30, 1844.

[52] *Cong. Globe*, 29 Cong., 1 Sess., App., p. 716.

[53] C. J. Ingersoll to Buchanan, September 20, 1844; G. Plitt to Buchanan, September 22, 1844; Buchanan Mss.

[54] *Pennsylvanian*, October 4, 1844.

[55] *Ibid.* October 3, 1844.

unmeasured denunciation. An indignant editor declared, "We do not believe that the popular mind as a whole is so thoroughly stultified as not to see through the abominable duplicity of which both Mr. Polk and his influential friends and organs are guilty as regards the Protective Policy. It is a game utterly inconsistent with common honesty or gentlemanly honor."[56] Wide publicity was given to a letter from Governor Jones of Tennessee, who asserted,

I can but regard the effort that is making in your state to pass James K. Polk off as the friend and advocate of Protection as an outrage, which for impudence and falsehood is unparalleled in the history of party warfare. . . Col. Polk can not, will not, dare not deny that he has always opposed the protective policy. . . Col. Polk at all times during both of my canvasses with him, opposed, denounced, and condemned the principle of protection, and during the last campaign, the tariff of 1842 received his most unqualified condemnation.[57]

Governor Letcher of Kentucky wrote Buchanan, "You owe it to your own Tariff principles, to your state, to your country, to your own character, not to engage in the dirty job of trying to elect such an *affair* as Polk to the greatest office in the world."[58] As to Polk's attitude upon protection, Letcher declared, "The idea of his being a tariff man is very provoking."[59]

According to the Whigs, the issue of the campaign was clearly and distinctly drawn between "Henry Clay, as a friend, and James

---

[56] *North American,* August 10, 1844.

[57] *Niles' Register,* LXVII, 125.

[58] R. Letcher to Buchanan, July 27, 1844; Buchanan Mss.

[59] *Ibid.* August 3, 1844. Concerning the alleged duplicity of the Kane letter, Prof. McCormac writes, "It was said that Polk in drafting his letter made a definite attempt to face both ways—that his emphasis on incidental protection was for the North while the substance was for the South. But if the tariff Democrats were in any sense deluded, it must have resulted from a meaning which they had read into the letter, for, as Polk had pointed out in the letter itself, his present views were to be found in his own record, the record of his party and the declarations that had been adopted at the Baltimore convention. In such a statement there was nothing equivocal—nothing to which a protectionist had reason to pin his hopes." (*James K. Polk,* p. 261). This is, perhaps, an unduly charitable interpretation. As compared with Polk's previous utterances during the campaign for governor in 1843 and his subsequent declarations as President, the Kane letter seems very equivocal and evasive. That it was intentionally so is shown by the important elision which Polk made in the original draft (see p. 161n, *supra*) and in his most circumspect handling of the Pulaski county interrogations (see p. 164n, *supra*). The impression persists that the Kane letter was designed not to elucidate but to conceal the writer's exact views upon the tariff in the hope of conciliating Northern protectionists.

K. Polk, as an enemy of the Tariff of 1842."[60] The protectionists
of the state were exhorted to choose between "Texas and No Tariff,
or Tariff and No Texas."[61] It was asserted that-

> If it is possible for the Loco Foco party to triumph, we may rest assured that
> whatever is dearest to Pennsylvania will be ruthlessly sacrificed. No avail will
> be her native wealth, the industry and enterprise of her inhabitants. Foreign
> competition to her infant manufactures will break them down, and she may
> become tributary to England for the articles in which reasonable protection
> would soon place her beyond injury from any rival. . . The manufacturer and
> mechanic need not be told that the annihilation of the present tariff is the grand
> end of Mr. Polk and his party. He has declared uncompromising hostility to it,
> and the first recommendation of his Executive life would be the repeal of the
> act on which the whole manufacturing system of the country rests.[62]

The gubernatorial election, which took place on October 8, had
been generally anticipated by both parties as an effective measure
of public sentiment upon the presidential question. The Whig
candidate was Joseph Markle, concerning whose political views little
was known. Henry A. Muhlenberg, the original Democratic nominee, died in the midst of the campaign and his place was taken by
Francis R. Shunk. In each case, the actual tariff views of the candidate seem to have received slight consideration; for all three were
indiscriminately denounced by the opposition as free traders and
foes of domestic industry. This was strikingly illustrated in the
case of Muhlenberg, who was repeatedly characterized as an anti-
protectionist by the Whigs, in spite of the fact that in Congress he
had voted against Clay's Compromise measure.[63] Shunk, as Muhlenberg's political legatee, inherited the stigmatization.[64] Nevertheless,
after Shunk had carried the state by a plurality of 4,282 votes,[65]
the Whigs sought to minimize the significance of the defeat by
declaring that he was an excellent tariff man and that Polk, as a free
trader, could not hope to share his popularity.[66]

The Democrats derived considerable political capital from the
results of the election in the first congressional district. The Whig

[60] *North American,* October 18, 1844.
[61] *Ibid.* June 3, 1844.
[62] *Ibid.* September 24, 1844.
[63] *Harrisburg Democratic Union,* July 3, 1844.
[64] *Old Warrior.* August 31, 1844.
[65] *Smull's Legislative Handbook,* 1921-22, p. 745.
[66] *North American,* October, 9, 18, 1844.

candidate was Edward Joy Morris, running for reelection after having established a reputation as one of the most active protectionists in the House of Representatives. Morris was opposed by George Lehman, Democrat, and Lewis Levin, nominated by the newly-organized Native American party. In order to obtain Native American votes for Markle, the Whig politicians agreed to abandon their candidate and throw their votes to Levin. As a result, Levin was elected, while Morris ran a poor third.[67] The Democrats enthusiastically seized upon the episode as conclusive evidence of the Whigs' hypocrisy upon the tariff question. In the words of one editor,

Nothing could better serve to expose the emptiness of whig professions of love for the tariff, than their desertion of E. Joy Morris in the first Congressional district. No man in Congress has exerted himself with more zeal for the tariff than Mr. Morris. He was the acknowledged Napoleon of the tariff forces; and yet to consummate a bargain with a third party, they basely deserted him at the last hour, for the support of a man, of whose opinions on the tariff question they knew literally nothing. . . They sat down and deliberately bargained away their *Congressmen who alone can make a tariff* in order to get votes for their Gubernatorial candidate, who could not, if elected, exercise the smallest kind of influence, one way or another! In a twinkling of an eye, the vaunted tariff, the "laboring man's bread" goes by the board, for the sake of adding a few votes to Markle for Governor.[68]

The Democratic victory in the state election, while encouraging to the party leaders, was not sufficiently decisive to warrant any relaxation of effort. Close observers noted a decline from the normal Democratic vote in some of the iron counties.[69] Kane felt it necessary to warn Polk that "we may lose somewhat in Allegheny, Centre and Huntingdon from the more direct bearing of the tariff question. . .The same remark is true of Montgomery at this end of the state, of Cumberland in the East middle, and of some others."[70] To curb this tendency, the Democrats gave wide publicity to the fact that Polk, while in the Tennessee legislature, had voted for liberal land grants to the iron manufacturers of the state.[71]

---

[67] *Ibid.* October 12, 1844.
[68] *Harrisburg Democratic Union*, October 12, 23, 1844.
[69] C. J. Ingersoll to Polk, October 15, 1844; Polk Mss.
[70] J. K. Kane to Polk, October 31, 1844; Polk Mss.
[71] *Pittsburgh Post,* October 26, 1844.

Corruption charges played an important part in the closing weeks of the campaign. The Whigs claimed that British manufacturers had subscribed a fund of $500,000 to help elect Polk and thus break down the tariff of 1842.[72] The Democrats cheerfully admitted the sum and the source, but declared that the money was being contributed to put over Clay and the assumption of the state debts.[73] It was likewise claimed that "more than $100,000 has been raised by the great Bank and Tariff aristocracy of Boston, New York and Philadelphia to crush the sturdy Democracy of Pennsylvania."[74] Charges were also circulated after the election that the Whig iron-masters of the state had compelled their employees to vote for Clay under threat of dismissal.[75] Clay's friends, on the other hand, countered with the assertion that but for the election frauds of the Democrats, he would have enjoyed a legal majority in Pennsylvania.[76]

The election returns gave Polk a plurality of 6,322 votes over Clay, with Birney, the Liberty party candidate, polling a negligible vote.[77] As compared with the preceding presidential election, the Democrats showed absolutely no loss of strength even in those regions where tariff sentiment was supposed to be strongest. Over one-half of Polk's plurality, for instance, was furnished by the four anthracite counties of the state; while in many of the iron counties, even in Allegheny, he made a better showing than had Van Buren four years previously.[78] Nevertheless, Buchanan believed that if

---

[72] *Miners' Journal,* September 21, October 26, 1844.

[73] *Harrisburg Democratic Union,* September 25, 1844.

[74] A. Beaumont to Polk, October 23, 1844; Polk Mss.

[75] A. Best to Polk, November 2, 1844; Polk Mss.; *Harrisburg Democratic Union,* November 6, 1844; *Pennsylvanian,* November 15, 1844.

[76] Clay, *Works,* II, 434-436, 447.

[77] *Smull's Legislative Handbook,* 1921-22, p. 740. Even the anti-slavery candidate had found it advisable to face both ways upon the tariff question in Pennsylvania. His views were set forth in a letter to a friend in Pittsburgh, in which, after advocating free trade as a theory, he continued, "Were I now a member of Congress, I should oppose the repeal of the present tariff before it was fairly and fully tried. If it should be found to work well for the country . . . I should continue my support. In this case, my theory would be proved false by facts—against which no theory ought to be maintained. But should it work ill for the country . . . I should favor its reduction to the revenue standard—but so gradually that all the interests involved in it might, in the highest possible degree be saved from loss." (*Old Warrior,* October 13, 1844).

[78] *Harrisburg Reporter,* November 13, 1840; *Carlisle American Volunteer,* November 28, 1844.

the tariff question could have been completely eliminated, Polk's majority would have reached 25,000.[79]

The Whigs, meanwhile, were heaping redoubled vituperation upon the Kane letter as the most apparent cause of their political downfall. Vehemently, the editor of the *North American* declared, "To say that the people of Pennsylvania have been 'humbugged' by Loco foco demagogues on the subject of the Tariff would be to express in the mildest language our opinion of an infamous fraud practiced against their most vital interests."[80] Another journal asserted that Polk's victory had made Pennsylvania "a laughing stock to every Southern free-trader as the Tariff State which voted for free trade."[81]

It would be a mistake, however, to interpret Clay's defeat as a plebiscite of any kind upon the policy of protection. Actually, many other factors contributed to the defeat of the Whigs. As a suspected practitioner of "bargain and corruption," Clay was anathema to the still loyal Jacksonians of Pennsylvania. As a duelist and gambler, he was offensive to the ever-powerful religious element of the state. As a member of the Masonic order, he was objectionable to the former Anti-Masons within his own party. As the friend of a national bank, he was unacceptable to all those who yet treasured the economic precepts of Andrew Jackson. Moreover, the close cooperation between the Whigs and Native Americans during the presidential campaign served to alienate what Roman Catholic support Clay might otherwise have enjoyed.

These obvious points of weakness account for the eagerness of the Whigs to make the tariff the one great issue of the campaign. Even this attempt, however, involved serious difficulties. If Clay was the "Father of the American System," he could likewise claim paternity of the odious Compromise of 1833, which many Pennsylvanians believed to have ruined their commonwealth. Men who had cursed Clay in 1833 as an apostate and a free trader could not be convinced in the course of a brief campaign that the Kentuckian was indeed "a better tariff man than James K. Polk," who, whatever his faults, had never struck the protectionist flag in the very face of the enemy. Nor were Clay's more recent tariff utterances, espe-

---

79 Buchanan, *Works,* VI, 74.

80 *North American,* November 13, 1844.

81 *Pittsburgh Gazette,* November 5, 1844.

cially those designed for Southern ears, likely to allay the suspicion created by the Compromise Act. Moreover, the force of the Whig argument was greatly weakened by the fact that the act of 1842 had scarcely wrought the economic miracles predicted for it. Although a considerable expansion had taken place in the iron industry, there had been no material increase either in prices or in wages.[82] The average price of anthracite coal at Philadelphia had dropped from $5.79 per ton in 1841 to $3.20 in 1844; while miners' wages had fallen almost as rapidly.[83] Agricultural products, likewise, were selling at far lower quotations than had prevailed before the passage of the tariff of 1842.[84] As a result, the "home market" argument of the Whigs failed to arouse the customary protectionist enthusiasm among the farmers of the state.[85] For all these reasons, Clay's tariff appeal failed to attract enough converts to overturn the normal Democratic majority in Pennsylvania. It is altogether certain, however, that had the electorate foreseen the impending overthrow of the tariff of 1842, the verdict at the polls would have been very different. As Governor Porter, himself a Democrat, declared two months after the election, "I hazard nothing in asserting that neither of the presidential candidates could have hoped, for a moment, to get a majority of the votes in this state, had not his claims been based upon the assurance that he was friendly to the continuance of the present tariff laws, substantially as they stand."[86]

---

[82] *House Exec. Doc.*, 38 Cong., 1 Sess., No. 2, pp. 316-322; *Sen. Rep.* 52 Cong., 2 Sess., Vol. III, pt. 1, pp. 181, 183; pt. 4, pp. 1562-64, 1570; Swank, *Iron in All Ages*, p. 514.

[83] *Sen. Rep.*, 52 Cong., 2 Sess., Vol. III, pt. 1, 181; pt. 4, p. 1561; Swank, *Statistical Abstract*, p. 22.

[84] *House Exec. Doc.*, 29 Cong., 1 Sess., No. 6, p. 515; 34 Cong., 1 Sess., No. 2, pp. 83-85; *Sen. Rep.*, 52 Cong., 2 Sess., Vol. III, pt. 1, p. 107; *Pittsburgh Gazette*, August 29, 1844; *Pittsburgh Post*, February 12, August 29, 30, 1844.

[85] A Pennsylvania correspondent informed Polk that "there is a great change going on among the farmers upon the subject of the present tariff. . . They begin to inquire how it is that in 1841 they got $1.30 per bushel for wheat, while now they get but 80 cents." (J. Bradford to Polk, August 23, 1844; Polk Mss.)

[86] *Pennsylvania Archives*, Fourth Series, VI, 1071.

# CHAPTER IX

FIGHTING THE WALKER TARIFF, 1845-1846

The years covered by the tariff of 1842 represent a period of extremely rapid industrial expansion in Pennsylvania. The iron industry, in particular, enjoyed a remarkable growth, due to a steadily increasing demand, improved methods of production, and the highly protective provisions of the tariff of 1842.[1] The state's output of pig iron apparently more than doubled between 1842 and 1846.[2] From 1843 to 1846, inclusive, 29 anthracite furnaces and 63 charcoal furnaces were built; while only 8 anthracite and 11 charcoal furnaces failed.[3] It was estimated that by 1846 one-third of the total output was anthracite pig iron, which could be produced much more cheaply than the charcoal article.[4] At the same time, rapid progress was being made in some of the more advanced forms of iron manufacture. Pennsylvania's first rolling mill for the production of railroad iron went into operation in 1845 and was quickly followed by several other establishments of a similar nature.[5]

Iron prices, however, responded much more slowly than did production to the quickening tendencies of the period. Even after the passage of the new tariff, quotations upon the Philadelphia market continued to decline until the latter part of 1843. Then an upward trend set in which continued without interruption for several years and which seemed to justify the most enthusiastic predictions of

---

[1] The specific duties imposed by the tariff of 1842 were equivalent on the average to 63 per cent. on pig iron, 80 per cent. on rolled bar, and 34 per cent. on hammered bar. The rates on manufactured iron ran about 60 per cent., although on many items the duty was much higher. As a result, iron imports from 1842 to 1846 were definitely less than during the years immediately preceding and following the period of high duties. (*Sen. Doc.,* 28 Cong., 1 Sess., No. 3, p. 44; 62 Cong., 1 Sess., No. 72, pp. 1450, 1625, 2122; *Sen. Exec. Doc.,* 37 Cong., 2 Sess., No. 2, pp. 254-266).

[2] There are no accurate statistics for Pennsylvania pig iron production during these years. Estimates for 1842 range from 151,885 to 189,856 tons. The figures for 1846 vary between 368,056 and 406,027 tons. (*House Exec. Doc.,* 31 Cong., 1 Sess., No. 4, pp. 809-10; *Hunt's Merchants' Mag.,* XVI, 590; French, *History of the Rise and Progress of the Iron Trade,* p. 73). Grosvenor believes, however, that both estimates for 1846 are much too high. (*Does Protection Protect?,* p. 216).

[3] *Doc. Rel. to the Manu. of Iron in Penna.,* p. 109.

[4] *Hunt's Merchants' Mag.,* XVI, 590.

[5] *Miners' Journal,* April 11, 1846; Swank, *Iron in All Ages,* p. 434.

the protectionists.[6] By 1845, all observers were agreed that the price of pig and bar iron had reached an extremely high and profitable level.[7] One authority, for instance, estimated that

under the present prices there is a profit of ten dollars on each ton of iron manufactured in Pennsylvania. . . From information acquired from iron-masters, we consider the profit of $10 per ton at present prices, at rather less than the actual result. . . Probably in no year in her past history has the business of her citizens been so profitable. The times of '35 and '36 would not compare with the present year. Prices then rose from an expansion of the currency; now from the great and safe law of demand.[8]

The ironmasters also profited from the fact that during the era of rising prices there was no commensurate increase in wages. The workers of the Pittsburgh rolling mills obtained an increase of 15 per cent. as the result of a strike following the great fire of 1845. Wages were also raised, beginning about 1844, in the anthracite furnaces of eastern Pennsylvania. In many establishments, however, no increase was granted in spite of materially augmented prices.[9] Indeed, it was charged that many protectionists who most loudly declaimed in favor of a tariff to aid the American workingman were among the first to turn to cheap foreign labor in order to keep wages at a low level.[10]

This era of rapid development was not altogether an unmixed blessing to the iron industry of Pennsylvania. One ironmaster pointed out that 27 new furnaces were under construction in a single county and warned that the almost inevitable result would be "over production, low prices and ruin."[11] The situation was made more precarious by the fact that so many of the new establishments were charcoal furnaces, doomed to an early and inevitable obsolescence in the fact of cheaper and more efficient manufacturing processes. Such enterprises, called into unnatural existence by the

---

[6] See tables of prices in *House Exec. Doc.*, 38 Cong., 1 Sess., No. 2, pp. 320-328; Swank, *Iron in All Ages*, p. 514; Clark, *History of Manufactures*, III, 387.
[7] Cf. *Pittsburgh Gazette*, May 21, 1845; *Niles' Register*, LXVIII, 234.
[8] *Albany Argus*, quoted in *Niles' Register*, LXIX, 172. See also Calhoun, *Correspondence*, p. 355.
[9] *Sen. Rep.*, 52 Cong., 2 Sess., Vol. III, pt. 4, pp. 1562-64, 1570; *Pittsburgh Gazette*, May 21, 1845.
[10] *Pittsburgh Post*, April 28, May 12, 1843; April 20, 1850.
[11] *House Exec. Doc.*, 29 Cong., 1 Sess., No. 6. p. 516.

tariff, served only to divert capital from more productive channels and contributed nothing to the permanent industrial development of Pennsylvania. Most of them quickly sank into bankruptcy as soon as the repeal of the act of 1842 left them to work out their destinies upon a more strictly competitive basis. For the time being, however, they served to give the iron industry an exaggerated appearance of rapid growth and alluring prosperity.

The coal industry, likewise, enjoyed a remarkable development under the act of 1842. Anthracite production increased from 1,076,649 tons in 1842 to 2,284,659 tons in 1846.[12] This expansion was due in considerable measure to the growing use of anthracite in the iron industry. Another contributing factor was the extension of the Reading railroad to the Schuylkill region in 1841, with a consequent saving in both time and cost of transportation.[13] At the same time, foreign imports were reduced to negligible proportions by the duty of $1.75 per ton. As a result, Pennsylvania coal enjoyed a virtual monopoly all through the eastern portion of the country. Prices were generally low, but this was offset by decreased transportation costs and reduced wages.[14] Employment was steady, however, so that all concerned expressed satisfaction with the existing state of the coal trade. Indeed, C. J. Ingersoll went so far as to suggest in 1843 that American anthracite might profitably invade the European market, and he urged a state appropriation to finance a trial shipment.[15]

The era of industrial expansion, following so closely upon the passage of the new tariff law, greatly strengthened the protectionist movement in Pennsylvania. Many who had previously espoused free trade on theoretical grounds now swung around to a whole-hearted affirmation of tariff principles. The most important convert of this period was Henry Charles Carey of Philadelphia, soon destined to become the nation's outstanding literary exponent of the protectionist policy. Henry C. Carey, the son of Mathew Carey, had been for many years an active partner in his father's publishing business,

12 Pennsylvania Bureau of Statistics of Labor and Agriculture, *Annual Report*, 1872-73, pp. 213-216.
13 *Hunt's Merchants' Mag.*, XXI, 277.
14 *Sen. Rep.*, 52 Cong., 2 Sess., Vol. III, pt. 1, p. 181; pt. 4, p. 1561; Swank, *Statistical Abstract*, p. 22.
15 *Niles' Register*, LXV, 154-156.

but had withdrawn in 1835 in order to devote his entire time to a serious study of economic and social science. The first fruits of these deliberations were presented in several volumes, published between the years 1835 and 1840. Strangely enough, Carey appears in these early works as an implicit believer in free trade, at least in theory. Although he had already developed many of the fundamental conceptions upon which he later reared his edifice of protection, as yet he saw in them only a further justification of the laissez-faire principle. With a most unfilial perversity, he found his closest associates among such free traders as Condy Raguet and Clement C. Biddle and learned his economic precepts at the feet of Say and Adam Smith.[16] In his first published work, he declared,

Had this subject been properly understood, we should long since have seen the end of protective tariffs; but as nothing can be more evident to the unenlightened than the advantage to be derived from making their neighbors pay them high prices, so nothing is more easy than to excite popular feeling in favour of a system of protection; and the same man who would deem absurd such a system in his own family, would advocate its adoption by the large family, termed a nation; as if those principles of trade which were true with regard to ten or twenty persons, could be untrue when applied to twenty thousand or two hundred thousand.[17]

Carey joined with the Manchesterians in deriding "the absurd system of corn laws,"[18] and urged the negotiation of reciprocity treaties as "an improvement upon the old and barbarous system."[19] He asserted that free trade promoted peace, lowered taxation, increased wages, and contributed to the general welfare.[20] He did not advocate, however, that absolute free trade should be established overnight, but he maintained that a gradual reduction of duties (such as that embodied in the Compromise Tariff of 1833) would benefit all and injure none.[21] He believed that the 20 per cent. maximum rates provided by the Compromise Act might very well be made permanent. In 1840, he confidently wrote, "Happily, the question of protection is now settled forever."[22]

---

[16] Elder, *Memoir of Henry C. Carey*, p. 25.
[17] Carey, H., *Essay on the Rate of Wages*, p. 14.
[18] *Ibid.* p. 51.
[19] *Ibid.* p. 134.
[20] *Ibid.* p. 9.
[21] Carey, H., *Principles of Political Economy*, I, 207.
[22] *Ibid.* III, 224.

Carey's free-trade predilections, however, failed to survive the era of industrial activity ushered in by the tariff of 1842. As was to become his habit, Carey ignored all other factors and attributed this progress solely to the beneficent influence of the new tariff. By 1844, he had become convinced that protection was a necessary national policy, but he still was unable to reconcile it with his interpretation of economic theory. Not until 1847 did there flash upon him one morning as he lay in bed the conception of progressive land occupation which enabled him to throw overboard the whole laissez-faire system and to substitute for it an aggressive and unrelenting protectionism. To borrow his own words, "I jumped out of bed and, dressing myself, was a protectionist from that hour."[23]

Carey in later life made no attempt to conceal the fact that he had once deviated from the paths of protectionist orthodoxy. He explained that he had been led into erroneous conclusions by the delusive prosperity in America as a result of the European wars and that closer observation had brought him to a truer understanding of economic principles.[24] Some of his critics, however, attributed his conversion to more selfish motives and made much of the fact that his private investments were such as to give him a heavy stake in the maintenance of the protective policy.[25] Shortly before his conversion, in 1840, he lost a considerable investment in a paper mill which failed because of foreign competition.[26] He was also interested, in 1839, in one of the pioneer experiments in the making of iron with coke. This enterprise (at Karthaus in Clearfield county) was abandoned at the close of the first year because of inadequate transportation facilities.[27] More successful were his investments, from 1835 to 1865, in coal lands. The Carey shaft, sunk near Pottsville in 1852, was the first shaft in the Schuylkill region and disclosed a fifty-one foot thickness of coal—the richest

---

[23] Baird, "Carey and Two of his Recent Critics," *American Philosophical Society, Proceedings*, XXIX, 171.

[24] Carey H., *Principes de la Science Sociale*, p. xvii. See also Carey's letter to Buchanan, January 31, 1850; Buchanan Mss.

[25] The *Pennsylvanian* of October 6, 1860, compares "the free-trade Henry C. Carey, of 1832, who *was not then* the receiver of coal rents, and the tariff Henry C. Carey, of 1860 who *is now* the receiver of coal rents."

[26] Baird, "The Carey-Baird Centenary, January 25, 1885," *American Bookseller*, XVII, 103.

[27] Swank, *Iron in All Ages*, p. 369.

deposits then known.[28] The rents derived from this investment constituted Carey's chief source of income and naturally gave him a
first-hand interest in the state of the coal trade. That he was not
insensible to such considerations is shown by the following letter,
written on January 25, 1837, at a time when he was avowing
strong attachment to the theory of free trade:

I observe that a bill has been introduced into the Senate to repeal the duty
on Coal, and am induced to trouble you with this letter, because I believe
that any interference with that matter at the present moment cannot but be
highly injurious to your state. . . [If we are let alone until 1842] we shall
not care a farthing whether there is a duty upon it or not, but to interfere
with it now will do great harm. . . It would be iniquitous to compel us to
supply coal at free trade prices, when all the articles produced at the North
are burdened with duty. We (I mean my brother and myself) have paid
nearly One Thousand dollars duty upon the iron we have used in the last
year. . . How then can we supply coal at free trade prices? . . . It is difficult
to withhold the expression of one's feelings when the very men who derive
most advantage (If any do derive it) from the tariff system and navigation
laws, are the foremost in the endeavor to break down their neighbors.[29]

Carey, himself, does not seem to have felt that selfish considerations
lay at the root of his protectionism; for he wrote, "I never have
received a dollar, nor will I, as author. . . As I have much to say to
politicians I prefer to be able to say that I am not actuated by any
motive but that of a desire to reach the truth."[30]

Once having brought economic theory and fact into apparent
harmony, Carey hastened to promulgate his epochal discovery. He
completed his *The Past, the Present, and the Future* within three
months and gave it to the world as a confession of faith and a
revelation of hitherto unrecognized reality. Defiantly repudiating
the pessimistic dogmas of the Classicists, he assembled all social
phenomena into one beneficent and harmonious system of natural
law and then, almost without warning, turned the closing chapters
into a climactic justification of the protectionist doctrine. This was
the book which Elder declared to mark "an era in the history of

---

[28] Baird, "The Carey-Baird Centenary, January 25, 1885," *American Bookseller*, XVII, 103; *Pittsburgh Post*, April 14, 1852; *Miners' Journal*, July 3,
1858.
[29] H. C. Carey to G. D. Wall; Gratz Collection.
[30] H. C. Carey to R. W. Griswold, January 25, 1857; Gratz Collection.

political economy, from which it may count its A. U. C., its Hegira, or its Declaration of Independence."[31]

From 1848 until his death, thirty-one years later, Carey's pen was constantly employed in the cause of protection. All of his larger works and some sixty of his pamphlets were concerned primarily or incidentally with the advantages of the restrictive system. For sheer quantity, his writings on the subject exceed those of his father, and they are far more exhaustive in their treatment. He made the newspaper press his willing instrument, and through the ready editorial shears of the period gained a national circulation for his arguments. He was virtually the protectionist editor of the New York *Tribune* from 1850 to 1856 and wrote constantly for the Philadelphia *North American,* the most vehement tariff journal in Pennsylvania. He assisted his friend, John S. Skinner, to establish *The Plough, the Loom, and the Anvil,* a monthly agricultural magazine with protectionist leanings and from 1848 to 1852 contributed to it some of his most elaborate statistical studies. Through constant reiteration and patient exposition he sought not only to make manifest the practical advantages of protection but also to formulate an attractive theoretical basis for the system he espoused.

Carey rested his whole protectionist system upon a categorical denial of Ricardo's historical assumption that in the settlement of new lands the best soils are first cultivated.[32] He held that the first settlers of necessity shunned the rich soils of the river bottoms—with their dense vegetation to be cleared and their miasmic swamps to be drained—and settled upon the open but less fertile hillsides where immediate cultivation was possible. Only as population increased, and with it control over the forces of nature, could the richer and more productive lands be brought under cultivation. With increased population came more perfect social organization, more effective mastery of the machinery of production, and a constantly accelerated conquest over poverty, disease, and ignorance. He scorned the "dismal science" of Malthus and Ricardo, who found a persistent tendency for population to outrun the means of subsistence. His optimistic nature preferred to see in an expanding population a progressive impetus for material and intellectual advance-

---

31 Elder, *Memoir,* p. 26.
32 Carey, H., *Past, Present, and Future,* p. 23.

ment.[33] He affirmed this principle for every nation and for every period of national development. Absolute over-population, he believed, would be averted by the restrictive effect of civilization upon the procreative powers of the race.[34]

Carey believed that a healthy concentration of population could exist only where producer and consumer were located side by side. He compared them to the positive and negative plates of an electric cell which becomes dynamic only when they are brought in proximity.[35] Wherever possible, transportation should be avoided; for transportation was a tax which had to be paid by the producer.[36] The greatest folly of all was to export raw products and import manufactures.[37] Not only did such procedure result in an unfavorable balance of trade with consequent loss of specie,[38] but it also impoverished the land, since the refuse could not be restored in the form of fertilizer.[39] True economic policy, therefore, demanded that factories should be established which would bring the consumers of iron and cotton and food to the side of the producers of those commodities. Thus new markets would be created, the tax of transportation would be eliminated, the essential elements would be restored to the native soil, wealth would accumulate at home, and population would increase.[40]

The protective tariff was of course the rod with which Carey would smite against the rock of national resources to bring forth this beneficent stream. All considerations of revenue should be deliberately ignored in framing the nation's customs laws. To use the tariff as an instrument of indirect taxation he considered as "petty larceny."[41] He believed that the needs of the government should be supplied through direct taxation and that then duties could be raised to a point where they should be really protective.[42] National self-sufficiency was the goal he sought for all nations. So

---

33 *Ibid.* pp. 48, 56, 246; *Unity of Law*, p. 390.
34 Carey, H., *Principles of Social Science*, III, 302, 305.
35 Carey, H., *Unity of Law*, p. 293.
36 Carey, H., *The Plough, the Loom and the Anvil*, IV, 132.
37 Carey, H., *Manufactures, an Evidence and a Measure of Civilization*, p. 6.
38 Carey, H., *Money*, p. 50.
39 Carey, H., *Past, Present, and Future*, p. 299.
40 *Ibid.* p. 103.
41 *Ibid.* p. 464.
42 *Ibid.* p. 468.

far as possible, domestic commerce should be substituted for international trade. Each nation should strive, therefore, to make its
agriculture and industry adequate for all legitimate needs. England
must learn to produce her own food supply and cease her pernicious
strivings to become the industrial monopolist of the world.[43] The
United States, on the other hand, should strive for an industrial
development which would free her people from a humiliating and
costly dependence upon foreign ships and foreign merchants.[44] He
believed that "the road toward perfect peace, perfect union, perfect
freedom of trade, and perfect political independence, lies through
the establishment of perfect industrial independence."[45] As Held has
pointed out, Carey's ideas, if carried to their logical conclusion,
would arrive at something very similar to Fichte's closed commercial state.[46] Carey never specifically carried his system to such an
extreme, but neither did he designate any particular point beyond
which his Chinese wall policy of commercial exclusion should not be
carried.

Protection, according to Carey, was not only the cement by
which producer and consumer should be bound together, but also
might have been the cohesive element which would have united the
nation and averted the Civil War. A consistent protective policy
would have encouraged the establishment of manufactures in the
South and by making the inefficient slave labor unprofitable would
have solved the question through gradual and voluntary emancipa-
tion.[47] Not long before the outbreak of hostilities, he wrote, "Mr.
Calhoun sowed the seeds of sectionalism, abolitionism, and disunion,
on the day on which he planted his free trade tree. . . All have
thriven, and all are now yielding fruit—in exhaustion of the soil
of the older States, and consequent thirst for the acquisition of distant territory; in Kansas murders and Harper's Ferry riots; in
civil and foreign wars."[48] When the conflict came, he hastened to

---

[43] *Ibid.* p. 443; *Harmony of Interests,* p. 67. Henry Carey's writings, like
those of his father, were bitterly vindictive against all things English. The
title of his pamphlet *Commerce, Christianity, and Civilization versus British
Free Trade* speaks for itself.
[44] Carey, H., *Shall We Have Peace?,* p. 6.
[45] *Ibid.* p. 5.
[46] Held, *Carey's Socialwissenschaft und das Merkantilsystem,* p. 164.
[47] Carey, H., *The Slave Trade,* pp. 392-394.
[48] Carey, H., *Financial Crises, their Causes and Effects,* p. 56.

admonish Secretary Chase that "the Union may again be reestablished, but if it be so, it will be as a consequence of the permanent and assured maintenance of the protection policy. . . Let us, on the contrary, return to the free trade policy of 1846, and the day will not then be far distant when the Union will be split up into half a dozen fragments."[49] After the war, he reaffirmed his position, and asserted that if adequate protection had been maintained, "not only should we have had no secession war, but at this hour the South would exhibit a state of society in which the landowners had become rich while their slaves had been gradually becoming free."[50]

The same economic influences which brought Henry C. Carey into the ranks of the protectionists were responsible for the general unwillingness of Pennsylvanians to accept any modification of the tariff of 1842. The strength of this feeling has already been noted in connection with the defeat of the McKay Bill and the presidential campaign of 1844. The twelve months which followed Polk's election were marked by something of a lull in the tariff agitation in Pennsylvania. This was due partly to the distracting influence of the Mexican situation; and partly to the peculiar position in which both parties found themselves upon the question. The Democrats, who had good reason to fear the tariff policy of the new administration, found it expedient to handle the subject with extreme circumspection. Some members of the party bluntly denied that the existing law was in any danger and declared that rumors to that effect originated with speculators seeking to create a "tariff panic."[51] Others deemed it wise to cushion the shock of a possible revision by cautiously finding flaws of detail in the act of 1842.[52] The outstanding leaders of the Democratic party, however, maintained a most discreet silence upon the entire subject. At the same time, the Whigs, as sponsors of the existing duties, were of necessity forced to play a passive role until the opposition committed some overt act. The Pittsburgh *Gazette* seized upon Polk's inaugural message as the opening gun of the attack and declared, "It is now clearly evident to all that nothing can save the Tariff but the neces-

---

[49] H. C. Carey to S. P. Chase, June 19, 1861; Chase Mss.
[50] Carey, H., *Resources of the Union*, p. 17.
[51] *Pittsburgh Post*, November 21, 1844; *Pennsylvanian*, September 2, 1845.
[52] *Pennsylvanian*, November 19, 1844; October 30, 1845.

sities of the country. If we are driven into a war, the Tariff may be preserved."[53] Most of the Whig journals, however, reserved their fire for the main assault, which was expected to come with the convening of the new Congress in December, 1845.

Although popular discussion of the tariff lagged during 1845, the issue was vigorously drawn in the Pennsylvania legislature, where a new United States Senator was to be elected to fill the vacancy created by Buchanan's resignation. The Democrats, who had a majority upon a joint ballot, nominated G. W. Woodward as the party candidate. Simon Cameron, however, had built up a considerable personal following among the Democratic members of the legislature through a judicious distribution of the canal patronage, and had long been laying plans to secure his own election by a coalition of Cameron Democrats, Whigs, and Native Americans.[54] The tariff was seized upon as the only bond sufficiently strong to hold together so unnatural a political alliance. Accordingly, a loud clamor was raised that Woodward was a free trader and a foe of the tariff of 1842, a charge scarcely justified by his own utterances upon the subject.[55] At the same time, a group of Whig members of the legislature addressed a note to Cameron, inquiring as to his views upon the subject of the tariff and distribution. In answer to this interrogation, Cameron wrote,

During the recent Presidential election the Tariff of 1842 was much discussed. The Democratic party of this State took a decided stand in favor of this measure. The leading interests of the State are involved in its preservation. The people, without distinction of party, concur in desiring that its provisions should remain unaltered, and regard any attempt to change them as hazardous to the interests of American industry. Supported by the Democratic party of the State in my views, and feeling the importance of the measure to Pennsylvania, I have no hesitation in declaring that I am in favor

---

[53] March 7, 1845.

[54] McClure, *Old Time Notes*, I, 94; *Address of the Peoples' Club of Philadelphia in favor of Gen. Simon Cameron*, p. 6.

[55] Concerning the tariff, Woodward had declared, "I consider the tariff of '42 a revenue tariff, and I believe it affords, in a judicious manner for the most part, that incidental protection which it is the right of government to give to home interests. No doubt its details will need modification from time to time; but stability in a reasonable tariff policy is what the country most wants and I feel solicitude, therefore, for the maintenance of the general principles and main features of the law of 1842." (*Niles' Register*, LXVIII, 263; *Pennsylvanian*, April 8, June 21, 1845).

of the Tariff of 1842, and if elected to the Senate of the United States I will sustain it without change . . . I am . . . in favor of the distribution of the proceeds of the public lands, and if elected, will support that measure.[56]

Fortified with this declaration, the Cameron leaders whipped unwilling protectionists into line, and on the following day their candidate was elected with the support of forty-four Whigs, sixteen Democrats, and seven Natives.[57] Cameron's triumph, although denounced as party treason by the Democrats, was hailed by the Whig press as a great victory for protection over free trade.[58]

The tense partisan feeling which was injected into the protectionist controversy at this time was further illustrated by the proceedings of the state tariff convention which met at Hollidaysburg on November 12, 1845 with ex-Governor Porter in the chair. The convention was sponsored by the Democratic leaders of the Pittsburgh district, and was designed to influence the Polk administration against any revision of the existing duties. Although the gathering was ostensibly non-partisan, the Democrats were in a large majority, since many Whigs stayed away for fear of political trickery.[59] Those Whigs who were present carried on a constant denunciation of the convention's alleged moderation. They bitterly condemned all attempts to characterize the tariff of 1842 as a revenue measure and asserted that the hypocrisy of the Democrats was manifest in their unwillingness to pledge the delegates "to stand by the Tariff at all hazards, to discriminate by their suffrages and support, in favor of the party and administration, whether of the State or Union which shall assure to the country the fair measure of protection it requires."[60] Undeterred by criticism, the Democratic majority adopted a vigorous set of resolutions, which declared,

Resolved, That the State of Pennsylvania is deeply interested in the maintenance and preservation of the protective policy afforded by the existing Revenue Tariff.

[56] *Address in favor of Gen. Simon Cameron*, p. 8; *Niles' Register*, LXVIII, 132, 264.

[57] Mueller, *Whig Party in Pennsylvania*, p. 116.

[58] *North American*, March 17, 1845; *Pittsburgh Gazette*, March 18, 1845; *Pennsylvanian*, June 21, 1845.

[59] *Pittsburgh Commercial Journal*, October 27, 1845; *Niles' Register*, LXIX, 142.

[60] *Pittsburgh Commercial Journal*, November 17, 1845; *Pennsylvanian*, November 17, 1845; *Miners' Journal*, November 22, 1845.

Resolved, that the people of this state cannot be seduced into abandonment or betrayal of that policy which in the brief period of three years has reanimated the almost desponding energies and restored the prostrate credit of this Commonwealth.

Resolved, That we are opposed to a horizontal or twenty per cent. ad valorem tariff, inasmuch as it neither affords fair, just, nor adequate protection to many of the great interests of the State of Pennsylvania, nor can it afford revenue sufficient to defray the expenses of the government economically administered.

Resolved, That justice and sound policy forbid the Federal Government to repeal, or in any way materially alter or modify the Tariff of 1842, so long as the same yields sufficient revenue to defray the expenses of the government.[61]

The insatiable Whigs, however, characterized these strongly protectionist declarations as "milk-and-water" resolutions, and they proceeded to walk out of the convention hall in well-simulated disgust.[62]

The Polk administration, during the months intervening between the inauguration and the opening of Congress in December, 1845, was careful to drop no hint as to its intended tariff program. Much speculation existed as to the part which Buchanan, as Secretary of State, would play in determining the executive policy. Many friends of the tariff regarded the Pennsylvanian's presence in the cabinet as assurance that the existing duties would not be disturbed. Governor Letcher coupled his congratulations to Buchanan with the admonition, "Keep your eye upon the Secretary of the Treasury."[63] One strongly protectionist paper sought to reassure its readers by declaring,

There is good reason to rely upon Mr. Buchanan's adherence to his professions of regard for Pennsylvania interests. In addition to his public committals during the campaign of 1844, which it is not believed Mr. Buchanan will in any degree falsify, he is held to a common cause with our manufacturers by a direct pecuniary interest. He is one of the owners of Lucinda Furnace in Clarion Co., Pa., an establishment in active operation.[64]

[61] *North American,* November 18, 1845; *Niles' Register,* LXIX, 181.
[62] *Pittsburgh Commercial Journal,* November 27, 1845.
[63] R. P. Letcher to Buchanan, March 12, 1845; Buchanan Mss.
[64] *Pittsburgh Commercial Journal,* December 1, 1845. The Lucinda furnace was of the comparatively inefficient charcoal type, which would be the first to feel the pressure of foreign competition. It was built in 1833 and abandoned about 1857 because of the growing scarcity of timber. (Lesley, *Iron Manufacturer's Guide,* p. 102).

As a result of this feeling, the persistent rumor that Buchanan was about to resign his cabinet position for a place upon the Supreme Court bench caused considerable alarm in protectionist circles. The *North American* asserted that "Pennsylvania will not relieve Mr. Buchanan from his post as guardian of the Tariff."[65] John W. Forney warned him that if he accepted the judicial appointment, he would certainly be accused of having abandoned the interests of his state in order to secure a comfortable position for himself.[66]

Buchanan seems to have used his cabinet position to make a strong, although ineffective, opposition to the drastic reductions favored by the President and his Secretary of the Treasury. On November 1, 1845, Polk submitted to the cabinet the tariff portion of his annual message. Buchanan approved the President's recommendations for the abandonment of the minimum principle and for a general substitution of ad valorem for specific duties, but he strongly urged that specific rates should be retained on certain articles such as iron, coal, and sugar.[67] When the draft of Secretary Walker's celebrated report was presented to the cabinet, Buchanan declared "that it was a strong free trade document, and was in its doctrine opposed to his whole course on the subject during his whole public life."[68] He had already warned Polk that he would not be able to control the Pennsylvania Democrats in Congress if a reduction were attempted, and he predicted that a return to the horizontal ad valorem duty of the Compromise Act would "prostrate the Democracy of the Middle and Northern States in a single year."[69] Dallas, too, had advised Polk that the Democrats should avoid the disruptive tariff issue and seek rather to unite the northern and southern branches of the party by launching an attack against the abolitionist menace.[70]

As the event was to prove, the forebodings of Buchanan and Dallas were fully justified. At the very same time, however, certain Pennsylvania Democrats were furnishing the President with a very different picture of the tariff situation in the Keystone State. Some

---

[65] January 28, 1846.
[66] J. W. Forney to Buchanan, October 30, 1845; Buchanan Mss.
[67] Polk, *Diary*, I, 85.
[68] *Ibid*. p. 94.
[69] *Ibid*. p. 46; Buchanan, *Works*, VI, 74.
[70] G. M. Dallas to Polk, October 16, 1844; Polk Mss.

of the leading Democratic politicians seem to have been lulled into a false security by their victory at the polls in 1844. Immediately after the election, J. K. Kane wrote the President-elect,

Our only real embarrassment has proceeded from the tariff question. Our political guides in this state were to blame for this. They had never met the subject fairly before the people; and when the Convention adjourned, there was no time left for abstract discussion. . . Almost everywhere, we were forced by the manufacturing Interest to argue the policy of *protection,* and I am convinced, that so far as there was danger on that subject, we have encountered it all. Hereafter, with a little more nerve on the part of our leading men, Pennsylvania may be secured against all risk of being divorced by the Tariff from the Democracy of the Union.[71]

At the same time, Henry Horn interpreted Clay's defeat to mean "that the people of Pennsylvania are too enlightened upon the subject to believe in high protective duties when the expenditures of the government does not require them."[72] Simon Cameron, who later became the unrelenting foe of the Walker tariff, pleasantly assured the President, in December, 1845, that "we Pennsylvanians may scratch a little about the tariff but we will not quarrel about it."[73] David Wilmot, during the congressional debates on the act of 1846, expressed regret; that

this restrictive system has not been met in Pennsylvania as it ought to have been. Prominent partisan leaders—those who gave tone and direction to public opinion—who in a great degree moulded the political faith of our people—have shrunk from looking it full in the face. Rather than labor for the reform of abuses, they have found it easier to sanction and promulgate error.[74]

It is very evident that Polk's own predilections led him to accept the views of Kane and Wilmot rather than those of Buchanan and Dallas. On the day of the final passage of the tariff of 1846, the President wrote in his diary,

The Pennsylvania Democracy have been placed in a false position upon this subject. Her public men have not had the moral courage to take bold ground and proclaim the true doctrines to her people. Pennsylvania is essentially an

---

[71] J. K. Kane to Polk, November 4, 1844; Polk Mss.
[72] H. Horn to Polk, November 2, 1844; Polk Mss.
[73] Polk, *Diary,* I, 110.
[74] *Cong. Globe,* 29 Cong., 1 Sess., App. p. 771.

agricultural state & as a community cannot be interested in imposing enormous taxes on the many for the benefit of the few. I do not doubt that Pennsylvania will continue to be democratic if her public men and presses shall have the independence and moral courage to avow the truth as they know it to exist.[75]

This feeling undoubtedly made Polk less willing than he might otherwise have been to listen to Pennsylvania's demands for preferred treatment in framing the provisions of the Walker tariff.

The Administration's tariff policy was very clearly defined in the President's annual message in December, 1845, and in Secretary Walker's report which accompanied it. Both documents were frankly anti-protectionist in spirit. It was recommended that the existing duties should be drastically reduced so that no single rate should exceed the maximum revenue standard. Only within that limit was incidental protection desirable. It was further recommended that all minimum valuations and all specific duties should be abolished and replaced with strictly ad valorem rates. More specifically, Secretary Walker asserted that on most articles 20 per cent. would represent a fair maximum revenue standard.[76] As was to be expected, Polk's message and Walker's report met with a storm of protest from Pennsylvania protectionists. One paper declared, "Let the honest Loco Focos who voted for Polk under the belief that he would support the Tariff read the message and weep."[77] Another journal observed, "It is and must be a poignant and mortifying reflection that the shaft which quivers in the heart of Pennsylvania is plumed with her own feathers."[78] It was asserted that the publication of the Walker report had resulted in a marked decline in the iron trade.[79] One Whig editor exclaimed, "Let Congress adjourn! That is the universal feeling of our people of all parties. If Congress were suddenly to be dispersed by an earthquake (not that we wish the least personal injury to any of its members) it would prove a blessing to our country."[80] It was freely asserted that the tariff was being offered up as a sacrifice to Great Britain to placate her upon the subject of

[75] Polk, *Diary*, II, 55.
[76] Richardson, *Messages and Papers of the Presidents*, IV, 403-406; *Sen. Doc.*, 62 Cong., 1 Sess., No. 71, pp. 8-24.
[77] *Harrisburg Telegraph*, December 3, 1845.
[78] *North American*, December 4, 1845.
[79] *Harrisburg Democratic Union*, December 31, 1845.
[80] *Harrisburg Telegraph*, January 10, 1846.

Oregon, and it was seriously questioned whether actual war would not constitute the lesser evil.[81]

The Administration pronouncement produced an interesting clash of tariff and politics in the Pennsylvania legislature. The state Senate adopted by unanimous vote a set of resolutions instructing the Senators and requesting the Representatives "to oppose all attempts to alter or modify" the existing tariff act.[82] The Democrats of the House, however, perhaps acting under instructions from Washington, attempted to drive the Whigs into opposition by adding a clause against the distribution policy, against a national bank, and in favor of a subtreasury.[83] The Whigs defeated this maneuver by the simple expedient of refusing to vote on the question of final passage and leaving the Democrats to adopt the amended resolutions without opposition.[84] The only sincere objection to the tariff resolutions came from the representatives of Bradford and Tioga counties, which, located in the remote northeastern portion of the state and interested chiefly in lumbering, constituted the last free-trade stronghold in Pennsylvania.[85]

The first outbreak of protectionist indignation against the Administration was followed by a period of comparative quiet; while the country awaited the tariff bill being drafted by the Committee on Ways and Means. This measure, as reported to the House, clearly reflected the views of President Polk and Secretary Walker. It abolished all minimum valuations and all specific duties and replaced them with a comprehensive ad valorem classification. The 30 per cent. schedule contained most of the products in which Pennsylvania was particularly interested—iron and its manufactures, wool and woolens, coal, leather, paper and glass. On coal and iron, especially, this meant a very drastic reduction from the existing duties.[86]

---

[81] Polk, *Diary*, I, 261; *North American*, January 24, 1846; *Harrisburg Telegraph*, February 28, 1846; *Pittsburgh Commercial Journal*, January 28, February 25, 1846.

[82] *Pamphlet Laws*, 1846, p. 511; *Senate Journal*, I, 58.

[83] *Harrisburg Telegraph*, January 21, 1846; *Miners' Journal*, February 28, 1846. One of the Democratic leaders in the House wrote Buchanan, "We have Tariff Resolutions also, instructing for the Act of 1842. This we are competent to fix." (V. E. Piollet to Buchanan, January 7, 1846; Buchanan Mss.)

[84] *House Journal*, 1846, I, 184, 185.

[85] *Harrisburg Telegraph*, January 28, February 11, 1846.

[86] *House Exec. Doc.*, 29 Cong., 1 Sess., No. 6, p. 63; *Miners' Journal*, February 14, 1846; *Harrisburg Telegraph*, October 28, 1846.

With the single exception of David Wilmot, who represented the free-trade Bradford-Tioga-Susquehanna district, the Pennsylvania delegation rose as one man to denounce the proposed reduction. Several of the members sponsored an exhibition of American manufactures designed to impress their fellow legislators with the advances made by domestic industry under the tariff of 1842.[87] Stewart, who took a leading part in the debate, declared that Secretary Walker's project to increase the revenue by lowering the tariff was "the greatest absurdity that ever entered into the imagination of man."[88] Another speaker asserted that if the bill passed, the ensuing ruin would compel Pennsylvania to repudiate her state debt.[89] The Whig members were loud in their denunciation of Polk and Buchanan and the Kane "fraud", and they freely predicted that the enactment of the proposed bill would result in the permanent overthrow of the Democratic party in the Keystone State.[90]

The Democratic members of the delegation naturally were more reserved than the Whigs in their criticism of the Administration's policy. Nevertheless, with the exception of Wilmot, they left no doubt as to their opposition to the bill, and they even refused to attend the party caucus where the subject of the tariff was under discussion.[91] Concerning the attitude of the Pennsylvania Democracy, Brodhead asserted,

We occupy the same position on this question of the tariff which was occupied by Jefferson, Madison, Monroe, and Jackson, the same position which we have occupied since the organization of the Government, and we are not now to be driven from it; and I advise those who desire to obtain or retain political power to take heed how they trifle with the industrial pursuits of the people of that great State.[92]

---

[87] *Niles' Register*, LXX, 51; *Miners' Journal*, June 6, 1846. Polk, at least, was not particularly impressed by this exhibition. He concluded from the wealth and skill which were represented there that American manufacturers were strong enough to stand upon their own resources instead of relying upon the bounty of the government. (Polk, *Diary*, I, 421.)

[88] *Cong. Globe*, 29 Cong., 1 Sess., App., p. 938.

[89] *Ibid.* App., p. 1005.

[90] *Cong. Globe*, 29 Cong., 1 Sess., App., pp. 712, 716, 726, 1005. Henry Clay, writing to Stewart while the bill was before the House, instructed him to "give my respects to some of our Democratic friends in the Pennsylvania delegation, and ask them whether they *now* think that the President is a better tariff man than I am." (Stewart, *Speeches*, p. 71.)

[91] *Niles' Register*, LXX, 224.

[92] *Cong. Globe*, 29 Cong., 1 Sess., App., p. 979.

The Administration seems to have been rather disturbed by the attitude of the Pennsylvania Democrats and apparently was willing to make certain concessions in regard to iron and coal if they would agree to vote for the Walker bill. Wilmot later declared,

I am of the firm belief, that if six democrats from Pennsylvania would have acted with me, instead of adhering immovably to the act of 1842, our State would have obtained all that reasonably could have been asked, and her great interests placed on a satisfactory and permanent basis. In the early stages of the bill, before its friends had counted and marshaled their forces, we could, in my judgment have secured adequate *specific* duties. In this I may be mistaken, but think not. It is certain that we could have obtained 50 per cent. ad valorem. Even in the latter stages of the bill, and when its passage was certain without any of our votes, so anxious were its friends to secure Pennsylvania's support (from party considerations) that McKay, who had charge of the bill as chairman of the Committee of Ways and Means offered to move 40 per cent. on iron if half the democrats from our state would then vote for the bill. It always seemed to me strange when the passage of the bill was certain, that our men would not make sure of all they could get. They, however, were pledged to the tariff of 1842, and it was easier to stand by their pledges than to explain to their constituents the reason for a departure from them.[93]

Wilmot's own attitude toward the tariff of 1846 is puzzling, to say the least. He had been elected by a free-trade constituency upon a definite pledge to work for a modification of the act of 1842. Yet his principal speech, delivered on July 1, contains the most curious inconsistencies. In the first few paragraphs he seeks to demolish the protective principle in theory and in fact; by the middle of the speech he has become a "protectionist within the revenue standard;" and he concludes the address with a plea for "at least" 40 per cent. protection for Pennsylvania coal and iron. The following excerpts will serve to indicate the decidedly evolutionary nature of Wilmot's discourse:

It is said by the protectionists that the "industry of the country" must be protected. This claptrap phrase, together with others, such as "home markets,"

---

[93] Quoted in Going, *David Wilmot,* pp. 92-93. See also *Cong. Globe,* 29 Cong., 1 Sess., App., p. 771. Wilmot's views were probably over-optimistic. Polk was personally opposed to any kind of specific duties. (Polk, *Diary,* I, 267). Moreover, subsequent attempts at compromise in the Senate indicate that although the Administration might have been willing to make ad valorem concessions on iron and coal, the Southern extremists showed no disposition to yield. See also J. S. Yost to Coryell, November 14, 1846; Coryell Mss.

protection against pauper labor, etc., have lost their power over intelligent and reflecting men. Is that protection to the interests of the country which levies contributions upon nine-tenths of its labor to build up a favored and privileged class. . .

Sir, I am in favor of protection. I here avow myself a protectionist in the highest and truest sense of the word. I demand protection for labor against the cruel exactions of capital. I demand protection for the equal rights of the people, against a privileged and monopolizing class, upheld and sustained by partial legislation. I claim protection for the hard earnings of the poor against an insidious system that plunders by stealth, and eats out his substance. . . Yet, under the thin and flimsy disguise of protection to American labor, such a policy is attempted to be fastened upon the country. I will war against it while I have breath. . .

Labor is best protected when its productions are allowed to seek their natural and best markets, purchasing in return where it can buy cheapest. . . In my judgment, this restrictive policy is ruinous to the labor and industry of the country, and if persisted in will, in a brief time, paralyze the great agricultural and planting interests. . .

I am in favor of a tariff for revenue; of an equal, just and constitutional tariff; one that shall protect all interests equally, granting favors to none. By a revenue tariff, I understand one levied upon revenue principles, and in which those principles are adhered to in its details. . .All imposts are necessarily protective; and when protection is the incident, and not the primary object of the duty, it is legitimate, and within the letter and spirit of the Constitution. I am, then, a protectionist within the revenue standard or principle. When the duty laid does not by its stringent operation diminish the revenue, it is not in my opinion open to objection, although it might be deemed by some too highly protective. . .

If . . . there is any interest within the range of American productions, in favor of which the principle of restrictive duties can be tolerated, I confidently claim iron is that interest . . . I shall probably support this bill on the question of its passage through the House. I trust, however, that the duties upon iron and coal will be increased at least 10 per cent. above the present rates of the bill, if they are not made specific, which I prefer.[94]

Even upon the question of final passage, Wilmot showed a disposition to stand upon both sides of the issue. He was the only Pennsylvanian to vote in favor of the bill, doing so on the grounds that he was pledged to a modification of the act of 1842; at the same

---

[94] *Cong. Globe,* 29 Cong., 1 Sess., App. pp. 767–771.

time he declared that if he held its fate in his hands, it should not pass until amended in favor of Pennsylvania's particular interests. Then when the measure was returned to the House with an inconsequential Senate amendment, he voted against concurrence in the hope, as he later declared, that it might be sent to a conference committee with one more chance for revision on coal and iron.[95] In this way, he was able subsequently to present himself to his immediate constituents as a free trader and to the state at large as a protectionist.[96]

The passage of the Walker bill by the House was made the occasion for considerable sardonic comment from the Whig side of the chamber. Schenck of Ohio moved as an amendment that the Kane letter should be inserted in the measure as a tariff law for Pennsylvania only.[97] Andrew Stewart suggested that the title of the bill should be changed to read,

A bill to reduce the duties on the *luxuries* of the rich, and increase them on the *necessaries* of the poor; to bankrupt the treasury; strike down American farmers, mechanics, and workingmen; to make way for the products of foreign agriculture and foreign labor; to destroy American *competition* and thereby establish a foreign *monopoly* in the American market; and, by adopting the principle of "free trade," to reduce the now prosperous labor of this country to the degraded level of the pauper labor of Europe; and, finally, to destroy the property and *independence* of these United States and again reduce them to the condition of *colonies* and *dependencies* of Great Britain.[98]

Both parties in Pennsylvania united in vehement denunciation of the bill as passed by the House of Representatives.[99] It was said that

---

[95] *Cong. Globe*, 29 Cong., 1 Sess., pp. 1053, 1165; Going, *David Wilmot*, p. 92.
[96] It is possible that the key to Wilmot's tariff attitude in 1846 will be found in the following letter, written shortly after the opening of Congress: "I learn by letter that Miller speaks unfavorably of the President's views upon the subject of the Tariff. This if so is disgraceful. I have no charity for those who knowing the *right* will not or dare not pursue it. If I am to stand entirely alone on that question, receiving no countenance or support or encouragement from any quarter, I shall look out sharply for myself." (Wilmot to John Laporte, December 15, 1845; Society Collection, Hist. Soc. of Penna.).
[97] *Cong. Globe*, 29 Cong., 1 Sess., p. 1051.
[98] *Ibid.* p. 1050.
[99] Southern extremists, on the other hand, felt that too much concession had been made to Pennsylvania in framing the measure. After its passage by the House, James Gadsden wrote Calhoun, "The Pennsylvanians really seem to control you. If Iron and Coal is to enable them to tax at will the whole of the U. S. it is as well that we separate from our Pennsylvania false Democracy." (Calhoun, *Correspondence*, p. 1085).

seventy-six of the eighty Democratic papers in the state were opposed to the measure.[100] Even the generally anti-tariff *Pennsylvanian* believed that the protection it afforded was inadequate.[101] The Whigs were disconsolate and sought to relieve their emotions by the most unrestrained tirades against the Democratic party in general and against David Wilmot in particular. Concerning the latter, the Harrisburg *Telegraph* declared, "This recreant son, who basely betrayed her interests and voted with the free traders should be banished from her territory. His infamous treachery should be revenged by disowning and turning him upon the South for support. His name and his deed will stink in the nostrils of every true-hearted Pennsylvanian forever."[102] Nevertheless, Wilmot's vote seems to have been approved by a majority of his constituents.[103]

Many Pennsylvanians, especially among the Democrats, took refuge in the hope that the bill would suffer either defeat or drastic revision in the Senate. Accordingly, a host of lobbyists descended upon Washington in a desperate last-minute effort to defeat or amend the measure. Some were Pennsylvania Democrats, anxious to escape the political consequences of a drastic reduction of duties; but most of them were manufacturers or their agents seeking to preserve existing legislative favors.[104] A Washington correspondent reported that "Pennsylvania . . . had a cohort of lobbys here from almost every Iron Foundry in the state . . . straining every nerve and taxing every expedient to continue the odious tax law of 1842."[105] Polk wrote, "The most tremendous efforts I understand are being made by the Capitalists who are engaged in manufactures to defeat the Bill. . . Scores of them I understand are flocking to Washington for the purpose."[106] After the bill had passed the Senate, the President observed, "The capitalists & monopolists have not surrendered the immense advantages which they possessed and the enormous profits which they derived under the tariff of 1842, until after a

[100] *Pittsburgh Post,* July 28, 1846.
[101] July 10, 1846.
[102] July 8, 1846.
[103] *Pennsylvanian,* July 22, 24, 1846.
[104] Cf. Polk, *Diary,* II, 33, 42; *Niles' Register,* LXX, 309; *Public Ledger,* April 9, 1846; *Pittsburgh Commercial Journal,* July 16, 1846; *Miners' Journal,* August 8, 1846; Calhoun, *Correspondence,* p. 353.
[105] *Cleveland Plain Dealer,* quoted in *Pittsburgh Post,* August 18, 1846.
[106] Polk, *Diary,* II, 27.

fierce and mighty struggle. This City has swarmed with them for weeks. . . Their effort will probably now be to raise a panic (such as they have already attempted) by means of their combined wealth, so as to induce a repeal of the act."[107]

Meanwhile, innumerable protectionist petitions were being poured into the Senate from Pennsylvania, a circumstance which led Senator Sevier of Arkansas to remark that "on the meeting of the Senate every day, first they had prayers by the chaplain, then the reading of the Journal, and next an hour and a half consumed in the recital of a sort of funeral dirge from the pensioners of Pennsylvania."[108] Cameron, in particular, maintained a persistent opposition to the Administration's tariff policy; indeed, his intensely vocal protectionism at this time served in considerable measure to lay the foundations of his subsequent popularity in the Keystone State.[109] As the debate progressed it became evident that the final vote in the Senate would be extremely close, with the outcome probably depending upon the casting vote of Vice President Dallas. The Pennsylvanians in Washington, therefore, deemed it prudent to work for amendments, which, in the event of passage, would render the measure less obnoxious to the industrial and mining interests of the state.   Dallas, especially, was anxious to find some basis of agreement which would make the responsibility of the casting vote less onerous. After the passage of the bill, the Pennsylvanian wrote, "I labored night and day indefatigably to bring about a compromise, and had a dozen shapes for it, any one of which I made no hesitation to declare should command the casting vote of the V. P."[110] One plan which received his sanction proposed that the reductions provided by the Walker bill should take place gradually over a ten-year period.[111] Other projects provided for general reductions of from 20 to 33 1/3 per cent. on all duties over 30 per cent., with the stipulation that no rate was to be brought below that figure.[112] At first, such proposals made little

---

[107] *Ibid.* p. 55.
[108] *Cong. Globe,* 29 Cong., 1 Sess., p. 1132.
[109] Cf. Blaine, *Twenty Years of Congress,* I, 195.
[110] Dallas to H. Phillips, July 28, 1846; Dreer Collection.
[111] Polk, *Diary,* II, 46.
[112] *Ibid.* pp. 33-35; Webster, *Writings and Speeches,* VI, 462; *Niles' Register,* LXX, 324; *Pittsburgh Commercial Journal,* August 5, 1846; *Pittsburgh Post,* July 27, August 7, 1846; Calhoun, *Correspondence,* p. 354.

headway, due to the combined opposition of the Administration, the hostility of many prominent Whig leaders, and the unwillingness of the two Democratic Senators from Pennsylvania to assume the responsibility for accepting any compromise in the face of their legislative instructions. On July 27, however, the Administration suffered a serious reverse, when, by a single vote, the bill was referred back to the Committee on Finance with instructions to make some very material changes. Since the session was rapidly approaching a close, such reference seemed to presage the defeat of the measure. This reverse immediately brought the Administration into a much more concessive frame of mind. That same evening, Cave Johnson, who was one of the President's closest political associates, wrote Buchanan,

The great question can be compromised with a proviso that the duties on coal and iron shall not be reduced exceeding 25 per cent. from the present rates of duty. If you think well of it, send for Cameron and Sturgeon to breakfast. I will breakfast with the President and call by a little after 8 o'clock. Whatever is done must be done by 10 o'clock.[113]

The following morning, Secretary Walker visited the Capitol and definitely promised several members of the Pennsylvania group that he would sponsor an amendment designed to effect a considerable increase in the proposed duties on coal and iron.[114] The amendment was never introduced, however; for no sooner had the pledge been given than clever political maneuvering brought the tariff once more before the Senate. Amidst great excitement the measure was hastened to a final decision, with the certainty that its ultimate fate would depend upon the casting vote of Vice President Dallas.

Dallas, during his early public career, had been generally recognized as a staunch protectionist. In 1831 he had signed a call for a tariff meeting along with such friends of the restrictive system as Mathew Carey and Charles Jared Ingersoll.[115] As a member of the Twenty-second Congress he had voted for the Act of 1832 only with extreme reluctance and had vigorously opposed the Compromise of

---

[113] C. Johnson to Buchanan, July 27, 1846; Buchanan Mss.

[114] *North American*, August 1, 1846; *Harrisburg Telegraph*, August 19, 1846; *Pittsburgh Post*, September 12, 1860. The Administration had determined several days previously to compromise rather than to allow the bill to be defeated. (Polk, *Diary*, II, 35, 46.)

[115] *Poulson's American Advertizer*, September 23, 1831.

1833.[116] At that time he was characterized as a "high" rather than a "moderate" protectionist.[117] The Charleston *Mercury*, moreover, had referred to him as "a notorious protective tariff man."[118] On the other hand, Dallas' earlier career had revealed a marked tendency to sacrifice his personal convictions upon the altar of party loyalty. While in the Senate in 1832, he had introduced and strongly supported the bill for rechartering the national bank; yet immediately after Jackson's veto of the measure, Dallas was one of the speakers at a Philadelphia meeting which adopted resolutions approving the President's act.[119] When Jackson sought to hasten the overthrow of the bank by removing the government deposits, Dallas wrote, "I mourn over its downfall as over the offspring of my father: —but I think I can perceive that its directors have ensured its destruction by perverting its principles, and by shamelessly as well as unwisely throwing away the very grappling irons which my father had given them to hold on to popular favor and good will."[120]

The same party loyalty which had swung Dallas into opposition to the national bank now called him to support the Walker tariff. Moreover, he was bound to the Secretary of the Treasury both by family ties and personal friendship.[121] On the other hand, for a Pennsylvanian to consummate the overthrow of the cherished tariff of 1842 might well be regarded as an act of political suicide.[122] Nevertheless, Dallas appears to have met the situation without flinching. Even before the Walker bill passed the House of Representatives, he wrote an intimate friend,

I say to you privately that I am determined whenever the casting vote is elicited, that it shall conform as closely as I can make it, to the resolutions of the Baltimore Convention on all the great questions of policy distinctly involved in those resolutions. This I *will* do, *conte qui conte*,—in obedience to the

---

[116] See pages 111 and 122, *supra*.
[117] *American Sentinel*, February 18, 1833.
[118] *Niles' Register*, LXVII, 43.
[119] *Cong. Debates*, 22 Cong., 1 Sess., pp. 530, 943-950, 1073; *To the Citizens of the State of Pennsylvania*, (1832); *Pittsburgh Post*, June 3, 1844.
[120] Dallas to G. Wolf, March 2, 1834; Wolf Mss., Hist. Soc. of Penna.
[121] R. J. Walker to Polk, May 31, 1844; Polk Mss.
[122] Dallas' political foes in Pennsylvania seem to have derived considerable satisfaction from his dilemma. Early in the Senate struggle, John W. Forney wrote Buchanan, "It would be fun if Dallas had to untie the Tariff knot! Rare fun." When the passage of events had transformed the possibility into a certainty, Forney wrote, "Dallas is in a fix. God help him!" (J. W. Forney to Buchanan, July 9, 27, 1846; Buchanan Mss.)

dictates of a conscience that will not permit me to swerve from a pledge. I can bear abuse—I can cheerfully go back to the practice of the law & to private life—but I cannot bear to falsify my promise to those who elected me as their representative. Read over again the resolutions of the Baltimore Convention, and you will see the extent of my obligation, voluntarily assumed, in accepting the nomination, on the subject of the Tariff.

My desire is to watch attentively every phase of the Tariff movement, and to be prepared to act, on every emergency, as a sense of justice and responsibility to the Country—the *whole* of the American People—may dictate. . . I submit to your judgment—and to that of Judge Kane—and Col. Page— whether it would not be proper and expedient, after the views I have now stated to you, to stem in some degree and by a few paragraphs, the idea which adversaries are endeavoring to get up, that I am disposed or bound to square my official action on the Tariff to what are termed the Pennsylvania doctrines.[123]

As early as July 7, Dallas was certain that he would be required to give the casting vote, and he warned that "they who feel any interest in my futurity must prepare themselves for the Consequences of seeing the Baltimore convention resolution strictly carried out."[124]

The crisis came on July 28. When the Senate assembled that morning it was clear that the Administration forces were once more in control of the situation and were determined to push the tariff through to a speedy vote. Cameron, in a last despairing attempt at compromise, offered two amendments. The first proposed a 25 per cent. reduction on all duties over 30 per cent., but stipulated that no such duty should be brought below 30 per cent. The second provided that the existing duties on coal and iron and all iron manufactures should be reduced only 25 per cent.[125] Both proposals were rejected outright; for, as Dallas wrote, "the Cataract was tumbling, and his offer was a mere straw opposed to its impetus."[126] A few moments later, the question of passage to a third reading produced the long-anticipated tie vote and placed the issue squarely before the presiding officer. Dallas, before giving his vote, briefly explained the motives which guided him in his difficult decision. He interpreted the proceed-

---

[123] Dallas to H. Phillips, July 3, 1846; Dreer Col.
[124] *Ibid.* July 7, 1846.
[125] *Cong. Globe*, 29 Cong., 1 Sess., p. 1155.
[126] Dallas to H. Phillips, July 28, 1846; Dreer Col. The Democrats subsequently maintained that these amendments would have carried but for the opposition of Whig Senators who were anxious for the bill to pass in a form which would cause the overthrow of the Democratic party in Pennsylvania. (*Pittsburgh Post*, August 4, 1846).

ings in the House to mean that a majority of the American people favored a modification of the nation's tariff laws, and he declared that as a representative of the whole country, he could not stand in the way of the popular desire. Moreover, he believed that most branches of American industry had become sufficiently vigorous and powerful "to enter with confidence the field of free, fair, and universal competition." He admitted that the act went farther than he deemed altogether wise, but added, "I cannot resist the impression that the bill is more equal, more tempered, and more just, than the act of 1842, which it supersedes. That it deals with some pursuits and resources of my native Commonwealth less kindly than she might well expect, does not relieve me from my duty, but only makes its performance personally reluctant and painful." Accordingly, he gave his vote in the affirmative.[127] Final passage followed shortly thereafter, with both Cameron and Sturgeon voting in the negative.[128] Dallas was not called upon to repeat his casting vote; since Senator Jarnagin of Tennessee, who had previously refrained from voting, was now compelled by his instructions to support the measure.

Polk signed the new tariff law on July 30, 1846. He seems to have anticipated no serious reaction against the measure, even in Pennsylvania.[129] Nevertheless, Pennsylvanians of both parties had given fair warning during the debates in Congress that the passage of the Walker bill would mark the beginning, not the end, of the struggle. Stewart, in the House, had threatened,

Pass this destruction bill and he would call on the people—the honest hard-handed farmers, mechanics and laboring men of the land to fling their banners to the breeze, with the inscription "The British free-trade tariff of 1846— Repeal! Repeal!! Repeal!!!" and never lower it till it triumphed—as triumph it would most gloriously—in the renewal of the tariff of 1842 and with it the restoration of our national prosperity and independence.[130]

After Dallas had given the casting vote, but before the final passage of the new tariff, Cameron had risen to enter his solemn protest against the measure and to declare "that from henceforth repeal would be the word among the Democracy of the North, and that it would not cease until it triumphed."[131]

---

127 *Cong. Globe*, 29 Cong., 1 Sess., p. 1156.
128 *Ibid*. p. 1158.
129 See pages 186 and 187, *supra*.
130 *Cong. Globe*, 29 Cong., 1 Sess., App., p. 943.
131 *Cong. Globe*, 29 Cong., 1 Sess., p. 1157.

CHAPTER X

THE PROTECTIONIST REVOLT, 1846-1848

The passage of the Walker tariff brought forth a torrent of angry protest from Pennsylvania protectionists. The *Miners' Journal* and other papers appeared in mourning to announce the overthrow of the act of 1842. The *North American*, characterized by a Richmond editor as "the most rabid Tariff paper in the union,"[1] thundered,

Let the cry of "Repeal" be rung forth from the anvil, the loom, the shuttle, the mine, the furnace, the plough handle, and the workshop. Let there be no pause, nor weariness, until this fungus of British extraction is expunged from our statutes and its place occupied by a bill which shall protect every American interest, so as to render us independent in war and prosperous in peace.[2]

Temporarily demoralized by the event, many Democrats followed Cameron's example in demanding the repeal of the new law. One Democratic paper exclaimed, "REPEAL is the word! Take it up Democrats! echo it iron men! echo it miners and laborers; shout it mechanics! There shall be no rest, no reposing until the British Tariff Bill is repealed."[3] Similar sentiments, expressed by meetings and journals in all parts of the state, afforded eloquent evidence of a complete breakdown of party discipline within the Democratic ranks.[4]

Many dismal pictures were drawn of the sad future awaiting Pennsylvania industry under the reduced duties. The *North American* declared, "Pennsylvania, like Joseph of old, has been bound by her brethren and sold to a strange land. Her forge fires may go out, but those of England will burn the brighter for it; her mines may be deserted, but those of England and Nova Scotia will prosper the more."[5] The same journal ventured to predict that the new tariff, in its workings,

---

[1] *North American*, September 23, 1846.
[2] *Ibid.* July 30, 1846.
[3] *Spirit of the Times*, July 30, 1846.
[4] *North American*, August 21, 22, September 3, 7, 10, 1846; *Pittsburgh Commercial Journal*, September 16, 1846.
[5] *North American*, September 18, 1846.
[6] *Ibid.* August 13, 1846.
[7] *Niles' Register*, LXX, 307.
[8] *Ibid.* p. 356.

will be calamitous—very calamitous to every interest which Pennsylvania cherishes. It will diminish by millions the value of our staples. . . It will lower the rates of wages—it will throw thousands out of employment—it will induce general distress, and incalculable individual suffering. It will lessen the value of property in the State; it will depreciate the value of agricultural products; it will ruin thousands of mechanics; it will check improvements, public and private; it will plunge the state into an inky pit of repudiation, and produce without a single benefit, promised or hoped, universal loss and suffering![6]

It was asserted that the adoption of the bill by the House of Representatives had caused an immediate drop of $2 per ton in the price of pig iron.[7] Less than two weeks after the enactment of the new tariff, it was reported that Philadelphia factories were being closed down and that wages were being reduced.[8] It was claimed, likewise, that within sixty days of the passage of the bill a thousand workers had left the coal regions to seek employment elsewhere, and that among those who remained "scarcely a smiling face, except in infancy, was to be seen."[9]

Much of the abuse was centered upon the hapless figure of the Vice President, who, it was asserted, had basely betrayed the interests of his native state. So strong was the feeling that doubts were expressed for his personal safety when he should reach Philadelphia.[10] Dallas, himself, complained that he had been "inundated with threatening anonymous letters of the vilest character."[11] He was burnt in effigy in Philadelphia and elsewhere; while the barrels placed over the chimneys of closed factories were derisively referred to as "Dallas Night Caps."[12] It was freely charged that he had been bribed with British gold to give the casting vote, and his name was frequently linked with that of Benedict Arnold as a traitor to his country.[13] A Whig paper fulminated,

He has now fully proven what he is, a wretched demagogue—a base truckler to power—a small intellect encased in a bust of pompous clay. . . The South have flattered him with the hope of being elevated to the presidency, and he

---

9 *Miners' Journal,* September 12, 26, 1846.
10 S. Harris to Buchanan, August 5, 1846; Buchanan Mss.
11 Dallas to H. Phillips, July 28, 1846; Dreer Col.
12 *North American,* September 30, 1846; *Pittsburgh Commercial Journal,* August 3, 4, 1846; *Pennsylvanian,* August 7, September 26, 1846.
13 *Pittsburgh Commercial Journal,* September 21, 1846; *Miners' Journal,* August 1, October 3, 1846; July 26, 1851.

has basely bowed the knee and sold Pennsylvania to secure his own elevation. . . . He is, however, politically dead, as he should have been long ago,
and the next state will immediately follow when his traitorous spirit quits
the miserable clay tenement that it occupies.[14]

A Democratic journal, not to be outdone, declared, "Should Mr.
Dallas live to the age of Mathuzalah, he will never be able to make
ample atonement for his severe onslaught upon the home industry
of Pennsylvania. Farewell to all vice presidents for the future from
Pennsylvania.—We have had enough of one to last us, while all who
live now shall continue to breathe the breath of existence."[15]

It is clear that the Democracy of Pennsylvania was for the
moment completely demoralized by the passage of the Walker tariff.
Nevertheless, the leadership and discipline which so frequently had
saved the party from disaster was not slow to reassert itself.
Buchanan was the first of the Democratic leaders to turn to a consideration of measures to retrieve the situation. His privately expressed opinion of the tariff of 1846 was by no means flattering. He
declared that it "cannot be sustained by principles which ought to
govern the conduct of a wise statesman in the present condition of
the country." He believed that the new law would not produce adequate revenue, would be difficult to administer, and would be ruinous
to industries dependent upon foreign raw materials. He maintained,
moreover, that through its heavy reductions on iron and coal, it
would "operate more prejudicially on Pennsylvania than any other
state." For all these reasons, if forced to choose between the tariff
of 1842 and the Walker measure, he admitted that he would prefer
the former.[16] Buchanan was too astute a politician, however, to play
into the hands of the Whigs by uttering such sentiments publicly.
With the important congressional and state elections less than three
months ahead, it was imperative that immediate measures be taken
to rally the shattered forces of the Democracy. At the same time,
it was evident that the party must choose its ground with extreme
caution if it was to escape the avenging wrath of an enraged electorate. Buchanan hastened, therefore, to draw up a list of suggestions for the guidance of John W. Forney in determining the editorial

---

[14] *Harrisburg Telegraph*, July 29, 1846.
[15] *American Sentinel*, quoted in *Niles' Register*, LXXI, 46.
[16] Buchanan, *Works*, VII, 44.

policy of the *Pennsylvanian,* the most influential Democratic paper in the state. It would be well, Buchanan believed, to build their tariff argument upon the following salient points:

1. An approbation of our Senators and Representatives for resisting the passage of the Tariff Bill, as dictated alike by public duty and their instructions.

2. The impossibility of obtaining a restoration of the Tariff of 1842, it having been condemned by public opinion, and even by the manufacturers themselves. . .

3. That many who voted for the present Tariff did so, not because they were satisfied with all its provisions, but because by means of it, they would get clear of the Tariff of '42.

4. That a disposition exists among the Democracy to do justice to Pennsylvania by increasing the duties on coal, iron and mechanical labor; and a united and vigorous effort to accomplish this purpose may, and probably will, prove successful at the commencement of the next Session of Congress, and a very short time after the present law will go into operation, which will be on the first day of December.[17]

5. That this desire will be greatly increased should the State adhere to its Democratic faith; it being much more probable that this will be granted by a Democratic majority, on an appeal from their political brethren, than from the Whigs.

6. The Manufacturers ought to be warned not to make it a political question, and not to attempt to excite a panic; but to go on with their business, and all may yet go well.

7. If the issue shall be made between the present law, and the Tariff of 1842, defeat is inevitable. The Tariff of 1842 never will be restored. By making the attempt we lose all the advantages within our reach. Repeal is not the word, but modification. A protective Tariff is not the word; but a revenue Tariff with sufficient discrimination to maintain our home industry.

8. Still convinced as I am that specific duties are not the best, it may be better not to make the point distinctly, at the present moment.[18]

Buchanan's suggestion was promptly and whole-heartedly taken up by the *Pennsylvanian.*   Gradually, as party devotion overcame the first shock of disappointment, other Democratic editors followed

---

[17] Forney wrote back warning Buchanan against too definite a promise of modification on coal and iron. He pointed out that it would be difficult to fulfill such a pledge in the face of a free-trade President and a hostile majority in Congress. (Forney to Buchanan, August 23, 1846; Buchanan Mss.)

[18] Buchanan, *Works,* VII, 46-47.

[19] J. W. Forney to Buchanan, August 23, 1846; Buchanan Mss.; *Pennsylvanian,* August 4, 5, 8, 10, 1846.

Forney's lead and came out in at least qualified approval of the Walker tariff.[20] One paper commented, "It is indeed gratifying to notice the chance that is taking place in the tone of the Democratic press of Pennsylvania on the subject of the Tariff. Those papers which at first denounced the passage of the new bill, have, upon examination, discovered many redeeming qualities in it, and have become satisfied that its protection to Pennsylvania interests is abundant."[21] In many counties, Democratic meetings began to express gratitude for the overthrow of the act of 1842 and to hail the new law as "an honest effort to reconcile and unite all the various and heretofore conflicting interests of these United States, to check monopoly, encourage every branch of home industry, and place our revenue laws on a permanent basis, above and beyond the strife of party politics."[22] At the same time there developed a noticeable tendency to deal more charitably with Dallas and his casting vote.[23] An open letter signed by a large number of Philadelphians commended him for his "unflinching adherence to Democratic principles —especially to that cardinal point: 'the greatest good to the greatest number.'"[24] The Democrats of Chester county asserted that the casting vote exhibited "a degree of moral firmness which has scarcely a parallel in the pages of our legislative record. . .The day is assuredly coming when that casting vote will be celebrated as equalling

---

[20] One Democratic observer, noting this tendency to abandon the act of 1842 in favor of the Walker tariff, declared, "How far this feeling is the result of investigation and comparison or that of party fealty may be somewhat difficult to decide." (J. Miller to Buchanan, November 9, 1846; Buchanan Mss.)

[21] *Waynesburg Messenger,* quoted in *Pennsylvanian,* September 15, 1846.

[22] *Pennsylvanian,* August 25, 1846.

[23] Forney, who hated the Vice President, complained to Buchanan that "in touching this question it is impossible to avoid sustaining Dallas. These people here are building him up by their abuse and threats." Forney to Buchanan, August 4, 1846; Buchanan Mss.)

[24] Among the signers was William D. Kelley, later known as "Pig Iron" Kelley because of his ultra-protectionism. At this time Kelley was a free-trader. Dallas, replying to this letter, declared, "I gave that vote because not to have given it would wound my conscience; wound my self respect, wound my principles, and incurably wound my country. . . Is it possible that our upright Commonwealth can for one moment demand that an officer, elected by the suffrages of all the twenty-eight States, and bound by his oath and every constitutional obligation faithfully and fairly to represent, in the execution of his high trust, all the citizens of all the Union, should narrow his great sphere and act with reference only to her peculiar wishes?" (*Pennsylvanian,* August 5, 1846).

the iron will, the foresight, the patriotic service of General Jackson, in removing the deposits and vetoing the re-charter of the United States Bank."[25] A Luzerne county meeting commended the casting vote as a "noble, magnanimous and high-minded act, worthy of the admiration and approval of mankind."[26] From Potter county came the prediction that, so far as Dallas was concerned, "the fires raised by federal Whiggery will only serve to lighten his footsteps to the Presidential chair."[27]

The shift of sentiment in favor of the new tariff was by no means universal among the Democrats. There were many sections in which the party spokesmen sternly refused to compromise with their convictions upon the subject. Buchanan reported, on August 22, that "whilst several of the Journals, under the lead of the *Pennsylvanian*, and some of the people, advocate the law as it now stands, a large portion of the remainder are in favor of restoring the Tariff of 1842."[28] A month later, an observer declared, "The Democratic party in this state seem to be about equally divided on the tariff of '46. It seems to go by counties."[29] A Whig editor noted that "the administration journals in Pennsylvania are divided upon the tariff question into all manner of doctrines according to the temperature of the location."[30] In spite of Buchanan's conciliatory efforts, therefore, the Democracy of Pennsylvania approached the fall elections in an ominously divided condition.

The political struggle of 1846 centered around the election of a canal commissioner and Pennsylvania's twenty-four Congressmen. For the former office, the Whigs nominated James M. Power of Mercer county; while the Democrats renominated William B. Foster of Bradford county. So far as the Whigs were concerned, the tariff was made the one ànd only issue of the campaign. It was asserted, "The issue is now fairly made between the friends of Free Trade on the one hand, and those who are in favor of protecting their own industry on the other. The strife now is between Tariff men and anti-Tariff men. All other questions are for the present subordinate

---

25 *Harrisburg Democratic Union*, August 26, 1846.
26 *Ibid.* August 25, 1846.
27 *Pennsylvanian*, October 22, 1846.
28 Buchanan, *Works*, VII, 73.
29 A. Ramsey to Buchanan, September 23, 1846; Buchanan Mss.
30 *Niles' Register*, LXXI, 4.

to this one."[31] According to the Whigs, "The only general ticket in the field is that for Canal Commissioner—that then will be the test. Let every man in Pennsylvania who desires repeal of the British tariff cast his vote for James M. Power."[32] Wide publicity was given to Horace Greeley's assertion that "every Loco Foco elected to Congress from Pennsylvania will be hailed as a sign of approval of the new bill, no matter whether the successful candidate be for the Tariff Bill of 1842 or for the foolish Free Trade Bill of 1846."[33] Indeed, the prediction was boldly advanced that "the British Tariff will not survive a Whig victory in Pennsylvania three months."[34]

The Democratic leaders realized that their prospects for success were very dubious. One observer reported to Buchanan, "The gradual rise of breadstuffs may help us some, but very little, because thousands of people know nothing of it."[35] Buchanan, realizing the gravity of the situation, carefully prepared an open letter to the Pennsylvania electorate in which he took strong ground in favor of higher duties on coal and iron.[36] This statement was submitted to Polk, who declared that although he was not averse to a "reasonable modification" on coal and iron, "the general scope of Mr. Buchanan's proposed letter adheres too much to the protective principle."[37] Forney also believed that any expression upon the subject would simply make a bad matter worse, and he strongly urged that the letter should not be sent.[38] It was feared that any such criticism of the new law would be resented by Dallas' friends and would only serve to widen the party breach.[39] Buchanan, with characteristic caution, yielded to this advice and the proposal was accordingly dropped.

Almost of necessity, the disunited Democracy had to content itself with ridiculing the idea that Foster was a free trader or that the election of a canal commissioner had anything to do with the tariff question. The Whigs were reminded that the "Board of Canal

---

[31] *North American,* October 5, 1846.
[32] *Pittsburgh Commercial Journal,* August 28, 1846.
[33] *Ibid.* September 4, 1846.
[34] *Ibid.* August 27, 1846.
[35] J. Ziegler to Buchanan, October 5, 1846; Buchanan Mss.
[36] Draft of letter to Morris Longstreth, August 21, 1846; Buchanan Mss.
[37] Polk, *Diary,* II, 106.
[38] Forney to Buchanan, August 21, November 2, 1846; Buchanan Mss.
[39] J. Miller to Buchanan, November 9, 1846; Buchanan Mss.

Commissioners had other duties to perform than to interfere with the duties specially allotted Congress," and that the tariff had no more to do with the office "than it has with the next President in Mexico, or the next King of France."[40] In the various congressional districts, the lack of Democratic unity upon the tariff was very clearly apparent. The *Miners' Journal* reported,

In Philadelphia city and county, Messrs. Brown, Florence, and Stokes, Loco candidates for Congress advocate the British Bill of 1846—and C. J. Ingersoll goes for the tariff of 1842. In Montgomery and Delaware counties, in Berks, in Chester, in Lancaster, in Bradford, in York, and Adams, and a number of other counties of the state, the Loco Foco candidates have also arrayed themselves in favor of the British bill. In Northampton, in Dauphin, Lebanon, and Schuylkill, in Northumberland, Union, and Lycoming, in Columbia and Luzerne, and a number of other counties, the candidates go for the Tariff of 1842.[41]

The struggle in Wilmot's district attracted general attention, but it soon became evident that he had the situation well in hand. The Democrats of Bradford county renominated him unanimously upon the first ballot, and strong resolutions were adopted commending his vote in favor of the tariff of 1846.[42]

The result of the election of 1846 was a decided victory for the entire Whig ticket. The Democrats elected only seven of the twenty-four Congressmen, as compared with twelve at the preceding election.[43] Wilmot was reelected, but his majority, as compared with two years before, was cut from 2971 to 747.[44] Power, the Whig nominee for canal commissioner, received a plurality of 8,899 votes; a year previously, the Democratic candidate for the same office had been elected with a plurality of 30,392 over his Whig opponent, and a clear majority of 5,107. To complete the rout, the Democrats lost both houses of the state legislature; their representation fell from

---

[40] *Pittsburgh Dispatch,* quoted in *Pittsburgh Commercial Journal,* September 3, 1846; *Pennsylvanian,* July 24, 1846; *Harrisburg Democratic Union,* August 26, 1846.

[41] October 3, 1846.

[42] *Pennsylvanian,* September 16, 18, 1846; Wilmot to Buchanan, September 21, 1846; Buchanan Mss.

[43] *Harrisburg Democratic Union,* October 28, 1846.

[44] *Harrisburg Telegraph,* October 28, 1846. Ex-Governor Porter was said to have attributed Wilmot's reelection to the fact that "in that region of country the only things the people manufactured were shingles, and they stole the lumber to make them, and the only *protection* they wanted was protection from the officers of justice." (*North American,* November 18, 1846).

sixty-seven to forty-four in the House, and from eighteen to fourteen in the Senate.[45]

As was to be expected, there was no uncertainty in the Whig ranks as to the cause of their overwhelming victory. Most of the Democrats, likewise, frankly admitted that the tariff of 1846 had been the instrument of their political downfall. One Democratic journal declared that it was

idle to lay our late defeat to a storm of wind and rain, when it must be ascribed to a political hurricane, whose course could be traced with the closest accuracy upon a geological map of the state. A reduction of two-thirds of the duty on iron and more than one-half on coal, is an all-sufficient cause, without censuring the elements for their interference.[46]

Many Democrats, including Governor Shunk, expressed the fear that if the tariff of 1846 continued to be made a campaign issue, their party would be thrown into a permanent minority.[47] One paper, looking forward to the next presidential election, declared, "If the support of the Tariff of '46 is to be still the rallying cry, it will be worse than idle to engage in the contest, and we should save much trouble and expense by permitting the Whigs to walk unmolested over the course. Neither rain nor sunshine could save us from another defeat."[48] Buchanan was more optimistic; for he wrote,

Disapproving, as you know I have always done, of the Tariff of 1846, I yet do not concur in opinion with you that it will make the State permanently Whig. The circumstances under which it will go into operation are favorable. Iron & coal for some time to come, must command a high price; & the universal failure of the last harvest throughout Europe will keep up the prices of our bread stuffs & other agricultural productions. I trust that a modification of the Tariff of 1846 will be effected before the Manufacturers & Coal Dealers can be seriously injured.[49]

[45] *Pennsylvanian*, October 25, 1845; *North American*, October 31, 1845; *Harrisburg Democratic Union*, October 28, 1846.
[46] *Harrisburg Democratic Union*, November 11, 1846. For similar Democratic testimony see Polk, *Diary*, II, 217; *Pottsville Democratic Press*, quoted in *North American*, October 24, 1846; also letters to Buchanan from J. W. Forney (October 21), J. Miller (November 9), J. P. Brawley (November 22); Buchanan Mss.
[47] J. Miller to Buchanan, November 9, 1846; Buchanan Mss.
[48] *Harrisburg Argus*, quoted in *North American*, November 10, 1846.
[49] Buchanan, *Works*, VII, 117.

Another observer, who shared Buchanan's views as to the close correlation between economic conditions and the immediate future of the Democratic party, predicted that

if the price of Flour, Iron and Coal should continue fair as they may until the next fall's elections the chances are that we will beat them. But if a fall of prices should take place in any of these articles to any material extent between this and then the result in all probability will be different. . . We may . . . sustain ourselves until a revulsion in prices actually takes place. But when it does come whether sooner or later the democratic party will have to bear the consequences politically.[50]

Actually, economic conditions throughout 1847 played into the hands of the Democrats even beyond the most optimistic expectations of the party leaders. Iron and coal prices were, on the whole, higher than they had been under the tariff of 1842.[51] Eight anthracite and twelve charcoal furnaces were opened during the year, many of them by experienced iron men.[52] Famine conditions in Europe produced a tremendous increase of food exports, which resulted in a corresponding rise of agricultural prices. As a result, farm products were worth from 25 to 50 per cent. more in 1847 than during the previous era of high protection.[53] Summing up the economic situation, one journal declared, "Never since the Declaration of Independence have there been more solid prosperity and cheering plenty existing throughout our land than at the present time."[54]

The Democrats of Pennsylvania joyously hailed existing conditions as affording unanswerable proof of the validity of their tariff contentions. A Pittsburgh paper declared, "The complete success of the Tariff of 1846 is now candidly admitted by every honest man."[55] The Democrats of Chester county believed "that the present prosperity . . . cannot fail to convince the minds of all candid and unprejudiced citizens of the utter falsity of those predictions of ruin to the country made by federal presses in '44 and at the time of the

---

[50] J. Miller to Buchanan, November 9, 1846; Buchanan Mss.
[51] Swank, *Iron in All Ages*, p. 514.
[52] J. Findley to Buchanan, December 8, 1846; Buchanan Mss.; *Doc. Rel. to the Manu. of Iron in Penna.*, p. 109.
[53] *Sen. Rep.*, 52 Cong., 2 Sess., Vol. III, pt. 1, p. 107.
[54] *Harrisburg Democratic Union*, April 28, 1847.
[55] *Pittsburgh Post*, August 13, 1847.

enactment of the Tariff of '46."[56] The heavy export of agricultural produce was hailed with particular delight because of the attitude taken by the protectionists at the time of the repeal of the British corn laws. Prior to 1846, the tariff party in America had repeatedly argued that if England would abandon her commercial restrictions, the United States might immediately do likewise.[57] When the remote contingency suddenly became an actuality, however, Pennsylvania protectionists hastened to shift their ground. In the first place, it was argued, cheaper foodstuffs would enable English manufacturers to pay lower wages and thus cut their costs of production.[58] In the second place, it was held, England would henceforth obtain her breadstuffs from Europe, instead of importing American grain by way of Canada under a system of preferential duties.[59] Thus, it was argued, the repeal of the corn laws would actually injure both the American industrialist and the American farmer. The Democrats, however, greeted the unprecedented exportation of agricultural produce during 1847 as unmistakable evidence that once more the direful prognostications of the Whig protectionists had been falsified by the event. Governor Shunk gave official sanction to this view, when he declared in his last annual message,

There is good reason to believe that the prosperity of the people of the United States, particularly those connected with the agricultural interests, has been promoted by the removal, on the part of the British government, of the high duties upon our exports of grain, and other agricultural productions, and the modification of our own tariff, by which the commercial exchanges of the two countries have been greatly augmented, without affecting injuriously, so far as I am informed, any of the great manufacturing interests, or other industrial pursuits of our people.[60]

The Whigs, notwithstanding high prices and expanding trade, remained adamant in their hostility to the Walker act. They declared that the prevailing prosperity existed in spite of, not because of, the tariff of 1846. The Whig state convention resolved, "that

[56] *Harrisburg Democratic Union,* May 12, 1847.
[57] *Cf. North American,* August 30, 1842.
[58] *Pittsburgh Commercial Journal,* July 13, 1846.
[59] *Harrisburg Democratic Union,* August 4, 1847; *Cong. Globe,* 29 Cong., 1 Sess., App., p. 941.
[60] *Pennsylvania Archives,* Fourth Series, VII, 203. See also Calhoun, *Correspondence,* p. 327.

the tariff of 1842 was the source of unexampled prosperity to the country, and that its repeal has been attended with results detrimental to the true interests of all sections and classes."[61] The rise in the price of breadstuffs was attributed, not to the tariff, but to the European famine; or, as one journal phrased it, "The President has invoked ruin; Providence has interposed to avert it."[62] As for those who had the temerity of deny this contention a protectionist editor declared, "We might marvel that the lightnings of Heaven have not already blasted the impious jugglers, as Ananias of old was struck down for a less wicked lie."[63] It was commonly held that only a complete restoration of the act of 1842 would save the economic structure of the country from inevitable disaster. The *Miners' Journal,* for instance, announced itself as "utterly opposed to any and all efforts which may be made to patch up the bill of abomination passed at the last session of Congress. . .The task of Hercules when called upon to cleanse the Augean stable was a trifle compared with that of freeing the Tariff of 1846 from faults."[64]

The Whig landslide of 1846 had given that party complete control of the state legislature, and they eagerly seized the opportunity to carry the tariff war to Harrisburg. By a vote of 55 to 41, the House adopted resolutions in favor of the restoration of the tariff of 1842. The vote was strictly along party lines except that two Democrats abandoned their colleagues and supported the measure.[65] The Whig majority in the Senate, instead of acting upon these resolutions, introduced a series of much stronger declarations, accusing Polk, Dallas, and Shunk of perfidy upon the subject of the tariff. Three Whigs and one Native American, however, allied themselves with the Democrats to prevent consideration of these vigorous resolves.[66] The session, therefore, brought forth no direct action upon the tariff. The Whigs, however, did use their legislative control to repeal the state's fugitive slave law—a deliberate blow at the South, which represented, in a very real sense, Pennsylvania's reply to the overthrow of the tariff of 1842.[67]

[61] *North American,* March 13, 1847.
[62] *Ibid.* January 27, 1847.
[63] *Pittsburgh Commercial Journal,* May 14, 1847.
[64] November 14, 1846.
[65] *House Journal,* 1847, I, 90; *Harrisburg Democratic Union,* January 23, 1847.
[66] *Senate Journal,* 1847, I, 254, 471.
[67] Mueller, *Whig Party in Pennsylvania,* p. 135.

Encouraged by their tariff-born triumph of the previous year, the Whigs labored industriously to inject the same question into the gubernatorial election of 1847. To facilitate the process, there was talk of nominating either Walter Forward or Andrew Stewart, both closely identified with the protectionist cause in Pennsylvania.[68] The ultimate choice, however, fell upon James Irvin, a wealthy ironmaster of Centre county. The Whig nominee was known as a staunch protectionist and enjoyed the important political asset of having helped to pass the act of 1842 in the House of Representatives. Nevertheless, the Democrats, with Governor Shunk as a candidate for reelection, entered the campaign with real hope of victory. Party discipline and the prevalent prosperity had completely healed the tariff schism responsible for the disaster of the preceding year, and even in the most strongly protectionist areas of the state, Democratic spokesmen found it no longer hazardous to express open approval of the Walker act.

Throughout the campaign, the Whigs maintained that "the true issue before the people is Irvin and Protection vs. Shunk and British Free Trade."[69] More specifically, Shunk was bitterly condemned for his annual message of the preceding January, in which he had been only mildly critical of the Walker tariff.[70] The Democrats, on the other hand, heaped endless ridicule upon the efforts of their opponents to make the tariff the one great issue of the campaign. A Washington county meeting believed

that the Tariff of 1842 is and ought to be entirely defunct, and that the absurd idea of our political opponents to galvanize the corpse by making its resuscitation the watchword of their camp and the rallying cry in their ranks is but another evidence that they will continue ostinately to adhere to an exploded notion or an obsolete idea long after the country had left it far behind.[71]

The *Pennsylvanian*, in a passage heavy with sarcasm, made the observation,

The *North American* would go into the contest in Pennsylvania on the tariff issue alone. It would go out among the blighted fields of poor ruined, seduced Pennsylvania—among the deserted workshops—her blown out furnaces—her

[68] *Pittsburgh Commercial Journal*, December 16, 1846; *Miners' Journal*, December 5, 1846.
[69] *Harrisburg Telegraph*, September 14, 1847.
[70] *Pennsylvania Archives*, Fourth Series, VII, 129-130.
[71] *Pennsylvanian*, August 26, 1847.

beggared mechanics—and would then invoke upon the offending Democracy the curses and the vengeance of a deceived and deluded people. The youth who fired the Ephesian dome—the incendiary with his gunpowder plot—Fieschi with his infernal machine—men who open railroad switches—people who poison reservoirs—became suddenly embodied saints in comparison with those who had lighted the train for the complete ruin of the country in passing the Tariff of 1846 . . . These prophecies have all been falsified. The country never was happier or more prosperous.[72]

The confidence of the Democrats was fully justified by the results of the election. Shunk carried the state over Irvin by a plurality of nearly 18,000 votes.[73] The Democrats also recaptured the lower House of the legislature, but the Whigs retained control of the Senate.[74] It would be a mistake, however, to interpret the result, as certain Democratic papers attempted to do, as a clear-cut referendum in favor of the tariff of 1846.[75] In the face of continued prosperity, the majority of Pennsylvanians could not be made to believe that the tariff was the burning issue of the campaign. The electorate apparently preferred to accept the Democratic contention that the great issue of the canvass was not protection but the question of upholding the Administration in time of war. Moreover, it was obviously difficult to arouse enthusiasm over the tariff in an election in which no national offices were at stake. For all these reasons, the campaign of 1847 represents an interlude rather than an episode in the Pennsylvania tariff struggle. As the presidential election of 1848 was destined to show, the protectionists of the state were neither reconciled to the workings of the Walker tariff nor prepared to extend full political absolution to those responsible for its passage.

The Democrats, in spite of their gubernatorial triumph, approached the state and national elections of 1848 with considerable trepidation.[76] Economic conditions, which had become a sort of

---

[72] *Ibid.* April 28, 1847.

[73] *Smull's Legislative Handbook,* 1921-22, p. 745.

[74] *Pennsylvanian,* October 25, 1847.

[75] *Harrisburg Democratic Union,* November 3, 1847; *Washington Union,* quoted in *Niles' Register,* LXXIII, October 23, 1847.

[76] From the standpoint of the practical politician, the Pennsylvania election of 1848 was an extremely important one. It was expected—correctly, as the event proved—that the fate of the presidential contest would hang upon the vote of the Keystone State. Moreover, the deathbed resignation of Governor Shunk made it necessary to choose a new state executive. Control of the legislature also assumed more than ordinary importance; since a United States Senator was to be elected at the next session.

political barometer for the party, were not encouraging. English iron prices fell off heavily during 1848; at the same time the duties were automatically reduced under the workings of the ad valorem system.[77] As a result, imports of raw and manufactured iron were 39 per cent. larger than during the preceding year.[78] This, combined with domestic overproduction, caused a decided decline of prices on the American market as well.[79] It was estimated that five anthracite and twenty charcoal furnaces failed during the year in Pennsylvania alone, and many other ironworks were compelled to suspend operations.[80] The mining regions likewise suffered from a marked decline in the price of coal.[81] At the same time, the numerically important agricultural interest was also affected adversely by a noticeable drop in the price of farm products.[82] Naturally, the trend of the economic situation caused real concern to those Pennsylvania Democrats who had been relying upon continued prosperity to save them from the avenging wrath of the protectionists. As early as February, one of the party leaders warned Buchanan that if the depression continued until the election, "it will have a powerful effect upon the result."[83]

Democratic prospects in Pennsylvania were not improved by the choice of Lewis Cass to head their presidential ticket. Cass in the Senate had voted in favor of the Walker tariff, and upon other occasions had shown himself to be decidedly lukewarm toward the policy of protection. Morris Longstreth, the Democratic nominee for governor, while a man of considerable ability, had never shown a disposition to exalt the tariff above the interests of his party. Nor was there much comfort to an ardent protectionist in the declaration of the Democratic state convention that

the Tariff of 1846 has realized the most sanguine expectations of its advocates

[77] Swank, *Statistical Abstract*, p. 24; Wilkie, *Manufacture of Iron in Great Britain*, p. 10.

[78] *Sen. Exec. Doc.*, 37 Cong., 2 Sess., No. 2, pp. 254-266.

[79] *House Exec. Doc.*, 38 Cong., 1 Sess., No. 2, pp. 328, 330; Swank, *Iron in All Ages*, p. 514; *Iron and Steel Industries of the U. S.*, p. 9; *Pittsburgh Gazette*, April 5, 1848.

[80] *Doc. Rel. to the Manu. of Iron in Penna.*, p. 109; *Pittsburgh Post*, January 2, 1848; *Pittsburgh Gazette*, April 1, 8, 1848.

[81] Swank, *Statistical Abstract*, p. 22; *Public Ledger*, February 9, 1848; John M. Read to Buchanan, February 22, 1848; Buchanan Mss.

[82] *Sen. Rep.*, 52 Cong., 2 Sess., III, pt. 1, p. 107.

[83] John M. Read to Buchanan, February 13, 1848; Buchanan Mss.

and friends and as signally falsified all the woeful predictions of its enemies. The Democracy of Pennsylvania cling to it as one of the crowning measures that has rendered the present national administration illustrious on the page of history, and are proud to record it as a demonstration established by the infallible tests of truth and time, that a restrictive commercial policy . . . has degenerated into an "obsolete idea."[84]

The Whigs, under these circumstances, would have preferred to enter the campaign with a strongly protectionist ticket, such as Clay for President and Andrew Stewart for Vice President.[85] They were reasonably satisfied, however, with the national convention's choice of Zachary Taylor and Millard Fillmore. Taylor's tariff views were unexceptionably vague, and Fillmore, while in Congress, had been chairman of the committee which had reported the tariff of 1842. The protectionist appeal of the Whig ticket was further strengthened by the choice of William F. Johnston as the party candidate for governor. Johnston was an iron manufacturer and a former Democrat, who had abandoned his old party as a protest against the enactment of the Walker tariff.[86] The Whig state convention, therefore, was able to declare, without fear of embarrassing contradiction that "we firmly adhere to the principles of protection embodied in the tariff of 1842."[87]

Largely because of the Democrats' anomalous position on the tariff, the Whigs were able to conduct a much more aggressive campaign than their opponents. More than a year before the election, Clay had recommended that protection and the Kane "fraud" should be made the foremost issues in Pennsylvania.[88] This suggestion was enthusiastically taken up by the Whig leaders, except in the northern counties where tariff sentiment was weakest and antislavery feeling most prevalent; there it was found expedient to stress the Wilmot proviso as the principal issue of the campaign.[89] Little could be said about Taylor's personal views upon the tariff; since the General had never committed himself beyond the mere

[84] *Pittsburgh Post*, March 13, 1848.
[85] *Harrisburg Telegraph*, May 9, 1848; *Pittsburgh Commercial Journal*, June 12, 1848.
[86] *Pennsylvanian*, September 26, 1848; Mueller, *Whig Party in Pennsylvania*, p. 150.
[87] *Harrisburg Telegraph*, March 17, 1848.
[88] Clay, *Works*, IV, 544.
[89] *Pennsylvanian*, September 15, 1848.

statement that he would not veto any revenue law which received the sanction of Congress.[90] Instead, the election was heralded primarily as a long-sought opportunity to wreak summary vengeance upon the authors of the Kane "fraud" and to register an unmistakable mandate for "the repeal of the abominable British bill of 1846, which. . .has impoverished the condition and impaired the prosperity of our own state."[91] It was freely predicted that a Whig victory in Pennsylvania would compel the Democrats in self-preservation to submit to the restoration of the tariff of 1842.[92] More specifically, it was asserted that a Whig majority in the legislature was essential to ensure the election of a loyal protectionist to the Senate, where the overthrow of the Walker tariff might well depend upon a single vote. Whig voters who had been led to believe that the protective system had been struck down by the unfilial hand of George M. Dallas now learned for the first time that it was in reality the vote of Lewis Cass which had consummated the act of destruction.[93] The *North American* went so far as to assert that "from Bangor to Corpus Cristi there is no public man more distinctly, openly, and unqualifiedly committed against the protective policy in all its forms and features, than Lewis Cass. . .He never made a speech, wrote a letter or gave a vote favorable to the interests of Pennsylvania or the manufacturing states."[94]

The Democrats, by way of rebuttal, declared that it was a "villainous cheat to represent General Taylor as a Tariff man."[95] It was pointed out that

Taylor's position and interests are all unmistakably southern; and if elected, he will be in the hands of the most uncompromising free trade and slavery partizans in the country . . . It is preposterous for the Tariff men of Pennsylvania to look to anything from a candidate who is a southern man and a cotton planter and supported by the most ultra free-trade nullifiers of the South.[96]

In language reminiscent of 1844, the voters were assured that

[90] *Harrisburg Telegraph*, May 9, 1848.
[91] *North American*, September 15, 1848.
[92] *Miners' Journal*, September 30, 1848.
[93] *Ibid.* September 23, 1848; *Harrisburg Telegraph*, October 31, 1848.
[94] November 6, 1848.
[95] *Harrisburg Democratic Union*, November 1, 1848.
[96] *Pennsylvanian*, October 16, 1848.

"General Cass is a better tariff man than General Taylor."[97] On the whole, however, both the character of their candidate and the unsatisfactory trend of the economic situation served to keep the Democrats very largely upon the defensive so far as the tariff question was concerned.

The state elections in October generally favored the Whigs, but by an extremely narrow margin. Johnston, who was elected governor, carried the state by only 297 votes.[98] The Whigs also captured fifteen out of twenty-four congressional seats, although the aggregate popular vote showed a slight Democratic majority.[99] Wilmot, reelected as a Free Soil Democrat, rolled up a tremendous majority of 3,802 votes, but the decisive factor in his district was the slavery issue, not the tariff.[100] The Whigs gained control of only one house of the legislature, but their margin was sufficient to insure the election of a Whig to succeed Cameron in the United States Senate.[101] The Democrats did succeed, however, in electing their candidate for canal commissioner, as a result of the Whig nominee's opposition to the state ten-hour factory law.[102] Spurred on by the closeness of the gubernatorial poll, both parties redoubled their efforts to capture Pennsylvania's electoral vote in the impending presidential election. Even the Whigs, however, scarcely anticipated the plurality of 13,537 which Taylor received three weeks later. The greatest Whig gains were recorded in the hard coal regions, where the prevailing economic depression was especially acute. The most dramatic political revolution in the state occurred in Schuylkill county, which gave a majority to a Whig presidential candidate for the only time in the history of the party.[103]

The jubilant Whigs spared no pains to drive home the tariff implications of their victory. The *North American*, with typical enthusiasm, declared that the outcome of the election

has settled . . . forever, the principle of protection . . If any now be disposed to deny this, let him look at Pennsylvania—brave and honest and glorious old

---

97 *Harrisburg Democratic Union*, November 1, 1848.
98 *Smull's Legislative Handbook*, 1921-22, p. 745.
99 *Pennsylvanian*, October 24, 27, 1848; *North American*, October 25, 1848.
100 *North American*, October 26, 1848.
101 *Pennsylvanian*, October 19, 20, 1848.
102 *Ibid*. October 28, 1848.
103 *Harrisburg Democratic Union*, November 22, 1848.

Pennsylvania, who has, at last, so signally buffeted down from their high places the fraud-mongering free traders of '44—let him look at her and be satisfied.

Did that mighty voice, coming, like the roar of an explosion of fire-damp, from the depths of her coal mines, shaking the hills above them—that wrath cry from abandoned furnaces and silent mills and workshops—that loud tone of indignation, sounding from so many fertile fields not yet actually reached by the fast-spreading death blight—did these, then, mean nothing?[104]

Democratic observers, likewise, admitted that the tariff question had been in large measure responsible for their defeat. As one of the party leaders wrote,

There are two causes to which the result may be attributed—gunpowder and the tariff! Which of them had the greatest influence, it will be hard to ascertain. . . . There is one thing to be done and if it is not, then there may be a long time between the revolution and the restoration. It is a revision of the tariff as to the staples of Pennsylvania. . . . They said it was bread and they would not stand to principle.[105]

Although it was not realized at the time, the election of 1848 was to constitute the last important Whig triumph in Pennsylvania. Thereafter, the party was compelled to shift an increasing portion of its attention to the slavery question and to subordinate in corresponding measure its greatest political asset—the tariff issue. During more than two decades of stormy existence, the Whig party of Pennsylvania won only three decisive triumphs—the elections of 1840, 1846 and 1848—and in every case it was the tariff question which appears to have furnished the margin of victory.[106] The growing dissatisfaction with the inexorable workings of the Compromise Act doubtless swung the handful of votes necessary to give the state to Harrison in 1840. That the passage of the Walker tariff was the decisive factor in 1846 and 1848 was generally recognized by observers of both parties. This short-lived political revolt not only elevated Zachary Taylor to the White House, but also gave the Whigs of Pennsylvania their only canal commissioner, their one governor, and their sole United States Senator. The defeat of the party in the intervening election of 1847 was obviously due to the

---

[104] November 11, 1848.
[105] H. B. Wright to Buchanan, November 13, 1848; Buchanan Mss.
[106] The gubernatorial victories of Ritner in 1835 and Pollock in 1854 were both the result of Whig coalitions with other parties.

submergence of the tariff issue by the Mexican war and the unusual prosperity which prevailed. It was sound political instinct, therefore, which led the Whig politicians of Pennsylvania to make protection the dominant note of every political campaign, even for the most humble of local offices.[107] The national bank in the early years of the party and anti-slavery at a later period were elements of real strength, but neither issue, when divorced from the tariff, could make much headway against the natural numerical advantage and superior leadership of the Democracy. Only through actual incursions into the ranks of the tariff Democrats could the Whig minority hope to obtain a majority at the polls. In one election after another, therefore, the issue resolved itself into a struggle between the stern party discipline of the Democrats and the protectionist lure enticingly displayed by their political adversaries.

---

[107] *Cf.* Whig campaign for sheriff in Schuylkill County in 1849. (*Miners' Journal*, September 29, 1849.)

# CHAPTER XI

# PROTECTIONISM'S DARKEST HOUR, 1849-1857

American industrial statistics before the Civil War, especially those concerning the manufacture of iron, are neither so complete nor so accurate as might be desired. The inadequacy of the available data becomes especially apparent when one seeks to determine the exact conditions prevailing in Pennsylvania's basic industries during the years immediately following 1848. Contemporary testimony, always open to suspicion where the tariff is in controversy, becomes unusually contradictory and confusing during these years. The *North American,* for instance, informed its readers in adjoining columns of a single issue that:

The tariff of 1846, which has fulfilled the expectation and intention of its projectors by protecting British interests, has reduced us to this extremity. All over Pennsylvania the furnaces are out of blast, the forges are silent, and the sheriff and his tipstaves are the only tenants of our once flourishing manufactories.

Early and late we hear now the roar of the great hive of industry resonant with the cheering, exciting noises of its myriad laborers, and behold, on all sides, the evidences of that opulence which mercantile enterprise and mechanical skill are creating in our midst.[1]

The same discrepancies appear in the testimony of Pennsylvania's spokesmen at Washington. Speaking of the industries of the state, Senator Cooper declared that there was "a degree of suffering prevalent among them which has not existed at any period within many years past—not even in 1842, previously to the passage of the act known as the tariff act of that year." Thereupon, Senator Sturgeon arose to assert that although the producers of pig iron might be in difficulties, "more iron has been manufactured at Pittsburgh the present season, and at a greater profit, than ever was the case before" and that the state as a whole "was never more prosperous than at present."[2] The truth, as usual, appears to lie between the two extremes here represented. Economic conditions generally were un-

---

[1] September 22, 1851.
[2] *Cong. Globe,* 31 Cong., 1 Sess., p. 1551.

doubtedly much less satisfactory between 1849 and 1851 than during the period immediately preceding. Nevertheless, the depression, coming in natural sequence after an era of extremely rapid industrial expansion, was by no means so universal nor so acute as extremists in the protectionist camp wished the country to believe.

The iron industry, especially, was seriously affected by overproduction and declining prices on both sides of the Atlantic. Between 1847 and 1851, pig iron on the Philadelphia market fell from $30 to $21 per ton and bar iron dropped from $86 to $55 per ton. This represented for both commodities the lowest price prevailing at any time prior to the Civil War.[3] So far as the rolling mills were concerned, the low price of their raw material compensated in some degree for the depressed price of bar iron, but for the producer of the pig metal, there was no corresponding relief.[4] It was claimed that during 1849 and the first four months of 1850, five anthracite and forty-five charcoal furnaces failed in Pennsylvania alone.[5] It was further estimated that of the 304 furnaces in the state, 167 were out of blast on November 1, 1850.[6] It was asserted that in Armstrong and Clarion counties, forty out of forty-two furnaces were closed during the worst stages of the depression.[7] When President Taylor visited Pittsburgh in August, 1849, he was informed that four-fifths of the ironworks in Allegheny county had failed during the previous eighteen months.[8] In general, the anthracite furnaces fared much better than did their charcoal competitors. Although many of the anthracite establishments deemed it expedient to close down temporarily, few failed, and most of these were small concerns, dating from the days of experiment with coal as a fuel.[9] The charcoal furnaces, however, were handicapped by much higher costs of production, and the advent of unprecedentedly low prices drove

---

[3] Swank, *Iron in All Ages*, p. 514; *Iron and Steel Industries of the United States*, p. 9.
[4] *Miners' Journal*, September 29, 1849.
[5] *Doc. Rel. to the Manu. of Iron in Penna.*, p. 109.
[6] *Hunt's Merchants' Magazine*, XXV, 576.
[7] *Plough, Loom and Anvil*, V, 265.
[8] *Public Ledger*, August 23, 1849.
[9] See list of anthracite furnaces in *Doc. Rel. to the Manu. of Iron in Penna.*, Appendix.

many such enterprises into bankruptcy.[10] For three years, in the words of one ironmaster, the charcoal producer was confronted with a "struggle for life and not for profit."[11] With a large number of furnaces out of blast, it is probable that Pennsylvania's total production of pig iron fell off materially during these years of extremely low prices.[12]

Fundamentally, the iron depression in America was merely one phase of a world-wide revulsion, due to overproduction and low prices.[13] A contributing factor, however, was the exceptional influx of foreign iron, which, beginning about 1848, was ruthlessly dumped upon the American market to relieve the surplus stocks of English manufacturers. Measured by quantity, the annual importation of pig and bar iron was more than four times greater during these years than it had been under the tariff of 1842.[14] Spurred on by steadily mounting imports, the iron interest of Pennsylvania hastened to launch a strong agitation in favor of higher duties. A group of ironmasters assembled at Pittsburgh in August, 1849, and expressed the belief that "the present depressed state of the iron trade has its origin and is entirely caused by the low rate of duty at which English iron is admitted into this country." At the same time a call was issued for a national convention of furnace owners to be held

---

[10] Under normal conditions, the furnace cost of anthracite pig iron was about $13 to $16 a ton, as compared with $18 or $20 a ton for the charcoal product. A poor quality of pig metal could be made for much less. For various estimates as to furnace and transportation costs at this period see *Doc. Rel. to the Manu. of Iron in Penna.*, pp. 52, 56, 89; *Pittsburgh Post*, November 10, 1849; *House Exec. Doc.*, 31 Cong., 1 Sess., No. 4, p. 813; Fritz, *Autobiography*, p. 95; Clark, *History of Manufactures*, I, 385.

[11] Hewitt, *On the Statistics and Geography of Iron*, p. 25.

[12] There are no trustworthy figures for the pig iron production of either state or nation during these years. A Pennsylvania ironmaster estimated that the state's production dropped from 389,350 tons in 1847 to 198,813 tons in 1850. (*Doc. Rel. to the Manu. of Iron in Penna.*, p. 103). This estimate, although widely circulated and generally accepted by Pennsylvania protectionists, probably greatly exaggerates the extent of the depression. The United States census for 1850 gives the state's production at 285,702 tons. (*Statistical View of the United States, Seventh Census*, p. 181). Even the census figures, however, are not overly accurate during these early years.

[13] It was reported in 1850 that one-third of the furnaces in England had likewise gone out of blast. (*Pittsburgh Post*, June 18, 1850).

[14] Computed from statistics in *House Exec. Doc.*, 30 Cong., 2 Sess., No. 33, pp. 2-15; *Sen. Exec. Doc.*, 31 Cong., 1 Sess., No. 3, pp. 178-179; *Annual Report on Commerce and Navigation*, 1850, pp. 176-177; 1851, pp. 182-183.

in the same city in November.[15] This general convention was attended by 166 delegates, representing ironworks in New Jersey, Virginia, New York, Ohio, Kentucky, Illinois and Pennsylvania.[16] All agreed that increased protection was necessary, but there was a serious division of opinion as to the kind and amount of duties to be levied. One group favored a flat specific duty upon iron, while others urged the adoption of a sliding scale, under which the tax would be increased as the price declined.[17] It was finally decided, however, that a tax of $10 per ton on pig iron and $20 per ton on bar iron would be necessary to afford adequate protection to the American producer.[18] The following month, another convention met at Philadelphia, made up of ironmasters from eastern Pennsylvania, New Jersey, and Maryland.[19] A memorial was addressed to Congress, calling for a permanent adjustment of the rates on iron, with either a specific duty or a sliding scale.[20] Like the two previous conventions, this gathering attracted little attention in the national legislature, already deeply engrossed in the tense deliberations which produced the Compromise of 1850.

The difficulties of the coal industry during this period arose principally from too-rapid expansion, with consequent overproduction and low prices. Anthracite output increased from 3,287,970 tons in 1850 to 4,428,916 tons in 1851, the largest growth for any one year prior to the Civil War.[21] As a result, prices by the fall of 1851 had declined to extremely low levels; while the rapid expansion of the industry served to keep wages comparatively high.[22] The operators also had to contend with an inefficient sales system, a

---

[15] *Miners' Journal*, August 25, 1849.
[16] *Proceedings of the Iron Convention held at Pittsburgh*, pp. 13-14.
[17] *Ibid.* pp. 8-11.
[18] *Ibid.* p. 12. At existing prices, the 30 per cent. ad valorem rate was equivalent to a tax of $3.81 per ton on pig iron and $8.94 per ton on bar iron. (Computed from statistics in *Annual Report on Commerce and Navigation*, 1850, 176-177).
[19] *Public Ledger*, December 22, 1849.
[20] *Doc. Rel. to the Manu. of Iron in Penna.*, pp. 19-21.
[21] Pennsylvania Bureau of Statistics of Labor and Agriculture, *Annual Report*, 1872-73, pp. 213-216. The mere fact that this amount could be marketed, even though at extremely low prices, is further evidence that the anthracite iron industry of Pennsylvania was by no means completely prostrated at this time. For comment upon this point, see *Hunt's Merchants' Magazine*, XXVI, 770.
[22] Swank, *Statistical Abstract*, p. 22; *Sen. Rep.*, 52 Cong., 2 Sess., Vol. III, pt. 4, p. 1561.

short-sighted credit policy, and fluctuating transportation charges, which combined to produce an embarrassing condition of alternate stagnation and oversupply in the coal trade.[23] In an effort to raise prices, the Schuylkill district suspended the mining and shipping of anthracite for several weeks during the spring and summer of 1849, but the results of this early attempt to control production were not encouraging.[24] At the same time, the rapid exhaustion of the more shallow surface workings was driving many of the smaller operators out of business and was making necessary drastic changes in mining procedure.[25] In large measure, the situation was the product of that maladjustment which is inherent in rapid growth, but the coal regions did not hesitate to stigmatize the Walker tariff as the ultimate source of their difficulties.[26] A lobbyist was sent to Washington in 1849 with instructions to work for a specific duty of $1.25 per ton in place of the existing ad valorem rate, which was equivalent, at current prices to 65 or 70 cents per ton.[27] Since the total import of foreign coal at this time only amounted to approximately 3 per cent. of the domestic production, it is not surprising that this appeal fell upon deaf ears at Washington.[28]

The Pittsburgh region, for various reasons, appears to have been particularly affected by the general industrial depression. Allegheny county, with an investment in the iron industry exceeding that of any other county in the state, quickly felt the pinch of low prices and decreased demand.[29] The year 1849, moreover, was an extremely trying one for all the mercantile and manufacturing interests of the western metropolis, due to the interruption of the river trade as a result of the cholera epidemic and low water upon the Ohio.[30] Then, early in 1850, most of the Pittsburgh rolling mills were closed by a strike against the 25 per cent. wage reduction announced by

---

[23] *Public Ledger,* February 2, 1849; *Pennsylvanian,* April 3, 1849; *Miners' Journal,* April 21, 1849.
[24] *North American,* April 26, 1849; *Public Ledger,* March 21, April 9, May 9, July 7, 1849.
[25] *North American,* January 12, 1852.
[26] *Miners' Journal,* June 2, 1849.
[27] *Ibid.* November 17, 1849.
[28] Pennsylvania Bureau of Statistics of Labor and Agriculture, *Annual Report,* 1872-73, pp. 213-216; *Mineral Resources of the United States,* 1915, II, 358.
[29] *Harrisburg Telegraph,* March 3, 1852.
[30] *Pittsburgh Commercial Journal,* November 2, 1849.

the employers, who declared that the alternative was either more protection or lower pay.[31] The strike failed after a duration of more than three months, and the workers were forced to accept the reduction.[32] The long suspension of the rolling mills in turn caused a serious oversupply of pig metal, which added greatly to the difficulties of the charcoal furnaces of the vicinity.[33] Later in the same year, all the cotton mills in Allegheny City were forced to suspend operations. According to the Democrats, the stoppage was due to domestic overproduction and the high price of raw materials; while the Whigs maintained that a heavy influx of British cottons was responsible.[34]

The adverse trend of economic conditions between 1849 and 1851 effected little change in the traditional attitude of the two major parties upon the tariff question. The Whigs continued to denounce the Walker tariff as a "virtual repeal of the Declaration of Independence."[35] A meeting at Philadelphia asserted "that the Act of 1846, which taxed American labor to support the paupers of England, and to make the richest portions of Pennsylvania a howling wilderness, is regarded by us as a treason and a crime against the country."[36] The Whig state convention for 1850 held that "all the great interests of Pennsylvania, having their ultimate end in Labor, are languishing under the ruinous effects of the Foreign serf and pauper competition, invited and drawn over by the degrading Tariff of 1846, to a degree that has no parallel in the former history of the country."[37] It was declared further that only the influx of gold from California had saved the industrial interests of the country from utter and complete annihilation.[38] Even the Whigs, however, had receded by this time from their earlier demands for the unqualified restoration of the tariff of 1842. A resolution calling for the reenactment of that law was introduced in the state Senate in

---

31 *Ibid.* January 18, 1850; *Pittsburgh Post,* January 14, 1850.
32 *Pittsburgh Post,* April 27, 1850.
33 *Pittsburgh Post,* May 1, 1850; *Hunt's Merchants' Magazine,* XXV, 577.
34 *Pittsburgh Post,* August 6, 1850; *Pittsburgh Commercial Journal,* August 7, 1850.
35 *North American,* October 6, 1851.
36 *Ibid.* October 8, 1849.
37 *Harrisburg Telegraph,* June 30, 1850.
38 *North American,* June 24, 1851.

1851, but it received only one affirmative vote.[39] Instead, the Whigs now took strong ground in favor of a moderate upward revision, based upon a system of specific duties and American valuations.[40] The protectionist wing of the party greatly resented the ever-increasing encroachment of the slavery question, which served to divert Congress from a consideration of such legislation. Petulantly, one journal declared,

While our leading statesmen are willing to risk their reputation for wisdom and consistency by concocting unpalatable, if not disreputable, compromises, because a few dissatisfied spirits have blustered about disunion, they seem to care nothing for the desires and demands and necessities of hundreds of thousands of toiling freemen—which the present policy is fast impoverishing. . . Is it not time for this struggle to cease, and for some useful legislation to be entered upon?[41]

It was asserted that "the State of Pennsylvania alone has lost more in a pecuniary point of view, within the last four years, by the repeal of the tariff of 1842, than the value of all the slaves that have ever escaped from all the slave holding States, since the formation of the Union."[42] Another editor assured his anti-slavery readers that "a judicious Tariff will be found to be a more formidable barrier to the extension and progress of Slavery than any other instrument within the grasp of Congress."[43]

The Democratic press, on the other hand, delighted to ridicule the direful protestations of their political adversaries. One journal noted that the Whig agitation "has periodical spasms, not unlike Mr. Webster's 'hay' fever. . .It is, perhaps, a singular coincidence in the history of the tariff, that always preceding an election in Pennsylvania, the country is seized with a violent fit of depression—the manufacturers suddenly get the blues, the horrors, and all sorts of inauspicious devils."[44] The Washington *Union*, long a source of vexation to Pennsylvania protectionists, called attention to

---

[39] *Senate Journal*, 1851, I, 202.
[40] *House Journal*, 1851, I, 183-185; *Miners' Journal*, April 14, 1849, December 14, 1850.
[41] *Pittsburgh Gazette*, May 13, 1850.
[42] *Pittsburgh Commercial Journal*, June 6, 1850.
[43] *Miners' Journal*, July 6, 1850.
[44] *Detroit Free Press*, quoted in *Harrisburg Keystone*, September 16, 1851.

the periodical clamor got up by the leaders of the Federal party and the iron masters of Pennsylvania on the eve of every important election in relation to the pretended depressed state of the iron interest in Pennsylvania. . . They blow out their furnaces, dismiss their hands, and then raise a most lugubrious groan of distress. . . The causes of this periodical "pig iron" clamor raised by the iron masters of Pennsylvania are now so transparent that it has become disgusting to the community. It is now understood to be the conjoint cry of grim, insatiable avarice and political desperation and deserves and should receive the contempt and rebuke of the intelligent people upon whom it is designed to operate.[45]

It cannot be denied that these charges contained an element of truth. There is reason to believe, however, that the Democrats, themselves, were not entirely oblivious to political considerations in their handling of the tariff question. Prior to an election, the party in Pennsylvania took well-nigh unanimous ground in defence of the existing duties. At a time when the Whigs were loudest in their professions of universal ruin, one of the leading Democratic organs in the state declared that "the manufacturing interests of the country were never in a more prosperous condition than at the present time, the croaking of the Federalists and Conservatives to the contrary notwithstanding."[46] Even the iron industry was characterized as being in a flourishing condition.[47] The Democratic state convention in 1849 unanimously resolved "that the practical workings of the present revenue laws clearly demonstrate their superiority over those which immediately preceded them."[48] The Lebanon county convention in the same year held that "the howling of a few politicians and manufacturers in favor of the exploded doctrine of high protection would be ridiculous did not their selfish character raise them to the dignity of being contemptible."[49] A Pittsburgh paper ventured to assert that "nine-tenths of the people of Pennsylvania are opposed to a higher tariff than the one now in existence."[50] Another journal believed that "the tariff of '46 is the best tariff we have ever had, and will be the most popular until a further reduction of duties takes place," and

---

[45] Quoted in *Harrisburg Telegraph,* September 26, 1849; *Miners' Journal,* September 29, 1849.

[46] *Pittsburgh Post,* August 21, 1849.

[47] *Pennsylvanian,* January 27, 1849; *Pittsburgh Post,* November 15, 1849; *Harrisburg Keystone,* November 4, 1851.

[48] *Pittsburgh Post,* July 11, 1849.

[49] *Harrisburg Democratic Union,* August 29, 1849.

[50] *Pittsburgh Post,* February 2, 1850.

predicted that the protective system would come to be regarded as "one of the most pernicious schemes to enrich one portion of the American people out of the spoils of another, that ever was devised by profligate politicians, and will be held in the same execration as the alien and sedition law of 1798."[51] It was even urged that the party should be bolder in its attacks upon a system "which like slavery is being abolished by the public opinion of all civilized countries."[52]

While bound by ties of party loyalty to the support of the act of 1846, some foresighted Democrats realized that a failure to modify the tariff might result in the loss of the state in 1852. Accordingly, an agitation was launched immediately after the election of 1850 in favor of specific duties for coal and iron. The Pittsburgh *Post*, which originated the movement, declared that if they could "take the Tariff question out of the Arena of politics by imposing such duties upon iron and coal as the interests of the whole country require. . .the death knell of Whiggery in Pennsylvania will be sounded."[53] The proposal elicited considerable favorable comment from the Democratic press of Pennsylvania, but when Congress failed to act, it was discreetly dropped during the gubernatorial campaign of 1851.[54] After the election, the proposal was revived in behalf of iron alone, and in this form was approved by Democratic meetings in several counties.[55] Buchanan seriously doubted the advisability of this movement, which he feared would play into the hands of the enemy.[56] The approach of the presidential contest, however, quickly put an end to the agitation, and the sharp rise of prices which followed the election made further appeal unnecessary.

The remarkable recuperative power of the Democratic party in Pennsylvania was well illustrated in the trend of state politics between 1849 and 1851. The election of 1849 centered around the choice of a canal commissioner and members of the legislature. The Whigs, as usual, maintained that the election of their candidate would be regarded in Washington as an imperative mandate for the repeal of

---

[51] *Harrisburg Keystone,* October 28, November 25, 1851.
[52] *Pittsburgh Post,* October 12, 1849.
[53] *Ibid.* October 30, November 27, 1850.
[54] *Ibid.* November 30, 1850; *Pennsylvanian,* November 13, 26, December 6, 28, 1850.
[55] *Pittsburgh Post,* October 31, 1851; *Pennsylvanian,* November 20, December 12, 15, 1851.
[56] Buchanan to J. W. Forney, January 1, 1852; Buchanan Mss.

the Walker tariff.[57] It was also predicted that if the Democrats captured the legislature, one of their first acts would be to adopt instructing resolutions in favor of the act of 1846.[58] The Whig contentions were weakened, however, by the fact that no national offices were at stake, and the Democrats easily elected the canal commissioner and regained control of both houses of the legislature.[59] That the Democratic victory was no accidental triumph was indicated by the election of the following year, in which the party secured fifteen of the twenty-four congressmen.[60] Efforts of the Whigs to make the tariff a decisive factor in this contest were completely nullified by the irresistible force of the slavery issue.[61]

Nevertheless, the Whigs approached the gubernatorial election of 1851 with a renewed determination to make the tariff issue the instrument of victory. Governor Johnston, as a candidate for reelection, was universally recognized as one of Pennsylvania's most unyielding protectionists. The Democrats, on the other hand, nominated William Bigler, who, having made a fortune in lumbering, was supposed to have little interest in the tariff question.[62] The Whigs, accordingly, took strong ground against the existing duties and reiterated their familiar contention that a victory for their candidate would ensure a speedy modification.[63] Johnston, himself, solemnly assured the voters "that the question of a protective or non-protective tariff will be settled for years to come by the action of the people at the ballot box on the 14th of October next."[64] Bigler and his associates, however, ridiculed the Whig contention and pointed out that the Democratic majority in Congress would scarcely be inclined to extend tariff concessions to a state which had repudiated the party at the polls.[65] In spite of this argument, there is reason to believe that the Whigs were making real progress with their protectionist appeal until the Christiana riot suddenly broke out a month before the election.

[57] *Harrisburg Telegraph*, September 22, 1849; *Miners' Journal*, September 29, 1849.
[58] *North American*, September 22, 1849.
[59] *Pennsylvanian*, October 24, 1849; *Miners' Journal*, November 3, 1849.
[60] *North American*, November 1, 1850.
[61] *Ibid.* October 11, 1850; *Pennsylvanian*, October 4, 12, 1850.
[62] *Pittsburgh Post*, August 21, 1851.
[63] *North American*, June 25, September 6, 20, 1851; *Miners' Journal*, September 11, 1851; *Pittsburgh Gazette*, October 1, 1851.
[64] *North American*, September 16, 1851.
[65] *Harrisburg Telegraph*, February 11, 1852.

This disturbance, culminating in the murder of a slave-owner seeking to recover an alleged fugitive, served to discredit Johnston in many quarters of the state and immediately threw the Whig party upon the defensive. This episode seems to have cost the Governor many votes, especially among the conservative business men of Philadelphia, who dreaded the effect of such anti-slavery disorders upon their Southern trade. With the tariff question thus relegated to the background, the Democrats were able to carry their entire ticket by a comfortable margin. Although Johnston's vote showed a slight increase over that of the preceding election, Bigler received a plurality of 8455.[66] The Democrats recovered Schuylkill county, which they had lost in 1848, and materially reduced Johnston's former majority in Philadelphia city and county.[67] The Pittsburgh *Post* believed that the slavery question had been the decisive factor in the contest and rejoiced that "the Tariff of 1842 with all its gilded charms, could not save the fanatic from overwhelming defeat."[68]

The Whig protectionists of Pennsylvania, repeatedly repulsed in the state politics of this period, were equally unsuccessful in their appeals to the national government for legislative relief. Much was hoped from the administration of President Taylor, who expressed the belief, while visiting Pittsburgh in 1849, that the duties imposed by the Walker tariff were "utterly inadequate."[69] Many protectionists would have preferred the appointment of "Tariff Andy" Stewart as Secretary of the Treasury, but the choice of William M. Meredith of Philadelphia for that position was received with general approbation.[70] Meredith's annual report for 1849 took strong ground in favor of higher rates on iron, coal, woolens, cottons, and other articles, and urged a return to specific duties wherever possible.[71] Commenting favorably upon these recommendations, a Schuylkill county meeting took pains to point out the "contrast between his conduct on this question with that of Pennsylvania's once favorite, now traitor son, George M. Dallas."[72]

[66] *Smull's Legislative Handbook*, 1921-22, p. 745.
[67] *Harrisburg Telegraph*, October 16, 1851.
[68] October 16, 1851.
[69] *Pittsburgh Post*, August 21, 1849.
[70] *Harrisburg Telegraph*, December 27, 1848, March 24, 1849; *Miners' Journal*, March 10, 1849.
[71] *House Exec. Doc.*, 31 Cong., 1 Sess., No. 4, p. 15.
[72] *Miners' Journal*, June 15, 1850.

Encouraged by the attitude of the Administration, Pennsylvania Congressmen made several attempts to obtain a modification of the existing duties. Shortly before Taylor took office, a resolution was introduced by Eckert, who represented the anthracite regions, instructing the Committee on Ways and Means to inquire into the expediency of a tariff bill based upon the principles of the act of 1842. This resolution was adopted by a close vote, with only four Pennsylvanians—all Democrats—opposing it.[73] The Committee reported in favor of specific duties and a limited increase of rates, but the measure was permanently tabled by the House of Representatives.[74] During the following session of Congress, several attempts were made to secure increased protection through the substitution of American for foreign valuations. One resolution, instructing the Committee on Ways and Means to report a bill to effect this change, was actually defeated by the votes of four Pennsylvania Democrats.[75] Another resolution, proposed in 1851 by one of the Democratic members of the delegation, provided for a tax of 40 per cent. upon imported iron, to be assessed upon the average foreign price for the preceding ten years.[76] These and other similar attempts were doubtless intended primarily for home consumption, since the prevailing temper of the Thirty-first Congress clearly precluded any serious expectations of higher duties.

The tariff agitation in Pennsylvania was abruptly stilled after 1851 by the advent of an era of unprecedented industrial and agricultural prosperity. For all the great economic interests of the state, the period from the beginning of 1852 to the panic of 1857 was one of rapid expansion, high prices, and abundant profits. The iron trade, which had become a fairly accurate barometer of general industrial conditions, experienced the most rapid increase of prices it had ever known. Pig metal, which during the depression had sold as low as $20 per ton, was bringing $45 per ton for the better grades by the close of 1852.[77] The average price of bar iron likewise increased from $55 per ton in 1851 to $91 per ton in 1854.[78] Generally speaking, iron

[73] *Cong. Globe,* 30 Cong., 2 Sess., p. 26.

[74] *Ibid.* p. 616; *House Rep.,* 30 Cong., 2 Sess., No. 129.

[75] *Cong. Globe,* 31 Cong., 1 Sess., p. 1813.

[76] *Ibid.* 31 Cong., 2 Sess., p. 357; *Pittsburgh Post,* February 4, 1851.

[77] *Pittsburgh Post,* November 11, 18, 1852; *Harrisburg Keystone,* January 19, 1853.

[78] Swank, *Iron and Steel Industries of the United States,* p. 9.

prices at the peak of the movement were as high as those of twenty-five years before, in spite of the fact that during the intervening period the cost of production had decreased from one-fourth to one-half for pig iron, and from one-third to three-fourths for bar iron, depending upon the process employed.[79] The extravagant profits implicit in such prices quickly brought most of the abandoned ironworks back into operation, caused the erection of many new establishments, and induced many owners to throw their plants into day-and-night production.[80] Increased output after 1854 caused something of a recession from the maximum price levels of that year, but the iron industry as a whole continued in a flourishing condition until the panic of 1857. Other industrial establishments, especially those engaged in the manufacture of cottons, woolens, and glass, were reported to be exceptionally prosperous during this period.[81] The coal trade, likewise benefited greatly from the increased demand which followed the revival of business. Average anthracite prices at Philadelphia rose from $3.34 per ton in 1851 to $5.19 in 1854; while miners' wages attained the highest level in more than a decade.[82] Pottsville was characterized during this period as "the most prosperous town in Pennsylvania—perhaps in the United States."[83] Even Henry C. Carey, in a most uncharacteristic burst of optimism, declared that "we care not a button whether the coal duty be retained or taken off."[84] As in the case of the iron industry, the rapidly increased output led to a decline of coal prices beginning in the fall of 1854. In spite of the complaints of the operators that they were being ruined by the fall of prices, production statistics would seem to indicate that the anthracite trade afforded reasonable profits for several years thereafter.[85] The farmers, also, enjoyed a period of unusual prosperity as a result of the extremely favorable agricultural prices which pre-

---

[79] Clark, *History of Manufactures*, I, 386.

[80] *Hunt's Merchants' Magazine*, XXX, 438-39; *Pennsylvanian*, April 17, 1854; *Pittsburgh Gazette*, June 10, 1854; *Pittsburgh Post*, November 26, 1855.

[81] *Pennsylvanian*, November 8, 1852; *North American*, August 12, 1856; *Hunt's Merchants' Magazine*, XXX, 438.

[82] Swank, *Statistical Abstract*, p. 22; *Sen. Rep.*, 52 Cong., 2 Sess., Vol. III, pt. 4, p. 1561.

[83] *Public Ledger*, October 11, 1854.

[84] Carey, H., *Coal*, p. 1.

[85] Penna. Bureau of Statistics of Labor and Agriculture, *Annual Report*, 1872-73. pp. 213-216; *North American*, October 24, 1854; *Hunt's Merchants' Magazine*, XXXII, 256.

vailed from 1854 to 1857. Pennsylvania, as the leading wheat-producing state in the Union, profited especially from the rapid increase in the price of that commodity, which more than doubled in value between 1852 and 1855.[86] '

A number of factors combined to make the tariff a decidedly minor issue in Pennsylvania between 1852 and 1856. In the first place, the prevailing prosperity robbed the restrictionist of his most effective and most convincing economic argument. Indeed, the high price of food-stuffs convinced at least one protectionist editor that the country needed fewer consumers and more producers, and he urged the well-nigh heretical doctrine that the streams of labor must now be diverted from the factory to the farm.[87] In the second place, the realization was growing that the overthrow of the Walker tariff would probably mean lower rather than higher duties. As early as 1849, the Washington *Union* had warned the protectionists of Pennsylvania that "if you attempt to increase the duties of the present tariff, the battle will not end until they are still further reduced."[88] This admonition became something more than an idle threat with the return of the Democratic party to power in 1853. High prices precipitated a revived demand for the free admittance of railroad iron; while a recurrent surplus of revenue seemed to justify a general reduction of duties. Accordingly, many Pennsylvanians were forced into a reluctant support of the Walker act as representing the lesser of two evils. In the third place, the rapid dissolution of the Whig party after the election of 1852 was a stunning blow to the forces of Pennsylvania protectionism. During the years of disintegration, it became clearly apparent, as the Democrats had long contended, that the professional politicians had provided the tariff movement with its most vociferous adherents. The temporary defection of this element to the ranks of anti-Catholicism and anti-slavery automatically relegated the tariff to an entirely subordinate position in Pennsylvania politics. For several years after 1854, the Kansas-Nebraska issue dominated the political arena, and left the protective tariff, in the words of one news-paper, "as dead politically as a United States bank."[89]

---

[86] *Sen. Rep.*, 52 Cong., 2 Sess., Vol. III, pt. 1, pp. 105, 107; *North American*, July 16, 1855; *Harrisburg Keystone*, August 20, 1856.
[87] *Pittsburgh Gazette*, December 3, 1855.
[88] Quoted in *Harrisburg Telegraph*, October 3, 1849.
[89] *Public Ledger*, December 23, 1854.

The abatement of protectionist excitement during these years is reflected in the comparative calm with which Pennsylvania received the consummation of the Canadian reciprocity treaty in 1854. Henry C. Carey, it is true, vigorously opposed such an agreement as a base betrayal of American interests.[90] Both Pennsylvania Senators, likewise, voted against the treaty when it was presented for ratification.[91] Aside from this, the opposition to reciprocity with Canada appears to have been rather perfunctory.[92] Buchanan informed President Pierce that such a commercial agreement would afford him "great satisfaction."[93] Even the mining interest, which had feared an influx of Nova Scotia coal under the treaty, rejoiced to find a considerable market for Pennsylvania anthracite in some of the Canadian provinces.[94] Prior to the Civil War, the only serious opposition to the treaty appears to have come from the shipping interests of Philadelphia, who resented the resu'tant diversion of trade, and from such extremists as Carey, who denounced all reciprocity agreements as a matter of principle.[95]

Pennsylvania protectionists in Congress, confronted with an aggressively hostile majority, were reduced during these years to a purely defensive role. At every session of the national legislature, proposals were introduced and vigorously pushed for a general tariff reduction and for the free admission of railroad iron. A particularly serious threat to the protective system developed in 1855, when a bill was introduced in the Senate providing for a three-year suspension of duties on railroad iron. Despite the desperate efforts of the Pennsylvania Senators to defeat or modify this measure, it was easily passed by a coalition of Southern and Western votes.[96] At the same time, a bill was pending in the House, which provided for a general reduction of 20 per cent. on all existing duties. Normally, such a measure, which lowered the rates on coal and iron to twenty-four per cent., would

---

[90] Carey, H., *Reconstruction*, p. 20.
[91] *Sen. Exec. Jour.*, IX, 374, 376.
[92] *Cf. North American*, September 16, 1854; February 9, 1855; *Public Ledger*, October 11, 1854.
[93] Buchanan to Pierce, June 7, 1853; Buchanan Mss.
[94] *House Exec. Doc.*, 36 Cong., 1 Sess., No. 96, p. 60; *Public Ledger*, June 29, 1854; June 23, 1856.
[95] *House Exec. Doc.*, 36 Cong., 1 Sess., No. 96, p. 60.
[96] *Cong. Globe*, 33 Cong., 2 Sess., pp. 859-61, 886.

have encountered the almost unanimous opposition of Pennsylvania. Seven Democrats, however, consummated a logrolling agreement to support the bill in return for assurance that the iron interest of the state would be protected against free railroad iron.[97] Since the passage of the measure by the lower House was assured, even without these seven votes, the stratagem was generally approved by the protectionist press.[98] Both the House and the Senate bills, however, were ultimately killed through nonconcurrence, due in considerable measure to the unremitting opposition of Pennsylvania.[99]

The trend of Pennsylvania politics between 1852 and 1856 affords further evidence of the relative unimportance of the protectionist movement during these years. The moribund Whig party, it is true, made a deliberate attempt to fight the presidential campaign of 1852 upon the familiar ground of the tariff. Franklin Pierce was characterized as "one of the bitterest opponents to the Protection of American industry and Pennsylvania interest that could be selected in the whole country."[100] A Pittsburgh editor depicted the Democratic candidate as an uncompromising free trader and denounced him for his "obstinate adherence to certain antiquated absurdities."[101] Protectionist journals recalled that in the New Hampshire Democratic convention in 1846, Pierce had offered a resolution declaring that "believing the principle of protection to be  wrong, we go for a Revenue Tariff, adopted to the wants of the Government, imposing the burdens of taxation equally upon all."[102] The Whigs branded the Democratic nominee as the "British candidate" and sought to confirm the accusation by circulating extracts from the English press in favor of his election.[103] As usual, the closing days of the campaign were featured

---

[97] *Ibid.* p. 931. The real sentiment of the delegation was indicated by a test vote earlier in the session, which showed only one Pennsylvanian as favoring a reduction of duties. This was Galusha A. Grow, who was Wilmot's law partner and successor in Congress. (*Ibid.* p. 619.)

[98] *Public Ledger,* February 26, March 6, 1855; *Pittsburgh Gazette,* February 28, 1855; *Miners' Journal,* March 3, 1855.

[99] *Cong. Globe,* 33 Cong., 2 Sess., pp. 894, 910-14, 1088.

[100] *Miners' Journal,* June 12, 1852.

[101] *Pittsburgh Commercial Journal,* July 21, 1852.

[102] *Harrisburg Telegraph,* September 29, 1852.

[103] *North American,* July 28, August 5, 1852; *Miners' Journal,* August 7, 1852. The Democrats replied, rather weakly, that these excerpts had been inserted in the English press by American Whigs resident abroad, who hoped thereby to discredit Pierce. (*Pittsburgh Post,* September 23, 1852).

by the claims of both parties that British gold was being sent to America to influence the election in behalf of their opponents.[104]

The campaign evoked very little discussion of General Scott's tariff views, which were kept intentionally vague by his advisers.[105] Instead, the Democrats concentrated their fire upon Graham, the Whig candidate for Vice President, whose vote in the Senate against the tariff of 1842 made him especially vulnerable. A Whig victory, it was emphasized, would place the casting vote in the hands of an acknowledged free trader and would even elevate him to the presidency, if Scott should die in office.[106] As further evidence of their opponents' hypocrisy upon the subject, the Democrats pointed out that it was a Whig Secretary of the Treasury who ruled that freight charges should not be included in the assessed valuation of imports under the Walker tariff.[107] All such academic arguments, however, were completely overshadowed by the rapid improvement of economic conditions during the progress of the campaign. Gleefully, a Democratic editor exclaimed,

Iron is going up just as it should be going down, and the iron masters are threatened with prosperity when a due regard to the success of the whig party which has so deeply sympathized with their sufferings demands that they should be completely ruined and that the fire in every forge and furnace in the Commonwealth should be extinguished instead of burning brighter. Alas! for whiggery, such a state of affairs, though it may be sport for the iron master, will prove to be death for the whig party, whose only hold on life in Pennsylvania is the tariff.[108]

Aided by the opportune revival of business conditions and profiting from the inherent weaknesses of the opposition, Pierce carried the state in the November election by a plurality of 19,458 votes.[109] After scanning the returns, a Whig editor sadly remarked, "Winfield Scott,

---

[104] *North American,* October 7, 27, 1852; *Miners' Journal,* October 30, 1852; *Pennsylvanian,* November 2, 1852.

[105] Scott had written Thaddeus Stevens in 1842 that "I am not only in favor of a tariff for *revenue,* but also for *protection.*" (May 5, 1842; Stevens Mss.)

[106] *Pennsylvanian,* September 17, 1852; *Pittsburgh Post,* September 27, October 19, 1852.

[107] *Pennsylvanian,* September 30, 1852; *Pittsburgh Post,* October 8, 1852.

[108] *Harrisburg Keystone,* August 18, 1852. The Whig explanation that British manufacturers had deliberately raised iron prices in order to influence the result of the American election was not altogether convincing. (*Miners' Journal,* October 30, 1852).

[109] *Smull's Legislative Handbook,* 1921-22, p. 740.

after being always victorious against his country's enemies on the tented field has at last been defeated by British and Australian gold."[110] Another partisan observer declared,

The luck of the American democracy is miraculous. The accident of a famine in Ireland saved them in 1847 . . . In 1849 and 1850 the receipts of gold from California counterbalanced the exports of gold to England . . . Could the Whig party have come before the people then, with their candidate for President pledged to "specific duties" they would have swept the states in triumph. But lo ! the luck of the Democracy. As a first compensating consequence of the destruction of the iron furnaces and mills, their stored products, thrown off like the silkworm's, at the price of death, sprang to a post mortem value they could not have attained but for the general crushing of the factories. Pig metal jumped four, five, six, seven and eight dollars a ton. And fast on the heels of this dearly bought advance came the recoil upon our shores of the tempest raised in England by the gold discoveries in Australia, and the frightful emigration of laborers on iron to that land of gold . . . Rail bars leap and leap, until, a month before our late election, rails that had been laid down on New York landings at $33 per ton could not be placed there for a penny less than $65 a ton . . . The Democrats won the day by dilating and dwelling on the advance in iron as proof of the salutary operation of the British tariff.[111]

The triumph of Pierce was followed by a period of political quiet which continued until the election of 1854. This contest, which centered about the choice of governor and members of Congress, precipitated a bitter struggle upon the issues of anti-Catholicism and the Kansas-Nebraska act. The tariff, however, was scarcely mentioned. The Democratic state convention chose to ignore the subject entirely; while the Whigs merely adopted a perfunctory resolution declaring "that the policy of protecting our home industry against the depressing influence of foreign capital and labor is as sound in principle now as ever, notwithstanding the accidental causes which, for the moment, may seem to declare otherwise."[112] Although a Whig and Know Nothing coalition elected James Pollock to succeed Governor Bigler, the whole course of the campaign indicated that, for the time being, the forces of Pennsylvania protectionism were politically bankrupt.

---

110 *Bedford Inquirer*, quoted in *Harrisburg Telegraph*, November 10, 1852.
111 *Pittsburgh Commercial Journal*, November 10, 1852.
112 *Westmoreland Intelligencer*, March 23, 1854; *Pittsburgh Gazette*, August 11, 1854.

The tariff was likewise a decidedly minor issue in the presidential contest of 1856. The Democratic state convention struck the keynote of the Buchanan campaign when it asserted that "all other evils are insignificant in comparison with that of danger to the Union."[113] This pronouncement was reaffirmed by the state central committee, which maintained that "the time has passed for the discussion of Bank and Tariff questions."[114] Manufacturers were told that only the election of Buchanan would preserve their Southern markets, which were declared to be more important to Pennsylvania industry than the enactment of any tariff.[115] To refute the protectionist professions of their opponents, it was pointed out that many of the Republican leaders had taken an active part in the agitation for free railroad iron.[116] For the most part, however, the Democrats confined themselves to a glorification of Pennsylvania's favorite son, an arraignment of their adversaries as abolitionists and disunionists, and a scathing commentary upon the more unconventional episodes of Fremont's tumultuous career.

There were many ardent protectionists arrayed in opposition to Buchanan in both the Republican and the American camps. Henry C. Carey was a member of the national convention which nominated Fremont, and himself received three votes for Vice President.[117] Fillmore's adherents included such recognized friends of the tariff as Edward Joy Morris and Andrew Stewart.[118] Nevertheless, even the fanatically protectionist *Miners' Journal* admitted that the great issue of the election was "free territory, free labor, free speech and Fremont."[119] Only incidentally were references made to Buchanan's part in the Kane "fraud" and to his alleged subserviency to the free trade party of the South.[120] An effort was also made to revive the "ten-cent Jimmy" accusation, but none of these threadbare charges seem to have carried much weight.[121] In spite of a last-minute coalition be-

---

[113] *Pennsylvanian*, March 6, 1856.
[114] *Ibid.* August 30, 1856.
[115] *Words of Counsel to Men of Business*, p. 3.
[116] *Pennsylvanian*, October 8, 1856; *Last Appeal to Pennsylvania*, p. 4.
[117] *Pittsburgh Gazette*, June 19, 1856; *North American*, June 20, 1856.
[118] Shortly before the election, however, Stewart swung to the support of Fremont in the hope of uniting the opposition party. (*North American*, August 25, 1856; *Harrisburg Weekly Telegraph*, August 7, October 30, 1856).
[119] June 14, 1856.
[120] *Cf. Miners' Journal*, May 3, 1856; *Pittsburgh Gazette*, August 29, 1856.
[121] For an elaborate refutation of the "ten-cent Jimmy" allegation, see Coxe, *Short Answers to Reckless Fabrications*, pp. 17–24.

tween the Republican and American parties, Buchanan carried his native state with a plurality of 27,152 votes.[122] The Democratic vote exceeded that of the combined opposition in such protectionist strongholds as Philadelphia (city and county), Schuylkill, Clarion, Columbia, and many other of the leading coal and iron counties.[123]

When Congress convened for its short session after Buchanan's election, the Pennsylvania delegation was compelled, as before, to assume a purely defensive attitude upon the tariff question. It was evident that a vigorous attack, sponsored by two of the leading interests of the country, was to be launched against the existing duties. The woolen manufacturers were extremely anxious to have wool placed upon the free list; at the same time, the agitation for free railroad iron was reopened with unprecedented vigor. Pennsylvania protectionists, with considerable reason, feared that a working agreement might be effected between these two interests. Moreover, the plea for cheaper wool found enthusiastic support in Philadelphia, which had become the greatest single center of woolens manufacture in the country.[124] Accordingly, it was deemed expedient to save the duties on railroad iron by acceding to the demand for free wool.[125] After a rather discursive debate, the House passed a bill, the chief effect of which was to place on the free list all wool valued at less than twenty cents or more than fifty cents per pound. Although the Pennsylvania representatives, by concerted action, could have defeated the measure, their solicitude for the iron interest impelled them to support the bill unanimously.[126] An unexpected menace was encountered in the Senate, however, when Hunter of Virginia introduced a substitute measure providing for a general downward revision of the Walker duties. The 30 per cent. schedule, which most vitally concerned Pennsylvania interests, was to be reduced to 23 per cent. under this proposal. Debate in the Senate was extremely limited, due to the impending close of the session, but both Bigler and Brodhead found occasion to denounce the Hunter substitute in unqualified terms and to express their approval of the House bill as the lesser of two evils.[127]

122 *Smull's Legislative Handbook*, 1921-22, p. 740.
123 *Public Ledger*, November 15, 1856.
124 *Hunt's Merchants' Magazine*, XLIII, 558; *North American*, January 18, 27, 1855; *Miners' Journal*, March 29, 1856.
125 *Cf. Miners' Journal*, December 6, 27, 1856; *North American*, March 9, 1857.
126 *Cong. Globe*, 34 Cong., 3 Sess., p. 791.
127 *Ibid.* App., pp. 332, 346.

In spite of Pennsylvania's opposition, the general reduction was approved by a vote of thirty-three to twelve.[128] The two measures were then referred to a conference committee, which adopted the provisions of the Senate bill with a few slight modifications, one of which increased the 23 per cent. rate to 24 per cent. This compromise agreement, when referred back to the House for concurrence, was declared to be utterly unacceptible to Pennsylvanian interests.[129] This was due largely to the fact that the iron-makers of that state received none of the benefits of cheaper raw materials which served to reconcile many other manufacturers to a general reduction of the tariff.[130] Consequently, although the House accepted the committee report by a large majority, only three Pennsylvanians voted for its adoption, while sixteen were recorded in the negative.[131] The Senate also accepted the compromise, with Bigler supporting and Brodhead opposing the measure.[132] Bigler was later bitterly attacked by his political opponents for his vote on this occasion, but the Democratic Senator replied that he had supported the report in order to avoid an even more drastic reduction.[133]

The tariff question seriously reentered Pennsylvania politics, after a lapse of several years, in connection with the gubernatorial election of 1857. The issue was precipitated, not by the passage of the new revenue law earlier in the year, but by the choice of David Wilmot as the Republican candidate. Ever since his vote for the Walker act, Wilmot had been invariably classified by Pennsylvania protectionists as an unrelenting foe of the tariff system. He himself, had asserted in 1848, "I have been . . . charged with having abandoned the doctrines of the free-trade party. I have never abandoned them; I have held them from my youth. I adhere to them still."[134] The espousal of such a candidate by the party which posed as the residuary legatee of Whig protectionism afforded the Democracy of Pennsylvania a tempting opportunity to expose the inconsistencies of their opponents. Conse-

---

[128] *Ibid.* App., p. 358.

[129] *Cf.* Blaine, *Twenty Years of Congress,* I, 197.

[130] *Pittsburgh Gazette,* March 7, 1857; *North American,* March 9, 1857.

[131] One of the affirmative votes was cast by a protectionist who declared that he did so only in order to call for a reconsideration. *Cong. Globe,* 34 Cong., 3 Sess., p. 971; App., p. 358.

[132] *Ibid.* p. 1062.

[133] *Ibid.* 35 Cong., 1 Sess., p. 2085.

[134] *Ibid.* 30 Cong., 1 Sess., p. 305.

quently, Wilmot's tariff views, together with his anti-slavery record, became the center of a violent controversy, which left his Democratic adversary, William F. Packer, free to pursue the even tenor of his campaign in comparative tranquillity.

The Republicans, in view of their candidate's dubious tariff record, attempted, so far as possible, to make slavery and sectionalism the dominant issues of the campaign. Even when the panic of 1857 broke only three weeks before the election, the protectionist implications of the crisis had to be handled with extreme caution. Nevertheless, there were communities, such as Philadelphia, in which the slavery question could not be safely pressed, and in these localities, it was necessary to present their candidate's tariff views in as favorable a light as possible. Hence it was categorically asserted that "Mr. Wilmot is not and never has been, a Free Trade man."[135] To sustain this contention, it was pointed out that the protectionists of Pennsylvania were actually demanding the restoration of the identical tariff law for which the Republican candidate had voted in 1846.[136] Wilmot, himself, assured a Harrisburg audience that he was "now, as he has ever been, in favor of affording adequate protection to all the great industrial interests of the country, and especially the great iron and coal interests of Pennsylvania."[137] After the outbreak of the panic of 1857, he asserted,

That the tariff policy of the government has much to do with the revulsions that periodically convulse the country is doubtless true, intimately connected as that policy must ever be with all our financial and industrial interests. The very considerable reduction made in the tariff at the last session of Congress must have had a disastrous influence in bringing upon us the present state of things, as it greatly stimulated importations, causing heavier drafts upon the country for its precious metals.[138]

The Democratic press, on the other hand, hailed Wilmot's protectionist professions with scornful unbelief. A Pittsburgh paper declared that "David Wilmot's advocacy of open and absolute Free Trade is as notorious as his monomania upon the subject of Abolition; one being about as intense, impracticable and absurd as the other."[139]

---

135 *Harrisburg Semi-Weekly Telegraph*, April 24, 1857.
136 *Pittsburgh Gazette*, October 1, 1857.
137 *Ibid*.
138 *Ibid*. October 3, 1857.
139 *Pittsburgh Post*, October 2, 1857.

Senator Bigler commented upon the remarkable spectacle of "the distinguished advocate of free trade in the embrace of the protectionists, and the protectionists under the leadership of the distinguished free trader."[140] It was suggested that even if "the present crisis does show that the principles of free trade are ruinous to the country, the Republican candidate for governor is the last man who should be benefited by the discovery."[141] Another editor observed that "if they vote for Wilmot, manufacturers of iron will have no right to say the tariff is important to them."[142] At the same time, the Democratic press mercilessly assailed Wilmot's anti-slavery utterances and ridiculed his efforts to revive an "obsolete" issue.

Packer, who had no such violent antagonisms to encounter, easily carried the state by the almost unprecedented plurality of 42,707. Wilmot's popular vote was considerably smaller than that received by the Whig gubernatorial candidate in any of the three previous elections.[143] The Republican candidate developed his principal strength in the northern and western counties, where anti-slavery sentiment was most pronounced. He carried the protectionist stronghold of Allegheny county, but by much less than the normal Whig or Republican majority. In Philadelphia, where anti-slavery sentiments were not popular, he made an extremely poor showing.[144] It would be impossible to estimate with any degree of accuracy the relative influence of the slavery and tariff issues in contributing to Wilmot's decisive defeat. There is little doubt that Pennsylvania as a whole was much more aggressively protectionist than it was anti-slavery at that time.[145] Nevertheless, so anomalous was the Republican candidate's position upon the tariff, and so confusing was the conflict of that issue with the slavery question in various portions of the commonwealth, that even contemporary observers hesitated to compute the resultant of these two political forces.

Although it was not so recognized at the time, the election of 1857 was destined to mark the end of the Democratic party's long domination of Pennsylvania politics. In spite of the fact that its protection-

---

140 *Pennsylvanian,* September 14, 1857.

141 *Pittsburgh Union,* September 28, 1857.

142 *Clinton Democrat,* quoted in *Harrisburg Keystone,* September 2, 1857.

143 *Smull's Legislative Handbook,* 1921-22, p. 745.

144 *Public Ledger,* October 27, 1857; *Pittsburgh Union,* October 29, 1857.

145 *Cf.* Blaine, *Twenty Years of Congress,* I, 205.

ism had always been open to serious question, the Democracy of the Keystone State had never lost two consecutive elections during four decades of fiercely-contended party strife. This remarkable record of success, in the face of Pennsylvania's admitted enthusiasm for the tariff system, would seem to require a word of explanation. A very important factor was the superior leadership enjoyed by the Democrats during the entire period of their ascendency. Such masters of political strategy as Samuel Ingham, James Buchanan, George M. Dallas, and Simon Cameron were always at the helm, alert to seize every advantage and quick to retrieve every disaster. The only Whig with a comparable gift of leadership was Governor Johnston, who came forward too late to preserve his party from disintegration. Another significant factor was the remarkable spirit of disciplined loyalty which habitually prevailed among the rank and file of the Pennsylvania Democracy. This harmony may be attributed in part to the enduring influence of the Jacksonian tradition and in part to the lure of the state patronage, which continued success placed at the disposal of the party leaders. The Whigs, on the other hand, suffered repeatedly from factional difficulties and were never in control of the state long enough to build a smoothly-running machine of office-holders. Finally, it should be noted that there were few elections during this period in which the tariff issue was clearly and convincingly drawn. The Whig press solemnly assured the voters each fall that the outcome of the canvass would determine the fate of the protective system, but there is reason to believe that comparatively few Democrats were impressed by such arguments. Much of the effectiveness of this annual appeal was lost through sheer reiteration; especially, since the occasional Whig victories seldom produced the tangible results which had been so enthusiastically promised. Moreover, the Democratic control of Congress, which was seldom broken during these years, enabled that party to approach the Pennsylvania electorate repeatedly with the plausible argument that only through its favor could the state hope to obtain desired tariff legislation. The state organization naturally found its political affiliation with the free-trade Democracy of the South a source of constant embarrassment, but it possessed a fairly effective rebuttal in the fact that the principal agitation for free railroad iron came from the Whigs and Republicans of the North and West. Thus the inherent strength of the party enabled it for many years to escape the political consequences of its rather dubious position upon the tariff issue. Only in times of great popular excitement, as in 1846 and 1848, was the Democratic domination of the state seriously imperiled. Nevertheless, Buchanan had served warning, as early as 1852, that the tariff issue was making Pennsylvania a very close state politically, and that it would be necessary to treat the subject with the utmost caution.[146] All went smoothly, however, until the panic of 1857 suddenly snapped the long-tried patience of protectionist Pennsylvania and precipitated a political revolution of far-reaching significance to the state and to the nation.

---

[146] Buchanan to J. W. Forney, January 1, 1852; Buchanan Mss.

# Chapter XII

## THE TRIUMPH OF PENNSYLVANIA PROTECTIONISM, 1857-1861

The panic of 1857, which consummated the overthrow of the Democratic party in Pennsylvania, burst upon the state with devastating suddenness. The Philadelphia banks announced the suspension of specie payments on September 25, and similar action was immediately taken in many other parts of the commonwealth. The ensuing contraction of credit, diminution of demand, and decline of prices compelled many manufacturing establishments to close their doors. By the end of October it was estimated that between thirty and forty thousand persons were out of work in Philadelphia and the vicinity.[1] It was said that three-fourths of the textile machinery in the city was stopped temporarily, with more than ten thousand out of employment as a result.[2] Iron prices fell heavily, and it was asserted that approximately one-half of the forty thousand ironworkers in the state had been dismissed.[3] The stoppage was brief in many cases, but the total iron output for 1858 showed a marked decline from that of the preceding year.[4] At the same time, very drastic wage cuts were imposed in all branches of the industry.[5] The coal trade, likewise, quickly felt the blight of the general industrial stagnation. Anthracite production in 1857, for the first time since 1838, failed to show an increase over that of the preceding year.[6] Coal prices declined steadily until 1859, at which time the industry was declared to be "more depressed than at any former period in its history."[7] Miners' wages, likewise, fell to extremely low levels.[8] Throughout the state, therefore, the panic of 1857 appears to have fallen with particular severity upon the laboring classes, the very element from which the Democratic party had always drawn its most devoted following.

---

[1] *Pennsylvanian,* October 20, 1857; *North American,* April 29, 1858.

[2] *Harrisburg Telegraph,* October 9, 1857; *Hunt's Merchants' Magazine,* XLIII, 557.

[3] *Pennsylvanian,* March 27, 1858; *Pittsburgh Gazette,* September 18, 1858.

[4] *Hunt's Merchants' Magazine,* XLIII, 116-117, 563-567.

[5] *Sen. Rep.,* 52 Cong., 2 Sess., Vol. III, pt. 1, pp. 181, 183; pt. 4, pp. 1562-64, 1570.

[6] Pennsylvania Bureau of Statistics of Labor and Agriculture, *Annual Report,* 1872-73, pp. 213-216.

[7] *Testimonials to Henry C. Carey,* p. 24.

[8] *Sen. Rep.,* 52 Cong., 2 Sess., Vol. III, pt. 1, p. 181; pt. 4, p. 1561.

Fundamentally, the panic of 1857 was the product of an era of extravagant expenditures, wild inflation of credit, and premature investment of borrowed capital in enterprises that could give no immediate return. The depression was world-wide in extent, but was intensified in America by a system of unsound banking and unregulated currency. Although imports had been extremely heavy for several years before the crash, there is every reason to believe that these were a symptom rather than a cause of economic maladjustment. As Secretary Cobb pointed out in his annual report for 1858, the depression had affected every line of American industry, protected and unprotected alike, and he concluded that the tariff was in no wise responsible for the situation.[9] Buchanan, likewise, in his first annual message declared emphatically that the panic had "proceeded solely from our extravagant and vicious system of paper currency and bank credits, exciting the people to wild speculations and gambling in stocks."[10] This contention, which has been generally indorsed by students of economic history, found ready acceptance among the hard-pressed Democrats of the Keystone State. Senator Bigler declared that the effort to interpret the depression in terms of the tariff was "simply preposterous."[11] The *Pennsylvanian* took similar ground and pointed out that "the inevitable tendencies of an inflated system of paper money is to expand credit and enhance nominal values to such an extent as to completely counteract the protective influence of any rate of duties not entirely prohibitory."[12]

Pennsylvania protectionists, however, quickly hit upon the tariff as the one great source of the prevailing distress. The *North American* declared, without the slightest reservation, that "the calamitous visitation under which the mercantile and manufacturing interests of our city are now suffering is the result of a false and ruinous tariff policy."[13] The same view found official sanction in Governor Pollock's last annual message, which asserted,

If the principle of the act of 1842 had been preserved—even if its rate of duties had been reduced—our specie, by millions, would not have gone into coffers to build up and sustain the foreign manufacturer; home industry would be prosper-

[9] *House Exec. Doc.*, 35 Cong., 2 Sess., No. 3, p. 10.
[10] Richardson, *Messages and Papers of the Presidents*, V, 437.
[11] *Pennsylvanian*, September 10, 1858.
[12] October 5, 1857.
[13] October 1, 1857.

ous; and the cry "we want work", issuing from a thousand lips in our large cities and manufacturing districts, would not now be heard; nor would a foreign debt of nearly five hundred millions of dollars exist, to startle and alarm us.[14]

Less than a week after the suspension of specie payments by the Philadelphia banks, Henry C. Carey wrote to Buchanan, warning him that "the administration of Mr. Van Buren was the most calamitous one in our history; but unless its record be now carefully studied, with a view to profit by his errors, yours will stand conspicuous as the most unfortunate of all." At the same time, the ardent protectionist offered to assist the President in formulating an economic policy which would preserve the country from impending disaster.[15]

Firmly convinced by such utterances that the tariff was indeed the instrument of ruin, protectionists in all parts of the state hastened to demand a drastic upward revision of the existing duties. A noticeable feature of this revived agitation was its strength among the laboring classes, who were exhorted "to throw off the trammels of party and unite together, as one brotherhood, for the purpose of procuring the passage of such a Protective Tariff as will best subserve the interests of the Union."[16] Encouraged by the strength of this sentiment, the leaders of the People's party, as the Republicans then preferred to be known, approached the congressional elections of 1858 fully determined to make Kansas the moral issue and protection the material issue of the campaign. The *North American* declared, "The foremost practical question in the next Congress is to be the enactment of such a tariff as will save the interests of Pennsylvania from destruction. . . It is of the last importance that Pennsylvania should pronounce, in the coming election, in favor of a thorough revision of the tariff, and unmistakably declare for the principle of protection to American industry."[17] Whigs, Republicans, Americans, and Independent Democrats were urged to unite for the overthrow of those false representatives who gave their tariff votes "looking one way to their constituents and vigorously rowing another."[18] Simon Cameron, who toured the state in behalf of the

---

14 *Pennsylvania Archives,* Fourth Series, VII, 940.
15 H. C. Carey to Buchanan; October 1, 1857; Buchanan Mss.
16 *North American,* February 19, 1858.
17 *Ibid.* August 2, September 23, 1858.
18 *Ibid.* April 26, May 20, 1858.
19 *Harrisburg Telegraph,* October 1, 1858.

People's party, everywhere stressed the tariff issue and declared that he was "one of those old-fashioned men who believed in protection for protection's sake."[19] Much emphasis was laid upon "Viceroy" Buchanan's alleged subservience to British interests.[20] As proof of this contention, it was pointed out that a Scotch firm had been granted a contract to furnish 6,000 tons of iron water pipes for the new Washington aqueduct, even though, it was asserted, Philadelphia firms had submitted lower bids.[21] So effectively was this charge pressed in the iron districts that one Pennsylvania Democrat wrote Buchanan, imploring that the contract be canceled.[22] This was actually done, just prior to the election, upon the ostensible grounds of late delivery.[23]

The Democratic candidates, hard pressed by their adversaries, found it advisable to join in the agitation for higher duties.[24] At the same time, the protectionist professions of their opponents were held up to ridicule and scorn. If increased protection was desired, it was argued, it must be sought from the gracious hands of the Democracy, not from their opponents, who "care nothing for Pennsylvania interests and cannot be expected to legislate for them."[25] The pages of history were ransacked, moreover, to prove that the People's candidate for supreme court judge had voted against tariff resolutions in the state legislature in 1824 and had voiced approval of Dallas' casting vote in 1846.[26] The first charge was admittedly true; the second was denounced by Henry C. Carey and other Republicans as a vicious calumny.[27]

In spite of the heroic efforts of the Democracy, the election returns heralded a political upheaval of cataclysmic proportions. The fifteen Pennsylvania Democrats in the preceding Congress were reduced to five; while the Republican and American representation was increased from ten to twenty.[28] Of the eleven Democrats who

---

[20] *North American*, July 15, 1858.
[21] *Pittsburgh Gazette*, July 30, 1858; *Miners' Journal*, July 31, 1858; *North American*, October 2, 1858.
[22] J. B. Baker to Buchanan, October 4, 1858; Buchanan Mss.
[23] *Miners' Journal*, October 9, 1858.
[24] *Pittsburgh Gazette*, September 24, 1858.
[25] *Pennsylvanian*, July 23, September 29, October 8, 1858.
[26] *Ibid.* October 1, 1858; *Pittsburgh Post*, October 5, 1858; *North American*, September 28, 30, 1858.
[27] *House Journal*, 1823-24, p. 448; *Harrisburg Telegraph*, October 5, 1858.
[28] *Miners' Journal*, October 16, 1858.

were up for reelection, only three were successful, and one of these ran as an anti-Lecompton candidate.[29] All through the iron and coal regions, the People's party showed unprecedented strength, as it rolled up large majorities in such former Democratic strongholds as Schuylkill, Lucerne and Columbia counties.[30] The most stunning administration reverse, however, was the defeat of J. Glancy Jones in the Berks district, long known as the "tenth legion of the Democracy." Jones, who was serving his fourth term in Congress, had won general recognition as a man of real ability, chairman of the House Committee on Ways and Means, and a close friend of President Buchanan. His close identification with the Administration, however, had mobilized against him the strong protectionist and anti-Lecompton sentiment in his district. An independent candidate was accordingly put forward in the person of John Schwartz, a wealthy ironmaster of rather mediocre ability.[31] The tariff was made the chief issue of the campaign, and wide publicity was given to Jones' assertion that "I deem any movement in this country towards a protective tariff for protection sake, as nothing but an ingenious political device to lead both capital and labor to destruction."[32] As a result, the Democratic candidate was defeated by 19 votes, after having swept the district with a majority of 6,004 two years before.[33] The administration was deeply chagrined at Jones' defeat, which represented the first Democratic reverse in "Old Berks" since the days of Jefferson.[34] Two months later, the same district gave the People's party an even more decisive victory in a special election to fill the vacancy caused by Jones' sudden resignation to accept a diplomatic post.[35]

Several factors contributed to the political overthrow of the Democracy in the election of 1858. The defection of Forney, Buchanan's *fidus Achates*, over the question of the patronage, the persistent charges of inefficiency and corruption at Washington, and

---

[29] *North American,* October 14, 1858.
[30] *Ibid.* October 23, 1858.
[31] Buchanan characterized Schwartz as a "downright old Dunce." (Buchanan to G. M. Wharton, October 16, 1858; Buchanan Mss.)
[32] *Pennsylvanian,* July 3, 1858.
[33] *Cong. Globe,* 36 Cong., 1 Sess., p. 1951; McClure, *Old Time Notes,* I, 334; Jones, *Life and Public Services of J. Glancy Jones,* II, pp. 54-56, 80-91.
[34] Buchanan, *Works,* X, 230; *Pennsylvanian,* October 11, 1858.
[35] *North American,* December 2, 1858.

especially, the intense disssatisfaction with the Administration's Kansas policy, all doubtless played a part in the result. There is nothing to indicate, however, that the indignation of the anti-slavery forces in Pennsylvania was any stronger in 1858 than it had been twelve months before. Moreover, it is significant that the great Democratic losses were found, not in the preeminently anti-slavery counties, but in the coal and iron regions of the state.[36] It was generally recognized, therefore, that only the tariff issue, intensified by twelve months of industrial depression, could have produced the major political revolt which was to end the Democracy's long domination in Pennsylvania. This was the view adopted by such experienced political observers as ex-Governor Porter and President Buchanan.[37] The latter, explaining the causes of defeat, wrote,

This was caused by a suspension of nearly all the Iron works in the State & the great number of laborers thus cast out of employment. This has often before occurred. If the Tariff on Iron had been a hundred per cent the same distress would have existed. The administration are as justly responsible for the motions of the Comet as for the low price of Iron. In the natural course of events business will revive before the next election and then with similar justice we shall enjoy the benefit of producing a return of "good times."[38]

Buchanan's hopeful expectations were based upon sound historical precedent. Never had the Democracy failed to rally after a defeat; never had the party lost two consecutive elections. The President failed to realize that recurrent economic pressure had at last driven the Democrats of the state to renounce their Jacksonian heritage and to throw themselves permanently into the embrace of new political leaders, who were in a position to render more than lip service to the principles of Pennsylvania protectionism.

The leaders of the stricken Pennsylvania Democracy awaited with intense interest the announcement of the Administration's tariff policy in the President's annual message for 1858. A year before, Buchanan had taken the ground that the tariff of 1857 had "been in operation for so short a period of time and under circumstances

---

[36] A Philadelphia editor computed that in the twenty counties in which free soil sentiment was known to be strongest, the Democratic ticket showed a gain of 10,660 votes over 1856; while in fifteen counties dominated by mining and manufacturing interests, the party lost 29,616 votes. (*Pennsylvanian*, November 15, 1858).

[37] D. R. Porter to Buchanan, October 14, 1858; Buchanan Mss.

[38] Buchanan to G. M. Wharton, October 16, 1858; Buchanan Mss.

so unfavorable to a just development of its results as a revenue measure that I should regard it as inexpedient, at least for the present, to undertake its revision."[39] The economic revulsion, however, had caused a serious decline in the customs receipts and a rapidly growing deficit in the national finances, which seemed to justify higher duties, if only to meet the revenue requirements of the government.[40] It was hoped, moreover, that Buchanan would not be insensible to the exigencies of the Democratic party in his native state and would seize the opportunity to appease the disgruntled voters of Pennsylvania with a strong protectionist declaration. Immediately after the election, Duff Green warned the President that "Forney has created an impression that you are so much under *Southern* influence that you will not stand by Pennsylvania on the Tariff."[41] He further assured Buchanan that the iron interest of the Keystone state would be satisfied with a specific duty of $6 a ton on pig iron and $12 a ton on bar iron, and urged that some such conciliatory arrangement be effected.[42] A prominent Pennsylvania Democrat admonished, "I cannot see how we are to get Pennsylvania back in full rank and file by 1860 unless the Congress will give them protection for their coal and iron. This done by you, the enemy will be prostrated."[43] Another observer reported that "I have never seen so much unanimity of sentiment in regard to this matter as pervades at present all classes and shades of political association."[44] Nevertheless, ex-Governor Porter assured the chief executive that "if the democracy of the South would. . .give us a Tariff—a reasonable one, with specific duties, or a home valuation . . . and so framed as to give some assurance that it would remain stable, we could right up Pennsylvania again before the end of another year."[45]

Buchanan's annual message categorically denied that the tariff of 1857 was in any way responsible for the difficulties through which the country had been passing. He declared that "the same ruinous

---

[39] Richardson, *Messages and Papers of the Presidents*, V, 458.
[40] *Statistical Abstract of the United States*, 1912, pp. 743, 745.
[41] D. Green to Buchanan, October 14, 1858; Buchanan Mss.
[42] D. Green to Buchanan, October 29, 30, 1858; Buchanan Mss.
[43] J. Chambers to Buchanan, November 8, 1858; Buchanan Mss.
[44] J. M. Hopkins to Buchanan, November 24, 1858; Buchanan Mss.
[45] D. R. Porter to Buchanan, October 14, 1858; Buchanan Mss.

consequences would have followed in the United States whether the duties upon foreign imports had remained as they were under the tariff of 1846 or had been raised to a much higher standard." At the same time, the President urged that the revenue requirements of the government should be met through a reasonable increase in the existing tariff rates, and that, wherever possible, specific duties should be levied. He cautiously expressed the belief that "the incidental protection thus afforded by a revenue tariff would at the present moment to some extent increase the confidence of the manufacturing interests and give a fresh impulse to our reviving business."[46] These observations were enthusiastically welcomed by Pennsylvania Democrats, who saw in the presidential policy a possible formula for the political rehabilitation of their party. The members of the state legislature temporarily buried party differences and, by a virtually unanimous vote, approved Buchanan's recommendation in favor of specific duties.[47] At the same time, a vigorous Pennsylvania lobby descended upon Washington to give proper emphasis to the President's demand for a tariff revision.[48]

Congress had scarcely assembled when the first gun of the protectionist assault was fired by a Pennsylvanian. Even before the President's message had been read or the Committee on Ways and Means appointed, Representative Dewart introduced a resolution calling for higher duties on coal, iron, lead, wool and other articles.[49] This was the first of a long series of Pennsylvania resolutions, which, while varying greatly in detail, were all clearly protectionist in intent.[50] Several of these measures called for a restoration of the tariff of 1846, a circumstance which led Dallas to write from London,

It was a strange exhibition at the last session of Congress which shewed our Iron and Coal men urging a return to the Casting-Vote Tariff of '46. That of '57 was ill timed and perhaps too low:—even upon the exclusive principle of revenue:—but that in so short a period as eleven years, the tarred-and-feathered-

---

[46] Richardson, *Messages and Papers of the Presidents*, V, 520-522.

[47] *House Journal*, 1859, p. 100; *Senate Journal*, 1859, p. 86; *Sen. Misc. Doc.*, 35 Cong., 2 Sess., No. 25.

[48] *Pittsburgh Gazette*, January 19, 1859; *Pittsburgh Post*, January 25, 1859; *Harrisburg Patriot*, February 16, 1859.

[49] *Cong. Globe*, 35 Cong., 2 Sess., p. 5.

[50] *Ibid.* pp. 195, 686, 878, 1409, 1858, 2196; *Pittsburgh Post*, January 28, 31, 1859; *Pennsylvanian*, March 9, 1859.

and-hung-in-effigy one of '46 should become the rallying point—the "quadrilatre" as it were—of former foes, was hardly to be expected.[51]

All such proposals were rejected, however, and the session came to an end without any significant action. Senator Bigler, deeply provoked at the course of events, was reported to have declared that the failure of the Southern Democrats to sustain the President's recommendations would inevitably give Pennsylvania to the Republicans.[52]

Whether or not the Democratic Senator made the statement attributed to him, the results of the fall elections seemed to attest its validity. Although only minor state offices were at issue, the question of protection could not be submerged. The Democrats of the state aligned themselves squarely behind Buchanan's tariff policy as outlined in his second annual message.[53] The People's party, on the other hand, asserted that the Administration "has surrendered itself to the fire-eating, disunion-plotting free traders of the cotton states; and it stands to-day fully committed against the rights, interests and honor of free American labor."[54] The voters were exhorted, therefore, to defeat the entire Democratic ticket "and thus pave the way for the success of a Protective Tariff President in the contest of 1860."[55] The electorate, apparently, took the opposition leaders at their word; for the People's party won two-thirds of the seats in the lower house of the legislature, and filled ten out of eleven Senatorial vacancies.[56] For the first time in its history, the Democratic party of Andrew Jackson had failed to rally from defeat, and had lost two consecutive elections.

As soon as the new legislature assembled, the Republican members of the lower house set in motion an ingenious device to discredit the protectionist professions of their opponents. The conventional tariff resolutions were introduced, expressing the customary deep attachment to the tariff system in general and to the principle of specific duties in particular. A Republican member thereupon introduced

[51] Dallas to H. Phillips, August 10, 1859; Dreer Collection.
[52] *Pittsburgh Gazette,* February 3, 1859.
[53] *Harrisburg Telegraph,* March 18, 1859; *Pennsylvanian,* August 9, 12, 27, September 21, 1859.
[54] *North American,* April 12, 1859.
[55] *Harrisburg Telegraph,* September 30, 1859.
[56] *Ibid.* October 20, 1859.

the following amendment, the sole purpose of which was to compel the Democrats to vote against the resolutions as a whole:

> Resolved, That while we approve of that part of the President's annual message to the last Congress, expressing a preference for *specific* over *ad valorem* duties, we cannot believe these sincere, while he retains in office a Secretary of the Treasury who recommended and urged upon Congress an entirely different policy—one destructive of all Pennsylvania interests. Experience proves that no protection can be expected from the National Democracy, who have modified and repealed the only measure which afforded relief since eighteen hundred and forty-two.[57]

With this scathing addition, the resolutions were adopted by the House on a strict party vote, except for one Democrat who supported them on the grounds that the question of protection took precedence over all other considerations.[58] Ruthless in their exercise of power, the Republicans next refused to permit the Democratic minority to record upon the official journal an explanation of their votes.[59] The obnoxious resolutions were then passed by the Senate, which divided upon strict party lines.[60] Thus the Democrats found themselves, on the eve of a presidential election, publicly branded as anti-protectionists by the identical strategy which they had blithely invented and relentlessly employed in the days of their political ascendency.[61]

Mixed motives served to bring the tariff question emphatically to the fore in the first session of the Thirty-sixth Congress, which opened in December, 1859. Two years of greatly curtailed imports had produced an alarming treasury deficit, which impelled President Buchanan to renew his former plea for an upward revision of the tariff, based upon a comprehensive system of specific duties.[62] Furthermore, the knowledge that Pennsylvania's vote would probably decide the impending presidential contest compelled the Republican party, especially, to give attentive ear to the protectionist entreaties of the Keystone State. Accordingly, the House of Representatives turned to a serious consideration of a tariff bill drafted

---

[57] *House Journal*, 1860, p. 135.
[58] *Ibid.* pp. 136–138.
[59] *Pennsylvanian*, January 23, April 2, 1860.
[60] *Senate Journal*, 1860, pp. 749–750.
[61] See pages 143 and 188, *supra*.
[62] Richardson, *Messages and Papers of the Presidents*, V, 574.

by Justin S. Morrill of Vermont, a protectionist member of the Committee on Ways and Means. This measure, which became the basis for the Morrill Act of 1861, was ostensibly designed to restore, through the medium of specific duties, the general level of protection afforded by the tariff of 1846. The transition from ad valorem to specific duties, however, was made a pretext for a considerable increase in the rates actually levied on many articles. The measure provided for specific duties of $6 a ton on pig iron, $12 a ton on railroad iron, and $15 a ton on bar iron; while the specific duty on coal was fixed at $1 a ton. The proposal—which was ultimately dropped from the bill —for the virtual abolition of the warehousing system appealed especially to the commercial interests of Philadelphia, who complained that the existing arrangement tended to concentrate all the import trade at New York. The novel spectacle was presented, therefore, of a merchants' lobby at Washington, working in concert with the protectionist forces for the passage of a tariff bill.[63]

Pennsylvania protectionists, both in Congress and at home, hailed the Morrill bill with general enthusiasm as a step in the right direction. The prevailing sentiment was well expressed by the *North American,* which held that the measure "is somewhat too complex, we fear, and is not all we could wish. But it is a vast improvement on the present system and its passage will soon revive the business of our citizens and replenish the coffers of the nation. It is especially favorable to the interests of Pennsylvania."[64]    Edward Joy Morris exuberantly described the pending bill as one which "will operate like a magic wand upon Pennsylvania; which will set to work every idle loom— which will kindle the extinguished fires of every furnace—which will be a greater stimulus to Pennsylvania industry than ever was applied by the protecting legislation of our government."[65] A convention of iron manufacturers, assembled at Philadelphia, likewise approved its provisions and urged its enactment by Congress.[66] At the same time, Washington was reported to be overrun with Pennsylvania Democrats, justly fearful of the political consequences if Congress failed to pass the desired legislation.[67] Responding to the clearly expressed wishes

---

[63] *Public Ledger,* February 11, 1861.
[64] *North American,* May 24, 1860.
[65] *Ibid.* April 9, 1860.
[66] *Harrisburg Patriot,* March 29, 1860.
[67] *Ibid.* June 16, 1860; *Pennsylvanian,* June 7, 1860; *North American,* June 13, 15, 1860; *Miners' Journal,* May 26, June 9, 23, 1860.

of their constituents, the Pennsylvania representatives supported the bill by a unanimous vote upon its final passage.[68] The news that the Morrill bill had received the approval of the House was greeted with salvoes of artillery in many parts of Pennsylvania.[69] The Morrill bill encountered a decidedly cold reception when it reached the Senate, where the Democrats were in full control. Ultimately, in spite of the heroic opposition of Bigler and Cameron, it was voted to postpone consideration of the measure until the following session.[70] As a last resort, Senator Bigler attempted to introduce a compromise proposal, embodying the general provisions of the act of 1846, the free list of the tariff of 1857, and a system of specific duties on iron, sugar, liquors, and certain other articles.[71] This measure, characterized by the Republicans as a "subterfuge and a sham," won little support, and Congress finally adjourned, leaving the tariff situation in a state of suspense.[72] The *North American* declared that the fate of the bill clearly indicated that President Buchanan "either has not a particle of influence with his party or he is the most insincere and treacherous man ever placed in power."[73] The Democrats, on the other hand, asserted that the Republicans had deliberately framed the proposed tariff so as to ensure its defeat in the Senate and thus make political capital for themselves in such protectionist strongholds as Pennsylvania and New Jersey.[74] Whatever the merits of such partisan accusations, the rejection of the Morrill bill made it certain that, so far as Pennsylvania was concerned, the tariff and not slavery would be the dominant issue in the impending state and national elections.

The Pennsylvania Republicans—or People's party as they still called themselves—were exceedingly anxious to enter the campaign of 1860 with standard-bearers whose protectionism should be above reproach. As a result of this feeling, it was suggested that the party should draft Henry C. Carey as a candidate for public office. The *North American*, for instance, enthusiastically endorsed the Philadelphian as a possible successor to Buchanan.[75] This movement soon

[68] *Cong. Globe,* 36 Cong., 1 Sess., p. 2056.
[69] *Miners' Journal, Pittsburgh Gazette, Pittsburgh Post,* May 12, 1860; *Harrisburg Telegraph,* May 16, 1860.
[70] *Cong. Globe,* 36 Cong., 1 Sess., p. 3027.
[71] *North American,* June 22, 1860; *Miners' Journal,* June 23, 1860.
[72] *North American,* June 23, 1860.
[73] *Ibid.* June 9, 1860.
[74] *Harrisburg Patriot,* June 6, 1860; *Pennsylvanian,* June 20, 1860.
[75] April 26, 1859, September 6, 1859.

died out, however, as protection, except in Pennsylvania, became submerged by more serious issues. Carey's name was also mentioned as the Republican candidate for governor in 1860. A Pittsburgh editor observed,

In 1860, Pennsylvania desires to give great prominence to the principle of protection. Is there any way she can so easily give effect to it as by electing Henry C. Carey to the governor's chair? . . . He is not only an elaborate writer, but largely interested by his investments in the mines and manufacturies of this state. Let us . . . go in for the nomination of the man, who, since the death of Henry Clay, is the truest representative in theory and practice of the American system.[76]

Nothing came of this movement, however, or of the suggestion that the Philadelphia economist be sent to Washington as Senator Bigler's successor.[77] Unfortunately, Carey was not on the best of terms with those through whom any such political preferment must come. For Simon Cameron—political dictator of Pennsylvania Republicanism—he had nothing but contempt. He habitually referred to Cameron with one of his most vigorous epithets as a "shirt of Nessus."[78] Also he did not hesitate to express his disapproval of the political methods of some of the Pennsylvania manufacturers. He was quoted by an intimate friend as saying, "Go to a manufacturer if you want to buy a Congressman, but never if you want to educate a constituency. Thank God! the men who make the tariff are not responsible for the men whom the tariff makes. They are the only instance in Nature where cultivation reaches the worst soil last."[79] Without the support of Cameron and of those who furnished the sinews of war, no mere economic philosopher could hope to gain a footing in Pennsylvania politics.

It was to Cameron, rather, that the rank and file of Pennsylvania protectionists eagerly turned to represent them in the political arena. Ever since his election to the Senate in 1845, Cameron had deliberately based his bid for popular favor upon an assiduously-cultivated reputation for extreme protectionism. The success of this effort was fully attested by the appearance of a vigorous presidential boom in his

---

[76] *Pittsburgh Commercial Journal,* quoted in *Harrisburg Telegraph,* October 18, 1859.
[77] *Harrisburg Patriot,* December 1, 1860.
[78] "Carey and Greeley," *Social Economist,* VII, 141.
[79] *Ibid.*

behalf as early as 1858. Cameron's candidacy was supported, according to one estimate, by four-fifths of the Republican press in Pennsylvania.[80] One editor pointed out, "The first experiment of a Pennsylvania President has been a complete failure. Simon Cameron, another Pennsylvanian will have to be elected to redeem our character."[81] Another journal argued that while

Pennsylvania *might* be carried by some other candidate, with General Cameron as our standard bearer victory would be *certain*. Nominate him and the toiling masses of the old Keystone would come in swarms from the mines, the forges and the workshops, to labor and vote for the man who has been the lifelong advocate of their interests and the zealous advocate of the Free Labor movement—a man who, everywhere and under all circumstances is every inch a Pennsylvanian, never deserting her people nor betraying her interests, for purposes of self-aggrandizement.[82]

The People's state convention in 1860 endorsed Cameron's candidacy, and instructed the Pennsylvania delegation to the national convention to vote for him as a unit so long as his name remained before the body.[83] Pennsylvania Republicans were to find, however, that the tariff issue loomed less large at Chicago than at Harrisburg, and Cameron soon found it expedient to renounce his presidential aspirations in return for a less exalted preferment.

Although prepared to yield in respect to their candidate, Pennsylvania protectionists were adamant in their demand that the Republican platform should take strong ground in favor of the tariff system. The *North American* declared, "We tell the convention, so soon to meet at Chicago, squarely, roundly, and in every other shape that means earnestness, that their candidates cannot carry the States of Pennsylvania and New Jersey unless they stand publicly on protective ground. . .This State cannot be carried on an anti-slavery issue only. Fremont proved that."[84] Such Republican leaders as Horace Greeley and Abraham Lincoln, on the other hand, took the opposite view that, in the interests of party harmony, the tariff question should be ignored by the convention.[85] It was realized,

---

[80] *Erie Dispatch*, quoted in *Harrisburg Telegraph*, September 27, 1859.
[81] *Miners' Journal*, July 31, 1858.
[82] *Harrisburg Telegraph*, June 1, 1859.
[83] *Ibid*. February 24, 1860.
[84] March 30, 1860.
[85] *Harrisburg Patriot*, April 28, 1860; Lincoln, *Complete Works*, VI, 11.

however, that Pennsylvanian susceptibilities were not to be trifled with; and a strong, if somewhat ambiguous tariff resolution was duly adopted.[86] An eye witness at the convention reported that when the tariff plank was read, "Pennsylvania went into spasms of joy . . . . her whole delegation rising and swinging hats and canes."[87] David Wilmot was noted as having taken a particularly exuberant part in this extemporaneous manifestation of protectionist zeal.[88]

From the standpoint of the Pennsylvania protectionist, the Republican or People's ticket contained elements of both strength and weakness. Lincoln's tariff views, so far as developed, were entirely satisfactory. No major tariff legislation had come before Congress during his brief career as a national legislator, but on such minor questions as had arisen, he had consistently aligned himself with the protectionists.[89] A few months before the Chicago convention he had written a Philadelphia correspondent,

> I was an old Henry Clay-Tariff-Whig. In old times I made more speeches on that subject than any other. I have not since changed my views. I believe yet, if we could have a moderate, carefully adjusted protective tariff, so far acquiesced in as not to be a perpetual subject of political strife, squabbles, changes and uncertainties, it would be better for us. Still it is my opinion that just now the revival of that question will not advance the cause itself, or the man who revives it.
>
> I have not thought much on the subject recently, but my general impression is that the necessity for a protective tariff will ere long force its old opponents to take it up; and then its old friends can join in and establish it on a more firm and durable basis. We the Old Whigs have been entirely beaten out of the tariff question and we shall not be able to reestablish the policy until the absence of it shall have demonstrated the necessity for it in the minds of men heretofore opposed to it.[90]

After his nomination, the Republican candidate hastened to take his stand squarely upon the tariff plank of the Chicago platform.[91] Lincoln's views, in short, were sufficiently orthodox to warrant a

---

[86] The text of this tariff resolution, the first ever adopted by a Republican national convention, is given in Porter, *National Party Platforms*, p. 58.

[87] Halstead, *History of the National Political Conventions of the Current Presidential Campaign*, p. 135.

[88] *Harrisburg Telegraph*, May 18, 1860.

[89] *Cf. Cong. Globe*, 30 Cong., 1 Sess., p. 852; 2 Sess., p. 26.

[90] Lincoln, *Complete Works*, V, 256.

[91] *Ibid*. VI, 58, 61.

sincere protectionist appeal in his behalf. The Republican nominee for Vice President, however, was much more vulnerable upon the tariff question. Hannibal Hamlin, like Wilmot, had voted for the act of 1846 and had long been classified as a free trader. Like Wilmot again, his tariff views had been greatly modified by his Republican environment, but the ghost of former principles yet remained to haunt his political aspirations.[92] Hamlin's potential weakness, however, was more than offset by the staunch protectionist reputation of Andrew G. Curtin, the Republican candidate for governor. Curtin came from a family of ironmasters and in the popular mind was closely identified with the tariff policy.[93] No better candidate could have been found to carry the question of protection directly to the electorate and make it, so far as Pennsylvania was concerned, the one great issue of the Republican campaign.

All varieties of tariff sentiment were represented among Lincoln's three rivals for the presidency. Douglas had always been most outspoken in his hostility to the restrictive system in all its manifestations. Throughout his public career he had been the unremitting advocate of lower duties, of reciprocity with Canada, and of free railroad iron. Concerning the tariff views of Breckenridge, the candidate of the Southern Democracy, little was known, but his political affiliations alone were sufficient to discredit him in the eyes of Pennsylvania protectionists. Senator Bell's loyalty to the tariff system was universally recognized, but other considerations made him a negligible factor in the political situation.[94] So far as the gubernatorial contest was concerned, the adherents of Douglas, Breckenridge, and Bell united their forces in support of Henry D. Foster, the Democratic nominee. Foster was a good protectionist in his own right and possessed the valuable political asset of having voted against the act of 1846, but he was greatly handicapped by his affiliation with a party, which, in the minds of many Pennsylvanians, had come to represent the utter negation of the tariff system.

The Republicans of Pennsylvania sought to wage the campaign of 1860 upon many different fronts. They denounced slavery in the

[92] *Pittsburgh Gazette*, September 7, 1860; *Miners' Journal*, September 22, 1860.
[93] *Miners' Journal*, March 10, 1860.
[94] *Cf. North American*, May 12, 1860.

territories and the slave trade; they pledged themselves to a homestead law, a Pacific railroad, and the admission of Kansas as a free state; they pleaded for a renunciation of Buchanan and all his works; they advanced the plausible argument that only Lincoln's election could keep the final choice out of the House of Representatives; and they ridiculed the idea that a Republican victory would endanger the Union. Nevertheless, overshadowing all else, loomed the question of protection to domestic industry as the one great paramount issue of the struggle. As one Republican editor explained, "After all, the tariff is the vital question. All parties are for the Union and the Constitution, so that there can be no dispute about them. But all parties are not for protection to American industry."[95] Less than seven months before the Confederate batteries opened fire upon Fort Sumter, the *North American* assured its readers that slavery was no longer a "practical issue."[96] On the morning of the state election, the same journal confidently declared, "This political cry of the 'Union being in danger,' which is revived at every election, and which was heard shouted even more loudly four years ago, is an insult to the intelligence and patriotism of our people. . .The live question which the people of this state are called to pronounce upon to-day is the protection of our industry."[97] Secure in the valor of their unbelief, the Republican leaders enthusiastically depicted Lincoln as "the friend of Henry Clay, and the champion of Protection to American Industry."[98] Simon Cameron assured the electorate that "in regard to the great interests of Pennsylvania, the subject of Protection to labor, his record is clear, emphatic, and beyond suspicion."[99] The protectionist zeal of Hamlin and Curtin was described in equally glowing terms.[100] At the same time, the opposition candidates of all parties were impartially characterized as unfriendly to the best interests of Pennsylvania industry. The People's state committee compiled and circulated an imposing catalogue of Douglas' free trade votes, designed to show his unremitting hostility to the

95 *Philadelphia Bulletin,* quoted in *Pittsburgh Gazette,* May 24, 1860.
96 *North American,* October 18, 1860.
97 *Ibid.* October 9, 1860.
98 *Harrisburg Telegraph,* May 26, 1860.
99 *Miners' Journal,* June 2, 1860.
100 *Ibid.* September 22, 1860; *Harrisburg Telegraph,* March 8, 1860; *Pittsburgh Gazette,* September 7, 1860; *North American,* September 14, 1860; *Public Ledger,* October 3, 1860.

protective system. Summarizing this record, the committee concluded that "the 'peculiar institutions' of Pennsylvania—the iron mines and manufactories—have no more steady, implacable, and persevering enemy, from South Carolina to Texas, than Stephen A. Douglas."[101] Breckenridge was denounced as "the exponent of the anti-tariff party, and the candidate of the radical free traders."[102] Bell, as a recognized protectionist, was treated less harshly, but it was pointed out that "he has no platform, and as he relies chiefly on Southern States for support, he will have to conform to a considerable extent to Southern policy, which favors free trade."[103] Turning their attention to the gubernatorial contest, the Republicans noted Foster's protectionist professions only to deride them, and declared that no Democrat could be regarded as a sincere friend of the tariff.[104] The editor of the *North American*, after a careful survey of the political situation, reached the conclusion that "not all of the Opposition are protectionists, but almost all protectionists are of the Opposition, and the only hope of American industry is through them."[105]

While the Republicans sought to make the tariff the great issue of the campaign, their opponents were much more aggressive upon the slavery question. A Democratic orator declared, *"We say it is a question between nationalism and sectionalism. . .They say it is a question of tariff or no tariff."*[106] Commenting upon the *North American*'s attempt to ignore the slavery issue, a Democratic editor observed, "In the midst of this fearful agitation, shaking the foundations of society, arraying section against section, tearing asunder old organizations—political, religious and social—an oily antediluvian like Mr. M'Michael calmly implores the people of Pennsylvania to vote for Lincoln, the representative of interminable agitation, because he is said to be favorable to a tariff."[107] Moreover, the argument was used with marked effect among the mercantile interests of Philadelphia that the election of Lincoln would mean

---

[101] *Record of Hon. Stephen A. Douglas on the Tariff*, p. 1.
[102] *North American*, September 15, 1860.
[103] *Philadelphia Bulletin*, quoted in *Pittsburgh Gazette*, May 24, 1860.
[104] *North American*, August 20, September 6, 1860; *Pittsburgh Gazette*, October 3, 1860.
[105] April 14, 1860.
[106] *Pennsylvanian*, April 30, 1860.
[107] *Harrisburg Patriot*, September 14, 1860.

the loss of Pennsylvania's great Southern markets.[108] Nevertheless, the persistent tariff agitation of their opponents made it impossible for the Democrats to evade the issue entirely. The weakness of both Douglas and Breckenridge on the subject, however, made it much safer to attack the opposition candidates than to defend their own. Accordingly, it was declared,

In honest truth the tariff cry on the part of the Republicans is a humbug. Hannibal Hamlin, the candidate for the Vice-President, is a well-known anti-protectionist, Abraham Lincoln, their candidate for the Presidency is a free trader; all men of sense know that the section of the country in which he lives is agricultural and that every agricultural district is opposed to such taxation as the Republicans propose. Stephen A. Douglas and Henry D. Foster are sounder tariff men than Abe Lincoln and Hannibal Hamlin.[109]

To support this view, it was pointed out that the word "protection" had been deliberately omitted from the Republican platform, and that William Cullen Bryant, the editor of one of the most vehement free trade papers in the country, was one of the Lincoln electors in New York.[110] Foster, noting the opposition arguments, found it very strange that Hamlin, who had voted for the act of 1846, should be pictured as a protectionist; while he, who had opposed the measure, should be described as a free trader.[111] The hard-pressed Democracy even advanced the threat that a Republican triumph might induce the enraged South to use its voting strength in Congress to abolish all duties and to substitute a system of direct taxation to supply the revenue requirements of the government.[112]

The Douglas party in Pennsylvania found itself in a particularly unenviable position upon the tariff question. Not only the People's party, but even the Breckenridge Democrats vigorously denounced the free trade tendencies of the Senator from Illinois.[113] So far as possible, Douglas' adherents, headed by Forney, avoided the tariff issue, and concentrated their efforts upon the questions of popular

---

[108] McClure, *Our Presidents and How We Make Them*, p. 177; *Speech of the Hon. William B. Reed on the Presidential Question*, p. 12.
[109] *Harrisburg Sentinel*, September 20, 1860.
[110] *Pennsylvanian*, May 19, 22, 1860; *Harrisburg Patriot*, May 22, 1860; *Speech of the Hon. William B. Reed on the Presidential Question*, pp. 13-15.
[111] *Harrisburg Sentinel*, September 20, 1860.
[112] *Pennsylvanian*, October 9, 1860.
[113] *Ibid.* September 11, 1860.

sovereignty and the preservation of the Union. Their candidate, however, boldly invaded Pennsylvania and attempted to placate the irate protectionists of the state with an ingeniously-contrived line of argument. In his speech at Reading, for instance, Douglas declared,

Whenever a proposition has been brought into Congress to increase the tariff up to the grade of expenditure or to reduce the expenditure down to the rate of the revenue, you find the slavery question becomes the point of discussion, and the bill is lost at the end of the session for want of time. . . Now let me ask the people of Pennsylvania if they expect to ever get the question of the tariff revised and reconsidered unless they first drive this slavery question out of Congress. Every interest you have connected with the revenue and with the tariff is sacrificed by this eternal agitation of the negro question. . . We must maintain a tariff which will raise revenue enough to defray the expenditures of the Government, economically administered; and in that manner we must furnish all the protection to American industry that a revenue tariff will afford.[114]

This expression of solicitude for Pennsylvania industry was hailed by both Lincoln and Breckenridge men as "the most unblushing effrontery" and as "a signal instance of political trickery which cannot be defended on any principle of honor or fair dealing."[115]

The outcome of the gubernatorial contest was awaited with intense interest in all parts of the Union. The state election was popularly regarded as a test of party strength, which would accurately foretell the result of the national struggle. Indeed, it was believed that the success or failure of the People's candidate in Pennsylvania would have a real determining influence upon the presidential vote in several of the doubtful states. Because of this feeling, the gubernatorial struggle was fought almost exclusively upon national rather than local issues. As in the national contest, protection to domestic industry was made the dominant question, especially by Republican orators, who assured the electorate that "the October contest in Pennsylvania will settle the future tariff policy of the govern-

---

[114] *Harrisburg Sentinel,* September 12, 1860.

[115] *Harrisburg Telegraph,* September 20, 1860; *Pennsylvanian,* September 24, 1860.

[116] *North American,* September 6, 1860. Early in the campaign, both Foster and Curtin found it expedient to go to Washington and there carry on an ostentatious lobby in behalf of the Morrill tariff. (*Harrisburg Telegraph,* June 15, 1860).

ment."[116] For this reason, Curtin's decisive victory, by a majority of 32,116, was hailed as a glorious triumph both for Abraham Lincoln and the principle of protection.[117]

Curtin's easy victory made it practically certain that Lincoln would carry both state and nation in the presidential election.[118] The political discussion continued unabated during the intervening period, but with something of a shifting emphasis from protection to slavery, as the Southern situation became more acute. The tariff question, however, was by no means neglected. Shortly before the election, the Douglas and Breckenridge forces arranged a fusion electoral ticket, pledged to cast its votes as a unit if either Democratic candidate could be elected thereby. Perfect harmony was not obtained, however, and Pennsylvania gave Lincoln a plurality of 89,159 and a clear majority of 59,518.[119] Nevertheless, Pennsylvania protectionists were compelled to temper their joy at the presidential triumph with the knowledge that the new administration would not control either house of Congress. Consequently, the passage of the pending Morrill tariff still seemed an exceedingly

---

[117] *Smull's Legislative Handbook*, 1921-22, p. 745; *North American*, October 11, 1860; *Harrisburg Patriot*, October 19, 1860; *Pennsylvania Archives*, Fourth Series, VIII, 334; *Cong. Globe*, 36 Cong., 2 Sess., p. 1190.

[118] James G. Blaine, in his *Twenty Years of Congress*, writes of Curtin's election, "Had the Republicans failed to carry Pennsylvania, there can be no doubt that Mr. Lincoln would have been defeated. An adverse result in Pennsylvania in October would certainly have involved the loss of Indiana in November, besides California and Oregon and the four votes in New Jersey. The crisis of the national campaign was therefore reached in the triumph of Governor Curtin in the state election which preceded by four weeks the direct choice of President. It would be difficult to compute the possible demoralization in the Republican ranks if Pennsylvania had been lost in October. The division among the Democrats was a fruitful source of encouragement and strength to the Republicans, but would probably have disappeared with the positive assurance of success in the national struggle. Whether in the end Douglas or Breckinridge would have been chosen President is matter of speculation, but it is certain that Mr. Lincoln would have been defeated. . . In reviewing the agencies, therefore, which precipitated the political revolution of 1860, large consideration must be given to the influence of the movement for Protection. . . Hundreds of thousands of ballots, cast in aid of free territory and as a general defiance to the aggressions of the pro-slavery leaders of the South, would have been utterly ineffectual if the central and critical contest in Pennsylvania had not resulted in a victory for the Republicans in October." (Vol. I, pp. 206-207). There is little doubt that protection was actually the decisive factor in securing Curtin's election. Blaine's larger contention, like most ventures into the realm of historical hypothesis, can neither be proved nor disproved.

[119] The official popular vote was: Lincoln, 268,030; Fusion ticket, 178,871; Douglas, 16,765; Bell, 12,776. (*Smull's Legislative Handbook*, 1921-22, p. 740.)

remote contingency. When Congress reassembled in December, 1860, Pennsylvanians had little hope that the Senate would take any affirmative action upon the Morrill tariff. Before the session was many weeks old, however, twelve Democratic Senators had withdrawn to join their states in open secession, and the Republicans, much to their surprise, found themselves in control of the upper house. Due in large measure to Cameron's unceasing vigilance, the tariff bill was kept persistently before the Senate, and it was finally passed with amendments on February 20, 1861.[120] Senator Bigler was the only Democrat to vote in favor of the measure. The amended bill was then returned to the House of Representatives for concurrence. Free trade sympathizers seized this opportunity to engage in a series of acrimonious philippics against Pennsylvania as the real author and principal instigator of the measure. Cox of Ohio lamented that under the provisions of the bill, "the people of the South and the people of the West are made tributaries to the iron satraps of Pennsylvania."[121] Pryor of Virginia, with scathing sarcasm, hurled the accusation that

The importunate protectionists of Pennsylvania, more clamorous and insatiable than the daughter of the horse-leech, after higgling successively with every party for a stipend from the Treasury, at last caught the Republicans in a moment of exigent need, and from their lust for place, extorted the promise of a bounty to iron. This bill is the issue of a carnal coalition between the Abolitionists of New England and the protectionists of Pennsylvania. It is the result of a compact, whereby, at the expense of the public interest, Pennsylvania engaged to support an Abolitionist for the Presidency on the condition that the Abolitionists would repay Pennsylvania by the protection of iron. . . We on this side the House may lament our inability to prevent the passage of this bill; but, among other circumstances of consolation, as friends of good faith and fair dealing, we are indemnified by the reflection that Pennsylvania is not cheated of her price, but is at last rewarded for that utter abnegation of self and that disinterested devotion to principle which have so conspicuously characterized her political conduct (Laughter). Rarely, indeed, in these degenerate days, is it given to us to witness such an instance of fidelity to engagement, of the fulfillment of obligations without regard to consequences, as is exhibited by the Republican party

---

[120] *Cong. Globe,* 36 Cong., 2 Sess., pp. 46, 444, 1065; *Harrisburg Telegraph,* February 21, 22, 1861.
[121] *Cong. Globe,* 36 Cong., 2 Sess., p. 1192.
[122] *Ibid.* p. 1190.

in this bill of indemnity to the ironmongers of Pennsylvania. It is a draft on the Treasury of the United States for payment in full of service rendered the Republican cause by the protectionists of Pennsylvania.[122]

In spite of such phrenetic outbursts, the differences between the two Houses were easily reconciled by recession and by conference, and on March 2, 1861, the Morill tariff received the signature of President Buchanan. Thus by the official act of Pennsylvania's once-favorite son, the government of the United States definitely cast aside the economic precepts of Adam Smith and set its face resolutely in the direction of protection as a fundamental tenet of national policy.

Sobered by the impending disruption of the Union, Pennsylvania protectionists received the news of the passage of the Morrill tariff with emotions of quiet satisfaction. The *North American* declared, "It has come suddenly and brilliantly, and over it there should be a sound of rejoicing all over Pennsylvania, and, indeed, wherever American industry has friends."[123] The *Miners' Journal* characterized the new law as "unquestionably the best tariff bill which has been adopted since the bill of 1842 was passed."[124] Henry C. Carey hastened to write Morrill, "Accept my congratulations upon the happy termination of your tariff labours. You have now connected your name with what is destined, as I think, to prove the most important measure ever adopted by Congress."[125] Carey rejoiced with good reason. The triumph of Pennsylvania protectionism was complete.

---

[123] February 28, 1861.
[124] *Miners' Journal*, March 2, 1861.
[125] Quoted in Swank, *Notes and Comments*, p. 92.

CHAPTER XIII

THE DYNAMICS OF PENNSYLVANIA PROTECTIONISM

The evolutionary development of Pennsylvania protectionism may be regarded as complete by the outbreak of the Civil War. As never before, merchant and industrialist, Republican and Democrat had spoken with one voice in favor of the Morrill act. The tariff struggle was destined to continue—for the true protectionist is insatiable—but henceforth it was to be a foreign war, fought with united front at Washington, not a civil conflict such as had convulsed the state in the days of the Kane letter and the casting vote of 1846. A complexity of forces, operative over a long period of time, had at last obliterated all the traditional economic and party lines and left Pennsylvania firm and united in its adherence to the protective policy as an instrument of national security, economic prosperity, and human happiness.

Economic forces, without question, provided Pennsylvania protectionism with its most impelling dynamic. Throughout the antebellum period there was a marked correlation between prevailing economic conditions and the trend of protectionist sentiment in the state. In view of this interrelationship, certain persistent tendencies should be noted, which will help to explain the course of the tariff movement during these years. It is clear, for instance, that Pennsylvania protectionism was the outgrowth of industrial strength rather than of industrial weakness. Almost invariably, protectionist agitation in behalf of a commodity did not appear until the domestic production was fairly well established. Every period of rapid industrial expansion left in its wake an intensified demand for ever-higher tariff barriers. This tendency was well illustrated in the case of Pennsylvania's basic economic interests, iron and coal. The first suggestion of higher duties on coal did not come until 1827, when anthracite production was one and one-half times the total import; and the first really serious agitation did not appear until 1831, when the output was five times the entire foreign supply. Thereafter, the ratio of imports to total consumption declined rapidly, but protectionist sentiment in the mining regions, instead of waning as foreign competition grew steadily less pressing, appears to have been stronger just before the Civil War than at any previous period.[1] The iron interest also developed its most vehement protectionism after 1840, not because of adverse economic conditions, but as a result of the introduction of the anthracite process, which meant increased output, cheaper costs of production, and a greatly improved competitive position. It is not difficult to explain this apparent paradox. Every era of industrial expansion drew to the support of the protective system new capital and additional voting strength; while the ensuing increase of domestic production only too frequently culminated in an economic revulsion, which uncritical contemporaries hastened to attribute to excessive importations.

It should likewise be noted that there was no certain correlation between the quantity of imports and the strength of the protectionist agitation at any given time. In some instances, as after the Revolution and the War of 1812, an influx of foreign goods was actually accompanied by an intensified demand for higher duties. On the other hand, unprecedentedly heavy imports from 1834 to 1839 and from 1852 to 1857 found the protectionist agitation in Pennsylvania at its lowest ebb. There is good reason to believe, therefore, that prices rather than imports were the controlling economic factor in determining the fluctuating progress of the tariff movement in Pennsylvania. An era of low prices, for instance, was almost certain to produce a vigorous protectionist agitation, even though imports were already negligible.[2] For this reason, severe economic revulsions played an important role in the development of Pennsylvania protectionism. It was the post-war crisis of 1819 which for the first time brought the stricken agricultural interests of the state into an enthusiastic endorsement of tariff principles and thereby united farmer and manufacturer in common support of protection as a fundamental national policy. It was the recurrence of panic in 1837 and 1839 which aroused Pennsylvania protectionists from their quiet acquiescence in the Compromise Act and launched the militant tariff crusade which convulsed state politics throughout the succeeding decade. Finally, it was the crisis of 1857 which

---

[1] Pennsylvania Bureau of Statistics of Labor and Agriculture, *Annual Report*, 1872-73, pp. 213-216.

[2] Extremely low prices tended automatically to cut down imports, especially under a system of specific duties.

consummated the overthrow of the Democratic party in the Keystone State and thus dissolved the political misalliance which had so long undermined the influence of Pennsylvania protectionism at the national capital. Conversely, a period of extremely high prices, such as prevailed in times of reckless speculation and inflated credit, tended to silence the tariff agitation, in spite of the flood of foreign goods which such conditions inevitably attracted to the American market.

Paradoxically, the protectionist movement in Pennsylvania derived strength and impetus from the very futility of its objectives. It was, in the first place, hopeless to rear any enduring tariff wall upon the shifting sands of an inflated currency, which inevitably served as a bounty to the foreign importer. Buchanan saw this danger and warned against it; and for his pains he was mocked as "Ten Cent Jimmy," the foe of high wages and American labor. Even Henry C. Carey failed to recognize the menace, and simultaneously advocated high protection and cheap currency; an attempt to reconcile the irreconcilable, which led many of his contemporaries, notably William D. Kelley, into strange realms of economic fallacy. Pennsylvania protectionists, generally, seem to have failed to comprehend that unsound banking and insecure currency rather than the tariff were the primary causes of their recurrent difficulties and they habitually took refuge in the more superficial interpretation that higher duties alone would alleviate their distress.

Pennsylvania's tariff movement, in the second place, derived continual accessions of strength from its rigid adherence to another fundamental fallacy, namely, that existing industries can be permanently benefited by the imposition of high import duties. Temporary rewards, of course, accrue to the original beneficiaries of protective legislation, and the industry as a whole may profit from a permanent expansion, but the individual operator, though intrenched behind prohibitive tariff barriers, will ultimately find himself surrounded by a domestic competition which will quickly restore the marginal producer to his previous precarious position. Such, indeed, was the experience of Pennsylvania manufacturers during these years, especially under the extremely protective tariffs of 1828 and 1842. Both measures ushered in a period of extremely rapid industrial expansion and abundant profits. Nevertheless, it was not long before manufacturers were beginning to complain of increased domestic competition and reduced returns.[3] Even Mathew Carey, on one occasion, expressed serious misgivings as to the trend of industry under the act of 1828. Both laws were repealed, however, before Pennsylvania's faith in the efficacy of the tariff system could be seriously shaken by such untoward developments. The protectionists of the state, therefore, continued to regard the tariff as a certain road to permanent industrial prosperity and, in striving after the unattainable, became ever more insistent in their demand for legislative favors.

Important as economic factors undoubtedly were in determining the course of Pennsylvania protectionism, the movement cannot be interpreted solely in such terms. Politics have long played a dominant role in American tariff controversies, and even the ardent protectionist zeal of the Keystone State was not impervious to the distracting clamor of party strife. For many years prior to the Civil War, Pennsylvania protectionists had to contend with a series of inauspicious political developments which greatly weakened their influence in the determination of the nation's tariff policies. The first of these great obstacles was the wave of political Jacksonism, which, about 1824, swept the state with irresistible intensity. It is not within the scope of the present work to consider the causes of Pennsylvania's mad infatuation for the "Hero of New Orleans."[4] Suffice it to say that Jackson's popularity was based upon quite other considerations than the tariff. Although he voted for the act of 1824 and acted with masterful decision when confronted with South Carolina nullification, he could scarcely be regarded as an extreme protectionist. Moreover, insofar as the tariff was at issue between the two parties, Jackson's opponents had much the stronger claim to protectionist support. It is said upon unimpeachable authority that a man shall not serve two masters—neither may a commonwealth. Pennsylvania, so long as she remained loyal to Andrew Jackson, was in no position to give whole-hearted and unwavering allegiance to the tariff system. This was clearly in-

---

[3] See pages 102 and 173, *supra.*
[4] For discussions of Jacksonian politics in Pennsylvania, see Bartlett, *Chief Phases of Pennsylvania Politics in the Jacksonian Period;* Hailperin, "Pro-Jackson Sentiment in Pennsylvania, 1820-1828," *Penn. Mag. Hist. and Biog.,* L, 193-240.

dicated by the attitude of some of the Jackson leaders of the state toward the ill-fated woolens bill of 1827.

The political heritage of Andrew Jackson—as exemplified in the long Democratic domination of Pennsylvania—was equally inimical to the translation of the state's admitted protectionist sentiment into legislative reality. The attitude of the Pennsylvania Democracy toward the tariff question might fairly be characterized as pseudo-protectionism. Ever loud in their professions of solicitude for the tariff system, the party leaders never hesitated to sacrifice it upon the altar of political success. This disposition was clearly manifest in some of the more confidential correspondence of the Polk campaign, as well as in Forney's frank comment to Buchanan after the disaster of 1846, "We must recover our state at all hazards. It is more important to us than twenty tariffs."[5] Some prominent Democrats, such as Andrew Stewart, James Irvin, and William F. Johnston, were impelled to bolt the party on the tariff issue, but the rank and file stood firm except under most extreme provocation. The long-suffering loyalty of the Pennsylvania Democrats helps to explain why successive administrations paid so little attention to the persistent protectionist appeals from the Keystone State.

Pennsylvania protectionism during these years was unfortunate even in its political friends. The Whig party, which alone afforded a reasonable hope of favorable tariff legislation, was weak in both state and national politics. Seldom in control of the government at Washington, the Whigs had very few opportunities to give a practical demonstration of their loyalty to the protective principle. The party as a whole, moreover, was by no means so intensely protectionist as was the Whig organization in Pennsylvania. Clay's vacillating tariff course and the continual necessity to conciliate important free trade elements in the South and West sometimes compelled Whig candidates and platforms to become models of evasion upon the subject. No such equivocation marked the party appeal in Pennsylvania, where protectionist professions were shouted from the housetops with unremitting zeal. The state organization, however, was beset with internal dissensions and uncertain leadership, which sapped its vitality and made it, more often than not, the instrument of defeat instead of victory. So long as Pennsylvania protectionists, therefore, sought political expression through the medium of the Whig party, they were doomed to repeated disappointment.

The Republican party, for the first time, supplied the protectionists of Pennsylvania with a really effective political instrument. The Republicans, nationally, were not yet particularly interested in the tariff question. Their anti-slavery sympathies, however, automatically released them from the embarrassing Southern alliance which had constantly restricted the freedom of the older parties in dealing with the tariff issue. Moreover, their political exigencies made them willing to bid high for support in the Keystone State. The Pennsylvania Republicans, at the same time, were comparatively free from the factional difficulties which had beset their political predecessors. For all these reasons, the political revolution of 1858 threw the control of the state for the first time into the hands of an aggressive and united party organization, inspired both in principle and in self-interest to pursue the tariff issue fearlessly and relentlessly to an ultimate triumph.[6] The protectionist victory, hastened upon the wings of a great national catastrophe, came with unexpected suddenness. There is reason to believe, however, that, even if the Civil War had not occurred, the new spirit in Pennsylvania politics would have quickly exerted a far-reaching influence upon the tariff policies of the United States.

The realm of economic philosophy likewise made at least a minor contribution to the triumph of Pennsylvania protectionism. Beginning about 1840, it was evident that theoretical free trade was gaining support even in the Keystone State. Additional force was given to the contentions of the Classicists by the contemporary trend of English economic policies. It was becoming increasingly apparent, therefore, that the tariff party could not count upon the support of the more thoughtful element of the population until economic theory and practice could be brought into a more apparent harmony. It was a real contribution to the protectionist movement, therefore, when Henry C. Carey attacked this problem and evolved a system of economic thought which seemed to glorify the coldly

---

5 J. W. Forney to Buchanan, October 29, 1846; Buchanan Mss.

6 Henry W. Davis of Maryland assured Morrill as early as August 20, 1859 that his bill would pass since "we are now independent of Penn. Locofocos and all rotten sticks." (Quoted in Parker, *Life of Morrill*, p. 104).

materialistic appeal of the industrialist with the triumphant idealism of the philosopher.

Environmental influences, rather than the writings of other economists, seem to have constituted the chief source of Carey's inspiration. His protectionism was far more unrelenting than Hamilton's, who very clearly regarded the protective policy as a temporary expedient, and who was ready at all times to lower the tariff barrier by means of favorable reciprocity agreements. Nor is there any evidence that Carey was indebted to Raymond to any significant extent. Likewise, the early attempts to show that he was under decided obligations to List have been generally abandoned by later commentators.[7] Indeed, it is doubtful whether the Philadelphia economist had even read List's *National System of Political Economy* when his first protectionist works appeared.[8] Rather, it may be said that Carey's economic philosophy was deeply rooted in the protectionist soil of his native state. Pennsylvania bred him; Pennsylvania educated him; and when the time was ripe, Pennsylvania called upon him to become her chosen evangel of her chosen creed. As an English observer has well said, "Carey's system is, in fact, Pennsylvanian rather than national economy; it is a product of Pennsylvania like its iron and coal."[9]

Among economic scholars, Carey found more followers abroad, especially in Germany and Scandinavia, than he did at home.[10] American economists, for the most part, remained coldly aloof, either reaffirming the conventional free trade doctrines of the English school or accepting the more orthodox protectionism of Professor Bowen of Harvard.[11] But if Carey's disciples were few, they

[7] Elder, *Memoir*, p. 28; Meuser, *List und Carey als wissenschaftlich Nationalökonomen*, p. 112; Gide and Rist, *History of Economic Doctrines*, p. 284; Turner, *The Ricardian Rent Theory*, p. 23n.
[8] Baird, "Carey and Two of his Recent Critics," American Philosophical Society, *Proceedings*, XXIX, 171.
[9] Leslie, "Political Economy in the United States," *Fortnightly Review*, XXXIV o.s., 503.
[10] Portions of his writings have been translated into French, German, Italian, Swedish, Russian, Magyar, Japanese, and Portuguese.
[11] Cyrus Elder complained before the Tariff Commission in 1882 that in most of the colleges only free trade principles were being taught. He quoted a letter from a student at Williams College who complained that "this college always has been and is a hotbed of free trade;" that "Henry C. Carey's name has never been mentioned in the classroom except to be cursed;" and that not one of his works was in the college library. (*Rep. of U. S. Tariff Com.*, 1882, p. 2355).

followed him only the more passionately. Most prominent among his followers were Robert Ellis Thompson, Stephen Colwell, William D. Kelley, Joseph Wharton, Henry C. Baird, William and Cyrus Elder, and Simon N. Patten of Philadelphia, E. Peshine Smith of New York, J. H. McIlvaine of Princeton, W. D. Wilson of Cornell, and V. B. Denslow of Chicago. This small group of satellites, revolving about Carey as an intellectual and Philadelphia as a geographical center, have come to be known as the American or Pennsylvania school of political economy. For better or for worse, the work of this school represents almost the only distinctive contribution which the United States has made to the science of political economy.[12] These men and their adherents hailed Carey as the preeminent economic thinker of the age, second in no respect to Adam Smith as a daring explorer into the realms of unrevealed truth. William Elder declared, "Mr. Carey is the Political Economist of the age. He has delivered the science of Society from its darkness and bondage."[13] Professor Denslow called his works "the most potential force contributed toward economic science since Adam Smith."[14] The *North American* described his *Principles of Social Science* as "by far the ablest, the most lucid, and the most convincing on the subject that has ever been given to the press."[15] Another critic ventured to predict that "Ricardo and Malthus will be to Carey as Ptolemy to Copernicus."[16]

Outside of this small but ardent group of disciples, the general tendency among American economists has been to treat Carey's protectionism with respectful but unbelieving tolerance, with the rather obvious expectation that with the passage of time his system will collapse of its own weight.[17] It would be a mistake, however,

---

[12] Cf. Taussig in *Palgrave's Dictionary of Political Economy*, I, 38.

[13] Elder, "Henry C. Carey," *Sartain's Magazine*, X, 444.

[14] Denslow, "American Economics," *North American Review*, CXXXIX, 28.

[15] April 15, 1859.

[16] Griswold, "Henry C. Carey and his Political Economy," *International Monthly Magazine*, II, 402.

[17] For a critical discussion of Carey's economic theories see Gide and Rist, *History of Economic Doctrines;* Haney, *History of Economic Thought;* Held, *Carey's Socialwissenschaft und das Merkantilsystem;* Jenks, *Henry C. Carey als Nationalökonom;* Levermore, "Henry C. Carey and his Social System," *Pol. Sci. Quart.*, V, 553-582; Marshall, *Principles of Economics;* Meuser, *List und Carey als wissenschaftlich Nationalökonomen;* Mill, *Principles of Political Economy;* Rabbeno, *American Commercial Policy;* Turner, *The Ricardian Rent Theory.*

to measure Carey's influence upon public opinion by the philosophical validity of his theories. It is an axiom of human affairs that a dynamic fallacy is far more powerful than a static truth. Carey was in a peculiarly favorable position to influence the economic thought of the country. His strength lay in the fact that he was not only an economic philosopher but also an astute propagandist. His philosophical trend gave him a prestige above the ordinary political demagogue; his journalistic capacity won him an audience commonly denied to the scholar. It must be kept clearly in mind that his paramount object was not to justify an abstract economic theory, but to write upon the statute books a definite expression of national policy. He has been considered too much as an originator of startling, though dubious, economic doctrines, and not enough as a moulder of public opinion.

In the view of many contemporaries, no single individual contributed as much to the triumph of the protectionist cause as did Carey. Like Henry Clay in an earlier period, he came to represent in the popular mind a personification of the tariff principle. It was his writings which transformed William D. Kelley, the Philadelphia free-trader, into "Pig-iron" Kelley, leader of the protectionist forces in the House of Representatives.[18] Many of the arguments and statistics found in congressional tariff discussions may be traced directly to his writings. Senator Bell of Tennessee referred to him as "the man who, without official station or its encouragements, has performed services of greater value to his country than those of half the generals and statesmen who figure in its civil and military annals."[19] Thompson, referring to the general revolution throughout the world from free trade to protection, declared, "To this result no single man—no ten men—contributed so powerfully as did Mr. Carey. . .There is hardly a protectionist in the civilized world who did not in some sort look up to Mr. Carey, as the patriarch and the prophet of the movement, with feelings of personal regard and esteem."[20] When the Morrill tariff was finally passed, the *North American* asserted that "but for the untiring pen of Henry C. Carey, and his great personal influence, we doubt very much

18 Kelley, *Speeches, Addresses and Letters*, pp. vi-viii, xxiii.
19 *Testimonials to Henry C. Carey*, p. 40.
20 Thompson, "Henry Charles Carey," *Penn Monthly*, X, 824.

whether the present success would not have been postponed several years."[21] The owner of this journal, Morton McMichael, asserted that Carey had "done more to illustrate, to expound, to enforce, and to maintain that great principle [protection] than any other man in the United States."[22] Even the generally hostile *Pennsylvanian* said of him, "He has, for some twenty years past, devoted his eminent abilities to the elucidation of questions connected with his favorite science; and has done more than any author living to bring it within the scope of the popular mind in this country."[23]

One must, however, exercise considerable caution in attempting to evaluate Carey's part in the triumph of the protective principle. It is easy to overrate the influence of any propagandist. It is an open question how far any individual, however talented, can influence a movement based upon far-reaching social and economic forces. For himself, Carey claimed a Messianic role, but it would be a mistake to depict him thus.[24] His writings appeared in response to a demand; they did not create one. He was the offspring of the Pennsylvania idea, not its father. He was not a scientific observer, seeking to follow the beacon of truth wherever it might lead, but an economic dogmatist, trying to rationalize the faith that was within him. On such a foundation an enduring intellectual edifice is seldom reared. At most, he merely smoothed the way for the rising tide of protection which industrial development and civil strife made inevitable. He was swept on to triumph by the irresistible force of an idea whose time had come, and when, and if, the American protective system falls, much of Carey's reputation as an economist seems destined to fall with it.

Nevertheless, Carey performed a distinct service to the cause of protection. His contribution was to make the movement vocal when for years it had been voiceless. He provided the slogans and formulas under which the scattered and unorganized tariff sentiment of the country might rally. The new industrial era spoke a new language to the American people, and he interpreted that language in terms

---

[21] *North American,* February 28, 1861.
[22] *Ibid.* December 3, 1860.
[23] April 15, 1859.
[24] An acquaintance quotes Carey as frequently saying, "Salvation, it is in me and in my books." ("Carey and Greeley," *Social Economist,* VII, 141).

which made protection and prosperity synonymous. He made protection respectable by substituting for the taint of self-interest the picture of it as an instrument of a beneficent Providence working in accord with the universal harmonies of natural law. He made protection convincing by bringing to its support a vast armament of facts and figures, more exhaustive than anything previously assembled. In short, he guided and accelerated processes he did not create; he served as a reagent to precipitate a solution long compounded.

Upon these foundations, economic, political, and philosophical, Pennsylvania protectionists have reared an imposing and enduring edifice. From the passage of the act of 1785 to "Encourage and Protect the Manufactures of the State by Laying Additional Duties on the Importation of Certain Manufactures which Interfere with Them" to the enactment of the Hawley-Smoot law of 1930, Pennsylvania has ever been in the forefront of the tariff battle. There is some reason to believe that the protectionist movement in the Keystone State has today passed its zenith. New economic forces, nonexistent before the Civil War, are beginning to exert an influence even in the tariff citadel. The urge for foreign markets, the growing dependence of the iron and steel industry upon imported ores, the tariff-stimulated rise of domestic competitors, especially in the South, may gradually effect the revolution in public sentiment which Condy Raguet vainly labored to produce. That day is not yet, however, for the old guard still rally beneath the battle-scarred, protectionist standards of their fathers and still march on the lobbies of Congress in resolute phalanx. Moreover, he who would seek political preferment at the hands of Pennsylvania must still confront the electorate with the assurance that he is "as good a tariff man as Henry Clay."

THE END.

# BIBLIOGRAPHY OF CITED MATERIAL

## MANUSCRIPT COLLECTIONS

Papers of James Buchanan; Hist. Soc. of Penna.
Papers of James Buchanan; Lib. of Cong.
Papers of Salmon P. Chase; Hist. Soc. of Penna.
Papers of John M. Clayton; Lib. of Cong.
Papers of Lewis S. Coryell; Hist. Soc. of Penna.
Dreer Collection; Hist. Soc. of Penna.
Gratz Collection; Hist. Soc. of Penna.
Papers of Duff Green; Lib. of Cong.
Papers of Andrew Jackson; Lib. of Cong.
Papers of Josiah S. Johnston; Hist. Soc. of Penna.
Papers of James K. Polk; Lib. of Cong.
Papers of John Sergeant; Hist. Soc. of Penna.
Society Collection; Hist. Soc. of Penna.
Papers of Thaddeus Stevens; Lib. of Cong.
Papers of George Wolf; Hist. Soc. of Penna.

## PUBLISHED WORKS, DIARIES, AND CORRESPONDENCE

*Memoirs of John Quincy Adams.* 12 vols. Ed. by C. F. Adams. (Philadelphia, 1874-77.)
*The Correspondence of Nicholas Biddle dealing with National Affairs, 1807-1844.* Ed. by R. C. McGrane. (Boston, 1919.)
*The Works of James Buchanan.* 12 vols. Ed. by J. B. Moore. (Philadelphia, 1908-1911.)
"Correspondence Addressed to John C. Calhoun, 1837-1849." *Report of the American Historical Association,* 1929. (Washington, 1930.)
"Correspondence of John C. Calhoun." *Report of the American Historical Association,* 1899. Vol. II. (Washington, 1900.)
*Works of Henry Clay, Comprising His Life, Correspondence and Speeches.* 7 vols. Ed. by C. Colton. (New York, 1897.)
"A Letter by Henry Clay." *Quarterly Journal of Economics.* Vol. II, pp. 490-491.
*The Complete Works of Benjamin Franklin.* 10 vols. Ed. by J. Bigelow. (New York, 1887-88.)
*The Writings of Benjamin Franklin.* 10 vols. Ed. by A. H. Smyth. (New York, 1905-07.)
*Works of Alexander Hamilton.* 12 vols. Ed. by H. C. Lodge. (New York, 1904)
*Correspondence of Andrew Jackson.* Vols. I-IV. Ed. by J. S. Bassett. (Washington, 1926-29.)
*Writings of Thomas Jefferson.* 20 vols. Memorial Ed. (Washington, 1903-04.)
Kelley, W. D., *Speeches, Addresses and Letters on Industrial and Financial Questions.* (Philadelphia, 1872.)
*Complete Works of Abraham Lincoln.* 12 vols. Ed. by J. G. Nicolay and J. Hay. (New York, 1905.)
*Journal of William Maclay, United States Senator from Pennsylvania, 1789-1791.* Ed. by E. S. Maclay. (New York, 1890.)
*Writings of James Madison.* 9 vols. Ed. by G. Hunt. (New York, 1900-10.)
*William Plumer's Memorandum of Proceedings in the United States Senate, 1803-1807.* Ed. by E. S. Brown. (New York, 1923.)
*The Diary of James K. Polk during his Presidency, 1845 to 1849.* 4 vols. Ed. by M. M. Quaife. (Chicago, 1910.)

*Letters of James K. Polk to Cave Johnson*, 1833-1848. Ed. by St. G. L. Sioussat.
Reprint from *Tennessee Historical Magazine*, September, 1915.
Stewart, A. *Speeches on the Tariff Question and on Internal Improvements.*
(Philadelphia, 1872.)
*Writings and Speeches of Daniel Webster*. 18 vols. (Boston, 1903.)

## NEWSPAPERS

Carlisle *American Volunteer*, 1844.
Chambersburg *Franklin Repository and Chambersburg Whig*, 1840-1842.
Greensburg *Westmoreland Intelligencer*, 1853-1855.
Harrisburg
    *Chronicle*, 1815-1817, 1822-1824, 1833.
    *Democratic Union*, 1843-1849.
    *Keystone*, 1840-1843, 1849-1858.
    *Old Warrior*, 1844.
    *Patriot and Union*, 1859-1861.
    *Pennsylvania Intelligencer*, 1820-1822, 1824-1831.
    *Pennsylvania Reporter and. Democratic Herald*, 1827, 1828, 1830-1832.
    *Pennsylvania Reporter and Democratic State Journal*, 1840.
    *Pennsylvania Telegraph*, 1832-1833, 1845-1853, 1856-1859.
    *Republican*, 1817-1819.
    *State Sentinel*, 1860.
Philadelphia
    *American Sentinel*, 1828, 1829, 1832-1839.
    *Aurora*, 1815-1822.
    *Democratic Press*, 1821, 1823-1827.
    *North American*, 1842-1861.
    *Pennsylvania Gazette*, 1785, 1787, 1789.
    *Pennsylvanian*, 1840-1861.
    *Pennsylvania Packet*, 1788, 1789.
    *Poulson's American Daily Advertizer*, 1830, 1831.
    *Public Ledger*, 1840-1861.
    *Spirit of the Times*, 1846.
    *United States Gazette*, 1815-1841.
Pittsburgh
    *American Manufacturer*, 1841, 1842.
    *Chronicle*, 1842-1844.
    *Commercial Journal*, 1845-1850, 1852, 1853.
    *Gazette*, 1815-1820, 1829-1834, 1839-1841, 1844, 1845, 1848, 1851, 1853-1857,
        1861.
    *Mercury*, 1815-1824, 1826-1828, 1835-1842.
    *Post*, 1843-1861.
    *Statesman*, 1819-1826.
    *Union*, 1857.
Pottsville *Miners' Journal*, 1825-1834, 1839, 1841-1852, 1855, 1856, 1858-1861.

## PERIODICALS

*The American Laborer, Devoted to the Cause of Protection to Home Industry.*
Vol. I. (New York, 1842-43.)
*The American Museum or Universal Magazine*. Vols. I-XII. (Philadelphia,
1787-1792.)
*Banner of the Constitution*. (Washington, December 5, 1829-November 24, 1830;
New York, December 1, 1830-April 27, 1831; Philadelphia, May 4, 1831-De-
cember 31, 1832.)
*The Emporium of Arts and Sciences*. New series, Vol. I. (Philadelphia, 1813.)

*The Examiner and Journal of Political Economy; devoted to the Advancement of the Cause of States Rights and Free Trade.* Vols. I, II. (Philadelphia, 1833-35.)

*The Free Trade Advocate and Journal of Political Economy.* Vols. I, II. (Philadelphia, 1829.)

*Hunt's Merchants' Magazine and Commercial Review.* Vols. I-XLIV. (New York, 1839-1861.)

*Niles' Weekly Register.* Vols. I-LXXV. (Baltimore, 1811-1849.)

*The Plough, the Loom, and the Anvil.* Vols. I-X. (Philadelphia and New York, 1848-57.)

*The Political Economist.* Vol. I. (Philadelphia, 1824.)

*The Register of Pennsylvania, devoted to the Preservation of Facts and Documents and Every Other Kind of Useful Information Respecting the State of Pennsylvania.* Edited by S. Hazard. Vols. I-XVI. (Philadelphia, 1828-35.)

## CLIPPINGS

Mathew Carey's Scrapbooks. Philadelphia Library Company. About one-half of the 145 volumes contain material relating to the tariff.

## PUBLIC DOCUMENTS: NATIONAL

*Annals of Congress,* 1789-1824.

*Register of Debates in Congress,* 1824-1837.

*Congressional Globe,* 1833-1861.

*Journal of the Executive Proceedings of the Senate of the United States of America.* Vols. VI, IX. (Washington, 1887.)

*American State Papers, Finance,* Vols. I-V; *Miscellaneous,* Vol. II. (Washington, 1832-59.)

*Senate Journal,* 20 Congress, 1 Session.

*Senate Executive Document,*
31 Congress, 1 Session, No. 3.
34 Congress, 3 Session, No. 55.
37 Congress, 2 Session, No. 2.

*Senate Document,*
21 Congress, 2 Session, No. 67.
28 Congress, 1 Session, No. 3.
62 Congress, 1 Session, No. 21.
62 Congress, 1 Session, No. 71.
62 Congress, 1 Session, No. 72.

*Senate Report,* 52 Congress, 2 Session, No. 1394.

*Senate Miscellaneous Document,* 35 Congress, 2 Session, No. 25.

*House Executive Document,*
22 Congress, 1 Session, No. 308.
22 Congress, 2 Session, No. 50.
29 Congress, 1 Session, No. 6.
30 Congress, 2 Session, No. 33.
31 Congress, 1 Session, No. 4.
34 Congress, 1 Session, No. 2.
35 Congress, 2 Session, No. 3.
36 Congress, 1 Session, No. 96.
38 Congress, 1 Session, No. 2.

*House Document,* 22 Congress, 1 Session, No. 285.

*House Report,* 30 Congress, 2 Session, No. 129.

*Annual Report on Commerce and Navigation,* 1850-1855.

*Compendium of the Enumeration of the Inhabitants and Statistics of the United States as obtained at the Department of State from the Returns of the Sixth Census.* (Washington, 1841.)

*A Compilation of the Messages and Papers of the Presidents,* 1789-1908. 11 vols. Edited by J. D. Richardson. (n.p., 1909.)
*Report of the United States Tariff Commission,* 1882. 2 vols. (Washington, 1882.)
*Statistical Abstract of the United States,* 1888, 1912.
*Statistical View of the United States, being a Compendium of the Seventh Census.* (Washington, 1854.)
United States Geological Survey, *Mineral Resources of the United States,* 1915, pt. 2. (Washington, 1917.)

PUBLIC DOCUMENTS: STATE

*Laws of Pennsylvania,* 1809-1861.
*Journals of the Senate of Pennsylvania,* 1815-1861.
*Journals of the House of Representatives of Pennsylvania,* 1815-1861.
*Journals of the House of Representatives of the Commonwealth of Pennsylvania,* 1776-1781. (Philadelphia, 1782.)
*Minutes of the Tenth General Assembly of the Commonwealth of Pennsylvania.* (Philadelphia, 1785.)
*Votes and Proceedings of the House of Representatives of the Province of Pennsylvania.* Vols. I, II. (Philadelphia, 1752.)
*Pennsylvania Archives,* Fourth Series, Vols. IV-VIII. (Philadelphia and Harrisburg, 1852-1902.)
*Pennsylvania Colonial Records.* 16 vols. (Philadelphia, 1852-53.)
*Charter to William Penn, and Laws of the Province of Pennsylvania passed between the Years* 1682 *and* 1700. (Harrisburg, 1879.)
*The Statutes at Large of Pennsylvania from* 1682 *to* 1809. 18 vols. (Harrisburg, 1896-1915.)
Commonwealth of Pennsylvania. *First Annual Report of the Bureau of Statistics of Labor and Agriculture for the Years* 1872-1873. (Harrisburg, 1874.)
*Smull's Legislative Handbook and Manual of the State of Pennsylvania,* 1921-1922. (Harrisburg, 1922.)
*Laws of the State of Delaware.* 2 vols. (Newcastle, 1797.)
*Laws of the State of New Jersey.* (New Brunswick, 1800.)

UNOFFICIAL COLLECTIONS OF SOURCES

Farrand, M., *The Records of the Federal Convention.* 3 vols. (New Haven, 1911.)
Halstead, M., *A History of the National Political Conventions of the Current Presidential Campaign.* (Columbus, 1860.)
McMaster, J. B. and Stone, F. D., *Pennsylvania and the Federal Constitution,* (Lancaster, Pa., 1888.)
New York Corresponding Association for the Promotion of Internal Improvements, *Public Documents Relating to the New York Canals.* (New York, 1821.)
Norton, A. B., *Reminiscences of the Log Cabin and Hard Cider Campaign.* (Mt. Vernon, O., 1888.)
Porter, K. H., *National Party Platforms.* (New York, 1924.)

CONTROVERSIAL AND THEORETICAL WORKS

Bastiat, F., *Sophismes Economiques.* (Paris, 1847.)
Carey, H.,
*Essay on the Rate of Wages.* (Philadelphia, 1835.)
*Principles of Political Economy.* 3 vols. (Philadelphia, 1837-1840.)
*The Past, the Present, and the Future.* (Philadelphia, 1848.)
*Harmony of Interests, Agricultural, Manufacturing, and Commercial.* (New York, 1852.)
*The Slave Trade, Domestic and Foreign.* (Philadelphia, 1853.)

*Coal, Its Producers and Consumers.* (Philadelphia, 1854.)
*Money.* (New York, 1857.)
*Financial Crises, Their Causes and Effects.* (Philadelphia, 1860.)
*Principles of Social Science.* 3 vols. (Philadelphia, 1858-60.)
*Principes de la Science Sociale.* 3 vols. (Paris, 1861.)
*Resources of the Union.* (Philadelphia, 1866.)
*Reconstruction—Industrial, Financial, and Political.* (Philadelphia, 1867.)
*Shall We Have Peace? Peace Financial and Peace Political?* (Philadelphia, 1869.)
*The Unity of Law; as exhibited in the relations of Physical, Social, Mental, and Moral Science.* (Philadelphia, 1872.)
*Manufactures—At once an Evidence and a Measure of Civilization.* (Philadelphia, 1875.)
*Commerce, Christianity, and Civilization versus British Free Trade.* (Philadelphia, 1876.)
Carey, M.,
*Addresses of the Philadelphia Society for the Promotion of National Industry.* Fourth Ed. (Philadelphia, 1819.)
*An Appeal to Common Sense and Common Justice.* (Philadelphia, 1822.)
*Essays on Political Economy.* (Philadelphia, 1822.)
*Reflections on the Subject of Emigration from Europe.* (Philadelphia, 1826.)
*Memorial of the Citizens of Philadelphia to Congress, November 9, 1827.* (Philadelphia, 1827.)
*Common Sense Addresses to the Citizens of the Southern States.* (Philadelphia, 1828.)
*Autobiographical Sketches.* (Philadelphia, 1829.)
*The Protecting System.* (Philadelphia, 1829.)
*The New Olive Branch. A Solemn Warning on the Banks of the Rubicon.* (Philadelphia, 1830.)
*The Crisis. An Appeal to the Good Sense of the Nation against the Spirit of Resistence and Dissolution of the Union.* (Philadelphia, 1832.)
*The Olive Branch, No. III.* (Philadelphia, 1832.)
*The Olive Branch, No. IV.* (Philadelphia, 1832.)
*Collectanea: Displaying the Rise and Progress of the Tariff System of the United States.* (Philadelphia, 1833.)
*Pamphlet Dedicated to the Great Manufacturing Capitalists of the United States.* (Philadelphia, 1833.)
*Autobiography.* Published serially in *New England Magazine,* Vols. V-VIII. (1833-1835.)
*The Querist.* (Philadelphia, 1839.)
List, F.,
*Outlines of American Political Economy in a Series of Letters to Charles J. Ingersoll.* (Philadelphia, 1827.)
*Appendix to the Outlines of American Political Economy in three additional Letters to Charles J. Ingersoll.* (Philadelphia, 1827.)
*Das Nationale System der Politischen Oekonomie, von Friedrich List, mit einer historischen Einleitung, von K. T. Eheberg.* (Stuttgart, 1925.)
Marshall, A., *Principles of Economics.* Eighth Ed. (London, 1920.)
Mill, J. S., *Principles of Political Economy.* Ed. by W. J. Ashley. (London, 1909.)
Raguet, C., *The Principles of Free Trade, illustrated in a Series of Short and Familiar Essays.* (Philadelphia, 1835.)

## MISCELLANEOUS PAMPHLETS

*The Plan of the Pennsylvania Society for the Encouragement of Manufactures and the Useful Arts.* (Philadelphia, 1787.)

*The Constitution of the Germantown Society for Promoting Domestic Manufactures.* (Philadelphia, 1790.)
*A Communication from the Pennsylvania Society for the Encouragement of Manufactures and the Useful Arts.* (Philadelphia, 1804.)
*Journal of a Convention of Delegates of the State of Pennsylvania held for the Promotion of the State Agricultural and Manufacturing Interests, Harrisburg, June 27, 1827.* (Harrisburg, 1827.)
*Proceedings of the General Convention at Harrisburg, July 30, 1827.* (n.p., n.d.)
*Review of the Report of a Committee of the Citizens of Boston and Vicinity, opposed to a Further Increase of Duties on Importations.* (Philadelphia, 1828.)
*Journal of the Free Trade Convention Held in Philadelphia from September 30 to October 7, 1831 and their Address to the People of the United States.* (Philadelphia, 1831.)
*General Convention of the Friends of Domestic Industry, assembled at New York, October 26, 1831.* (Baltimore, 1832.)
*Speech delivered by Horace Binney, Esq. at the Anti-Jackson Meeting, Held in the State House Yard, Philadelphia, October 20, 1832.* (n.p., 1832.)
*An Exposition of the Unequal, Unjust, and Oppressive Operation of the Present Tariff System in Relation to Iron, Wool, Hemp, Paper and the Manufactures Thereof.* (Philadelphia, 1832.)
*To the Citizens of the State of Pennsylvania.* (Philadelphia, 1832.)
*Answers of Ex-Gov. Polk, to two series of interrogatories propounded to him and Gov. Jones, through the presses of Memphis; together with a Letter to the People of Tennessee, disclosing his views on the Subject of the Public Expenditures, the Public Debt, the Tariff and the Bank of the United States.* (Memphis, 1843.)
Iron and Coal Trade Committee, Philadelphia. *Letter to the Hon. George Evans against the Repeal of the Duty upon Railway Iron.* (Philadelphia, 1844.)
*Prospect Before Us, or Loco Foco Impositions Exposed.* (Washington, 1844.)
Williams, T., *Address on the Subject of the Tariff, and the Relations of the Two Great Parties and Their Candidates Thereto.* (Pittsburgh, 1844.)
*Proceedings of the Iron Convention, held at Pittsburgh, November 21st, 22d and 23d, 1849.* (Pittsburgh, 1849.)
[Coxe, B.], *Short Answers to Reckless Fabrications, against the Democratic Candidate for President, James Buchanan.* (Philadelphia, 1856.)
*The Last Appeal to Pennsylvania.* (n.p., 1856.)
*Words of Counsel to Men of Business.* (n.p., n.d.)
*Address of the People's Club of Philadelphia in favor of Gen. Simon Cameron for the Next Presidency of the United States.* (Philadelphia, 1859.)
*Testimonials to Henry C. Carey, Esq. Dinner at the La Pierre House, Philadelphia, April 27, 1859. Receptions in the counties of Luzerne, Columbia, Montour and Carbon, Pennsylvania.* (Philadelphia, 1859.)
*Speech of the Hon. William B. Reed on the Presidential Question, delivered before the National Democratic Association, Philadelphia, September 4, 1860.* (n.p., n.d.)
*Record of Hon. Stephen A. Douglas on the Tariff. Compiled from the Official Records of Congress, for the People's State Committee of Pennsylvania* (n.p., 1860.)

## BOOKS OF TRAVEL OR DESCRIPTION, STATISTICAL WORKS AND DIRECTORIES

Acrelius, I., *Description of the Former and Present Condition of the Swedish Churches in what was called New Sweden, afterwards New Netherland, but at the Present Time Pennsylvania, etc. 1759. Reprinted in Memoirs of the Historical Society of Pennsylvania. Vol. XI.* (Philadelphia, 1874.)

Anderson, A., *Historical and Chronological Deduction of the Origin of Commerce, from the Earliest Accounts*. 6 vols. (Dublin, 1790.)
Birkbeck, M., *Notes on a Journey in America*. Third Ed. (London, 1818.)
Bowen, E., *The Coal Regions of Pennsylvania; being a General, Geological, Historical and Statistical Review of the Anthracite Coal Districts*. (Pottsville, 1848.)
Brissot de Warville, *New Travels in the United States of America. Performed in 1788*. (New York, 1792.)
Burnaby, A., *Travels through the Middle Settlements in North America, in the Years of 1759 and 1760*. (London, 1775.)
Coxe, T., *A View of the United States of America in a series of papers written at various times between the years 1787 and 1794*. (London, 1795.)
Cramer, Z., *The Navigator: containing directions for Navigating the Monongahela, Allegheny, Ohio and Mississippi Rivers*. Seventh Ed. (Pittsburgh, 1811.)
Douglass, W., *A Summary, Historical and Political, of the First Planting, Progressive Improvements and Present State of the British Settlements in North America*. 2 vols. (London, 1755.)
Fearon, H. B., *Sketches of America. A Narrative of a Journey of five thousand miles through the Eastern and Western States of America*. Second Ed. (London, 1818.)
French, B. F., *History of the Rise and Progress of the Iron Trade of the United States from 1621 to 1857*. (New York, 1858.)
Hewitt, A. S., *On the Statistics and Geography of Iron*. (New York, 1856.)
Jones, S., *Pittsburgh in the Year Eighteen Hundred and Twenty-Six*. (Pittsburgh, 1826.)
Kalm, P., *Travels into North America*. 2 vols. (London, 1772.)
Lesley, J. P., *The Iron Manufacturer's Guide to the Furnaces, Forges, and Rolling Mills of the United States*. (New York, 1866.)
Macpherson, D., *Annals of Commerce, Manufactures, Fisheries and Navigation*. 4 vols. (London, 1805.)
Scrivenor, H., *A Comprehensive History of the Iron Trade throughout the World from the Earliest Records to the Present Time*. (London, 1841.)
Seybert, A., *Statistical Annals of the United States of America*. (Philadelphia, 1818.)
Swank, J. M., *The Iron and Steel Industries of the United States. A Series of Statistical Statements showing the production and prices of iron and steel for a long series of years*. (Philadelphia, 1891.)
————, *Notes and Comments on Industrial, Political and Historical Subjects*. (Philadelphia, 1897.)
————, *Statistical Abstract. A collection of statistics relating to the Iron and Steel Industries of the United States*. (Philadelphia, 1888.)
Thwaites, R. G. (ed.), *Early Western Travels, 1748-1846*. 32 vols. (Cleveland, 1907.)
Wilkie, G., *The Manufacture of Iron in Great Britain*. (London, 1857.)
*Documents Relating to the Manufacture of Iron in Pennsylvania. Published in behalf of the Convention of Iron Masters which met in Philadelphia, December 20, 1849*. (Philadelphia, 1850.)

## BIOGRAPHIES AND REMINISCENCES

Benton, T. H., *Thirty Years' View*. 2 vols. (New York, 1854-56.)
Binney, C. C., *The Life of Horace Binney, with Selections from his Letters*. (Philadelphia, 1903.)
Blaine, J. G., *Twenty Years of Congress*. 2 vols. (Norwich, Conn., 1884.)
Elder, W., *A Memoir of Henry C. Carey*. (Philadelphia, 1880.)
Fritz, J., *Autobiography of John Fritz*. (New York, 1912.)
Going, C. B., *David Wilmot, Free Soiler*. (New York, 1924.)

[285]

Hirst, M. E., *Life of Friedrich List.* (New York, 1909.)
James, I., *Memorial of Thomas Potts, Jr.* (Cambridge, 1874.)
Jones, C. H., *The Life and Public Services of J. Glancy Jones.* 2 vols. (Philadelphia, 1910.)
McClure, A. K., *Old Time Notes of Pennsylvania.* 2 vols. (Philadelphia, 1905.)
——, *Our Presidents and How We Make Them.* (New York, 1900.)
McCormac, E. I., *James K. Polk, a Political Biography.* (Berkeley, Cal., 1922.)
Malone, D., *The Public Life of Thomas Cooper, 1783-1839.* (New Haven, 1926.)
Parker, W. B., *The Life and Public Services of Justin Smith Morrill.* (*Boston,* 1924.)
Sargent, N., *Public Men and Events from the Commencement of Mr. Monroe's Administration in 1817 to the Close of Mr. Fillmore's Administration in 1853.* 2 vols. (Philadelphia, 1875.)
White, G. S., *Memoir of Samuel Slater.* Second Ed. (Philadelphia, 1836.)

## GENERAL WORKS

Bartlett, M. G., *The Chief Phases of Pennsylvania Politics in the Jacksonian Period.* (Allentown, Penna., 1919.)
Bishop, J. L., *A History of American Manufactures from 1608 to 1860.* 2 vols. (Philadelphia, 1861.)
Clark, V. S., *History of Manufactures in the United States.* 3 vols. (New York, 1929.)
Eiselen, M. R., *Franklin's Political Theories.* (New York, 1928.)
Gide, C. and Rist, C., *History of Economic Doctrines from the Time of the Physiocrats to the present Day.* (Boston, n. d.)
Grosvenor, W. M., *Does Protection Protect? An Examination of the Effect of Different Forms of Tariff upon American Industry.* (New York, 1871.)
Haney, L. H., *History of Economic Thought.* (New York, 1911.)
Held, A., *Carey's Socialwissenschaft und das Merkantilsystem.* (Wurzburg, 1866.)
Jenks, J. W., *Henry C. Carey als Nationalökonom.* (Jena, 1885.)
Laughlin, J. L. and Willis, H. P., *Reciprocity.* (New York, 1903.)
Meuser, E., *List und Carey als wissenschaftlich Nationalökonomen.* (Mainz, 1914.)
Meyer, H. B., *History of Transportation in the United States before 1860.* (Washington, 1917.)
Mueller, H. R., *The Whig Party in Pennsylvania.* (New York, 1922.)
*Palgrave's Dictionary of Political Economy.* 3 vols. Ed. by H. Higgs. (London, 1925.)
Rabbeno, U., *American Commercial Policy.* (New York, 1895.)
Ringwalt, J. L., *Development of Transportation Systems in the United States.* (Philadelphia, 1888.)
Sherwood, S., *Tendencies in American Economic Thought.* (Baltimore, 1897.)
Stanwood, E., *American Tariff Controversies in the Nineteenth Century.* 2 vols. (Boston, 1903.)
Swank, J. M., *History of the Manufacture of Iron in all Ages, and particularly in the United States from colonial times to* 1891. (Philadelphia, 1892.)
——, *Progressive Pennsylvania, a Record of the Remarkable Development of the Keystone State.* (Philadelphia, 1908.)
Taussig, F. W., *The Tariff History of the United States.* Sixth Ed. (New York, 1914.)
Turner, J. R., *The Ricardian Rent Theory in Early American Economics.* (New York, 1921.)
Wilson, E., *Standard History of Pitsburgh, Pennsylvania.* (Chicago, 1898.)

# MAGAZINE ARTICLES

Baird, H. C., "Carey and Two of His Recent Critics, Eugen v. Böhm-Bawerk and Alfred Marshall," *Proceedings of the American Philosophical Society,* XXIX, 166-173.

Baird, H. C., "The Carey-Baird Centenary, January 25, 1885." *American Bookseller,* XVII, 59-64, 102-106, 125-126.

Denslow, V. B., "American Economics." *North American Review,* CXXXIX, 12-29.

Elder, W., "Henry C. Carey." Sartain's Magazine, X, 444-449.

Griswold, R. W., "Henry C. Carey and His National Economy." *International Monthly Magazine,* II, 402-407.

Hailperin, H., "Pro-Jackson Sentiment in Pennsylvania, 1820-1828." *Pennsylvania Magazine of History and Biography,* L, 193-240.

Leslie, T. E. C., "Political Economy in the United States." *Fortnightly Review,* XXXIV o. s., 488-509.

Levermore, C. H., "Henry C. Carey and his Social System." *Political Science Quarterly,* V, 553-582.

Thompson, R. E., "Henry Charles Carey." *Penn Monthly,* X, 816-834.

"Carey and Greeley." *Social Economist,* VII, 134-145.